HISTORIANS AND NATIONALISM

Historians and Nationalism

East-Central Europe in the Nineteenth Century

MONIKA BAÁR

OXFORD

UNIVERSITY PRESS

Great Clarendon Street, Oxford OX2 6DP

Oxford University Press is a department of the University of Oxford.
It furthers the University's objective of excellence in research, scholarship,
and education by publishing worldwide in

Oxford New York

Auckland Cape Town Dar es Salaam Hong Kong Karachi
Kuala Lumpur Madrid Melbourne Mexico City Nairobi
New Delhi Shanghai Taipei Toronto

With offices in

Argentina Austria Brazil Chile Czech Republic France Greece
Guatemala Hungary Italy Japan Poland Portugal Singapore
South Korea Switzerland Thailand Turkey Ukraine Vietnam

Oxford is a registered trade mark of Oxford University Press
in the UK and in certain other countries

Published in the United States
by Oxford University Press Inc., New York

© Monika Baár 2010

The moral rights of the author have been asserted
Database right Oxford University Press (maker)

First published 2010

British Library Cataloguing in Publication Data
Data available

Library of Congress Cataloging in Publication Data
Data available

Typeset by Laserwords Private Limited, Chennai, India
Printed in Great Britain
on acid-free paper by the
MPG Books Group, Bodmin and King's Lynn

ISBN 978–0–19–958118–4

3 5 7 9 10 8 6 4 2

This book is dedicated to the memory
of my grandmother, Lola.

Acknowledgements

First and foremost, I would like to thank my supervisor, Professor Robert Evans, for providing inspiration for my doctoral thesis and subsequently advising its metamorphosis into the present book. Some of the debts I have incurred extend back to my undergraduate years in Budapest. I am especially grateful to Endre Bojtár, who provided me with valuable insights on the cultures of East-Central Europe. Mária M. Kovács aroused my interest in some questions which subsequently became important themes of this book. Much of the thesis revision was undertaken in the two years that I spent as a Postdoctoral Fellow in the Max Planck Institute for the History of Science in Berlin, where my work benefited both from the thriving intellectual milieu of Lorraine Daston's Department and from the librarians' assistance with the location of material held in obscure places. I wish to thank my colleagues and friends who commented on the manuscript at various stages and/or helped in other ways: Claudia Baldoli, Stefan Berger, Tibor Frank, Gábor Klaniczay, Richard Overy, Steve A. Smith and Balázs Trencsényi. Last but not least, Lisa McKee's assistance with proofreading has been greatly appreciated.

Contents

Introduction

This book investigates the writings, thoughts and preoccupations of five historians in comparative perspective and aims to ascertain their place in the intellectual landscape of nineteenth-century historiography. They are: Joachim Lelewel (Polish, 1786–1861), Simonas Daukantas (Lithuanian, 1793–1864), František Palacký (Czech, 1798–1876), Mihály Horváth (Hungarian, 1804–78), Mihail Kogălniceanu (Romanian, 1818–91). As historians these scholars played prominent roles in articulating perceptions of their national past. As leading figures in their national movements they contributed to contemporary political debates and shaped visions of the future. Their impressive achievements attracted generous attention from their respective national communities. Nonetheless, their work has remained largely unknown to international scholarship. Accordingly, it has not been accommodated in a more comprehensive perspective and therefore continues to occupy a marginal place within historiographical production. The primary ambition of my study is to counter this oversight. To this end, the comparison of these scholars' writings, the elucidation of similarities and differences in their thoughts, represents only the first stage of my analysis. The second, final stage necessitates the evaluation of my findings within the context of the nineteenth-century historiographical canon. This calls for reflection both on attributes that corresponded to mainstream developments and on characteristics that were distinctive to their oeuvre. In a more general context, the underlying question of my study addresses the extent to which historical writing in a given era and genre is characterized by universal attributes and the extent to which it is influenced by regional conditions.

I am especially motivated by recent initiatives in historical research which seek to release marginal traditions from their isolated position and bring about a new, more encompassing vision of the European historiographical heritage. This is because, undoubtedly, the above-mentioned lacuna is not exclusive to the five historians featured in this study, but exemplifies a pattern. On the one hand, it is frequently lamented in literature that 'small' or 'peripheral' traditions have remained neglected fields of research. On the other, the tacit assumption that the essence of European historiography can be uncovered by the appraisal of a handful of 'mainstream' traditions seems to have survived. This limitation is unfortunate as it sacrifices the rich and complex diversity of European historical writing to an arbitrarily established standard. National historiography is typically defined as 'a specific form of historical representation which aims at the formation of the nation-states, accompanies the formation of the nation-states or seeks to influence the existing self-definitions of national consciousness'.[1] It seems justifiable, therefore, to pay more attention to national historiographies which developed in territories where national movements sought emancipation from within existing empires.[2]

Books on comparative historiography are scarce and informed by the predominance of the national paradigm. A notable exception to this trend is the volume *Writing National Histories, Western Europe since 1800*, which promises to investigate the hitherto overlooked common European dimension of historiographic nationalism.[3] The contributions in this book, which focus on four 'core countries', i.e. Britain, France, Germany and Italy, yield remarkable conclusions. However, as the chapters are dedicated to individual national contexts, the national paradigm cannot entirely be overcome. Studies in comparative historiography with a focus on East-Central Europe are especially rare. To my knowledge, there are only two existing accounts in this field, and unsurprisingly both were authored by scholars from the region. The first was written in 1946 by a Czech historian, Josef Macůrek, under the title *Dějepisectví evropského východu* (The Historiography of Eastern Europe, Prague, 1946). Macůrek's work offers an unprecedented survey of both East European history and historiography from the Byzantine era to just before the period in which he lived. The second book, *A történetírás története Kelet-Európában* (The History of Historical Writing in Eastern

---

[1] Stefan Berger, 'Representations of the Past: The Writing of National Histories in Europe', *Debatte* 12:1 (2004), 75.

[2] This constitutes an important ambition of the international research project *Writing National Histories in Europe* (2003–8), which is sponsored by the European Science Foundation.

[3] Stefan Berger, Mark Donovan and Kevin Passmore, 'Apologias for the Nation State in Western Europe since 1800', in Stefan Berger (ed.), *Writing National Histories: Western Europe since 1800* (London and New York, 1999), 3.

Europe, Budapest, 1996) was produced by a Hungarian scholar, Emil Niederhauser. This volume contains a sound outline of East European historiography, from its beginnings until modern times, but lacks explicit comparison.

The names of the historians upon whom this study focuses remain absent from general surveys, and the sporadic instances when they receive a mention are notable for their dismissive tone. G. P. Gooch's somewhat dated but still often quoted book, *History and Historians in the Nineteenth Century*, dedicates a few pages to what he calls 'minor countries' and touches cursorily on Lelewel, Palacký and Horváth in that context. Acknowledgement is given to Horváth for having produced a brief history from a democratic standpoint, but on the whole, criticism is levelled at his generation for allegedly being unable to escape the shackles of narrow patriotism.[4] In a similar tone, the paragraph dedicated to Lelewel argues that his analysis of medieval Polish history suffered from a lack of access to the archives, and that he was an ardent democrat who attributed more popular influences to early Polish history than had ever actually existed.[5] Another classic and monumental work on historiography is Eduard Fueter's *Geschichte der Neueren Historiographie*. This covers a long period from the scholastic tradition to the age of Burckhardt and has a very German focus. In the book Palacký's name receives just one cursory mention, and that in a pejorative sense. The author draws a comparison between the German historian Ludwig Häusser and Palacký and condemns both scholars for grounding their judgement entirely on patriotic sentiments and disregarding historical validity.[6]

Other overviews pay still less attention to marginal traditions, or even none at all. Harry Elmer Barnes's *A History of Historical Writing* mentions Palacký and Lelewel in passing in a chapter which is dedicated to 'other' countries (i.e. other than France, Germany and England),[7] and Ernest Breisach's book, *Historiography: Ancient, Medieval and Modern*, focuses exclusively on the German, British, French and American realm in the discussion of the modern period.[8] These accounts are also characterized by a lack of scholarly engagement, giving the overall

---

[4] G. P. Gooch, *History and Historians in the Nineteenth Century* (London and New York, 1952), 433–4.

[5] Ibid., 452.

[6] Eduard Fueter, *Geschichte der Neueren Historiographie* (Munich and Berlin, 1936), 541.

[7] Harry Elmer Barnes, *A History of Historical Writing*, 2nd edn. (New York, 1963), 220–6.

[8] Ernst Breisach, *Historiography. Ancient, Medieval and Modern*, 2nd edn. (Chicago, 1983).

impression that the writers never came into direct contact with my historians' work and based their judgements exclusively on secondary and tertiary sources. The consequence of this is an awkward situation, whereby my protagonists are condemned for imposing pre-existing conclusions on their material by scholars who seem to follow the same 'methodology'. A recent erudite addition to general surveys in modern historiography, Donald Kelley's *Fortunes of History* represents a refreshing change from this prevailing attitude inasmuch as it refrains from such value judgements. Kelley does not subscribe to the view that scholars representing marginal traditions can automatically be relegated to second- or third-rank historians. He also indicates that Iberian, Scandinavian, East European and Balkan states or would-be states all followed a similar trajectory of development.[9] Nevertheless, no attempt is made to establish those marginal traditions' relation to the mainstream scholarship of the age. The chapter in which East European, Iberian, Scandinavian and Balkan developments are bracketed together carries the telling title 'beyond the canon' and subtitle 'on the margins'.

That my historians, and in more general terms, representatives of 'marginal' traditions have not gained more widespread recognition can be at least in part attributed to methodological and practical difficulties, of which the most persistent is undoubtedly the language barrier. One of the greatest achievements of my protagonists was the replacement of the previously used Latin, German and Greek with the vernacular language, rendering their writings more accessible to the national community. At the same time, paradoxically, this novelty seriously restricted their availability to international scholarship. As Donald Kelley points out: 'these interstitial traditions also had their literary masterpieces, though they were hardly known outside their particular cultural spheres except through translation into at least one of the major languages'.[10]

However, it is not sufficient to explain this situation purely in terms of linguistic difficulties. Behind the linguistic barrier another obstacle appears to be lurking, which is ideological in nature. As I have briefly discussed above, the assessment of the historians' work is informed by clichéd value judgements and an a priori dismissal of their views. This is because such statements purport the existence of a 'proper' or 'more proper' historiography of the era, and it is in relation to

---

[9] Donald Kelley, *Fortunes of History: Historical Inquiry from Herder to Huizinga* (New Haven and London, 2002), 272.

[10] Ibid.

this putative, normative version that the awkwardness of Hungarian historiography 'in the shackles of patriotism', Palacký's nationalistic zeal and the idealization of the past in Lelewel's work, represented a distortion. This is not to question the validity of those critical remarks. But an intimate knowledge of nineteenth-century historiography is not necessary in order to realize that the criteria on which such criticism is founded, i.e. strong patriotic feeling, insufficiency of archival research and the idealization of the past, are general attributes of the era rather than the distinctive shortcomings of a few historians.

The unqualified attribution of political partisanship and unscholarly attitudes to historians of East-Central Europe may be connected with another general assumption about the 'special' role of the historian as a political force in nineteenth-century Central and Eastern Europe. The most concise formulation of this thesis originated from R. W. Seton-Watson, whose inaugural lecture, *The Historian as a Political Force in Central Europe*, at the School of Slavonic Studies in 1922, was entirely dedicated to this problem. According to Seton-Watson's old but still influential claim, present political miseries acted as an incentive to the revival of historical studies, enabling the present to be unfavourably contrasted with past glories. In Central and Eastern Europe the historical tradition was to play an 'absolutely decisive' part, even rescuing whole nations from oblivion.[11]

Doubtless, my protagonists' sensitivity to the acute problems within their societies manifested itself not only in their historical writings but also in public life: apart from Daukantas they were all highly committed politically. As Kogălniceanu put it: 'today we are not only writing, but also making history'.[12] On the international scene they sought to liberate their own nations from foreign ties and improve their international standing. Such ambitions were intertwined with domestic demands for the extension of individual rights to a larger part of the population and the abolition of the remnants of feudalism, in short for political and economic modernization. Lelewel played a crucial role in the Polish uprising of 1830. Subsequently, he became a charismatic leader of the exiled Poles. Palacký's political activity received extensive scholarly treatment due to his famous letter in which he rejected the invitation to attend the Frankfurt Parliament of 1848 (claiming that

[11] R. W. Seton-Watson, *The Historian as a Political Force in Central Europe* (London, 1922), 27.
[12] Alexandru Zub, *Mihail Kogălniceanu istoric* (Iași, 1974), 262.

he was not German but a Czech of Slavonic descent). Horváth became a bishop and Minister of Education during the revolution and war of independence in 1848–9, after which, like Lelewel, he was forced into exile. Kogălniceanu served as Prime Minister, then later as Foreign Minister and Minister of the Interior in one of the most crucial eras of Romanian history, the period of unification and attainment of national independence.

Nevertheless, these instances appear to provide little evidence about the exceptionality of my historians' political commitment. The historian who saw writing history as a way of practising politics and therefore deliberately set out not only to write and teach history but also to make it, appears to be representative of an archetype in an age when many historians both espoused political views in their writing as well as occupying powerful political posts. In his book referred to above (again, from which the East-Central European region is entirely absent!), Ernst Breisach concludes with regard to the era in question that 'one could have thought that the ancient period had returned, as history writing and public service once more were frequently linked'.[13] Among the abundant examples of historians 'turning Clio into the preceptor of the nation'[14] are the German historians at the Frankfurt Parliament in 1848 (the Professors' Parliament) and subsequently the Prussian schools' concern for German unification. A representative of the latter, Heinrich Sybel, famously declared that he was four-sevenths politician, three-sevenths professor.[15] The French Romantic school's use of history as a weapon in political struggles is also widely known, as is the fact that many of its members held prominent political positions, including François Guizot, who served as Prime Minister, and Thiers, who became the first President of the Third Republic.[16] Furthermore, one may ask whether political experience is inevitably harmful to historical writing, or whether, at least in some instances, it may have the potential to help comprehend the past. This question is especially worth asking in light of the fact that most historians of the era saw their own involvement

---

[13] Breisach, *Historiography: Ancient, Medieval and Modern*, 262.

[14] Herbert Flaig, 'The Historian as Pedagogue of the Nation', *History* 59 (1974), 18.

[15] Ibid., 19.

[16] See Jacques Barzun, 'Romantic Historiography as a Political Force in France', *Journal of the History of Ideas* 2:3 (1941), 318–29; Stanley Mellon, *The Political Uses of History: A Study of Historians in the French Restoration* (Stanford, 1958); Lionel Gossman, 'Augustin Thierry and Liberal Historiography', in Gossman, *Between History and Literature* (Cambridge, MA, and London, 1990), 83–151.

in politics not as an obstacle to understanding the past, but, on the contrary, as a catalyst for genuine historical insight.[17]

However, arguments about political partisanship as a distinctive hallmark of historiography in Central and East Europe are embedded in a more comprehensive discourse emphasizing political and cultural inferiority.[18] According to the foremost representative of this thesis, Hans Kohn, Western nationalism can be interpreted as a product of the Enlightenment, a rationalist ideology, centred around the notions of political legitimacy, active citizenship and the *Staatsnation*, while its Eastern counterpart was based on a romantic collectivism organized around the irrational, pre-civilized folk concept and the *Kulturnation*.[19] The former is deemed individualist and universalist, and compatible with liberal ideals, whereas the latter is regarded as collectivitist, exclusivist and therefore dangerous. Kohn's distinction and latent criticism, which was originally directed against Germany, soon became transferred into the context of Central and Eastern Europe. The shortcomings of this theory, especially its sweeping generalizations, have themselves been frequent targets of criticism. In addition, it has also been shown that almost all nations displayed some feelings of inferiority towards their competitors.[20]

Nevertheless, this line of argument continues to occupy a strong position in scholarly literature. Especially visible among its supporters are theorists who associate the development of nationalism with modernity and modernization and hence subscribe to a vanguard version of national development, which was later imitated by latecomers in a distorted form, resulting in dependence and underdevelopment: 'In Central and Eastern Europe the character of nationalism changed according to local conditions: the farther an area was from the lands in which nationalism developed, the less its nationalism resembled the original model. Even basic expressions of nationalism such as constitution, freedom, or republic acquired different meanings in more eastern areas of Europe.'[21] Nonetheless, the contradiction inherent in arguments about the distorted nature of nationalism in East-Central Europe is

---

[17] Gossman, *Between History and Literature*, 95.

[18] Andrzej Walicki, *Philosophy and Romantic Nationalism: The Case of Poland* (Notre Dame, 1944), 66.

[19] Hans Kohn, *The Idea of Nationalism* (New York, 1945), 329–31.

[20] Liah Greenfeld, *Nationalism: Five Roads To Modernity* (Cambridge, MA, 1992), 178.

[21] Peter Sugar (ed.), *Eastern European Nationalism in the Twentieth Century* (Washington DC, 1995), 8.

obvious (and symptomatic): when a nation is considered 'backward', such a verdict is arrived at by the imposition of a norm, from which backwardness is seen as a deviation. Yet, at the same time, the nation is typically labelled 'imitative', precisely for trying to adhere to that norm. Furthermore, an argument of this kind has serious implications when it becomes reiterated in the context of cultural production: if national movements were underdeveloped and imitative, it follows that their manifestations in historical writing must have shared the same characteristics: even at their best, they could only represent pale reflections of the European 'core'. Such may be the logic behind the conclusions about the simplistic and unscholarly nature of historical writing in the region.

Alternative approaches have diagnosed a methodological error in judging images of all national histories by the same criteria. For example, Miroslav Hroch maintains that the image of history in the Latvian and the Bulgarian national movement should not be assessed by the same standards and viewed through the same prism as English or German history. Rather, in analysing the image of a national history, account must be taken of the fundamental typological differences present in the process of nation-building in different parts of Europe.[22]

According to his approach the essential typological difference is that a number of peoples had already established themselves as nation-states by the onset of the period of modern capitalist transformation (e.g. the French, English, Dutch and Portuguese), while others remained in the position of 'non-dominant ethnic groups'. Within this context, Hroch distinguishes between dominant and non-dominant nations. Admittedly, this terminology has its limitations, as many nations do not fall into either of these two distinct categories. To give a few examples, Italians, Germans, Hungarians and Poles form an 'intermediate' or 'transitional' type. Yet, even with this reservation, Hroch's distinction appears to be more meaningful than alternative terminologies, such as 'non-historical', 'impoverished' nations and 'nations with empty histories'.

Nonetheless, even Hroch's approach contains a certain aspect of teleology. What distinguished non-dominant ethnic groups from their dominant counterparts is that they *lacked* three features characteristic of a fully formed nation: political autonomy; a standardized language used

---

[22] Miroslav Hroch, 'Historical Belles-Lettres as a Vehicle of the Image of National History', *National History and Identity, Studia Fennica Ethnologica* 6 (1999), 97.

to express all forms of high culture; and an established class structure. To this end, it is worth remembering that most European nations in the first half of the nineteenth century lacked one, two or three of these features, which makes it questionable to what extent we can speak about one normative development. What nevertheless renders this approach more attractive for my purposes is that it challenges the hegemonic (Kohnian) canon of nation-building which centres around the state and questions whether nations without states actually have relevant histories at all or whether they just have myths. According to this concept, having history means 'to have shared a common fate within a relatively coherent territory irrespective of whether this shared experience included a lack of political autonomy, or an interrupted autonomy, or whether it did not'.[23]

Furthermore, historians frequently seem to take for granted that the ultimate aim of each national political movement was the independent nation-state.[24] They tend to forget that many scholars and politicians in the nineteenth century would have been satisfied with a limited degree of independence, for example, autonomy within the confines of an empire or a multinational federation. On the other hand, the international recognition of an independent nation-state did not necessarily put an end to national aspirations: often the limited frontiers of that state stimulated irredentist sentiments. To this end, the variety which my five cases reveal can serve as a useful warning against conflating experiences in the region (and beyond) into a homogeneous whole.

My protagonists' vantage point was similar as they were representatives of the vast majority of European peoples who lived in multinational empires. Poland, Lithuania, Bohemia and Hungary, as well as Moldavia and Wallachia (the two principalities from which the Romanian nation-state subsequently evolved) were geographically and politically meaningful terms and all could claim a tradition of medieval statehood. Nonetheless, in the early nineteenth century these geographical terms no longer signified independent states. The 'national' territories were comprised of various lands, often belonging to different states and only loosely related to each other. Poland lost its political existence towards the end of the eighteenth century when it was partitioned between Russia, Prussia and Austria. Afterwards, the fundamental target of the

---

[23] Ibid., 98.
[24] This is noted by Maciej Janowski, 'Wavering Friendship: Liberal and National Ideas in Nineteenth Century East-Central Europe', *Ab imperio* 3–4 (2000), 77.

Poles became the restoration of the former state, or at least a fraction of it. The Bohemian lands formed part of the Habsburg Empire with a limited form of self-government. Hungary was likewise part of the Habsburg Empire but maintained a more independent political system within it, and in both cases, the nobility enjoyed certain historical privileges. Importantly, neither my Czech nor my Hungarian protagonist supported the idea of an independent nation-state as a desirable goal in the present. As we shall see later, they both maintained that the international conditions in post-1848 Europe rendered such claims unrealistic. The Grand Duchy of Lithuania formed an independent entity in the Middle Ages, but became part of the Polish Commonwealth with the Union of Lublin in 1569. After the partitions of Poland, the Lithuanian territories were incorporated into the Russian Empire. Daukantas's vision of a sovereign Lithuanian state was virtually unprecedented in the nineteenth century. Romania was the only one of the five countries which became an independent state during our period. Prior to that, the two principalities of Wallachia and Moldavia had been ruled by Greek princes who were imposed upon by the Ottoman rulers.

The use of the mother tongue for literary and scholarly purposes represented a crucial ambition of scholars in the nineteenth century and therefore constitutes an important theme of the book, although even in this matter we encounter significant individual variations. In Poland, the literary language upheld a continuous tradition and as a consequence no attempt at linguistic 'renewal' was necessary. On the other hand, Lithuanian was mostly spoken by the peasantry because the Lithuanian nobility had become overwhelmingly Polonized. It was Daukantas who created the initial broad concept of the standard written Lithuanian language. Similarly, Palacký contributed to the Czech linguistic renewal. Although the Czech language provided a medium for literary masterpieces in the sixteenth century, after the Battle of White Mountain (1620) it gradually disappeared from the public domain. Some members of the Bohemian aristocracy were proficient in Czech, but by the eighteenth century they usually reserved this language solely for communicating with their social inferiors. In Hungary the literary language already had a more established tradition, but had to be 'updated' in order to become suitable for more sophisticated scholarly usage. Last but not least, the standardization of the Romanian language gained momentum after the unification of the principalities. Romanians belonged to the world of Eastern Christianity and had initially used the

Cyrillic alphabet. It was only after the unification that the Latin alphabet was introduced, and this shift can also be observed in Kogălniceanu's writings.

As has been shown above, backwardness (as seen from the 'centre') is perhaps the best-known peculiarity of Central and East Europe, even though regional variations were significant in this matter. The survival of feudal structures, the weakness of the middle classes and a predominantly peasant population are among the most frequently cited peculiarities. I find it especially difficult to establish a stance towards these postulates, because, on the one hand, as we have seen, the application of the backwardness paradigm without qualifications results in sweeping generalizations. But on the other, backwardness was a condition which my protagonists themselves diagnosed, as they sought to improve unfavourable circumstances in their countries. Within the context of my study, the question that concerns us is (using Hroch's words) how to take account of these 'typological differences' in the assessment of historical writing. As the structures and institutions of national and cultural life in the region were still incomplete, their efforts and attention therefore had to be divided between several tasks. As Palacký put it: 'I might complain that in Bohemia I alone have been burdened with work which in other countries is shared by governments, academies, and educational institutions . . . I must be hod-carrier and master builder in one person.'[25]

Taking Palacký's 'complaint' on board, I propose that on the basis of these regional peculiarities, my historians' activities cannot be restricted solely to historical writing but must be accommodated within the overall cultural context of nation-building. They did not act just as historians in a narrow sense, but were engaged in the promotion of a unified vision of national culture. Therefore, in any study of their work, in addition to the analysis of the historical narrative, attention must be paid to their achievements in the field of language and literature, their pursuits in editing sources and publishing journals, and their contribution to the institutionalization and professionalization of the discipline.[26] Such an approach not only appears to do more justice to their achievements but

[25] Palacký, *Zur Böhmischen Geschichtschreibung* (Prague, 1871), 90; quoted in Joseph Zacek, *Palacký: The Historian as Scholar and Nationalist* (The Hague, 1970), 29.

[26] This ambition resonates with the approach taken by Joep Leerssen in *National Thought in Europe: A Cultural History* (Amsterdam, 2006), a book which gives ample consideration to the European 'margins'. Leerssen prefers to speak of 'national thought', which is a wider and less specific term than 'nationalism'.

can help to avoid the risk of imposing an anachronistic standard on their work. Although my historians' contribution to professionalization was fundamental, they lived in an era when this process was not yet completed and it would therefore be a mistake to interpret their work from the vantage point of our contemporary professionalized perspective alone.

On the methodological front I opted for the comparative method because, despite its obvious advantages for 'marginal' traditions, it has not been exploited to its fullest potential in the study of the historiography of East-Central Europe. Nonetheless, it should be acknowledged that comparison comes with difficulties and occasionally contradictions, as becomes manifest from my attitude to the historical canon. This is because, as I have stressed above, I believe that it does no justice to the five historians if the canon is imposed on their work as a norm, without qualifications. It seems much more convincing to propose that they should be judged on their own terms and not on the basis of criteria which emerged without taking their writings into account. However, precisely because I am seeking to describe an unknown terrain, a common denominator, a 'common language' is necessary, in relation to which their work can be positioned. It is only through making references and establishing connections to well-known representatives of mainstream historiography that my historians' work can be rendered more familiar and accessible. I am aware that this can only be achieved at the cost of generalizations, because the canon itself is complex and heterogeneous. With this reservation, I have tried to incorporate parallels and contrasts with major 'well-known' representatives of the era, especially the scholars of the German and Scottish Enlightenment, the French liberal school and English Whig historians. I have taken into account recent attacks on the comparative method and alternative methodological approaches, including intellectual transfer and *histoire croisée*.[27] In my opinion, these methods cannot replace the comparative perspective but can complement it. To this end, I have attempted to utilize some of the devices favoured by alternative methodologies in my study, especially in the parts that deal with the intellectual influences of my protagonists. This was not a simple task, however, since such methodologies have so far almost exclusively been applied in a bilateral

---

[27] Michael Espagne, *Les transferts culturels franco-allemands* (Paris, 1999); Michael Werner and Bénédicte Zimmermann, 'Beyond Comparison: Histoire Croisée and the Challenge of Reflexivity', *History and Theory* 45 (2006), 30–50.

(mainly French–German) context and their 'multilateral' applicability is still not entirely evident.

The scope of my research, the study of five cases, already allows for some generalizations. At the same time it allows for a close, in-depth engagement with the texts. However, moulding five historians into one framework unavoidably means cutting corners. My findings cannot hope to cover the breadth of detailed monographs on one single historian and reveal little about the complexities of individual national historiographical traditions. The original version of this work, my doctoral thesis, dedicated a separate chapter to the life-work of each historian, an arrangement which allowed more space for the discussion of the twists and turns of their intellectual development over the course of their lives and the indication of their position within their own national heritage. In the current, thematic arrangement the emphasis is shifted towards synthesis, as this is the field where I perceived a gap in historical literature. In adopting this structure, which is horizontal rather than vertical, I am aware that some things had to be glossed over or left out altogether.

The choice of the five historians may call for explanation. It is undoubtedly impossible to find five 'neatly comparable' cases, and certain practicalities also imposed limitations on my eventual options. Without implying that countries belonging to the same region may necessarily be best suited for comparison, when making my choice, it was important that my historians share a similar spatial and temporal setting as well as certain life experiences, which allows me to treat them as a group. All came from Central and Eastern Europe and were roughly contemporaries. Their activities mostly took place in the first two-thirds of the nineteenth century, a period which is often identified with the liberal phase of nationalism.

As far as the region is concerned, the comparison of a Polish, Czech and Hungarian scholar requires little justification.[28] The inclusion of a Romanian and a Lithuanian historian is perhaps more disputable. It may be argued that Romania belongs to South-East, rather than to East-Central Europe but these regional boundaries appear to be artificial.[29] Furthermore, I believe that in the absence of a South-East

[28] Palacký and Lelewel appear to be especially suited for comparison. See Halina Beresnevičiūte's MA dissertation, 'The Idea of the Nation in Joachim Lelewel's and František Palacký's Historical Works' (Central European University, Budapest, 1995).

[29] According to the most widely used definition, the lands of the former Habsburg Empire and those of the former Polish-Lithuanian Commonwealth constitute East-Central Europe.

European region from my work, the inclusion of the Romanian context may be worthwhile. The Lithuanian case is not self-explanatory either. There is no doubt that the comparison is not applicable to Daukantas in certain respects. Unlike his four other colleagues, he was not in a position to get involved in politics and to significantly contribute to the institutionalization of the discipline. Furthermore, since only one of Daukantas's historical writings (alongside several works of a linguistic and pedagogical nature) was published in his lifetime, his impact was to a large extent posthumous. Yet, I believe that precisely because he is entirely unknown beyond the confines of Lithuanian scholarship, his work may benefit most from the comparison.

There is no doubt that my historians' arguments were occasionally marred by contradictions and ambiguities, but it was not my intention to render them more rounded by explaining away those shortcomings. Furthermore, because of the connections and overlaps between my themes, occasional repetitions and frequent cross-references were unavoidable in the text. Finally, I do not wish to deny that the book may be affected by a subjective tone. Just as my historians intended to emancipate their nations in the nineteenth century, my aim is to release their work from isolation. I am happy to declare my enthusiasm for the subject which, in the light of its sensitivity, may raise some eyebrows. Historians working on nationalism in Central and East Europe often feel obliged to take cautionary measures by way of markedly distancing themselves from their subject matter. This is because an emphatic account may run the risk of creating the impression that the author supports exclusivist claims. As I hope will become obvious from the book, I am sympathetic to the ethical mission which seeks to deconstruct claims for exceptionality in any nation's history. At the same time, one of the benefits arising from the comparative method is the realization that *all* national histories lay claims to such exceptionality.

In the following paragraphs I set out the most important themes which constitute the focus of my investigation. The first part of my study examines the intellectual and cultural background and the second concentrates on the historical narrative. In view of the book's thematic arrangement, I found it necessary to dedicate a chapter to the discussion of the historians' lives and writings on an individual basis. Thus, Chapter 1 contains the intellectual and political mini-biographies of the historians. It considers their political and academic careers and the relationship between the two. It looks at the social milieu to which they were born, their education, what motivated them to become historians and the intellectual atmosphere in which they pursued their studies and which may well have been influential in their subsequent scholarly ventures. It touches on the milestones in their lives and professional careers, their salient writings and activities, and the most important shifts in their life-work.

Chapter 2 discusses the historians' expectations of history-writing and explores how their ambitions related to those of the representatives of Enlightenment-style general history and representatives of Romantic national history elsewhere. These goals included the democratization of the content (by writing the history of the people and not that of the ruling dynasty), the democratization of the medium (through writing in the national language) and the democratization of the audience (as they addressed not a handful of specialists but the national community). They sought to write histories in a pragmatic, impartial manner and believed that history was *magistra vitae*. This calls for a reflection on the question of whether it is possible to reconcile claims of impartiality with obvious political preferences. Relating my protagonists' goals to mainstream developments, I put forward the argument that there existed a general blueprint of national history-writing in this period, one which emphasized the ancient, continuous, unified and unique nature of national history. I also undertake a comparison between self-congratulatory accounts in mainstream historiography and my historians' change-oriented emancipatory rhetoric.

Chapter 3 examines the institutional setting of the scholars' activities and investigates their role in the professionalization and institutionalization of the discipline. Within this framework I look at the ways in which they entered academia, for example, with the help of sponsorship and by participation in academic contests. I explore the role of patriotic and scholarly societies in the organization of national culture: the advertisement of competitions, running of lectures, publication of periodicals, etc., and my historians' contribution to those activities. This is followed by the study of the universities' limited role in the promotion of historical studies in the region. Thereafter, I discuss the historians' contribution to the creation of periodicals and explain how such ventures were instrumental in the formation of a unified national culture and language. Their role in the collection and editing of sources is also taken into account. Finally, I look at examples of censorial intervention in their work, alongside the strategies which they devised in order to alleviate the impact of censorship.

In Chapter 4 I attempt, as far as possible, to reconstruct the intellectual background which informed the historians' mindset. I argue that the vantage point of such study must be their own national traditions. I look at the influence of the Enlightenment in its national variations, as well as the impact of Romanticism on their work. Within the analysis of foreign intellectual influences, special attention is given to the Göttingen school and in broader terms to the *Spätaufklärung*, as it provided perhaps the most decisive stimulus for my historians. Herder's influence is also investigated as I argue that his impact was not as crucial as one would expect. I also look at the inspiration which the Scottish Enlightenment provided for my historians and explore in what ways and to what extent they were indebted to the French liberal school and the writings of the Russian historian Nikolai Karamzin. Throughout the discussion I seek to explain the relevance of these intellectual currents for their purposes.

Chapter 5 is dedicated to the role of language in the scholars' life-work, as both the medium and the message. I discuss their contribution to the renewal of the national language. I demonstrate the possibilities which language provided for arguments about the antiquity, continuity, unity and uniqueness of national history. I then go on to address problems of intellectual transfer, originality and imitation. On the basis of textual analysis I attempt to illustrate how translations and adaptations, an independent and creative activity, were exploited as shortcuts in the process of creating national culture.

The following four chapters (6–9) are dedicated to the analysis of the historical narrative. I commence by looking at the problems of origins (especially prominent in the Romanian and Lithuanian cases) and the representation of early societies in my historians' work. I discuss various versions of 'antiquity': Nordic, Indo-European, Latin, 'Semi-Nomadic' and a putative Slavic variant. I demonstrate that early societies were portrayed by an appeal to Tacitean topoi and were strikingly similar to representations in mainstream historiography. Social justice, equality, common ownership of lands and chiefs who selflessly represented their community characterized this idyllic ahistorical situation. The period of feudalism, as explained in Chapter 7, was believed to represent a rupture in national life: the historians maintained in unison that it was a foreign development, which never fully penetrated their societies. I assess the humanitarian and utilitarian arguments with which they supported their demands for the abolition of serfdom, endowment of peasants with the right of property ownership and civic liberties. Further, I explore how my historians utilized a mainstream argument of the age according to which trade and industry and medieval towns played a seminal role in the weakening of the feudal system. Last but not least, I focus not only on the content but also on the form of the proposed changes and tackle the historians' attitudes to liberalism, democracy, reform and revolution.

Chapter 8 on the 'golden age' compares the periods which the historians saw as the most successful eras in national history. Throughout my analysis I highlight the difficulty inherent in the historians' aim of promoting national unity in societies which were characterized by social, geographical and ethnic heterogeneity. A similar challenge lay in the assumption of continuity in the light of the ruptured and fragmented nature of national history. For Lelewel, the most glorious period in Polish history was to be found in the days of the Polish–Lithuanian Commonwealth. Daukantas venerated the early, pagan period in the history of Lithuania, and in a more extended sense, the era before the Union of Lublin (1569). Palacký identified the pinnacle of Czech history with the Hussite movement in the fifteenth century, which he understood not only as a religious but also as a national and social movement. Kogălniceanu associated the 'golden age' with moments of unity in Romanian history, in particular with the reign of Michael the Brave in the late sixteenth century. Horváth saw contemporary Hungary, the Reform Age (1823–48), as an exceptional era. By means of the analysis of these five cases I demonstrate that the scholars reached nearly identical conclusions when defining the attributes of the 'golden age'. These included individual and collective freedom, a fair treatment of the unprivileged classes, a tolerant environment, hospitality to people of other nations and national unity.

Chapter 9 addresses overlapping national histories, using the examples of the Czech–German, the Polish–Lithuanian and the Romanian–Hungarian cases. The historians' attitudes to foreigners and enemies are also scrutinized, with special attention given to their views on the Jewish population, women and the role of the Jesuits in national history. Finally, the normative and anti-normative attitudes to Western civilization are discussed, together with the mission that the historians attributed to their nations in European history. I argue that they employed different argumentative strategies when addressing a domestic and a foreign audience. The concluding chapter attempts to accommodate my historians' accomplishments in the wider context of the European historiographical heritage. It addresses this problem by extending the regional and temporal scope of the examination. Thereafter follows an overview of my historians' reception by the succeeding generation. Lastly, the underlying questions of the book are revisited in light of my overall findings.

1

Five Biographical Profiles

The following pages offer a brief account of the key episodes in my historians' lives and of the milestones in their intellectual output. A pragmatic, rather than analytical, approach is adopted and the information presented here follows the dictates of my comparative perspective, as well as my objective of providing a backdrop to the principal concerns of the book. Thus, whilst these mini-biographies seek to be as informative as possible, they necessarily involve an element of selectivity and are by no means exhaustive. A more comprehensive picture can be constructed through recourse to the secondary literature listed in the Bibliography.

LELEWEL

Born in 1786 into a family with a heterogeneous ethnic background, Lelewel liked to claim that he did not possess a drop of Polish blood: his father's ancestors were Huguenots who settled in Warsaw in the early eighteenth century, whilst his mother descended from a Polish-Ruthenian land-owning family.[1] Lelewel's father, an alumnus of Göttingen University, rose to prominence in public life and participated in the reform programme introduced by the court of King Stanisław August. He sent the eldest of his nine children, Joachim, to be educated in the leading Polish educational institution of the age, the Collegium Nobilium Scholarum Piarum. Opened in 1740 by the eminent Piarist reform pedagogue Stanisław Konarski, this was a distinguished boarding

---

[1] My account of Lelewel's life draws heavily on Joan Skurnewicz's monograph, *Romantic Nationalism and Liberalism: Joachim Lelewel and the Polish National Idea* (New York, 1981). I also relied on Stefan Kieniewicz's book, *Joachim Lelewel* (Warsaw, 1990) and on the chapter 'Joachim Lelewel' by John D. Stanley in Peter Brock, John D. Stanley and Piotr J. Wrobel (eds.), *Nation and History: Polish Historians from the Enlightenment to the Second World War* (Toronto, Buffalo and London, 2006), 52–84.

school where pupils were instructed in the spirit of the Enlightenment.[2] Between 1804 and 1808 Lelewel studied at the University of Vilna. This institution, which evolved out of a Jesuit Academy in 1801 as part of Tsar Alexander I's efforts to modernize his Empire, will feature extensively in the book. At Vilna Lelewel read sciences, as well as ancient and modern languages, including Sanskrit and Arabic. He attended classes in drawing and engraving, and subsequently several high-quality hand-drawn maps testified to his artistic talent. He was also an active member of secret student societies, whose intention was to cultivate the traditions of the fatherland. Lelewel's early scholarly attempts revealed a passion for history. His student essay, *Rzut oka na dawność litewskich narodów i związki ich z Herulami* (An Overview of the Antiquity of the Lithuanian Peoples and Their Relations with the Heruli), addressed the origins of the Lithuanians. Meanwhile, *Edda, cyzli księga religii dawnych Skandynawii mięszkańców* (Edda, or the Book of Religion of the Ancient Inhabitants of Scandinavia, 1807), a translation of Paul Mallet's famous book on the Edda, constituted his first (anonymous) publication.

After graduation Lelewel taught for two years at a lyceum in Krzemieniec (near the Ukrainian border) and in 1811 he returned to Warsaw, where he regularly attended the meetings of the foremost learned society of the age, Towarzystwo Przyjaciół Nauk (Society of the Friends of Learning). In 1815 Jan Śniadecki, the rector of the University of Vilna, invited him to lecture in general history, an appointment which inaugurated the study of history as an independent discipline. Lelewel's intellectual preoccupations at this time concerned the theory of history, as well as the history of ancient civilizations and the early Slavs. His interest in theoretical issues yielded a (single-volume) collection of essays, *Historyka, tudzież o łatwym i pożytecznym nauczaniu historii* (The Theory of History: On the Easy and Useful Teaching of History, 1815). An ability to condense and conceptualize intricate problems rendered his book an unparalleled pioneering work in contemporary East-Central Europe. Publications on the history of ancient India, Greece and Rome followed, drawing primarily on his university lectures.

In 1818 Lelewel's career resumed at the newly established University of Warsaw, where he was appointed Professor of Bibliography and Curator of the University Library. In accordance with his new responsibilities, he developed familiarity with the field of bibliography and produced

---

[2] S. Kot, *Five Centuries of Polish Learning* (Oxford, 1914), 13.

the first major history of libraries and library science in the Polish language, *Bibliograficznych ksiąg dwoje* (Two Books on Bibliography, 1823 and 1826). He also delivered lectures on the comparative history of Poland and Spain, which laid the foundation for his essay *Historyczna paralela Hiszpanii z Polską, w XVI, XVII, XVIII wieku* (A Historical Parallel of Spain and Poland in the Sixteenth, Seventeenth and Eighteenth Centuries). The year 1821 saw him return to Vilna, serving as a very popular Professor of General History for three years. The essay entitled *O Historii jej rozgałęźieniu i naukach związek z nią mając* (On History, Its Branches and Related Disciplines, 1826), completed the young scholar's major contribution to the theory and methodology of history. In the early 1820s, largely due to publications in German and Russian, Lelewel's reputation gradually extended beyond the confines of his homeland and a critical evaluation of the prominent Russian historian, Nikolai Karamzin's *Istorija gosudarstva rossijskago* (History of the Russian State), later published in Polish as *Porównanie Karamzina z Naruszewiczem* (Comparison of Karamzin with Naruszewicz) won the praise of Russian liberal scholars. This productive era ended abruptly in 1824 when Lelewel, following a false allegation by the tsarist authorities that he had participated in an anti-Russian conspiracy, was expelled from the university and ordered to return to Warsaw.

In the absence of secure employment, Lelewel immersed himself in research in Warsaw, focusing increasingly on national history, which also presented an important issue on the agenda of the Towarzystwo Przyjaciół Nauk. He completed his first attempt in this field, the rudimentary *Historia Polski aż do końca panowania Stefana Batorego* (The History of Poland to the End of the Reign of Stefan Bathory) in 1813, but it was published only after his death in 1863. Another study, *Panowanie Stanisława Augusta* (The Reign of Stanisław August, 1818) presented a generally favourable assessment of the legacy of the Polish king (who ruled between 1764 and 1795), although it also contained some criticism. In its original form, this essay was interwoven with autobiographical elements which made it seem more like a personal recollection than a historical account. Initially banned by the censor, a subsequent and significantly improved version was published in 1831, and later in a further eight editions, including those in German and French. In 1828 my protagonist produced a small historical sketch, *Historia: Obraz dziejów polskich* (History: An Image of Polish History), which set out the main tenets of his interpretation of Polish history. This was superseded by the more complete *Dzieje Polski potocznym sposobem opowiedziane* (A History of Poland Related in a Colloquial Manner, 1828), a popular history for children, which sought to address aspects of political, as well as of social and cultural, history. Nine editions of this book had appeared by 1859, and it also served as a school textbook, thereby exerting considerable influence on several generations. Its German version, *Geschichte Polens*, sought to popularize Polish history among the foreign public. By the 1820s Lelewel had acquired a reputation as a proponent of liberal ideas and became actively involved in politics, culminating in his election as representative to the *Sejm* (Diet).

In response to Tsar Nicholas I's violation of the constitutional guarantees of the Congress Kingdom, and prompted by the eruption of the July Revolution in France and the Belgian revolt, an insurrection broke out in Warsaw in November 1830. Lelewel's role in the events assumed great significance; for a short time he acted as a member of the provisional government led by Prince Adam Czartoryski, a position which enabled him to abolish censorship. He later briefly served as Minister of Education in another revolutionary government. As president of the revolutionary Towarzystwo Patrioticzne (Patriotic Society), Lelewel authored numerous pamphlets and manifestos promoting the Polish cause abroad. During the uprising he composed a comparative study of the three Polish constitutions of 1791, 1807 and 1815: *Trzy konstytucje polskie* (Three Polish Constitutions), which sought to offer pragmatic guidance on how to establish an effective government. Translated into French, and later into other languages, it introduced the Polish question onto the agenda of liberals in Western Europe.

After the fall of the Congress Kingdom following the military capitulation of the Poles, Lelewel shared the fate of several thousand émigrés who sought asylum in the liberal capitals of Europe and continued their fight for the restoration of the Polish state from abroad. He was later sentenced to be hanged *in absentia* in his homeland. His first destination was Paris, where he received warm welcome from republicans such as the Marquis de Lafayette and Camille Odilon-Barrot. Lelewel joined the Polish émigré organization, Komitet Narodowy Polski (Polish National Committee), which advocated a free, independent and multinational Poland with pre-partition boundaries, a republican government and a democratic society. Lelewel's concern with Poland's fate is evident in the numerous but largely futile proclamations and declarations which he addressed to various bodies, such as the French Chamber of Deputies, the British Parliament, the Italians, the Hungarians, the Jewish people and 'Our Russian Brothers'. Alarmed by these activities, Louis Philippe's government expelled him from France on the demand of the Russian ambassador.

Lelewel then moved to Brussels, and apart from shorter journeys he remained there for the rest of his life. Belgium obtained independence in 1830 and several émigrés found protection under its liberal regime; as we shall see, at one stage Horváth also featured among them. Lelewel prized independence so highly that he even refused a professorship at the newly established University of Brussels, preferring instead to live in poverty. His political credo, founded on republicanist-democratic principles, represented a counterpoint to the aristocratic faction of Polish émigrés led by the monarchist Adam Czartoryski, who believed the Polish problem could by resolved by diplomacy. Lelewel initially expressed reservations about the agenda of the mainstream Towarzystwo Demokratyczne Polskie (Polish Democratic Society), but ultimately joined their ranks in 1846, when his preferred organization, the more radical Młoda Polska (Young Poland), disbanded.

In 1836 Lelewel completed a brief history, *Polska odradzająca się, czyli dzieje Polski od roku 1795 potocznie opowiedziane* (Poland in the Throes of Rebirth: A History of Poland since 1795 told in a Colloquial Manner). This autobiographical piece was primarily aimed at young people, recounting events from the time of the third partition in 1795 to the November uprising of 1830–1. It concluded that the re-establishment of the Polish state could only be achieved by the Poles' own efforts, which also necessitated the emancipation of the peasantry. An especially powerful and concise manifestation of my historian's political conviction, underlined by a reverence for Poland's ancient republican values, was *Prawność narodu polskiego* (The Legitimacy and Rights of the Polish Nation), an essay which was originally published in 1836, in the French *Journal de Rouen* and in the Polish émigré journal *Narod Polski* (Polish Nation). In 1843 he published *Dzieje Polski, które stryj synowcom swoim opowiedział* (History of Poland Told by an Uncle to His Nephews). Benefiting from the less severe censorship in Prussia, the book was printed in Poznań and then smuggled into Russian-occupied Poland, where it came to enjoy immense popularity.

Lelewel's most mature and sophisticated synthesis first appeared in 1844 as *Histoire de Pologne*, a year later as *Geschichte Polens* and finally, in 1855 (translated from the French original), as *Uwagi nad dziejami*

Polski i ludu jej (Observations on the History of Poland and its People).[3] As an account imbued with a strong republican leaning, and primarily focusing on social history, it has remained a classic text ever since. Lelewel welcomed the Cracow uprising of 1846 and it was at this time that he wrote *Stracone obywatelstwo stanu kmiecego w Polsce* (The Lost Citizenship of the Peasant Estate in Poland), an essay discussing the relationship between the peasantry and nobility in Polish history. His argument revolved around the erosion of what he believed had been the primordial rights of the peasant class from the Middle Ages onwards. In 1847 my historian joined the Société Démocratique Internationale. He fostered contacts with major players on the international political scene, such as Karl Marx, who wrote highly of *Histoire de Pologne*, and the Russian anarchist Mikhail Bakunin. Nevertheless, the psychological and material effects of émigré life took their toll, and the indifference of European powers towards the Poles greatly disheartened him. Thus, from the 1840s onwards, Lelewel's political rhetoric shifted towards a stronger emphasis on co-operation between the Slavic people. In 1848, in the hope of finding a satisfactory resolution to the Polish problem, he sent a representative to the Frankfurt Assembly and also to the Slav Congress in Prague, but it proved to be in vain.

Upon his retirement from politics after 1848, scholarly activity again became Lelewel's priority. His fascination with numismatics dated back to his youth: shortly before the uprising of 1830 he catalogued the entire collection of the Towarzystwo Przyjaciół Nauk and later that of Brussels' municipal library. In 1835 he published the two-volume *Numismatique du Moyen-Âge* and, a year later, a two-volume account of Celtic numismatics, *Études numismatiques et archéologiques* (1836). Geography and cartography constituted another area of interest. The ground-breaking *Géographie du moyen âge* (4 volumes, Brussels, 1850–2) marked a pioneering achievement in the field, even meriting a reprint in 1967 (published in Amsterdam). The four-volume *Polska wieków średnich* (Poland in the Middle Ages, 1846–51, with a further volume added in 1853) was an anthology of his earlier writings on medieval Polish history. Lelewel's collection of maps, which he bequeathed to Vilna University, belonged to the most notable in Europe. In addition

---

[3] *Uwagi nad dziejami Polsku i ludu jej* was published in Lelewel's collected works *Polska, dzieje a rzeczy jej*, Vol. III (Poznań, 1855), 31–469. Simultaneously, I also make references to the German version of his book, *Betrachtungen über den politischen Zustand des ehemaligen Polens und über die Geschichte seines Volkes* (Leipzig, 1845).

to an autobiography, he wrote his memoirs of the November uprising, *Pamiętnik z roku 1830–31* (Memories of 1830–31), first published in 1924. Lelewel died during a sojourn in Paris in 1861, two years before the outbreak of the January Uprising, another failed attempt to re-establish the Polish state. Despite his isolation from his homeland, where his writings were banned, he was mourned by thousands of people both abroad and in Poland and memorial services were held for him in Catholic and Protestant churches, and even in synagogues. He was initially buried in Paris, and in 1929 his remains were transferred to Vilna.

Lelewel was arguably the most influential Polish historian of the nineteenth century, exerting a lasting impact on Polish scholarship. The main tenets of his concept of history: his republican conviction; concern for the peasantry; reverence for the supposedly democratic nature of ancient Polish society; and belief that harmful foreign influences caused Poland's decline, constituted vantage points for future scholars, irrespective of whether they agreed with those views. The most exhaustive edition of Lelewel's oeuvre, initially produced under his own supervision, was published between 1855 and 1868 in Poznań, *Polska, dzieje a rzeczy jej* (Poland, Its History and Affairs, in twenty volumes), although Volumes XIV and XV never appeared. In the 1950s the Polish Academy launched a modern edition; however, this venture failed to fulfil its intended scope, with only nine volumes of *Dzieła* (Works) published between 1957 and 1973. In addition to the German, French and Russian versions of the Polish scholar's seminal writings, an anthology in the French language, *Joachim Lelewel: Textes Choisis*, containing excerpts from his writings, appeared in Brussels in 1986. An annotated bibliography of Lelewel's formidable scholarly output, *Bibliografia utworów Joachima Lelewela* (Bibliography of Lelewel's Works), was published in Wrocław in 1952.

DAUKANTAS

Simonas Daukantas's life story diverges from those of my other four protagonists in certain respects.[4] A solitary figure, who never found

---

[4] There exist two monographs on Daukantas in Lithuanian: Vytautas Merkys, *Simonas Daukantas* (Vilnius, 1991) and Saulius Žukas, *Simonas Daukantas* (Kaunas, 1988). Additionally, chapter 5 of Virgil Krapauskas' *Nationalism and Historiography: The Case of*

fame in politics, as the cliché goes, his sword was his pen. Leading an uneventful life, and denied the chance to publish many of his works, he received only modest acclaim in his lifetime. The occasional journey notwithstanding, Daukantas enjoyed scant opportunity to travel, and certainly not for the purposes of historical research. Whilst his colleagues helped to found scholarly societies, source collections and learned journals, such achievements stubbornly eluded him.[5] Yet, behind this seemingly uninteresting figure lies a remarkable man who produced multifarious musings. Although today he is best known as the first scholar to write history in the Lithuanian language, the range of his activities extended far beyond this, encompassing dictionaries, school textbooks, a prayer book, an anthology of folklore, translations of ancient and modern authors, as well as of agricultural manuals. All these were undertaken by a scholar who admittedly did not correspond to the archetypal Romantic-revolutionary hero but, rather, resembled an enlightened savant-educator. Daukantas was born in 1793 in Kalvai, a small village in Samogitia (Žemaitija, Żmudź), a region which spawned several contributors to the Lithuanian national revival. He was the eldest of five children and his father worked as a forester. Daukantas was initially educated at a nearby school run by the Dominican order, and, between 1814 and 1816, at the Vilna Lyceum. In 1816 he enrolled at the University of Vilna, creating a precedent for someone from his social background: with very rare exceptions the university only admitted students of noble origin. Tradition has it that Daukantas was even required to present a certificate of nobility before receiving his university degree, a problem which he solved by forging one.

Between 1816 and 1825 my historian studied at both the Faculty of Arts and the Faculty of Law and Politics. He was trained in Roman, civil and canon law and state theory, and ultimately received a degree in law, although his favourite subjects were classics and Russian and

Nineteenth-Century Lithuanian Historicism (New York, 2000), 63–84, is dedicated to Daukantas. An old essay by Vincas Trumpa, 'Simonas Daukantas, Historian and Pioneer of Lithuanian National Rebirth', *Lituanus* 11:1 (1965), 5–17, also contains useful information.

[5] Miroslav Hroch, in his book *Social Preconditions of National Revival in Europe: A Comparative Analysis of the Social Composition of Patriotic Groups among the Smaller European Nations* (Cambridge, 1985) establishes three phases of the national revival. In the first phase (A), nationalism is the concern of a small elite. In the third (C), it becomes a mass development. The connecting link between these two phases is the patriotic agitation of the intelligentsia by which national consciousness becomes a concern of the broad masses (phase B). Daukantas's lifetime fell to phase A of the Lithuanian national movement, whilst my other four historians' activities fell to phase B of their respective national revivals.

Polish literature. His interest in Lithuanian history was awakened by Ignacy Onacewicz, a professor of theology who undertook pioneering research into local history. Daukantas's final years at the University coincided with Lelewel's early years as a lecturer and he even enrolled on some of the latter's courses and consulted his works.[6] Yet, despite their shared intellectual milieu and fascination with history, the two scholars' accounts of Lithuanian history diverged significantly. The work of his friend and correspondent, Theodor Narbutt (1784–1864) an amateur historian who wrote a voluminous history of Lithuania in the Polish language, bore closer resemblance to Daukantas's approach. Daukantas chose not to participate in the activities of the secret student societies at the University. Nevertheless, he maintained close ties with a student group whose members were of Samogitian origin and later became catalysts in the Lithuanian cultural revival. His first historical account, 'Darbai senųjų lietuvių ir žemaičių' (The Deeds of the Ancient Lithuanians and Samogitians) was completed in 1822. It was not published until 1929, although the manuscript was copied and circulated among Lithuanian intellectuals throughout the nineteenth century.

After graduation in 1825 Daukantas visited Königsberg and conducted research in the archives of the Teutonic Knights. Later that year he became a secretary and translator at the office of the tsar's Governor-General in Riga. In all likelihood his departure was prompted by his inability to find employment in his homeland. The choice to settle in Riga might have also been influenced by the fact that the city housed significant primary sources of Lithuanian history; nonetheless the local archives ultimately remained inaccessible to him. In 1834 Daukantas moved to St Petersburg, where he found work as an assistant to the registrar of the Lithuanian Grand Ducal archives, which contained the most important sources for Lithuania's history, the Lithuanian Metrika (the state archive of the Grand Duchy, collected in the fourteenth to seventeenth centuries, written in a language similar to Belorussian). Ironically, as in Riga, Daukantas, despite being literally next door to his sources, and sometimes even using them to carry out his day-to-day bureaucratic tasks, found them frustratingly unavailable for his own scholarly purposes.

Daukantas's two manuscripts, 'Istorija Žemaitiška' (Samogitian History, 1838), and 'Pasakojimas apie veikalus lietuvių tautos senovėje'

---

[6] Daukantas's reference to Lelewel can be found in *Raštai* 1 (Vilnius, 1976), 51.

(The Story of the Deeds of the Ancient Lithuanians, 1850), repeated, developed and completed those ideas which he had set out in his first book, *Darbai*. All three accounts related the deeds of Lithuanians in chronological order. In 'Istorija Žemaitiška' (Samogitian History) the author narrated Lithuanian history until 1569, the Union of Lublin, which marked the cessation of Lithuania's independent statehood. However, on the final pages he announced his intention to continue his narrative beyond that date, but this aspiration remained unfulfilled.[7] *Pasakojimas* first appeared in 1893 and 'Istorija Žemaitiška' (in two volumes) was originally published under the title *Lietuvos istorija* in the United States in 1893–7. *Būdas senovės lietuvių, kalnėnų ir žemaičių* (The Character of Ancient Lithuanians) appeared in 1845 in St Petersburg. Published under the pseudonym of Jokūbas Laukys, it portrayed the material and spiritual life of ancient Lithuanians and became Daukantas's most innovative work, also distinguished for its literary quality and poeticized language. Unlike his other historical accounts, it followed a thematic arrangement and focused on topics such as religion, customs, commerce, geography and agriculture. In 1850 an extract from the book appeared in the Polish journal *Rocznik Literacki* (Literary Yearbook), and in 1926 the German scholar Victor Jungfer published *Alt-Litauen: Eine Darstellung von Land und Leuten, Sitten und Gebräuchen* (Berlin and Leipzig), an account which relied extensively on *Būdas*, but was also intended to rectify some of its inaccuracies.

Daukantas's concerns with the Lithuanian language were apparent in his ground-breaking efforts to codify written language, culminating in a three-volume Polish–Lithuanian dictionary and a Lithuanian–Latin dictionary (both published posthumously). An educational mission informed his Lithuanian prayer book, an ABC for elementary schools which became widely used in Lithuanian schools and a Latin exercise book, *Epitomae historiae Sacrae* with Lithuanian comments. The majority of his translations were specifically intended for children and young people, such as those of Cornelius Nepos's *De viris illustribus* and the fables of Aesop and Phaedrus. In addition, Daukantas translated the overwhelmingly popular adaptation of Defoe's *Robinson Crusoe* by the German scholar Joachim H. Campe, *Robinson der Jüngere* (1779), although his Lithuanian version, 'Rubinaičio Peliūzės gyvenimas' (The

---

[7] Daukantas, *Istorija Žemaitiška* (Vilnius, 1993), II. 552.

Life of Rubinaitis Peliuze), remained unpublished in his lifetime. Daukantas spent the summers in Samogitia where he collected folk-lore, which amounted to approximately 650 songs and 1,250 proverbs, sayings and tales. Many of these appeared in his anthology *Daines Žemaičiu* (Samogitian Songs, published in Petropilis, 1846). The same mission to educate also informed his translation of agricultural advice books from Russian, Polish and German. In 1850 Daukantas retired from state service and returned to his homeland, where he initially stayed with bishop Motiejus Valančius, who supported several scholars engaged in the Lithuanian national revival and wrote books of his own about Lithuanian history. Following a conflict with the bishop in 1855 Daukantas moved to Latvia and in 1861 to Papilė in Samogitia, where he died alone and impoverished in 1864.

Because many of Daukantas's works remained unpublished, his greatest impact was posthumous. Relying predominantly on conventional and secondary sources, he succeeded in devising a new conceptual framework for Lithuanian history. Apart from the originality of his medium, this scheme included the assertion that the Lithuanians sprang from Indo-European origins, an emphasis on the history of the common people, and a historical vision which venerated the Grand Duchy of Lithuania in the medieval epoch, whilst simultaneously disentangling his country's past from that of Poland. Overall, Daukantas's new direction paved the way for the Lithuanian cultural revival, as evidenced in the article dedicated to his legacy in the inaugural volume of the first Lithuanian national journal, *Aušra*, in 1883. The Lithuanian scholar's most popular history, *Būdas* was published several times, whilst the other three versions of his national history, originally published in the United States, reappeared in a series launched by the Lithuanian Academy. Its first two volumes, *Raštai I–II* (1976), contain Daukantas's national histories with the exception of *Istorija Žemaitiška* (1995), which was published separately. Furthermore, *Vertimai ir Sekimai* (Translations and Imitations, 1984) includes his translations and *Žemaitiška Tautosaka* (Samogitian Folklore, 1983–4) is a modern edition of his folklore anthology.

PALACKÝ

Palacký came into the world in 1798 as the second child of a Lutheran pastor-teacher in the Moravian town of Hodslavice, a frontier region inhabited by both Germans and Czechs.[8] He was first educated at a German school in a nearby town and subsequently at the Lutheran school of Trenčín (now Slovakia). He went on to study at the Lutheran Lyceum of Pressburg (Bratislava), a prominent theological institution which resembled, on a small scale, German Protestant universities and maintained links with them. Palacký learnt a wide range of subjects such as mathematics, theology, Hungarian public law and classics. He received no formal instruction in history and gained a considerable amount of knowledge through self-education. An exceptional command of languages (including proficiency in classical languages, English, German, Romance and Slavonic languages as well as Hungarian) enabled him to absorb an eclectic but impressive range of intellectual trends and authors, including foremost representatives of the Enlightenment and early Romanticism alike.[9]

In 1813 a flood compelled the 15-year-old pupil, on his way home from Pressburg, to spend a week with a family friend. The old man enlisted Palacký's help in translating passages from a Czech newspaper, because his own knowledge of Slovak and the old Czech language was insufficient. Palacký's competence in modern Czech turned out to be even weaker than the old man's, a shocking realization which marked a turning-point in his cultural orientation, prompting him to engage more thoroughly with the Czech language. As he later recalled: 'Up to this point I did not care for my mother tongue, I did not even like it: I preferred Latin and German.'[10] As a young man in Pressburg, he was one of the most popular visitors to local salons and his first scholarly attempts also date from this period. These included a translation of two letters from *Ossian* (which, at this stage, he believed to be original) and an essay on the Polish freedom-fighter Tadeusz Kościuszko. A study co-authored with Pavel Josef Šafářík, *Počátkové českého básnictví, obzvláště prozódie* (Elements of Czech Versification, especially Prosody, 1818, published anonymously), testified to the young scholar's interest in the history of prosody. He was also fascinated by philosophy and strove to devise his

---

[8] My account of Palacký's life draws heavily on the information presented in Josef Zacek, *Palacký: The Historian as Scholar and Nationalist* (The Hague, 1970). I also relied on the definitive monograph, which is Jiří Kořalka, *František Palacký (1798–1876) Životopis* (Prague, 1999). This book is also available in German translation: *Frantisek Palacky (1798–1876): Der Historiker der Tschechen im österreichischen Vielvölkerstaat* (Vienna, 2007).

[9] These influences receive extensive treatment in Josef Fischer, *Myšlenka a dílo Františka Palackého*, 2 vols. (Prague, 1926–7).

[10] Vojtěch Jaromír Nováček (ed.), *Františka Palackého korrespondence a zápisky* (Prague, 1898), I. 13.

own theory of aesthetics. Although this ambitious intention remained unfulfilled, a number of imaginative essays in the field reintroduced the use of the Czech language in philosophical treatises. Driven by a religious zeal, the young Palacký initially wanted to become a missionary, but later he aspired to be a poet. However, after some mediocre literary attempts, he decided against it, and increasingly dedicated his time to the study of history, especially to the Czech Protestant tradition and the Hussite period.

A new phase in Palacký's career commenced in 1823, when he left Pressburg for the Czech capital. As he later recalled: 'I was born in Moravia, educated mostly in Hungary and came to Prague because of my affection for Czech literature and history.'[11] In Prague he enjoyed the hospitality and support of the most prominent scholars of the age, such as Josef Jungmann and Abbé Dobrovský. With the mediation of these mentors he forged links with the representatives of enlightened Bohemian nobility, including Counts Kaspar and Franz Sternberg, eventually becoming the latter's personal archivist. In 1825 the Sternberg brothers, Palacký and Dobrovský decided to launch the journal of the Bohemian Museum, with the main aim of publicizing its holdings and, in more general terms, Bohemian history. The initial plan had been to publish this in German, but Palacký persuaded his friends of the need for a companion version in Czech, and from 1827 onwards, he became the editor of both the *Zeitschrift des böhmischen Museums* and the *Časopis Ceského Muzea* (Journal of the Bohemian Museum). Palacký's career as historian was 'officially' launched in 1826, coinciding with his triumph in an academic contest run by the Royal Bohemian Academy. His critical evaluation of the achievements of Bohemian historians since ancient times, *Würdigung der alten böhmischen Geschichtschreiber* (published in 1827) was praised by the jury as an outstanding entry which far exceeded the organizers' expectations.

In 1827 Palacký married Terezie Měchurová, the daughter of a wealthy landowner and attorney of Irish-Catholic origin. The union provided him with financial security as well as with valuable social contacts. It was at this time that he was approached by the Bohemian Estates, and in 1831 he successfully negotiated to become their official Historiographer. In this role, he was commissioned to produce a

[11] Palacký's letter to Graf Moritz Ditrichstein, 5 August 1827, quoted in Zdeněk Šamberger, 'Mladý Palacký a jeho zakladatelský význam pro českou vědu', *Strahovská knihovna* 11 (1976), 20.

history of Bohemia in the German language. This necessitated visits to several domestic and foreign archives: he consulted sources in numerous German, Hungarian and Italian towns, including the archives of the Vatican. The first volume of *Geschichte von Böhmen, grösstentheils nach Urkunden und Handschriften*, was launched in 1838. The stance which my historian adopted in relation to a controversy about two forged manuscripts, *Rukopis* (manuscript) *Zelenohorský* and *Královédvorský*, a major intellectual battle within Czech culture, stands in contrast to his advocacy of critical research. Palacký stubbornly defended the authenticity of these allegedly medieval documents, exposing himself to vitriolic criticism from German scholars as well as more subdued voices of dissent among his Czech colleagues. Palacký made a formidable contribution to institutionalization and professionalization. In addition to his instrumental role in the foundation of the German and Czech journals of the Bohemian Museum, he held prominent positions in the Royal Bohemian Society of Sciences, and was the driving force behind the foundation of a major scholarly-national society, Matice česká (Czech Matice), as well as initiating the establishment of the National Theatre. Another mission was the publication of seminal sources on Bohemia's history, resulting in the six-volume *Archiv český* (Czech Archive), and the first volumes of the series *Scriptores Rerum Bohemicarum*.

In the momentous year of 1848 Palacký found himself drawn to the focus of political life. Enjoying a solid reputation among German academics, who considered him a German historian, he was asked to join the Committee of Fifty, preparing for the All-German Constituent Assembly in Frankfurt. In his letter of response Palacký refused the invitation, stating that he was Czech and not German. This declaration directed people's attention to the very existence of the Czech nation, whilst simultaneously antagonizing the German political community, prompting the *Augsburger Allgemeine Zeitung* to comment that 'the entire German nation knows no more hateful name . . . than Palacký'.[12] Palacký's rejection of the Frankfurt invitation also defended the rationale of the continuous existence of Austria in the shadow of German unification; as he put it: 'if the Austrian state had not existed for ages, in the interests of Europe and indeed of humanity itself we would have to endeavour to create it as soon as possible'.[13] This gesture of loyalty was honoured by Emperor Ferdinand's offer of the portfolio of Minister of

<hr>

[12] Zacek, *Palacký*, 25.   [13] Palacký, *Gedenkblätter* (Prague, 1874), 152.

Public Education. Nonetheless, in order to avoid further confrontation with the German political forces, Palacký turned down the mandate. June 1848 saw him chairing the Slavonic Congress of Prague, the principal aim of which was to counter-balance the Frankfurt Assembly. Palacký was involved in the work of the Austrian Constituent Assembly, opened in July 1848 in Vienna and then moved to Kremsier in October, as a member of a committee responsible for drafting the constitution. He devised two versions of a federalist arrangement, but both were rejected and soon afterwards the convention itself was dissolved.

After the failure of the revolution, in the neoabsolutist era Palacký was, in his words, 'exiled from national life'. Under the surveillance of the police, and occasionally even threat of imprisonment, he withdrew to the family estates and devoted much of this time to the completion of his *opus magnum*, a comprehensive history of his nation. He considered all his other writings to be preliminary studies or merely preparatory labours for this ultimate venture. His initial intention had been to complete the text in German and subsequently produce an updated version in Czech, but following the harsh treatment he received from German scholars in 1848, he resolved to continue his project, which was now titled *Dějiny národu českého v Čechách a v Moravě* (The History of the Czech Nation in Bohemia and Moravia), in the Czech language. The content of the Czech version did not diverge significantly from the German, but the emphases of the narrative were placed at different junctures, with the focus shifting away from the history of a territory, Bohemia, towards that of an ethnic group, the Czechs. In the new text greater significance was attributed to the Hussite movement as the pinnacle of Czech history. Palacký soon realized that primary source-based reinterpretation of national history would be too time-consuming to allow him to encompass the modern era. Thus, he was compelled to draw the line in 1526, the year when Bohemia was incorporated into the Habsburg Monarchy.

Palacký recommended political activity in the 1860s, following the restoration of constitutional frameworks in Bohemia, as a member of the Imperial as well as the Bohemian Diet. Together with his son-in-law he presided over the National Party (Old Czechs) and took part in the negotiations between the Czechs and Vienna. In 1865 my historian wrote *Idea státu rakouského* (The Idea of the Austrian State, in the German version *Oesterreichs Staatsidee*), second only in political importance to the Frankfurt letter, containing his famous declaration, 'We existed before Austria, we shall still exist when it is gone.' Adjusting his views to the altered political circumstances and protesting against the impending Austro-Hungarian Compromise, he again put forward a strong case for a federal programme. However, unlike in 1848–9, this was not based on ethnic principles, but instead took into account existing historical-territorial entities. Following the Compromise he pledged his support for the Czech delegates' passive resistance at the Bohemian and Imperial Diet. Overall, his political engagement at this time, underpinned by clashes with the rival Young Czech party, was just as momentous as it was contentious. In the 1870s, with his health deteriorating, Palacký retired from politics and invested his energies in the completion of his national history. In a series of essays and memoirs he re-evaluated his former convictions and sketched out directions for the future. Like the mature Lelewel, his political-cultural orientation came to emphasize the solidarity of Slavic people; he even led a delegation to the All-Slavic Ethnographic Exhibition in Moscow. His political testament, *Poslední mé slovo* (Last Word, in the German version *Politisches Vermächtnis*), expressed remorse about his earlier belief in the necessity and viability of a strong Habsburg Empire and invested hope in the Russian Empire's political liberalization.

Palacký passed away in 1876, just one month after a banquet to celebrate the printing of the last section of the *Dějiny* (History). Thousands of people mourned the 'Father of the Nation' in a funeral which, as a contemporary observer put it, was more glorious than that of a king. Palacký's most important and enduring legacy is undoubtedly the complete, 3,000-page edition of *Dějiny*, reprinted numerous times, which encompasses the most significant components of his interpretation: the early democracy of the ancient Czechs; the perennial conflicts between German and Slavic culture; and the magnitude of the Hussite movement. Despite the refutation of these assertions, it nonetheless constitutes the most powerful narrative of national history, and Czech tradition would be unimaginable without it. The definitive edition of *Dějiny*, which contains the most complete elaboration of the Hussite period, appeared between 1876 and 1878.[14] Even without his *opus magnum* Palacký's career would have been exceptional, as shown by an impressive array of other works, ranging from brief accounts to

[14] Throughout the book I have relied on a six-volume edition which is based on definitive 1876–8 version. It was published in 1939–40 in Prauge by the publishing house Kvašnicka a Hampl and is more readily available than the earlier editions.

full-length studies, which represent a significant contribution to Czech scholarship. A selection of these was published in *Gedenkblätter* (1874), the more comprehensive three-volume *Radhost* (1871–3), and the three-volume *Spisy drobné* (Minor Writings, 1898–1902). A bibliography of Palacký's monumental lifework is to be found on the website of the Czech journal *Dějiny a současnost* (History and the Present).[15]

HORVÁTH

Mihály Horváth was born in 1809 in Szentes, a provincial town in southern Hungary, as the fourth child of a family with seventeen offspring. His father had historically belonged to the lower nobility, but earned his living as a barber and his family lived in impoverished conditions. Like Lelewel, Horváth completed his secondary education in a school run by the Piarists and subsequently he entered a priests' seminary. His decision was admittedly not motivated by a strong vocation for the priesthood, but rather by the opportunity for higher education that this afforded him. He viewed the novices' overtly restrictive routine to be an unnecessary burden, later recalling that 'people were entirely deprived of their own will'.[16] Nonetheless, the seminary offered a chance to pursue his interest in history, a subject that had fascinated him since adolescence, which coincided with a particularly dynamic and eventful period in Hungarian politics, characterized by the resistance of the Hungarian estates to the unlawful actions of the Habsburg government.

Horváth received a doctorate in theology at the tender age of nineteen, and was ordained in the following year. He subsequently alternated between poorly paid clerical positions and working as a private tutor for the children of noble families. Neither job brought fulfilment, and he found the isolation of the countryside disheartening. However, some improvement occurred in 1834, when the Marczibányi Society, a literary-learned institution, advertised an academic competition on the civilization of the ancient Hungarians. Horváth was awarded the first prize and, as in Palacký's case, this brought his name to public attention. His submission, *Párhuzam az Európába költözködő magyar nemzet s az akkori Európa polgári és erkölcsi műveltsége között* (Parallel between the

---

15 http://www.dejiny.nlh.cz/Bibl/Palacky.html
16 Horváth, *Magyarország függetlenségi harcának története* (Geneva, 1865), I. 225.

Moral and Social Conditions of the Early Hungarians and the Peoples of Europe), was first published in 1835. In the following year, another competition was launched by the Hungarian Academy, requesting candidates to assess the state of Hungarian industry and trade in the Middle Ages. This time Horváth finished in runner-up position and his book-length essay, *Az ipar és kereskedés története Magyarországban a XVI. század elejéig* (The History of Commerce and Industry in Hungary until the Early Sixteenth Century) was later deemed worthy of publication in the Academy's book series in 1842. Its sequel, which addressed the same topic in the context of the sixteenth to late eighteenth century, *Az ipar és kereskedelem története Magyarországban a három utolsó század alatt* (The History of Commerce and Industry in the Last Three Centuries), appeared in 1840.

Unusual figures captured my historian's attention to a greater degree than traditional ones. He dedicated essays to the natural son of the Renaissance king Matthias Corvinus, to the remarkable sixteenth-century noblewoman Ilona Zrínyi, as well as to Cardinal Martinuzzi, an eminent statesman in the sixteenth century who rose to his position from a very humble background.[17] For Horváth, the study of the common people represented an opportunity to undertake pioneering and in-depth research. A major contribution to the history of the legal situation of the Hungarian peasantry was his series of three essays, *Vázlatok a magyar népiség történetéből* (Sketches on the History of the Hungarian Peasantry) which approached the problem in chronological sequence from the Middle Ages until the late eighteenth century. The same motivation informed his study of a sixteenth-century peasant uprising, *Az 1514.-i pórlázadás, annak okai és következményei* (The Peasant Uprising of 1514, its Causes and Consequences, 1841), and the essay *Mikor fosztatott meg a pórosztály a szabad költözés jogától s mikor nyerte vissza azt?* (When was the Peasantry Deprived of the Right of Migration and When was it Regained?, 1839). Horváth was well acquainted with contemporary developments in political science and historical writing, and disseminated his knowledge to the Hungarian learned public through translations and adaptations. These included articles such as *Az országtani theoriák eredete, kifejlése és befolyása az újabb Európában, Heeren után,* (The Origins, Development and Influence of State Theories in Modern Europe, drawn from Heeren, 1842) and *Gondolatok a*

---

[17] These essays can be found in *Horváth Mihály kisebb történelmi munkái,* 4 vols. (Pest, 1868).

történetírás theoriájából (Thoughts on the Theory of Historiography, 1838). Other essays addressed the advancement of democratic ideals in the nineteenth century and the progressive developments on the European political stage after the French Revolution.

In 1841 Horváth became a regular member of the Hungarian Academy and three years later he was appointed as a teacher of Hungarian in the Theresianum in Vienna, a prominent imperial educational institution. Despite the unglamorous nature of the job and meagre remuneration, he enjoyed the luxury of being able to dedicate considerable time to historical research. Essays on the history of the Hungarian diets, the army, and studies examining the relationship between Hungary and Austria featured on his intellectual agenda. Another remarkable achievement was his history textbook for secondary schools (published in 1841), the first to have been produced in the Hungarian language, which received favourable reception, attracting praise for its lucidity and pleasing style. He completed a major four-volume *Magyarország történelme* (History of Hungary) in 1846, following the law of 1844 which declared that Hungarian should be the language of instruction in schools. This version was published eight times altogether, including a German translation (*Geschichte der Ungarn*, Pest, 1851).

In 1847 my protagonist returned to Hungary and became a parish priest in Hatvan, a provincial town. By this time he enjoyed a reputation as an eminent scholar who staunchly supported the cause of Hungarian liberals (especially those associated with Louis Kossuth) and the memorial speech that he delivered in 1847 at the funeral of Palatine Joseph, a statesman unusually receptive to the Hungarians' desires, further raised his profile on the political scene. The outbreak of the revolution, in March 1848, marked a new phase in his life. In June 1848, much to his surprise, he was made a bishop. Subsequently he was also made Minister of Culture and Education in the short-lived Szemere government. He was actively engaged in parliamentary discussions and tried to mediate between the ruler and the 'nation'. He also contributed to the codification of the law regarding nationalities and remained involved in the War of Independence that followed the Revolution, even helping to draft the manifesto on the dethronement of the Habsburg dynasty. As Minister of Education he advocated the separation of Church and State, a principle which he also propagated two decades later in the book *Williams Roger, „a szabad egyház a szabad államban" elv megteremtője, s megtestesítője* (Roger Williams, the Initiator and Representative of the 'Free Church in a Free State' Principle, 1868).

After the suppression of the revolution, under adventurous circumstances, Horváth succeeded in narrowly escaping from an impending death penalty, crossing the border disguised as the butler of a Hungarian noblewoman. Subsequently, in his absence, his name was nailed onto the gallows. He initially settled in Paris and earned his living by tutoring the children of the widow of Louis Batthyány, the unlawfully executed Prime Minister of the first revolutionary government. The year 1856 saw his move to Brussels and regular visits to the municipal archive bore fruit in a collection of *Hungarica* (sources relating to Hungarian history). These were published in Hungary under the pseudonym of Mihály Hatvani as *Magyar történelmi okmánytár a brüsseli országos levéltárból és a burgundi levéltárból* (Hungarian Historical Documents from the Archives of Brussels and Burgundy, 1857–9). The special significance of this four-volume collection was that it inaugurated the *Monumenta Hungariae Historica* series, the foremost Hungarian historical source collection. Upon the invitation of another Hungarian aristocrat's widow to tutor her daughter, Horváth left Brussels for Genoa in 1859. It seems likely that he encountered Louis Kossuth during his three-year sojourn in Italy, although by this time Horváth's support for him had begun to wane, as he believed Kossuth's dream of a Danubian federation to be unfeasible. Between 1862 and 1866 Horváth again lived in Geneva, and during this time, the improved, six-volume version of his *Magyarország történelme* (History of Hungary, 1860–3) was published in Hungary, causing a political sensation. The cover of the book suggested that this was a re-edition of his former four-volume work, but in reality it disguised a new and substantially amended text.

Horváth's original intention was to conclude his narrative with the year 1812 or 1815, in line with his belief that everything which happened after that time was not history but part of an 'unfinished revolution', still unfolding during the 1860s. Nevertheless, a friend (the eminent literary scholar Ferenc Toldy) convinced him to carry on until January 1848 (the outbreak of the revolution in Paris), because 'it would render more useful service to the nation than Kossuth's stirring speeches at meetings in America'. The result was a seminal and monumental study of the era between 1823 and 1848, *Huszonöt év Magyarország történetéből* (Twenty-five Years in the History of Hungary, 1864). The two-volume book, which was published in Geneva and then smuggled into the country, assessed developments in the Reform Era through the prism of liberalism. Despite the unavailability of primary sources, he succeeded in producing a book which has remained a definitive account until the present day.

In 1865 a further major book followed, *Magyarország függetlenségi harcának története 1848 és 1849-ben* (History of the 1848–9 War of Independence, published in Geneva), in which he recounted the principal episodes in the War of Independence and analysed its failure, distancing himself further from Kossuth's ideal of full independence in favour of the political forces which subsequently brought the Compromise with the Habsburgs in 1867. Initially the government banned the book, but it soon became a favourite of Empress Elisabeth, Francis Joseph's wife, who shortly before her coronation (as Queen of Hungary) invited the historian to her residence in order to discuss the book with him.

Horváth abandoned his clerical vocation during his period in emigration, and therefore saw no impediment to marrying his Genevan housekeeper. The marriage produced five children, two of whom survived into adulthood. Homesickness made Horváth yearn to return to Hungary. After an unsuccessful clemency plea in 1857, he was finally granted amnesty in 1866, after the defeat of Königgrätz, which considerably weakened the position of the Habsburg dynasty. Upon his return he received a warm welcome from Hungarian scholars and the learned public alike. The Catholic Church refused to acknowledge his civil marriage and granted him an honorary bishopric together with an annual living allowance. During these years Horváth's research somewhat declined in significance; nevertheless he lent invaluable support to the institutionalization of the historical discipline. In 1867 he was elected as the vice-president of the newly founded Hungarian Historical Society and later became its president. The published version of his inauguration lecture launched the journal of the Society, *Századok* (Centuries) in 1868. In the same year he became a representative in the parliament as a member of Ferenc Deák's party (Deák played an instrumental role in negotiating the Compromise). In 1848 Horváth urged the representatives to initiate the foundation of the National Archives. His most comprehensive, eight-volume *Magyarország történelme* was published in 1871–3, representing a landmark achievement: for the first time, the Hungarian public was provided with a substantial national history ranging from the ancient era until contemporary times. Horváth was also encouraged to collect and publish his earlier minor writings, an idea which did not entirely please him initially, as he believed some of his writings had become outdated. Finally, he accepted the offer, and the four-volume *Horváth Mihály kisebb történelmi munkái* (Mihály

Horváth's Minor Historical Works) appeared in 1868. Horváth died in 1878, during a convalescent sojourn in Karlsbad.

Although Horváth's immediate successors greatly appreciated his legacy, in the twentieth century he received far less attention than my other protagonists in their respective countries. Somewhat surprisingly, not even his remarkable *Huszonöt év Magyarország történetéből* (Twenty-five Years in the History of Hungary, 1864) merited a reprint, and only a limited range of his writings is available today. Among these is an anthology, *Polgárosodás, liberalizmus, függetlenségi harc: válogatott írások* (Budapest, 1986) and a critical edition of his essay on the peasant uprising of 1514.

KOGĂLNICEANU

The Romanian scholar was born into an aristocratic family in 1817 in Iaşi, the capital of Moldavia, and he was related by family and political ties to the upper nobility; his father was a close collaborator of the post-1834 ruler of Moldavia, Prince Mihail Sturdza. Kogălniceanu was fortunate to be educated in a 'noble way'.[18] He first received private education locally and then, when the Prince's two sons commenced their studies in France in 1834, he was invited to accompany them. At first they stayed in Lunéville, a town in the vicinity of Nancy. They were intentionally kept away from Paris in order to prevent revolutionary ideas from infiltrating their minds and, for the same reason, their teachers were monarchist and conservative priests. Kogălniceanu learnt French, Latin, Greek, German and some of the humanities subjects; however, contrary to his teachers' intentions, he could not be kept insulated from the currents of the age and developed a fascination with the social philosophy of the Encyclopaedists. The sojourn abroad also provided him with a contrast to the conditions in his homeland, for example, regarding the freedom of the press. At his father's request, he also kept abreast of technological developments, such as silk-production and sheep-farming, although he was aware that these could not be implemented in Moldavia on the basis of mere observation.

Towards the end of 1835 the Romanian students were suddenly ordered to leave France. As Kogălniceanu recalled several decades later:

[18] The definitive account on Kogălniceanu is Alexandru Zub's *Kogălniceanu, istoric* (Iaşi, 1974).

'French education seemed too revolutionary to our great protector, Tsar Nicholas I, therefore we were redirected from Lunéville to Berlin.'[19] He then enrolled at the University of Berlin and took courses in natural law, Roman law and history; whereas Greek, Latin, philosophy and mathematics were taught by a private tutor. In contrast to his previous isolation, my protagonist suddenly found himself in a thriving university, boasting some of the most eminent professors of the age, including Leopold von Ranke, Friedrich Carl von Savigny, Wilhelm von Humboldt and Eduard Gans, a professor of Prussian civil and criminal law. Kogălniceanu lodged with a Lutheran pastor, whose apartment served as a focal point for attempts to create a unified Germany. He followed the course of German unification with his own desire for the unity of the Romanian principalities uppermost in his mind and also realized that, in order to counter-balance Turkish and Russian ambitions of power politics, it was essential to win over the support of the progressive European public for the Romanian cause. This determination led him to the study of history: he comprehended that the precondition for achieving this objective was to raise public awareness of the very existence and the history of the Romanian principalities. By the age of twenty Kogălniceanu grew increasingly conscious of his future aims: to create a unified Romanian state and to implement political and social reforms whereby feudalism would be abolished and his country transformed into a modern society. He considered Count Hardenberg's programme of enlightened reform, informed by the ideal of (a) 'monarchy based on democratic institutions', to be exemplary for a future political arrangement of his homeland.[20]

Like my other historians, Kogălniceanu commenced his scholarly activities at an early age. Hoping to fill a lacuna in the knowledge of the foreign educated public and allegedly inspired by Wilhelm von Humboldt, he wrote a pioneering study of the Gypsies, *Esquisse sur l'histoire, les moeurs et la langue des Cigains*, which appeared in 1837 in Leipzig. In the same year his single-volume national history, similarly aimed at the foreign learned public, was published in Berlin, entitled *Histoire de la Valachie, de la Moldavie et des Valaques transdanubiens*. Focusing primarily on the history of Wallachia up until 1792, it was originally intended to form the first volume of a two-part work, but his subsequent immersion in politics, lack of adequate sources, and the ruler Prince Sturdza's unwillingness to approve a work which

---

[19] Kogălniceanu, *Opere*, Vol. I (Bucharest, 1974), 605.   [20] Ibid., I. 609.

might have offended Russian interests, prevented Kogălniceanu from producing the envisioned sequel. Of the 500 printed copies, eighty reached the principalities, but initially, they proved unpopular and two translations of the manuscript also remained unpublished. In the longer term, however, the innovative potential of this synthesis, in particular the use of historical arguments to reinforce unity, came to be fully appreciated. The year 1837 saw another publication by my historian: a brief overview of Romanian cultural developments, 'Romänische oder Wallachische Sprache und Literatur' in Lehrmann's *Magazin für die Literatur des Auslandes*, which appeared two years later in French translation.

In 1838 Kogălniceanu was ordered to return home by Prince Sturdza, who was alarmed by the young man's sympathetic attitude to the reformist, or even radical, intellectuals of the age. As well as working for the Prince as his private secretary, in the following decades he became involved in the promotion of Romanian culture in numerous ways. One of these was through journals, and, although his initiatives were invariably short-lived, their significance extended far beyond their print-run. The most ambitious enterprise was *Dacia Literară*. Founded in 1840, it represented an innovative attempt to foster national unity through the medium of literature. Other titles included *Propăşirea* (Progress, 1843) and *Calendar pentru Poporul Românesc* (Almanac for the Romanian People, 1842). Kogălniceanu published several of his own articles in these journals, as well as translations of varying lengths, including the short essays *Despre Civilisaţie* (On Civilization) and *Despre Pauperism* (On Pauperism). Similarly to my other protagonists, Kogălniceanu strove to publish primary sources pertinent to Romanian history. This entailed another short-lived journal specializing in historical sources, *Archiva Românească* (Romanian Archive, 1840), and the inception of *Scriptores Rerum Romaniarum* in 1845. The publication of the chronicles of humanist historians in two editions, *Letopiseţele Moldaviei (şi Valahiei)* (Annals of Moldavia and Wallachia, 1860) and *Chronicele României* (the Chronicles of Romania, 1872), represented a watershed in the history of source publications; some of these had appeared earlier in French, as *Fragments tirés des chroniques Moldaves et Valaques* (Iaşi, 1845). My historian also had a keen interest in theatre: in 1840 he became co-director of the National Theatre in Iaşi and worked as a theatre critic. Besides, two comedies and an unfinished autobiographical novel, *Tainele inimei* (Mysteries of the Heart), testify to his literary pursuits.

In 1843 Kogălniceanu launched a course on national history at the Academia Mihăileană (Mihailean Academy) in Iaşi. His inaugural lecture, *Cuvânt pentru deschiderea cursului de istorie naţională în Academia Mihăileană* (Speech for the Opening of the Course on National History) contemplated the meaning and purpose of history. In the absence of a more comprehensive narrative, this essay provides the most concise account of Kogălniceanu's interpretation of Romanian history. In addition to the inaugural lecture's significance as an embodiment of my historian's views, its message was also highly politicized; in that context, its emphasis on the inevitability of unification found a strong resonance not just domestically, but also among Romanian students residing in Paris. Nevertheless, challenging the status quo upset Prince Sturdza; consequently, in 1844 the course was abruptly cancelled and later that year Kogălniceanu was briefly imprisoned for his part in plotting to overthrow the Prince. Between 1845 and 1847 Kogălniceanu travelled around Europe, spending extended periods in Paris and Spain, the latter of which inspired his travel observations, *Notes sur l'Espagne*.

In 1848, like Palacký and Horváth in their home countries, Kogălniceanu became involved in the short-lived revolution in Moldova, again incurring the Prince's wrath. He escaped to Bukovina (an Austrian territory) and became a chief ideologist of the Moldavian Central Revolutionary Committee in exile, and his manifesto, *Dorinţele partidei nationale din Moldova* (The Wishes of the National Party in Moldavia, August 1848), set out a constitutional programme, reiterating the call for the union of the two principalities, as well as for civic and political liberties. In April 1849 the Ottoman and Russian powers appointed a new Prince, Grigore Ghica, who was receptive to the liberal and unionist factions. Kogălniceanu returned from exile and accepted high-level administrative posts. He promoted the idea of unification through the magazine *Steaua Dunării* (The Star of the Danube), also published in Brussels as *L' Étoile du Danube*. Another mission was to eradicate feudalism and, more specifically, its particularly inhumane practice, serfdom. To that end, Kogălniceanu's study *Sclăvie, vecinătate şi boieresc* (Slavery, Serfdom and Statute Labour, 1853), published in its original version as a foreword to the translation of Harriet Beecher-Stowe's *Uncle Tom's Cabin*, and two years later in the *Dacia Literară*, assessed the types of serfdom in European history and presented a strong case for its abolition in all forms.[21]

---

[21] Ibid., I. 592–602.

The outcome of the Crimean War in 1858 facilitated the unification of the principalities under Alexandru Ioan Cuza. As a close associate of the new Prince, Kogălniceanu was responsible for some major reforms put forward in the fourteen points of his *Profesie di credinţă* (Political Credo, 1860). Among these featured the secularization of the vast areas owned by the Orthodox clergy, electoral reform, the reorganization of the internal administrative and legal systems, creating equality before the law by abolishing boyar ranks and privileges, and the introduction of the Napoleonic code. My historian also played an instrumental role in the foundation of the University of Iaşi (1860) and University of Bucharest (1864). In 1862 Kogălniceanu delivered a speech in Parliament on the improvement of the conditions of the peasantry, *Îmbunătăţirea soartei ţăranilor* (The Relief of the Burdens of the Peasantry, 1862). His argument was reinforced by frequent references to historical precedent: on the one hand he emphasized that the abolition of feudal remnants was an indispensable humanitarian, as well as pragmatic, requirement of the age; on the other, he declared that a future resolution must take into account the historical specifics of Romanian society. Serving as Prime Minister as well as Minister of the Interior between October 1863 and January 1865, Kogălniceanu initiated the agrarian reform of 1864, which sought, albeit with limited success, to address peasant land ownership. After Cuza's fall and the accession of Prince Charles I of Hohenzollern in 1866, Kogălniceanu continued his active participation in politics, serving as Minister of the Interior on three further occasions between 1868 and 1880. As Foreign Minister he also played a salient role in securing Romania's independence from Ottoman rule in 1878.

In the 1880s Kogălniceanu withdrew from political life and focused his energies on academic commitments. He was elected to the Romanian Academy in 1868 and served as its president between 1887 and 1889. He spent time collecting historical documents and promoting archaeological excavations. His last significant public appearance in 1891 was a speech commemorating the twenty-fifth anniversary of the Romanian Academy: *Dezrobirea ţiganilor, ştergerea privilegiilor boiereşti, emanciparea ţăranilor* (The Liberation of the Gypsies, the Abolition of Boyar Privileges and the Emancipation of the Peasantry) called attention to the unresolved issues of land ownership and especially the lowly status of the Gypsy population; it also contained personal recollections of the scholar's life. Kogălniceanu had suffered from ill-health since 1886 and died in 1891 in Paris, where he was undergoing an operation. He was buried in Iaşi.

Kogălniceanu is primarily remembered and celebrated as a politician, the main architect of Romanian unification. His historical output, at least in the narrow sense of the word, was not as illustrious as that of my other historians, even though, as we have seen, some of his numerous and weighty parliamentary orations could also be defined as historical studies. Some cornerstones of his understanding of the national past, such as the postulation of Roman origins, were embedded in earlier traditions, whilst the rendering of national unity as a leitmotif represented a novel element. In addition to reshaping the Romanian political landscape, my protagonist exerted significant influence on the vistas of national life in his role as a publicist, theatre critic, editor and an outstanding organizer of cultural life. Kogălniceanu's historical and belletristic work, together with his numerous parliamentary discourses, were published in *Opere* (Works, in five parts from 1974), and a comprehensive annotated bibliography of his oeuvre, *Mihail Kogălniceanu 1817–91 Biobibliografie* (Bucharest, 1971) was produced by Alexandru Zub.

2

Romantic Historiography in the Service of Nation-Building

THE DEMOCRATIZATION OF HISTORICAL WRITING

'If the study of history has ever been essential, then it must have become so in our present age, in the time of disturbances . . . an altar on which we can rely . . . a prophecy which foreshadows the future.'[1] The words of Mihail Kogălniceanu, echoed by many of his contemporaries, testify to the widely accepted assumption that nineteenth-century scholars attributed an exceptional role to the study of history. By extension, those who undertook that study enjoyed considerable prestige. The nineteenth century was without doubt the great era of the 'backward-looking prophets'.[2] Historical research in the Romantic epoch extended to a variety of genres and subjects, but a great number of historians showed affinity first and foremost with the history of their own nation. Defining their intentions in stark contrast to the achievements of earlier generations, their stated goal was to renew historiography. The eminent French historian Augustin Thierry captured the mood of general dissatisfaction when he demanded that historians must no longer repeat the old stories under a new guise. He asserted that previous histories of France could not claim to be accurate representations because they revolved around a number of princely families. This idea resounded in his complaint: 'Accustomed from childhood to this historical pattern, we not only are not shocked by it, we do not even imagine that another could be devised . . . But a true history of France should relate the

---

[1] Kogălniceanu, *Opere*, Vol. II (Bucharest, 1976), 448. The statement was inspired by Augustin Thierry.
[2] These were Friedrich Schlegel's famous words.

destinies of the entire French nation: its hero would be the whole nation.'[3]

My protagonists elucidated their expectations of historical writing within this framework: they did not intend to follow in the footsteps of their predecessors because they believed that those accounts were insufficient. The eschewal of the historical writing of preceding generations, whether erudite humanists or scholars of the Enlightenment, became their vantage point from which they expounded their desiderata. Their ambition resided in writing a complete history of their own nation from its origins until recent times from a new perspective, one which encompassed the 'democratization' of every aspect of historiography: its subject, stage, medium and audience. Just as Thierry pointed to the deficient nature of earlier histories of France, Kogălniceanu regretted: 'Perhaps it is unique in the case of the history of the Moldavian and Wallachian people that all the chronicles of this country, all the memoirs of by-gone times, describe the life of princes, nobles and the clergy. Nowhere do the people appear, yet the prince is everywhere, although it should be the other way around.'[4]

In keeping with this criticism, scholars aimed to extend the scope of their writing, so that it would encompass the history of the entire nation. In particular, they proposed to incorporate the life of the unprivileged common people into their study, in other words, they sought to *democratize their subject*. This intention was academic in form, but political in content. The concept of nationhood in early modern Europe was associated less with common ethnic bonds than with certain feudal *privileges*, which only a small segment of the population, usually the nobility and clergy, enjoyed. Liberal historians redefined the privileges of political representation and property ownership as *rights* that should be bestowed upon a much wider sphere of the population. This attitude emanated from their conviction that, within society, a balance must be achieved between rights and obligations. Accordingly, the ordinary people, who had to share in the burdens, were to be entitled to the enjoyment of rights and membership of the nation. As a consequence, the terms 'nation' and 'people' no longer denoted different social strata, but became conterminous. It was in this spirit that the foremost Whig

---

[3] Augustin Thierry, *Dix ans d'études historiques* (Paris, 1834), 307–8, quoted in Gossman, *Between History and Literature*, 93.

[4] Kogălniceanu, *Opere*, II. 186.

historian of the age, Thomas Babington Macaulay, considered the Reform Act of 1832 that resulted in the extension of the franchise to be 'a Revolution which brought the Parliament in harmony with the nation'.[5] Lelewel displayed a similar outlook when stating that '(up until now) the Polish *szlachta* (gentry) alone enjoyed privileges . . . In place of the *szlachta* put the common inhabitants, the people; eliminate all the differences based on caste and discover that . . . the foundation of our fatherland is the people.'[6]

The redefinition of the content and nature of national history inevitably led to the questioning of earlier values and hierarchies. Kings and military leaders, whose exploits old chronicles celebrated, were no longer regarded as the real agents in history. At best, they were seen as 'heroes of power and repression', in contrast to the genuine great men epitomized by the 'heroes of freedom', who usually remained unacknowledged in historiography.[7] The dissociation from dynastic lines gained rhetorical validation though the rejection of the traditional way of periodization. With the genealogy of the nation no longer related to that of the rulers, a new chronology was proposed, in which the milestones of national history were not (necessarily) identical with the year of foundation and extinction of dynasties. Such new symbolical divisions often drew on models traditionally employed in the genre of universal history. They were typically informed by a teleological perspective and treated the nation as a collective individual whose existence tended to follow the pattern of individual biography.[8] Instances of a chronology of history paralleling the life of an individual included the scheme of the Scottish Enlightenment historian William Robertson, which divided history into dark ages, infancy and maturity, and Johann Gottfried von Herder's demarcation of humankind into child, youth and adult ages. Reiterated in the context of national history, such chronological patterns related to the changing fate of the nation throughout the centuries. The German scholar August von Schlözer devised a periodization for Russian history which contained four epochs: *nascens, divisa, oppressa* and *victrix*. As we shall see, Lelewel charted Polish history into Conquering, Divided, Flourishing and

---

[5] George Trevelyan, *Life and Letters of Lord Macaulay* (London, 1847), 347.

[6] Lelewel, *Dzieła*, Vol. VIII (Warsaw, 1961), 485, quoted in Skurnowicz, *Romantic Nationalism*, 65.

[7] Gossman, *Between History and Literature*, 90.

[8] Lothar Gall, *Confronting Clio: Myth Makers and Other Historians* (London, 1992), 12.

Declining phases, to be followed by 'Poland in the Throes of Rebirth'. An alternative version of chronology, employed by Horváth, detected two constantly alternating periods in the history of the nation, those of 'foreign influence' and 'national counter-influence'.

Since new history-writing no longer intended to focus on the life of rulers and on military affairs, *the stage of history was also democratized,* and was to be shifted from the royal courts and battlefields to less spectacular spheres of life. Macaulay formulated this omnipresent theme of historiography in the following way: '(The historian) must not confine his observations to palaces and solemn days. He must see ordinary men as they appear in their ordinary business and in their ordinary pleasures. He must mingle in the crowds of the exchange and the coffee-house. He must obtain admittance to the convivial table and the domestic hearth . . . He must not shrink from exploring even the retreats of misery.'[9] It was in this vein that Horváth compared the history books which revolved around affairs at the royal court and governmental bodies to a traveller 'who was willing to visit the highest circles only and who gave preference to the boredom of cool marble rooms over the cordiality of a cosy peasant cottage'.[10] Such sympathy towards the common people was accompanied by the observation that quiet alterations often resulted in more revolutionary effects than attention-grabbing developments in the limelight. By extension, scholars argued that real progress was rarely achieved by armies or enacted by senates, rather, it was caused by noiseless revolutions.[11] As a consequence, innovations in social and economic life gained more credit than military glory. Schlözer saw in the nameless artisan who first hammered out for himself an iron spade, a greater innovator than Hannibal who first led armies over the Alps and gained the victories of Cannae and Trasymene.[12] He also subscribed to another guiding principle of his age when asserting that the discovery of brandy and introduction of the potato, sugar and coffee exerted a deeper impact on history than the defeat of the Great Armada. Motivated by such incentives, historians sought to broaden the field of investigation,

[9] Thomas Babington Macaulay, 'History', in Fritz Stern, *The Varieties of History, from Voltaire to the Present* (New York, 1973), 85–6.

[10] This sentence emulated the statement of Wilhelm Wachsmuth, a German liberal historian. Horváth, *Polgárosodás, liberalizmus, függetlenségi harc,* 20.

[11] A powerful manifestation of this trope can be found in Thomas Carlyle's 'On History', see Stern, *The Varieties of History,* 97.

[12] Hans Peter Reill, *The German Enlightenment and the Rise of Historicism* (Los Angeles and London, 1975), 155.

so that it would embrace the history of society, commerce, industry and civilization in its widest aspects.[13]

That historians in the nineteenth century preferred to distance themselves from earlier traditions does not mean that they remained uninfluenced by them. The fact that all these principles referred to above had already been formulated by scholars of the Enlightenment (and in part those of the Renaissance period), though not necessarily with the accompanying political implications, highlights the considerable debt they owed to their predecessors' achievements. Such elements of continuity survived not just at the level of ambitions but also in scholarly pursuits. Whereas Enlightenment scholars employed a conjectural and philosophical setting in their study of society, government and language, Romantic historians took up identical themes in an empirical, historicized, individual-national framework.

What nevertheless distinguished the objectives of scholars pursuing the genre of national history from those of Enlightenment scholars engaged in universal history lay in the medium of their work and their audience. They aspired to write their histories not just about the people, but also *for* the people. Enlightenment historians aimed their histories at the learned public, whilst dynastic histories addressed a small group of fellow-scholars. National historians *democratized their audience* by extending their targeted readership to the entire (literate) population. This was to be achieved not only by political means but also through an element that all historians stressed: education. Thierry expressed his belief that French patriotism would benefit greatly if the knowledge of history was more widely diffused among the people and was therefore to become more popular.[14] In keeping with the widespread appeal and educational mission of national history, Daukantas directed his writings not only to the learned people but 'to the Lithuanian mothers who would like to tell their children about the deeds of the ancient Lithuanians but without having written texts would often make mistakes'.[15]

Liberal historians of the Romantic age liked to express their empathy towards the common people by rhetorically identifying with their fate. Thierry claimed that it was because he himself was 'born as a commoner' that he sympathized with and understood the concerns

[13] Ibid.
[14] Augustin Thierry, 'Letters from the History of France', in Stern, *Varieties of History*, 67.
[15] Daukantas, *Raštai*, Vol. I (Vilnius, 1976), 39–40.

of the unprivileged people.[16] Jules Michelet, who became a celebrated writer, public figure and tutor to royalty, constantly reiterated that he was himself a son of the people.[17] Irrespective of their social background and status, my protagonists likewise associated themselves with the destiny of the commoners, especially the cause of the peasantry. The extension of the intended audience to the national community necessitated the harmonization of the medium of writing with the requirements of the readers. Since the Renaissance period, vernacular languages had slowly but increasingly gathered strength and came to replace Latin, which had previously been used in academic texts. In early modern societies linguistic pluralism was considered normative and no close association existed between language and nation. Towards the end of the eighteenth century most states experienced a degree of linguistic homogenization. With the rise of the vernacular, historians gradually began to assume that the national language was the most appropriate medium for the study of national history and that accounts in foreign languages almost necessarily imposed a foreign perspective on their subject matter.

Although in some cases it is possible to speak of a pre-existing vernacular tradition, in East-Central Europe, earlier histories had normally been composed in German and Latin, and in the Romanian principalities they were also written in Greek, which was not intelligible to the majority of the population. Therefore, a shift to the vernacular language, the *democratization of the medium* became necessary. However, precisely because the vernacular had not previously been exploited for scholarly purposes, a great deal of linguistic work had to be undertaken to render it suitable for learned communication. This involved the standardization of the language, the creation of a new scientific terminology and the enhancement of the language through the medium of translation. Albeit to a varying extent, the five historians were all involved in such activities. In the case of Daukantas, linguistic endeavours were especially significant, because he was obliged to create his medium alongside his message and consequently embarked on historical writing in tandem with compiling dictionaries. Nevertheless, as we shall see, the importance which my historians ascribed to the national language varied in each case and none of them regarded language as the sole component of nationhood.

---

[16] Gossman, *Between History and Literature*, 95.

[17] Ibid., 157. Nevertheless, those sympathies usually dovetailed with a hint of dismissal or suspicion towards certain social groups, typically the urban proletariat.

A further point of divergence between Enlightenment-style philosophical history and national history lay in attitudes to the audience. Enlightened historians retained a distance from the public, and communicated to an interested, but never entirely complicit audience.[18] They also dissociated themselves from their subject matter and acted as detached narrators. In contrast to this twofold disengagement, for historians of the Romantic era these perspectives converged, as they identified both with their subject matter, national history, and their audience, the national community. They thought of themselves not as cold commentators but as apologists for their subject.[19] In this spirit, they often cast aspersions on Enlightenment scholars for their abstraction in historical matters and their exclusiveness; 'What time and talent have men wasted on metaphysical lubrications!'[20] lamented Guizot, and his colleague and comrade-in arms, Thierry, further elaborated on that disparagement when defining his credo as a historian:

The vocation I embraced was . . . planting for nineteenth century France the standard of historiographical reform. Reform of the study of history, reform of the way history is written, war on the writers without learning who failed to see, and on the writers without imagination who failed to depict; . . . war on the most acclaimed writers of the philosophical school, because of their calculated dryness and their disdainful ignorance of our national origins.[21]

In accordance with this intention, the success of national history could only be guaranteed if scholarly content was to be combined with popular appeal, making readability and lucidity of paramount importance. It was imperative that a good history should be, in Thomas Arnold's words, 'tangible', 'palpable', *handgreiflich*.[22] During this period, the historian was far removed from the specialist he subsequently became. His role was that of a teacher and educator, a purveyor of popular history. Hence, he attuned his narrative to the conditions of the readers: his presentation was not highly technical as readability was a crucial expectation.

---

[18] Karen O'Brien, *Narratives of Enlightenment: Cosmopolitan History from Voltaire to Gibbon* (Cambridge, 1997), 8.

[19] Gossman, *Between History and Literature*, 96.

[20] François Guizot, *Historical Essays and Lectures*, ed. Stanley Mellon (Chicago and London, 1972), 6.

[21] Thierry, *Dix ans d' études historiques*, 12–13; Gossman, *Between History and Literature*, 88.

[22] Thomas Arnold, *Lectures on Modern History*, 4th edn. (London, 1849), 209.

COMMITMENT AND IMPARTIALITY

Thus, in contrast to the histories composed only of battle scenes and dynastic affairs, and unlike the histories of Enlightened *philosophes* which appealed only to the intellect, the Romantic historians' aim was, in Thierry's words, to offer a history which addressed the heart as well as the mind.[23] A similar aspiration to make an emotional impact, amalgamated with a practical incentive, was reflected in Palacký's desideratum to write 'a *pragmatic* history appealing to heart and soul'.[24] To this end, references to the pragmatic nature of historical writing were ubiquitous on the contemporary scene: Johannes von Müller wished to write a pragmatic history of Switzerland, whilst Kogălniceanu declared that his course on national history at the Mihailean Academy would be conducted in a 'pragmatic spirit', and Lelewel and Horváth similarly subscribed to the application of the pragmatic method. Although the definition of 'pragmatic history', as expounded by scholars in the Enlightenment and Romantic periods could display subtle variations,[25] it is possible to identify certain common denominators which constituted its ingredients. A scholar who aspired to adhere to such principles had to fulfil the function of both teaching and entertaining, whilst appealing to a broad spectrum of educated and non-educated people. Moreover, a work of truly pragmatic nature had to resonate with contemporary concerns. As Horváth put it, the results of historical research could only be rendered meaningful if they infiltrated the realm of everyday life.[26]

In light of the significance that my historians attributed to the instructive nature of history, it is not surprising that they all endorsed the *historia magistra vitae* concept. Many of their contemporaries shared that conviction, including the above-mentioned Thierry. Such beliefs may run counter to a mainstream argument in historical literature

---

[23] Thierry, *Dix ans d' études historiques*, 10–11, quoted in Gossman, *Between History and Literature*, 87.

[24] *Dílo Františka Palackého*, ed. Jaroslav Charvát, 4 vols. (Prague, 1941), I. 71, quoted in Zacek, *Palacký*, 3.

[25] For a definition of pragmatic history from the mid-eighteenth century see J. L von Mosheim, *Versuch einer unpartheiischen und gründlichen Ketzergeschichte* (Helmstett, 1746), 28.

[26] 'Horváth Mihály beszéde a Történelmi Társulat első közgyűlésén 1867-ki május 15-kén', *Századok* 1:1 (1867), 9–10.

according to which the *magistra vitae* concept, despite its almost unbroken success until well into the eighteenth century, lost relevance with the emergence of the new, professional standards of historical writing. Manifestations of this type in subsequent periods, especially in prefaces, are interpreted primarily as appeals to the popular cliché lacking in practical effectiveness.[27] There is no doubt that some of my protagonists' evocations of the concept fall into this category: the inaugural lecture which Lelewel delivered in 1815 in Vilna paid homage to history as a guide, providing beneficial advice for state and governments.[28] Kogălniceanu's inaugural address at the Mihailean Academy drew on the definition of history as the mirror of the past and a tribunal where the historian played the role of the judge, whilst both of these themes also occurred in the other historians' writings.

Nevertheless, the validity of the argument about the declining prominence of the *magistra vitae* concept can only be maintained with some reservations. Firstly, it has been made primarily in the context of German historical writing and therefore neglected to consider a foremost representative of this tradition, Bolingbroke's *Letters on the Study and Use of History* (1772). Even in the first half of the nineteenth century the model could well mean more than a timeless platitude: the idea of historical recapitulation continued to underline strenuous attempts to read the lessons of history as the foundation of political wisdom.[29] Secondly, even within the German context some exceptions apply. The Freiburg scholar Karl von Rotteck (1776–1840), whose work enjoyed great popularity in East-Central Europe, was a German champion of this tradition.[30] Last but not least, even scholars who approve the argument about the tradition's waning relevance recognize its remarkably elastic nature which enables it to accommodate the most diverse constructions.[31] To this end, it eminently suits the genre and purposes of national history.

[27] Reinhart Koselleck, 'Historia Magistra Vitae: The Dissolution of the Topos into the Perspective of a Modernized Historical Process', in Koselleck, *Futures Past: On the Semantics of Historical Time* (New York, 2004), 27.

[28] His inaugural address was later published as part of the *Historyka*: 'O łatwym i pożytecznym nauczaniu historii', in *Dzieła*, II/2. 507–25.

[29] John Burrow, Stefan Collini and Donald Winch, *That Noble Science of Politics: A Study in Nineteenth Century Intellectual History* (Cambridge, 1983), 187.

[30] Jörn Rüsen, Horst Walter Blanke and Dirk Fleischer, 'Theory of History in Historical Lectures: The German Tradition of *Historik*, 1750–1900', *History and Theory* 23 (1984), 335.

[31] Ibid., 336.

It is true that, similarly to their contemporaries, my historians no longer saw history as cyclical or constant; their unfailing belief in progress presupposed a vision of the past which was essentially different from the present.[32] Nevertheless, this did not render the past an irrelevant experience: they seemed genuinely to have faith in history as a casebook which, if studied with a critical eye, contained solutions to the problems of the present as well as helping to avoid repeating the mistakes of their predecessors.[33] For example, when Horváth pledged his support for the Austro-Hungarian Compromise of 1867, he devised his argument on the basis of relevant episodes in the course of Hungarian history. Furthermore, when my historians embarked on the study of unprivileged classes, they did so because of their belief that finding solutions for the situation of the peasantry in the present required knowledge about their status in the past. It was in this spirit that Kogălniceanu's introduction to the *Archiva românească* (Romanian Archive) expressed the credo of a national historian:

Let our guiding book be Romanian history, let it be the palladium of our nationality. Through it we are going to learn what we did and what we have to do, through it we are going to see our future, through it we are becoming Romanians. Because history is the measure which helps to differentiate which nation is progressing and which is lagging behind. Therefore ask history, and you will learn who we are, where we come from and where we are going.[34]

Despite some considerable achievements in theoretical subjects (such as Lelewel's *Historyka*) my protagonists essentially represented a 'technical' school of historiography and showed more bent for craftsmanship itself than for ruminations on its philosophical and theoretical bases. Nevertheless, they did not remain unreflective about the limitations inherent in their profession. Palacký offered an illuminating formulation of this concern when he declared in the foreword to his *Geschichte von Böhmen* that:

I am far removed from the presumption of believing that I have always found the truth. The historian who can believe that has certainly never understood the seriousness of research. God alone sees into the heart . . . man however, judges everywhere from appearances . . . which often deceive us in the case of

[32] John Breuilly, 'Nationalism and the Making of Nationalist Pasts', in François Gemenne and Susana Carvalho (eds.), *Nations and their Histories. Constructions and Representations* (London, 2009), 7–28.

[33] Horváth, *Polgárosodás, függetlenségi harc, válogatott írások*, 23.

[34] Kogălniceanu, *Opere*, II. 404.

contemporaries, even friends. How could we hope to derive nothing but truth from the . . . deficient transmissions from the past? Honest investigation and effort are all that can be demanded and given.[35]

The five historians expressed a wish to write 'proper' history, 'true history', a desideratum which they associated with the concept of *impartiality*. Palacký attempted to write about John Hus with the 'greatest possible impartiality',[36] whilst Horváth voiced his regret about the unfair judgment which some great historical personalities received and expressed his hope that such partiality would be corrected with the benefit of hindsight, because 'history is the impartial tribunal of the world'.[37]

Impartiality has been defined in various ways, which renders it impossible to find one authoritative version of the concept.[38] Typically, the historian sought to address the truth. This is illustrated by the introductory remarks to Kogălniceanu's national history: 'I have been impartial, I have told the truth, but did I do it well? Being the first among my nation to attempt a major work, I myself recognize the difficulty of the task.'[39] The various definitions of impartiality displayed subtle variations but tended to include an element of detachment from the subject matter, engaging with divided opinion and transcending a single perspective on events. Further, impartiality was often associated with the observance of events from an 'elevated status', and the ability to rise above party interests or immediate concerns with justifying contemporary positions.[40]

It is not so much the definition of impartiality that initially demands attention, but rather a paradox that has frequently been employed to uncover the very nature of national historiography. Hindsight reveals a discrepancy between historians' definite political aims and the ethos of their profession, which demanded a commitment free of preconceptions

[35] Palacký, *Geschichte von Böhmen* (Prague, 1836), I. vii, quoted in Zacek, *Palacký*, 79.

[36] Palacký, *Zur böhmischen Geschichtschreibung* (Prague, 1871), 101–2.

[37] *Horváth Mihály kisebb történelmi munkái*, IV. 3.

[38] Even within the same generation differences can be observed, as for example, in the case of Robertson, Hume and Gibbon. See Jeffrey Smitten, 'Impartiality in Robertson's History of America', *Eighteenth-Century Studies* 19:1 (1985), 55–67; for the German context Reinhart Koselleck, Wolfgang J. Mommsen and Jörn Rüsen, *Objektivität und Parteilichkeit in der Geschichtswissenschaft* (Munich, 1977).

[39] Kogălniceanu, *Opere*, II. 45.

[40] Smitten, 'Impartiality in Robertson's History of America', 56.

and value judgements.[41] From this vantage point, the close association of the Romantic historian with his subject matter would render such a task unfeasible. But historians in the nineteenth century saw no contradiction between an impartial stance and harbouring political tendencies. On the contrary, they firmly believed that it was impossible to write history except from contemporary experiences, as those concerns determined what questions the historian had to ask of the past.[42] In François Guizot's view, impartial investigation combined respect for the past with the desire to contribute to the progress of society. Additionally, impartiality involved judgement by the standards of the whole rather than the interests of the part.[43] My protagonists' quest for impartiality likewise included an aspect of social commitment. Furthermore, it appears that at least some of their appeals to impartiality were informed by the desire to correct a prevailing interpretation which they believed to be extremely unjust or 'partial'. This applies especially to their critique of feudal society. Horváth condemned the 'partial' and 'prejudiced' nobility for their unwillingness to relinquish their privileges. In that context, impartiality meant freeing oneself from partiality, from the one-sided perspective of feudal noble society.[44]

ROMANTIC PROGRESSIVISM

Appeals to impartiality, the *magistra vitae* concept and pragmatic history were also frequently made in Enlightenment historiography, whereas there was a fundamental difference between the primary loyalties that informed the genres of universal history and national history. Enlightenment-style history has frequently been associated with a cosmopolitan view, and cosmopolitanism in that context is understood as a term which simultaneously encapsulates an attitude of detachment towards national prejudice and an intellectual investment in the idea

---

[41] George G. Iggers, 'Nationalism and Historiography, 1789–1996: The German Example in Historical Perspective', in Berger (ed.) *Writing National Histories*, 19.

[42] Gossman, *Between History and Literature*, 83.

[43] Aurelian Craiutu, 'Introduction', in François Guizot, *The History of the Origins of Representative Government in Europe* (Indianapolis, 2002), xiii.

[44] Ágnes R. Várkonyi, *Pozitivista szemlélet a magyar történetírásban*, Vol. II (Budapest, 1973), 58.

of a common European civilization. The savants of the Enlightenment (such as Robertson, Voltaire and Hume) assumed that histories and identities intersected with, and completed, each other but that individual states and nations were not, in themselves, intelligible units of historical study.[45] Romantic scholars believed in the meaningfulness of the study of the nation as an independent entity. Moreover, many of them shared the conviction of the contemporary German historian Heinrich Luden that 'the historian has to dedicate his attention to the history of the fatherland above anything else'.[46]

This approach and, in broader terms, the belief in the intelligibility of writing the history of the nation as an independent entity has commonly been associated with parochialism and contrasted to the cosmopolitanism of the Enlightenment. Enlightenment scholars have also been credited with contextualizing events within a European framework, which is usually understood as an antidote to the parochialism of national history.[47] Nevertheless, a distinction must be drawn between the ambitions of those scholars as expressed at the level of rhetoric and the completion of their goals: it has become a widely accepted viewpoint in the literature that the cosmopolitan tendencies of Enlightenment scholars in effect represented the universalization of their own particularism. As will be demonstrated using the example of their attitude to Eastern Europe, their 'European framework' did not extend far beyond familiar domains and they were not necessarily any freer from prejudices than their successors. In addition, it is important to note that in this era the word 'cosmopolitan' often acquired a connotation that deviated from the meaning with which Enlightenment historians endowed it. Cosmopolitanism could take on a pejorative tone when associated with the conservative and aristocratic values of the nobility, condemned for its egoism and ignoring all the world exterior to their caste. In contrast, the national idea, incorporating reciprocal solidarity between various oppressed nationalities, was seen to embody the true cosmopolitanism. In fact, therefore, its remit was wider and more encompassing than the 'cosmopolitan' but socially circumscribed world of the aristocracy.[48]

It is also worth remembering that the Romantic equivalent of Enlightenment-style universalism was not necessarily parochialism:

[45] O'Brien, *Narratives of Enlightenment*, 2.

[46] Heinrich Luden, *Geschichte des teutschen Volkes*, Vol. I (Gotha 1825), 10.

[47] O'Brien, *Narratives of Enlightenment*, 4.

[48] Andrzej Walicki, *Philosophy and Romantic Nationalism: The Case of Poland* (Oxford, 1982), 74–5.

whereas Enlightenment-style universalism was associated with the uniform forms of reason, its Romantic counterpart associated universality with variety and thus sanctified the pluralism of national cultures 'as unique and irreplaceable individualities of mankind'. According to the Romantic conception, the history of mankind resembled a wonderful symphony, with each nation representing a single sound. Each nation was appointed with its own historical mission, and contributed to the universal goal in accordance with its individual character.[49] *Romantic progressivism* was simply the temporalization of Romantic universalism. For Palacký, nations played a natural role in counterbalancing the egalitarian shapelessness of civilization: they added variety and colour to the world.[50] Yet, in his famous Frankfurt letter, the Czech scholar proclaimed that 'with all my burning love towards my nation, still I praise the good of humanity and of learning higher than the national good'.[51] In a similar vein Horváth stated in his inaugural lecture, delivered at the first meeting of the Hungarian Historical Society in 1867:

Nationality itself must not be our aim, but a tool for the desire to achieve a higher goal, the advancement towards humanity. Our final goals must be progress. The individual character of nations is an endowment of divine providence. It provides the most effective stimulus for competition, which is the inevitable prerequisite of progress.[52]

It is, of course, possible to argue that such declarations paid lip-service to the good of humanity. However, as we shall see later, an appeal to universal values formed one of the basic strategies employed by my historians when identifying their own nations' contribution to the advancement of mankind. One of the main premises of progressive-romantic nationalism was the brotherhood and solidarity of nations in their common struggle for freedom and justice. The slogan of the Polish uprising of 1830 (often used by Lelewel), 'For our freedom and yours', referred to the inhabitants of the Lithuanian and Ruthenian lands, whose cause the Polish patriots also served in their struggles to overthrow tsardom. Furthermore, the Polish revolutionaries called for the support of all nations of Europe as they maintained that their revolution had to be the revolution of all nations.[53]

The above line of reasoning, which established a causal link between history and progress and identified diversity as the source of progress

---

[49] Ibid., 75.   [50] Palacký, *Gedenkblätter* (Prague, 1874), 190.
[51] Ibid., 152.   [52] 'Horváth Mihály beszéde', 4.
[53] Walicki, *Philosophy and Romantic Nationalism*, 78.

as well as a distinctive characteristic of modern Europe, belonged to the central tenets of nineteenth-century liberalism. To the eminent representatives of this conviction belonged Guizot, in whose hands it became an elaborated liberal philosophy of history which was subsequently transmitted to English liberalism.[54] Progress provided a leading theme for historians of the age which appeared in countless variations. Macaulay's claim that 'the history of England is emphatically the history of progress' was informed by a conviction of the superiority of English civilization.[55] Palacký repeatedly wrote of the 'undeniable progress of the human spirit toward enlightenment and freedom',[56] and Horváth maintained that since the French Revolution, privileges, prejudices and authoritarianism disguised under divine rights were on the decline, while the ideals of justice and freedom were gaining ground.[57] Even Daukantas, whose writing contained no explicit references to contemporary developments and whose writings on ancient Lithuania tended towards a nostalgic tone, registered change as an imperative element in history, and his book commenced with the sentence: 'Nothing in this world that God has created ever remains the same, everything is subject to change.'[58] It may also be significant that both Palacký and Kogălniceanu edited journals which were entitled 'Progress'.[59]

The necessity and inevitability of progress was typically justified by and associated with the irreversible direction of the *Zeitgeist* or the will of divine providence, and the two were frequently considered to be identical. Like many of their contemporaries, my protagonists saw the hand of God in contemporary developments.[60] For example, a deist conception of God informed Thierry's declaration that the rise of the *tiers état* was the work of divine providence, and the representatives of the German historical school likewise assigned a role to the will of God in history.[61] My historians' understanding of the role of divine providence in history was that God intervened indirectly in

---

[54] John Burrow, *Whigs and Liberals: Continuity and Political Change in English Political Thought* (Oxford, 1988), 122.

[55] John Burrow, *A Liberal Descent, Victorian Historians and the English Past* (Cambridge, 1981), 35.

[56] Palacký, *Poslední mé slovo* (Prague, 1912), 54; *Politisches Vermächtnis* (Prague, 1872), 23.

[57] Horváth, *Williams Roger, a „szabad egyház a szabad államban" elv megteremtője, s megtestesítője. Életrajzi vázlat* (Pest, 1868), 1.

[58] Daukantas, *Raštai*, I. 403.   [59] *Pokrok* and *Propășirea* respectively.

[60] Andrzej Wierzbicki, *Historiografia polska doby romantyzmu* (Wrocław, 1999), 117.

[61] Gossman, *Between History and Literature*, 114.

developments through natural laws.[62] To this end, Palacký detected God's intervention in some episodes of the Hussite wars and, as we shall see in Chapter 8, Horváth emphasized the providential character of the triumph of liberal-democratic ideas in the Reform Age in Hungary.

SELF-CONGRATULATION VERSUS EMANCIPATION

Thus, in many ways, the five scholars followed a similar trajectory to that of other Romantic-liberal historians in Europe. Theirs was an intention to produce a national history in the vernacular, one which ventured into the realm of the common people. They aspired to compose their works in a pragmatic and impartial way and maintained that history was *magistra vitae*. Their interest resided in the study of national history in the first instance, but at the same time they related such history to the history of mankind. What nevertheless distinguished their goals from those of their 'Western' colleagues concerned their attitude towards the contemporary status quo. In the above-mentioned inaugural lecture of 1867 Horváth declared: 'Our century is the century of nationalities. Nations independent of foreign rule strive to strengthen their liberty under responsible governments. Nations that had fallen under foreign rule seek to secure liberty through the restoration of their freedom.'[63] The two categories of nations, as identified by Horváth, can be termed 'established' and 'emancipatory' nations, whose interests and aspirations often overlapped. In addition to promoting the extension of liberties to the unprivileged domestic population, historians representing 'emancipatory' nations understood that the freedom of the people was impossible without the freedom of their own nation in the concert of other European nations (whether it meant complete independence or not). 'Free people' and a 'free country' constituted the two fundamental postulates of liberal historiography in East-Central Europe.

Nevertheless, demands for a change in the European status quo needed to be accompanied by a corresponding shift in public opinion towards my historians' countries. As has been hinted, Eastern Europe was viewed by Enlightenment scholars through a lens of intellectual mastery:

---

[62] Zacek, *Palacký*, 70.   [63] 'Horváth Mihály beszéde', 3.

it provided Western Europe with its first model of underdevelopment. Eastern Europe was located not as the antipode of civilization, but rather somewhere along a developmental scale that stretched from civilization at one end to barbarism at the other.[64] That image survived well into the nineteenth century. Ranke's *History of the Latin and Germanic Nations from 1494–1514*, in which the Latin and Germanic nations were identified as constituting 'the core of all modern history', was a powerful and revealing manifestation of that stance. Ranke admittedly disregarded everything foreign to that core as something peripheral and, in that context, enumerated the Slavic, Lettic and Magyar 'tribes'.[65] It was against this backdrop that Kogălniceanu sought to demonstrate in his writings that the Romanians were not clods, but people of ancient and honourable lineage:

Three years have already passed since I left Moldavia; since then I have traversed all of Germany and a part of France. Everywhere I have found that no one has the slightest true ideas about Wallachia and Moldavia; their geographic position is hardly known; as for their history, their customs, their institutions, their misfortunes, even the most learned do not know them. The smallest countries of Africa and America are better known than these principalities. In this century of enlightenment the Moldavians and Wallachians are still regarded as a savage people, brutalised, unworthy of liberty.[66]

Thus, my historians had to place themselves in opposition to ignorant or sometimes even hostile Western attitudes from the perspective of 'established' nations and empires. Such nations were confident of their leadership in Europe and beyond and defined their achievements in a self-congratulatory way. Whig historiography was by definition a success story, the story of the triumph of constitutional liberty and representative institutions.[67] British historians, such as Macaulay, saw in Britain the guardian of general liberties across Europe, the champion of progress, the patron of mankind. They believed that the providentially favoured position of their country qualified Englishmen to play the role of pathfinder and instructor of the nations.[68] French scholars boasted about their country's civilizatory supremacy. Guizot

---

[64] Larry Wolff, *Inventing Eastern Europe* (Stanford, 1994), 9.

[65] Leopold von Ranke, *Geschichten der romanischen und germanischen Völker von 1494 bis 1535* (Leipzig and Berlin, 1824), I. iii–iv.

[66] Barbara Jelavich, 'Mihail Kogălniceanu: Historian as Foreign Minister, 1876–78', in Dennis Deletant and Harry Hanak (eds.), *Historians and Nation-Builders in Central and Southeast Europe* (London, 1988), 89.

[67] John Burrow, *A Liberal Descent*, 3.   [68] Ibid., 35 and 182.

declared that 'it is without vanity, I think, we may say that France has been the centre, the focus of European civilization'.[69] Representatives of these nations envisaged the progress of civilization as the imitation of one vanguard nation—typically, their own. Such a civilizing mission—bringing Christianity and Enlightenment to the 'barbarian', heathen people—was also used as justification for the often violent exploitation of subject peoples in the colonies.

In contrast to this self-congratulatory stance, my historians' narrative was characterized by a change-oriented, emancipatory tone. Because their own existence was not necessarily taken for granted, they had to find a raison d'être to counter the contemporary widely held view that groups of people needed to be sufficiently large in size before they could be designated as a fully-fledged nation. Such an approach was by no means unique to Central and East Europe, and even the existence of Belgium, Switzerland and Portugal was looked upon as inconvenient *Kleinstaaterei*.[70] Furthermore, the absence of continuous statehood was regarded as a further impediment to viability. Perhaps the most well-known manifestation of that conviction is Friedrich Engels's distinction between historical and non-historical nations. This concept resonated with Hegel's conviction, according to which nationhood was identical with the tradition of statehood and consequently a nation without state formation had, strictly speaking, no history.[71] Even as late as 1849 Engels contemptuously dismissed many peoples of the region as 'historically absolute nonexistent nations', who were doomed to extinction:

We repeat: apart from the Poles, the Russians and at most the Turkish Slavs, no Slav people has a future, for the simple reason that all the other Slavs lack the primary historical, geographical, political and industrial conditions for independence and viability. Peoples which have never had a history of their own, which from time to time when they achieved the first, most elementary stage of civilization already came under foreign sway, or which were forced to

---

[69] François Guizot, *The History of Civilization in Europe*, (ed.) Larry Siedentop (London, 1997), 11.

[70] Jo Tollebeek, 'Historical Representation and the Nation-State in Romantic Belgium (1830–1850)', *Journal of the History of Ideas* 59:2 (1998), 335; Eric Hobsbawm, *Nations and Nationalism since 1780: Programme, Myth, Reality* (Cambridge, 1991), 30–2; Oliver Zimmer, *A Contested Nation: History, Memory and Nationalism in Switzerland, 1761–1891* (Cambridge, 2003), xiii.

[71] Georg Wilhelm Friedrich Hegel, *Elements of the Philosophy of Right*, (ed.) Allen Wood (Cambridge, 1991), 375.

attain the first stage of civilization only by means of a foreign yoke, are not viable and will never be able to achieve any kind of independence.[72]

In 1848 it was the liberals and, in particular, the democrats who were more outspoken opponents of Slav strivings for autonomy than the conservatives, and were even prepared to risk a general European war.[73] It is true that Marx and Engels thought of the Poles as a 'necessary nation' and the restoration of Poland was seen by them as a point of honour for all the democrats of Europe, as well as the only way of annihilating Russia's domination over Eastern and Central Europe.[74] However, such moral support made little impact on the contemporary status quo. Thus, the desire on my historians' part to achieve both greater independence and recognition precipitated an emphasis on the necessity for change. Established nations saw in the ideal of Europe as a harmonious system of balancing states, a justification for political action. In contrast, the way the status quo was regarded by emancipatory nations was succinctly expressed by Palacký: 'It is a farce to make high-sounding proclamations about equilibrium in the political system of Europe, and tear apart countries, raise up robbers' hands against the holy rights, against the lives of glorious but unhappy nations.'[75]

THE BLUEPRINT OF NATIONAL
HISTORIOGRAPHY

The self-asserting strategies inherent in the self-congratulatory rhetoric of established nations and those intrinsic to the rhetoric of non-dominant nations made recourse to the same criteria. This is small wonder: since the self-justification of emancipatory nations was directed not only at the national community, but also towards dominant nations, it had to accept 'the rules of the game', the standards set by scholars representing established nations. As a consequence, arguments for the maintenance of the status quo and claims for an adjustment to the

[72] Friedrich Engels, 'Democratic Panslavism', in Marx and Engels, *Collected Works*, Vol. VIII (New York, 1977), 367.
[73] Iggers, 'Nationalism and Historiography, 1789–1996', 17.
[74] Walicki, *Philosophy and Romantic Nationalism*, 362–3 and 368.
[75] Agnew LeCaine Hugh, 'Czechs, Germans, Bohemians? Images of Self and Other in Bohemia to 1848', in Nancy Wingfield (ed.), *Creating the Other in the Nineteenth Century: Ethnic Conflict and Nationalism in the Habsburg Empire* (Oxford and New York, 2004), 64.

status quo were made on the same or a similar basis. Expectations from a nation with an 'established position' included a glorious history, which was *ancient, continuous, unified and unique*. These leading themes appeared in countless variations, but on the whole, the core aspects were considered axiomatic and had to be articulated and justified through well-grounded historical arguments.[76] Certainly, achieving such benchmarks required a great deal of 'engineering' on the part of the historian. There is no doubt that Romantic history-writing primarily focused on the 'ought' rather than the 'is' and as a consequence acquired a prescriptive tone.

Attributes that testified to those standards were sought and found in the history of law, language, literature, religion, institutions and also in customs and folklore. They included arguments based on historical rights and those appealing to natural rights, and the most effective claims revolved around a combination of these two aspects. Historians often diagnosed the forerunners of the contemporary parliament and constitution in ancient or even primordial institutions and assumed a degree of continuity between the old and contemporary establishments. Emphasis was placed on demonstrating the authenticity of native laws and customs which sought to provide an alternative to foreign legal traditions, especially those of Teutonic-Roman origin. In addition, thanks to its capacity to cut across regional borders and social divisions, the national language provided an especially suitable medium for voicing arguments for antiquity, continuity and unity. Last but not least, a distinctive ecclesiastical tradition, whether the Saxon Church in English historiography, the ancient pagan-Baltic religion in Daukantas's writings or Hussitism in Palacký's narrative was similarly regarded as constituting part of a unique national heritage. Its veneration typically involved a latent or more explicit critique of the influence of the Catholic Church in national history.

Antiquity was rarely associated with the date of state foundation even in the case of nations which boasted an established state tradition. As the argument went, the history of the people was more ancient than that of the state. The period of national antiquity was identified with an 'original', 'natural' situation, with freedom from time immemorial. That era, deemed as a normative epoch, was often contrasted to the contemporary standing of the nation, especially with regard to liberty and

---

[76] For an illuminating and convincing study of these leitmotifs in the Romanian context see Lucian Boia, *History and Myth in Romanian Consciousness* (New York, 2001).

freedom. Precisely because of the above-mentioned implicit consensus about the limited number of eventual viable entities in Europe, the emphasis on antiquity involved more than a glittering jewel attached to national history by ambitious, fantasizing historians. For example, possessing sufficient credentials in terms of seniority was considered an essential component of the claims for the restoration of the Polish state. As we shall see later, of special significance was the question of early occupancy in the case of overlapping territories, when more than one nation laid claim to a certain region. In these cases the legitimate ownership of the land was deemed to belong to the first occupant of the territory.

The reconstitution of *continuities*, of a suitable history which links present to past, characterizes every society. The quest for historic continuities is to be located especially in those places and at those times in which a national identity emerges and crystallizes.[77] Historians were constantly confronted with discontinuities: periods of foreign invasion, social turmoil, changing borders. Their role was to eradicate or at least smooth over those ruptures with the past and promote reconciliation. They assumed that however discontinuous the history of their state might have been, 'underneath', the people had always possessed a continuous history. For example, contemporary French historians saw the history of France as continuous with that of ancient Gaul, whilst English historians argued for some degree of continuity with the Anglo-Saxon period. By the same token, Palacký drew a line of continuity between the 'democratic' ideals and institutions of ancient Slavs, those of the representatives of the Hussite movement, and his own liberal-national demands. An effective strategy for creating continuity lay in 'reading history backward' in a teleological way, to arrive at foundational dates for national history.[78] Following that route, the Magna Carta of 1215 came to be seen as the origin of the long parliamentary tradition in Britain by Whig historians, and the ancient Roman Empire was perceived as the precursor of the Italian nation-state. In a similar way, Kogălniceanu detected the first attempt at the creation of national unity in the dynastic ambitions of the Wallachian prince, Michael the Brave in the

---

[77] Billie Melman, 'Claiming the Nation's Past: The Invention of an Anglo-Saxon Tradition', *Journal of Contemporary History* 26:3–4 (1991), 575.

[78] Berger, Donovan and Passmore, 'Apologias for the Nation State in Western Europe since 1800', 11.

early seventeenth century, who managed to unite the principalities of Moldavia, Wallachia and Transylvania for a short time under his auspices.

Bearing in mind that the historians' narrative was imbued with a progressivist, change-oriented tone, the question arises: how was it possible to reconcile arguments revolving around antiquity and continuity with a modernizing discourse? This question appears to be all the more relevant because from the eighteenth century onwards, the idea of the progress of society inverted a great deal of the prestige hitherto attached to antiquity and assumed the necessity of divorcing the past from the present.[79] Furthermore, a historical-philosophical doctrine of the rights of man, including the ideals of popular sovereignty and self-determination, likewise challenged historians' claims to ancient rights.[80] Scholars devised various strategies in order to reconcile the conflicting nature of arguments centring on antiquity and those revolving around progress. An especially effective one was to wrap demands for change in recourse to the past and put forward the argument that the required change represented not dissociation with antiquity, but on the contrary the restoration of the ancient values of society. Following that train of thought, it was argued that the contemporary situation represented a rupture in continuity with the normative ancient tradition. As a consequence, only through the revision of the contemporary situation could conditions be rendered correspondent to the original situation. For instance, Lelewel supported his claim for the extension of civic liberties by appealing to antiquity, maintaining that in ancient Polish society membership of the nation extended to the entire population: 'As long as the peasants and townsmen do not *return* to the complete rights of citizenship, as long as they are not called to political life . . . as long as their needs are not met, one cannot expect the freedom and independence of Poland.'[81]

'What the Church and religion were to the sixteenth and seventeenth centuries such to our age is the idea of nationality' declared Palacký upon expounding his views on the conflicting centrifugal and centripetal forces that he saw as inherent in contemporary Europe.[82] His statement bears witness to the emergence of a new fundamental unifying historical myth in nineteenth-century Europe, one which saw in the nation-state

---

[79] Burrow, *A Liberal Descent*, 21.   [80] Ibid., 21.

[81] Lelewel, *Dzieła*, VIII. 482, quoted in Skurnewicz, *Romantic Nationalism*, 67.

[82] Palacký, *Spisy drobné*, Vol. I (Prague, 1898), 113.

a privileged form of unity. Pursuit of unity encompassed complex and multifarious layers: social, geographical, ethnic-linguistic and sometimes religious aspects. As I have discussed above, *social unity* was to be created through the study of the history of groups that were hitherto excluded from the subjects of historical writing as well as from membership in the nation and through the promotion of common interests and the reconciliation of various social groups. Nevertheless, in an era when borders were not yet fixed on grounds of ethnicity and language, and when regional identities survived, members of the envisaged national community often remained fragmented in different political entities. In order to tackle this fragmentation, historians had to create the illusion of *geographical unity* of various lands and provinces by moulding them into a coherent vision of history. Thus, hitherto distinct lands and regions were, for the first time, treated as national history, as a history of a national desideratum.[83] The gradual fading of internal borders in national history-writing went hand in hand with a more precise demarcation of the national territory vis-à-vis foreign lands.

However, from the time that the revolutionaries had aimed to unite France, the removal of the obstacles to unity had involved a supreme paradox: exclusion in order to unite.[84] A more precise definition of nationhood provided criteria not only for determining who belonged to the nation but also for ascertaining who did not. In particular, the desire for *ethnic-linguistic unity* rendered the status of different ethnic and linguistic groups questionable within the national community. Yet, as we shall see, the 'solutions' offered by national historiography in this era comprised both options which proposed cultural assimilation and ones which sought to accommodate the diverse ethnic and linguistic groups within the national community and, by extension, within national history. Last but not least, to varying degrees, *religious differences* could also be viewed as impediments to the scheme of national unity in the multireligious societies of East-Central Europe, and this was particularly problematic with regard to the position of the Jewish population within the nation.

All national histories showed a notable zeal in demonstrating the *uniqueness* of their national heritage. Whig historians in Britain venerated the tradition of parliamentary liberalism, French historians revered

---

[83] Boia, *History and Myth*, 42.
[84] Stanley Hoffmann, 'The Nation, Nationalism, and After: The Case of France'. *The Tanner Lectures on Human Values*, Vol. XV (Salt Lake City, Utah, 1994), 224.

the unique significance of the 'Great Revolution' and Italian scholars liked to think of their homeland as the birthplace of European civilization.[85] A parallel can be drawn with the characteristics that my historians identified and reserved for their own national past. For Lelewel the Polish Commonwealth represented the only true republic among larger European nations and Palacký saw in the Hussite movement the first attempt in history to undermine the two main pillars of the Middle Ages: the authority of the Church in the religious sphere and the decisive role of the Holy Roman Empire in the secular realm. Identifying unique attributes of national history and defining the nation's mission also served the aims of self-justification because such contributions rendered the nation 'irreplaceable' in the view of national historians. However, most nations sought to justify their existence by emphasizing the same 'unique' features. This resulted in a peculiar twofold attitude which non-dominant nations adopted vis-à-vis dominant nations: one which was simultaneously *negative* and *analogous*, in which great powers were seen as both models and menaces.[86] On one hand, they differentiated themselves from dominant nations on the basis of unique characteristics. On the other, those unique features were often identical with the criteria which dominant nations employed for their own self-definition. For example, as we shall see, Lelewel maintained that the history of Poland did not follow the path of 'Western' developments, but the qualities which he associated with Poland's distinct path—freedom, democratic values, tolerance, etc.—were identical with the characteristics which French and English historians employed to define the uniqueness of their own nation.

CONSOLATION AND ENCOURAGEMENT

In addition to the themes which constituted the common heritage of the European historiographical tradition, certain rhetorical strategies appear to have been distinctive to the argumentation of emancipatory nations. As I have demonstrated above, contrary to mainstream contemporary opinion, my protagonists did not consider 'size' an essential virtue. To this end, an episode from the beginning of Palacký's career illuminates

---

[85] Berger, Donovan and Passmore, 'Apologias for the Nation State', 10.

[86] Vladimír Macura, *Znamení zrodu. České obrození jako kulturní typ*, 2nd edn. (Prague, 1995), 36.

the dilemmas which a historian representing 'smaller' nations had to confront. In 1818 the young Palacký announced to his friends his intention to write 'a history of Bohemia in the fifteenth century à la William Robertson'.[87] This ambition received a sceptical response, his friends asserting that 'the Czechs could not have a great historian because they do not have a great history'.[88] Palacký disagreed, pointing out that the Scottish Walter Scott and William Robertson as well as the Swiss Johannes von Müller, while representing 'less glorious' historical traditions, nonetheless succeeded in becoming great historians. When his friends expressed further doubts, believing that Palacký's effort was too late because the true historical spirit had already been extinguished in Bohemia, Palacký rebutted their sceptical stance, asserting that despite great handicaps—their small numbers, their landlocked geographical position and the enmity of their German neighbours and their domestic upheavals—the Czechs had a noteworthy past. This was because, according to Palacký, 'the glory of nations is not based on their number or on their physical strength, it lies in their life, their spirit' (*duch*).[89] This statement reverberated in his letter to Frankfurt in 1848 where he proudly declared that '[my] nation is a small one, it is true, but from time immemorial it has been a nation of itself and existing of itself'.[90] Palacký's claim indicates that, where circumstances dictate, the historian will take equal pride in smallness as in grandeur, and will emphasize that the contribution of his nation to civilization is much greater than its size would suggest.

Furthermore, as the history of emancipatory nations typically abounded in tragic occurrences, in addition to its traditional role, the maintenance of memory, historical writing increasingly assumed the role of consolation and self-defence. Lelewel evoked episodes from the past because 'the nation which loses its existence and looks for its rebirth by remembrance of the past gains strength'.[91] In 1867, revisiting the gloomy epoch of neoabsolutism after the failure of the Hungarian revolution and war of independence in 1848–9, Horváth declared in a similar vein that the mission of historical writing lay in offering consolation and awakening hope. It had to remind people that just as the storms of the past deprived the nation only of its leaves but not its roots, the present was likewise covered by passing clouds

---

[87] Kořalka, *František Palacký (1798–1876) Životopis*, 46.   [88] Ibid., 46.
[89] Palacký, *Korrespondence a zápisky*, I. 36, quoted in Zacek, *Palacký*, 30.
[90] Palacký, *Gedenkblätter*, 150.   [91] Skurnewicz, *Romantic Nationalism*, 35.

only, and once they had broken, new leaves would appear on the crushed tree of the nation.[92] Kogălniceanu resorted to the past for self-defence: 'National history is absolutely necessary to us for the defence of our rights against foreign nations . . . They have denied our origin and our name, partitioned our land, trampled upon our rights, only because we have not had the consciousness of our nationality, only because we have not been able to establish and defend our rights.'[93]

The extended emphasis on the disastrous aspects could easily result in the victimization of the past, an element which nevertheless could also appear in the historiography of established nations. In that context Macaulay famously claimed that his nation had been exempt from the ills which other nations experienced: 'While every part of the continent, from Moscow to Lisbon, has been the theatre of bloody and devastating wars, no hostile standard has been seen here but as a trophy. While revolutions have taken place all around us, our government has never once been subverted by violence.'[94] In contrast to this, as we shall see, my protagonists' typical claims included the portrayal of the national territories as the 'crossroads' of nations and the 'battlefields' of Europe. The sufferings and sacrifices were rendered meaningful by advancing the conviction that other nations profited from them. This allowed historians to develop an argument according to which their nations were moral creditors and not debtors to European civilization. In turn, an assertion of that kind could provide at least partial justification for the backwardness of my protagonists' societies: if their nation was lagging behind, this was because valuable resources had to be sacrificed for the benefit of others. Furthermore, as we shall see in the following chapters, unsurprisingly for national historiographies seeking to reassert their individual standing, the theme of *self-support*, the conviction that reliance on foreign assistance could not provide solutions, constituted a further recurring motif in my historians' writings.

A great number of historians in the Romantic era wrote oppositional narratives and did not foresee the culmination of national history in the present. Notable exceptions included the Whig historians for whom the Reform Bill of 1832 marked the finale of English history, the ultimate result of that which had been initiated with the Glorious Revolution

---

[92] 'Horváth Mihály beszéde', 7.   [93] Kogălniceanu, *Opere*, II. 389.
[94] Thomas Babington Macaulay, *History of England*, 6 vols. (1849–61), I. 271–2.

of 1688.[95] In a similar way, for the French liberal historians (although not left-wing historians like Jules Michelet) the July Revolution of 1830 symbolized the concluding moment of national history. Following that watershed, they attempted to justify the existing regime in which they occupied prominent political roles.[96] As we shall see, the characteristic vein of my historians' narrative was oppositional, but Horváth's narrative acquired a more satisfied tone after the Compromise and Kogălniceanu's stance underwent a major transformation after Romania gained the status of an independent nation-state in which he became part of the governing elite.

CONCLUSION: DESIDERATA AND FULFILMENTS

Taking the ambitions of Romantic historians at face value and considering how effectively they were fulfilled reveals a wide lacuna. In fact, the goals that historians set for themselves were so ambitious that even the strenuous efforts of several generations supported by a well-established institutional setting could not have succeeded in achieving them. The task of writing the complete history of the nation, from its origins to the contemporary period, in an innovative style, often proved to be an endeavour that exceeded the life-span of individual historians. They often passed away before they could complete their narratives or realized in the course of their lifetimes that only a more limited programme could be manageable. Daukantas entertained the idea of writing the history of Lithuania after 1569, in which year his accounts terminated, but such a plan never materialized. Towards the end of his life Palacký concluded that 'it is certain that with the year 1526 my work is ended, but not at all completed'.[97] They were by no means alone. Macaulay intended to write the history of his country as far as the era in which he lived but only reached the glorious revolution of 1688, Heinrich Luden's German history terminated in the thirteenth century, and Johannes von Müller's narrative on Switzerland could likewise only cover the medieval period. In addition to the extremely ambitious nature of such projects

---

[95] Benedikt Stutchtey, 'Literature, Liberty and the Life of the Nation: British Historiography from Macaulay to Trevelyan', in Berger (ed.) *Writing National Histories*, 32.

[96] See Ceri Crossley, 'History as a Principle of Legitimation in France (1820–48)', in Berger (ed.), *Writing National Histories*, 55.

[97] Zacek, *Palacký*, 93.

the manifold tasks of nineteenth-century historians also restricted the time and energy they could invest in the study of history. Some of them could only pursue research in addition to earning their living in other ways, and political commitments similarly hindered scholarly work. For example, as we shall see in the next chapter, involvement in the organization of the state proved so time-consuming for Kogălniceanu that he was compelled to abandon his initial goal of completing a second volume of his national history and focused on source collection and editing instead.

But even those scholars who were fortunate enough to be able to pay regular visits to the archives encountered difficulties. As will be explained in the next chapter, the exploration of archives was just about to commence, and so the majority of sources still lay unexplored in the archives. Furthermore, even on those fortunate occasions when it proved possible to uncover new sources in the archives, the documents were usually written by protégés of royal dynasties. Consequently, they included almost nothing about the life of unprivileged people. Attempting to tell the story of Saxon resistance to the Conqueror, Thierry regretted that he had no other sources than the occasional malevolent comments of the Norman chroniclers.[98] Lelewel likewise complained that the life of the common people appeared to be uniform and uneventful, and therefore their deeds only rarely and momentarily attracted the attention of historians, who then immediately reverted to ignorance.[99] All these factors contributed to the paradox that despite heralding a new historiography, Romantic historians remained locked into old sources and indebted to the achievements of earlier generations. Nonetheless, this over- reliance on pre-existing assessments and interpretative frameworks as well as prejudices can be observed in the oeuvre of every historical generation, even in those who claimed to have radically questioned their predecessors' incentives.[100] Not only does such continuity appear to be normative, in fact, scholars who try too hard to break away from tradition rarely succeed in making valuable contributions.[101]

Furthermore, examining our historians' achievements from a different vantage point reveals them to be far from futile. If we accept that

---

[98] Gossman, *Between History and Literature*, 93–4.

[99] Lelewel, *Polska, dzieje a rzeczy jej*, III. 31; *Betrachtungen über den politischen Zustand des ehemaligen Polens und über die Geschichte seines Volkes* (Leipzig, 1845), 2.

[100] Gall, *Confronting Clio*, 17.   [101] Ibid., 17.

historical writing in our era was a way of exercising politics and if we interpret Romantic historiography in terms of cultural wish-fulfilment, their accomplishments seem both fecund and impressive. They provided a programmatic desideratum by reconstituting the nation as a historical subject and opened new horizons for research. In some instances they substantially contributed to inverting the 'historical wheel', by breathing new life into a slumbering national sentiment and endowing nations in the shadow of extinction with a legitimate future. In other cases, they succeed in improving the dwindling prestige of the national past, in the eyes of both the domestic and foreign audience. Against the backdrop of such accomplishments, whether or not historians succeeded in completing their narratives or relied on archival sources was of little relevance.

Taking into account both interpretative directions, it can be concluded that the destiny of historiography in this epoch was as much to prospect as to produce. Nevertheless, as Alexandru Zub noted: 'generously and boldly to prospect in such a domain meant to lay the foundation of an authentic creation'.[102] However, in order to further advance the study of national history, individual efforts were no longer sufficient. It became necessary to provide an institutional framework for organized research incentives. The professionalization and institutionalization of historical studies in my protagonists' region was a long and gradual process, just as everywhere else, and constitutes the subject matter of the next chapter.

[102] Alexandru Zub, *A scrie şi a face istorie* (Iaşi, 1984), 347.

3

Institutionalization and Professionalization

THE TRANSFORMATION OF HISTORIOGRAPHICAL STANDARDS

New expectations from historical writing, as heralded by historians in the first half of the nineteenth century, were to be met in accordance with new methodologies that emerged from a major transformation. In the earlier, humanist tradition, historical writing belonged to the branch of rhetoric, but the validity of this convention gradually came to be questioned as standards of methodological rationality developed. While style and presentation remained important facets, the factual accuracy of historical statements evolved into the central aspect of historiography. Historical writing and historical research were always interconnected, but in the humanist tradition writing enjoyed primacy. The new, 'scientific' historiography emancipated the research component. The historian's craft was now primarily defined in terms of skills, which included the ability to critically engage with primary sources, augmented by knowledge of auxiliary disciplines such as chronology, palaeography, geography, statistics (*Statistik* or *Staatskunde*) and genealogy.[1] Knowledge of this kind distinguished the trained historian from the amateur and also helped to draw clearer boundaries with neighbouring disciplines. Yet, the transition of historical thinking was not accompanied by the sort of conceptual revolution that was experienced

[1] Georg G. Iggers, *Historiography in the Twentieth Century* (Hannover, NH, and London, 1997), 23–30; for institutionalization in the German context, see Konrad H. Jarausch, 'The Institutionalization of History in 18th Century Germany', in Hans Erich Bödeker, Georg G. Iggers and Jonathan B. Knudsen (eds.), *Aufklärung und Geschichte: Studien zur deutschen Geschichtswissenschaft im 18. Jahrhundert* (Göttingen, 1986), 25–48.

at this time in the natural sciences.[2] Furthermore, since the process of professionalization and institutionalization was accompanied by an intensification of national sentiment, paradoxically, the increased emphasis on methodological rigour and the foundation of professional institutions was concurrent with the ideological exploitation of history to legitimize national aspirations.

Moreover, the consequences of this shift were diverse, but evolved only by degrees and the relationship between the two traditions was informed by continuity, rather than rupture.[3] In the first part of the nineteenth century no clear distinction between amateur and professional existed. Although the study of history featured prominently in university curricula, it was embedded in other branches of knowledge and not viewed as an independent discipline. Thus, the majority of scholars were at least partly self-educated. Only in exceptional cases was it viable to earn one's living as a historian; financial resources had to be secured through alternative means. Possible solutions entailed family support, a good marriage (Palacký and Horváth), private sponsorship, as well as the choice of certain professions, typically those of priest (Horváth), civil servant (Daukantas) and private tutor (Horváth and Palacký).

An appropriate institutional framework proved essential for the organization of activities which otherwise could not have been pursued individually. As has been hinted earlier, scholarly ambitions to write the history of the people entailed exploring new sources which, until now, remained buried in the dust of the archives. Source editions were instigated in the early modern period (an example being Muratori's *Rerum Italicarum Scriptores*), but gained new impetus in the first half of the nineteenth century. Launched in 1819, *Monumenta Germaniae Historica* inaugurated a groundbreaking and exemplary initiative in this field. European academies and learned societies and, later, more specialized institutions, such as the Société de l'histoire de France instituted by Guizot in 1833, led the way in this respect.

Another manifestation of professionalization was the publication of periodicals intended for a more specialized readership. *Historische Zeitschrift* was launched in 1859, *Revue Historique* followed in 1878, and the *English Historical Review* in 1886. Founders of these journals

---

[2] Hayden White, *Metahistory: The Historical Imagination in Nineteenth Century Europe* (London and Baltimore, 1973), 137.

[3] Georg G. Iggers 'The Crisis of the Rankean Paradigm in the Nineteenth Century'; in Georg G. Iggers and James M. Powell (eds.), *Leopold von Ranke and the Shaping of the Historical Discipline* (New York, 1990), 172.

were united in their intention to avoid contemporary controversies and bias, an aim which they regarded, nonetheless, as perfectly compatible with omitting certain ideologies, trends and values. To that end, editors of the *Historische Zeitschrift* famously excluded three ideologies as illegitimate: feudalism, because 'it imposed lifeless elements on progressive life'; radicalism, which 'substituted subjective arbitrariness for organic development'; and ultramontanism, which 'subjected the national spiritual evolution to the authority of an extraneous Church'.[4]

State and private institutions alike became sites for professionalization and institutionalization. Of the former, two foundations played preeminent roles: the University of Göttingen (established in 1737) and the University of Berlin (inaugurated in 1810). In the late eighteenth century the teaching of history rarely dovetailed with the pursuit of research. Göttingen evolved into the epitome of a modern educational institution by integrating these two functions and, importantly for our purposes, served as a prototype for the creation of several European universities, including Vilna, Warsaw and Moscow.[5] The University of Berlin, founded by Wilhelm von Humboldt, also provided a paradigm for new universities, and the reform of those already in existence. Berlin distinguished itself by seeking to provide pragmatic and secular education that prepared students for a wider range of careers than its counterparts. Furthermore, following the traumatic experience of the French revolution and Napoleonic occupation, Humboldt's ambition was to turn it into a treasure house for the gold of the German past.[6]

The exercise of close scrutiny by state authorities, however, prevented universities from becoming fertile sites for 'experimentation'. For example, Guizot was expelled from the Sorbonne in 1818 for teaching 'ideas' rather than 'facts', and in 1850 freedom of instruction was repeatedly rescinded in French universities, with the consequence that Michelet, Quinet and Mickiewicz lost their positions.[7] Likewise, in

---

[4] Heinrich von Sybel, 'Vorwort', *Historische Zeitschrift* 1 (1859), iii.

[5] A valuable account on the Göttingen academic community is Luigi Marino, *Praeceptores Germaniae: Göttingen 1770–1820* (Göttingen, 1995).

[6] Universities in the nineteenth century are discussed in Walter Rüegg (ed.), *A History of the University in Europe*, Vol. III: *Universities in the Nineteenth and Early Twentieth Centuries (1800–1945)* (Cambridge, 2004).

On the University of Berlin more specifically see Charles E. McClelland, *State, Society and University in Germany, 1700–1914* (Cambridge, 1980), 99–149.

[7] Gossman, *Between History and Literature*, 195.

1837 seven professors were expelled from Göttingen University, including Dahlmann and Gervinus, in response to their complaints that the Hanoverian king, Ernst August, had violated the constitution.[8] Historical pursuits could be hindered not just by such direct intervention but also by the everyday reality of censorship, especially in periods following revolutions and uprisings, although they proved less of an impediment to private and semi-private patriotic and scholarly societies.

LEARNED SOCIETIES

Academies and learned societies were not established specifically for the pursuit of historical research (and in that capacity differed from subsequent, more specialized organizations); rather, they placed the study of history in a wider framework of the national heritage, which included language, literature and folklore. Nevertheless, the focus on culture did not exclude the formulation of political goals. On the contrary, the cultural field provided a safer domain for the expression of political ambitions than the public arena. For example, Horváth believed that, during the Reform Era, discussions that took place in Hungarian patriotic societies and reading groups played an even greater role in the dissemination of 'reform ideas' than debates on the political stage.[9]

The learned societies of Poland, Bohemia and Hungary were products of Enlightenment-style patriotism and came into being in the late eighteenth to early nineteenth centuries. In all three respective contexts they assisted my protagonists' integration into the academic community. Far from being exclusive and inward-looking, these institutions attached great importance to reaching the wider public by hosting lectures and discussions. The publication of sources, book series and periodicals numbered among a broad range of activities, and, in many cases, they also housed a library. It may also be significant that in Hungary the Diet added the regulation of intellectual property to its agenda on the initiative of an important literary-scholarly institution, the Kisfaludy Society.[10] Familiarizing the national community with achievements

---

[8] This is discussed in Friedrich Christoph Dahlmann (ed.), *Die Protestation und Entlassung der sieben Göttinger Professoren* (Leipzig, 1843).

[9] Géza Fülöp, *A magyar olvasóközönség a felvilágosodás idején és a reformkorban* (Budapest, 1978), 125.

[10] Horváth, *Huszonöt év Magyarország történetéből 1823-tól 1848-ig*, 2 vols. (Geneva, 1864), I. 266.

abroad constituted another mission; to that end, societies instigated translation projects. Furthermore, in keeping with an established convention in prominent European academies, their counterparts in East-Central Europe organized scholarly competitions with the intention of unearthing talented but hitherto unknown scholars. Prize questions often reflected preoccupations of the age, as well as addressing problems specific to individual national contexts.

The Royal Bohemian Society was founded around 1774.[11] Its proceedings were originally conducted in German, but the use of the Czech language gradually increased until, by the end of the nineteenth century, it had come to predominate. The Polish equivalent was the Towarzystwo Przyjaciól Nauk (Society of the Friends of Learning), which commenced its activities in Warsaw in 1800, upon the initiative of a Polish aristocrat.[12] It operated as a salon where representatives of the nobility, upper clergy and intellectuals assembled to exchange views on cultural and scientific issues. In addition, public sessions were also organized and major scholarly works were accomplished under the aegis of the society.[13] In Hungary a patriotic aristocrat, Ferenc Széchényi, established the National Library in 1802, and his son, István Széchenyi, offered his one year's income for the creation of the Academy of Sciences in 1825. On a smaller scale, initiatives such as reading societies also became popular.[14]

In Warsaw, the historical section constituted a separate branch of the Towarzystwo. Its main ambition was to encourage the completion of a major national history, a study which would have concluded the work commenced by the Enlightened bishop Adam Naruszewicz.[15] Although Lelewel was not elected to full membership of the society until 1831, he attended its meetings from the outset and this provided fresh impetus for his—at this stage fragmentary—version of national history, *Historia*

---

[11] Mikuláš Teich, 'Bohemia from Darkness into Light', in Roy Porter and Mikuláš Teich (eds.), *The Enlightenment in National Context* (Cambridge, 1981), 149. The society functioned under various names, such as *Böhmische Gelehrte Privatgesellschaft, Böhmische Gesellschaft der Wissenschaften, Königlich-Böhmische Gesellschaft der Wissenschaften.*

[12] For a history of the society see Jerzy Michalski, *Z dziejów Towarzystwa Pryjaciól Nauk* (Warsaw, 1953), in which chapter 6, pp. 149–94, deals with the historical section of the society.

[13] These included Samuel Linde's Dictionary of the Polish language and Adam Naruszewicz's History of Poland.

[14] These were comparable to the French *cabinets de lecture* and the German *Lesegesellschaften.*

[15] The texts of various projects can be found in Marian Henryk Serejski (ed.), *Historycy o historii—Od Adama Naruszewicza do Stanisława Kętrzyńskiego 1775–1918* (Warsaw, 1963), 68–90.

Polski aż do końca panowania Stefana Batorego (The History of Poland to the End of the Reign of Stefan Bathory), from which he read extracts at the meetings. In addition, he wrote numerous book reviews for the society together with studies in numismatics and geography. He was also commissioned to produce the advertisement for an academic competition in Polish law.[16]

Palacký's and Horváth's careers likewise benefited from the inspirational effects of patriotic societies, and they 'reciprocated' by supporting these societies in their activities at a later stage. Both scholars made their academic debut by participating in contests. Palacký triumphed at a competition advertised in 1826 by the Royal Bohemian Society, inviting contestants to critically evaluate the attainments of Bohemian historians since ancient times. Although Palacký turned out to be the sole participant, this should not diminish the significance of the occasion. His submission, published in 1827 under the title *Würdigung der alten böhmischen Geschichtschreiber*, represented a ground-breaking enquiry into historiography. Nine years after the Bohemian initiative, the Marczibányi Society, an institution initiated by a Hungarian noble family in the early nineteenth century, advertised a prize question on a theme that addressed the Hungarians' arrival and settlement in the Carpathian basin in the ninth century: 'How did the social and moral conditions of the conquering Hungarians compare to the peoples of contemporary Europe?' Not only did Horváth win the prize for his submission *Párhuzam* (Parallel) but, a year later, in 1836, he became a runner-up in another of the Hungarian Academy's contests. This time the subject related to the history of Hungarian industry and commerce in the Middle Ages. It reverberated with public debates about the influence of towns on Hungarian civilization, whilst mirroring a general European interest in the contribution of towns to freedom and prosperity, a popular topic of prize questions on the agenda of European academies.

Both Palacký and Horváth distinguished themselves through their engagement with scholarly societies at a later stage of their careers. Palacký, in particular, had links with almost every significant institution of his era. As well as holding functions in the Royal Bohemian Society, he contributed to the pursuits of the Bohemian Museum. Inaugurated

---

[16] On the Society's attempts at organizing academic contests see the chapter 'Zadania konkursowe i próby prac zbiorowych', in Michalski, *Z dziejów Towarzystwo Pryjaciól Nauk*, 114–48.

in 1818, the founders of this institution drew inspiration from similar establishments created slightly earlier, especially the Hungarian National Museum, and the Museum of Moravia and Silesia in Brno.[17] As with the Royal Bohemian Society, the Bohemian Museum epitomized *Landespatriotismus*; its constitution and statutes were written in German and only members of the executive committee were required to be proficient in Czech. As has already been mentioned, the journal of the Bohemian Museum was launched by Palacký and his fellow patriots in German and Czech versions in 1817.

Palacký also made his mark on another scholarly-national society, Matice Česká (Czech Matice).[18] Originally constituting a section of the Bohemian Museum, in 1832 the Matice became independent. The first institution of this type was Matica Srbska (Serbian Matica, established in Pest in 1826 by Serbians living in the Hungarian realm). Albeit on a significantly smaller scale, it emulated the Hungarian Academy of Sciences, founded in the preceding year. Subsequently Slovak, Moravian, Croatian, Slovenian and Dalmatian and Polish *Matices* came into being.[19] These instances testify to the existence of regional initiatives which were not necessarily dependent on 'Western models' and could take the form of both cooperation and rivalry. The initial aim of the Matice Česká was to undertake preparatory work for a Czech Encyclopaedia, based on the Brockhaus *Konversationslexikon*. This project remained unrealized: in Palacký's lifetime only 750 entries for the letter 'A' were collected. Nevertheless, the institution evolved into a notable promoter of national culture. It subsidized and published seminal works of the Czech national revival; such as Palacký's *Dějiny*, which, from 1848, appeared under its aegis.[20] It occupied an authoritative position on theoretical issues relating to the Czech language and in regard to the production of schoolbooks in Czech. Matice Česká also operated a book exchange programme with Polish, Russian, German and Danish societies and libraries and, in 1849, an exchange scheme was arranged

---

[17] Palacký's involvement is discussed in Ales Chalupa, 'Frantisek Palacky and the National Museum', *East European Quarterly* 15:1 (1981), 85–101.

[18] *Matice* (in other Slavonic languages *matica)* is a generic term and implies meanings such as queen bee, mother, womb. For more on Matice Česká see Stanley B. Kimball, 'Matice Česká, 1831–1861: The First Thirty Years of a Literary Foundation', in Peter Brock and H. Gordon Skilling (eds.), *The Czech Renascence of the Nineteenth Century* (Toronto, 1970), 53–73.

[19] Kimball, 'Matice Česká, 1831–1861', 58.

[20] Other significant ventures included Joseph Jungmann's Czech–German dictionary and Pavel Josef Safářík's epochal book on Slavonic antiquities, *Slovanské starožitnosti*.

with the Smithsonian Institution in Washington DC (established three years earlier).[21]

Although the most active members were intellectuals, Matice was open to every social stratum (subject to membership fee) and succeeded in helping to integrate various elements within Czech society.[22] It attracted many foreign members, especially from the ranks of Slavic scholars. Matice's reliance on subscriptions and donations caused occasional financial difficulties; however, at the same time, financial independence guaranteed its survival even through the period of neoabsolutism, although Palacký's close relationship with the institution was interrupted during that era. After the restoration of constitutional life in 1860–1, new opportunities for the establishment of institutions emerged and Matice gradually lost its hegemony.[23] Palacký's other initiatives included Svatobor (Holy Grove) in 1861, a society designed to support impoverished Czech writers. He also served as chair of a committee set up to raise funds for the building of the National Theatre in 1850. After initial difficulties, this initiative bore fruit and, in 1868, the cornerstone of the Theatre was laid.

Palacký benefited from prestigious international contacts, including collaboration with the Göttingen scholar Johann Gottfried Eichhorn, and correspondence with Heinrich Sybel, university professor in Munich and founder of the *Historische Zeitschrift*, who sought his opinion on political developments in Europe and Austria's possible reaction to them.[24] Palacký was among the first scholars to be elected to the Austrian Academy of Arts and Sciences, which was founded in 1846 upon Metternich's initiative. Although the vested interest behind Metternich's support was to keep the intellectuals associated with liberal and national currents under governmental control, the Academy funded noteworthy scholarly initiatives. This included an edition of the documents of fifteenth-century church councils, the *Monumenta conciliorum generalium saeculi XV*, initiated by Palacký.[25]

[21] Kimball, 'Matice Česká, 1831–1861', 66.

[22] Anna M. Drabek, 'Frantisek Palacky and the Beginning of the Austrian Academy of Arts and Sciences (Österreichische Akademie der Wissenschaften)', *East European Quarterly* 15:1 (1981), 96.

[23] Kimball, 'Matice Česká, 1831–1861', 72.

[24] Jiří Kořalka, 'Palacký, Sybel a počátky Historische Zeitschrift', *Husitský Tábor* 9 (1987), 225.

[25] Drabek, 'Frantisek Palacky and the Beginning of the Austrian Academy', 107.

Horváth was elected to regular membership of the Hungarian Academy in 1841. His source collection, compiled in the Brussels archives (of which more below), was published under the auspices of the Academy. He also became involved in the ventures of the Természettudományos Társulat (Natural Science Society), launched in 1841. Despite its name, the society welcomed members from all disciplines and subsequently a sub-group for historians was established within its confines. Through this, historians enjoyed the opportunity to communicate with scientists, for example during the field trips which they undertook for studying the geology, botany and history of the country.[26] After returning from exile Horváth was elected to the Kisfaludy Society, an establishment named after a writer and founded in the Reform Era. His inaugural lecture in 1868 addressed the questions: 'Why is contemporary art so fruitless? Why does historiography produce many more masterpieces?'[27]

Most importantly from the point of view of institutionalization, Horváth became a founding member of the first professional society of Hungarian historians, the Magyar Történelmi Társulat (Hungarian Historical Society). Taking advantage of less turbulent political life, the society was launched shortly after the Compromise in 1867, one year before the Royal Historical Society in Britain. Horváth served as the Hungarian society's first vice-president and also chaired the editorial committee of its periodical, *Századok*. With its primary focus on historical studies, this institution differed from the patriotic societies which had flourished in the first half of the century. Founding members disputed whether the society should become a more exclusive institution with invited members from the historical profession, or if it should be open to the general public.[28] Horváth put forward a strong case for the latter and eventually his proposal was accepted. His inaugural lecture, delivered at the society's first meeting, defined the society's mission along these inclusive lines, emphasizing the need to produce research and publish sources in forms accessible to the educated reader and to involve the general

[26] Várkonyi, *Pozitivista szemlélet*, II. 38.

[27] Horváth, 'Miért meddő korunkban a művészet? S a történetírás miért termékenyebb remek művekben?', *Kisfaludy-Társaság Évlapjai* 4 (1868), 471–89.

[28] For an account on the association's outset see Steven Bela Borsody, 'The Foundation of the Hungarian Historical Association and its Impact on Hungarian Historical Studies', in Borsody, *Clio's Art in Hungary and in Hungarian-America* (New York, 1985), 17–34. The historical activities in the Academy are tackled in Imre Lukinich, *A Magyar Tudományos Akadémia és a Magyar Történettudomány* (Budapest, 1926).

public in the society's activities.[29] Shortly after its inception the society boasted around 600 members, a figure which tripled within a decade.

Most Romanian societies were formed after unification and the establishment of the independent state, and their counterparts were established in Transylvania with the express purpose of promoting Romanian culture. For instance, ASTRA, the Transylvanian Society for Romanian Literature and Culture, which was founded in Sibiu in 1861 and counted Kogălniceanu among its members. Kogălniceanu was also connected with the *Societate Academică Română* (Academic Society), the forerunner of the Romanian Academy established in 1867, with the primary goal of engaging in linguistic study and promoting a unified literary language through the publication of a Romanian grammar and dictionaries.[30] At the inaugural meeting a separate historical and archaeological section was created, with Kogălniceanu's involvement, and this played a seminal role in the publication of historical documents. In 1879 the Academic Society was renamed as the Romanian Academy.[31] One of Kogălniceanu's influential discourses, *Dezrobirea ţiganilor ştergerea privilegiilor boiereşti, emanciparea ţăranilor* (The Liberation of the Gypsies, the Abolition of Boyar Privileges and the Emancipation of the Peasantry) was delivered in 1891 in commemoration of its 25th anniversary.

UNIVERSITIES

Nineteenth-century universities in East-Central Europe saw their fundamental mission as the training of loyal civil servants, bureaucrats and teachers; hence practical knowledge was favoured over abstract learning. Prominent historians were not necessarily affiliated with universities; from among my protagonists only Lelewel had such an association. His positions as Lecturer (1815–18) and, later, Professor of History (1821–24) in Vilna, and as Professor of Bibliography in Warsaw (1818–21), provide valuable insights into the process of professionalization and institutionalization. Both universities were products of

[29] 'Horváth Mihály beszéde', 9–10.
[30] Dan Berindei, 'Societatea Academică Română (1867–1878)', *Revista de Istorie* 19:6 (1966), 1069–89.
[31] Kogălniceanu's contribution to the Romanian Academy is tackled in Zub, *Kogălniceanu, istoric*, 785–803; for the historical activities of the Academy see Dan Berindei, 'L'activité de la section d'histoire de la Société Académique et l'Académie Roumaine jusqu'au parachévement d l'unité nationale (1867–1918)', *Revue Roumaine d'Histoire* 5:6 (1966), 963–79.

Tsar Alexander I's attempt to establish a modern school system in his empire, together with their counterparts in Dorpat/Tartu, Moscow and Charkov. Vilna's predecessor institution, founded by the Polish king, Stefan Bathory, in 1579, belonged to one of the numerous Jesuit academies which were subsequently upgraded into universities in East-Central Europe, where the Jesuits' involvement in education was particularly pronounced.[32] In an attempt to win the support of the Poles, in 1803 Tsar Alexander re-established this academy as the University of Vilna and appointed the eminent Polish magnate and statesman Prince Adam Czartoryski as its curator.[33] Four faculties were created; theology, philosophy, law and medicine. Initially, the language of instruction was Latin; from 1816 it was Polish, and between 1825 and 1832, when the authorities closed the university, it was Russian.

Czartoryski made concerted efforts to attract reputable foreign scholars.[34] Authorities in Vilna (and also in Warsaw and Moscow) considered Göttingen a paragon and even attempted to recruit a professor and graduates from there. Czartoryski succeeded in enticing to Vilna the Göttingen philologist Ernest Gottfried Grodek, whose handbook of ancient Greek literature brought him widespread international acclaim. Grodek sowed the seeds of neohumanism at the university, an intellectual current that influenced both Lelewel and Daukantas. Subsequently, the appointment of József Gołuchowski, a former student of Friedrich von Schelling in Erlangen, as Professor of Philosophy showed the extent to which the ideals of Romanticism had permeated Vilna.[35] During his years as a student in Vilna, in the absence of 'professional' historians, a professor of theology directed Lelewel's historical endeavours. My protagonist's subsequent appointments as Lecturer in 1815 and Professor in 1821 marked history's debut as an independent discipline at the university. His charisma vastly improved history's prestige among the students, and a poem dedicated to him by Adam Mickiewicz testifies

[32] For the discussion of the Jesuits' decisive role in education in the Habsburg Empire see R. J. W. Evans, 'Die Universität im geistigen Milieu der habsburgischen Länder (17.–18. Jh.)', in Alexander Patschovsky and Peter Baumgart (eds.), *Die Universität in Alteuropa*, (Constance, 2000), 183–204.

[33] On the Vilna education district see Daniel Beauvois, *Lumières et société en Europe de l'Est: l'Université de Vilna et les écoles polonaises de L'Empire Russe* (1803–1832), 2 vols. (Lille, 1977).

[34] James T. Flynn, *The University Reform of Tsar Alexander I 1802–1835* (Washington DC, 1988), 114.

[35] An extensive history of the university is József Bieliński, *Uniwersytet Wileński 1579–1831*, 3 vols. (Cracow, 1899–1900).

not only to the subject's popularity but also to his own.[36] He inspired student societies, especially the Philomaths, who endeavoured to promote Polish culture in a patriotic spirit. The fate of the Philomaths' Society indicates the precarious nature of the university's autonomy and its vulnerability to state intervention. In 1823, members were accused of anti-Russian conspiracy and although no evidence for this was forthcoming, the society was forced to disband and many members were arrested and exiled. This incident marked the end of Polish educational self-government in the Western provinces of the Russian Empire and also had serious consequences for Lelewel. The investigation also addressed his involvement in the alleged plot and he was accused of contributing to the spirit of unrest at the university. As a result, he was expelled from the university and ordered to return to Warsaw.

Between 1818 and 1821 Lelewel was Professor of Bibliography and Curator of the University Library in Warsaw. In line with the educational goals of the university to train civil servants for the newly constituted Congress Kingdom, history was not granted a separate chair and was intended only as an auxiliary subject for students of philosophy, law and literature.[37] On the other hand, the creation of a professorship of bibliography reflected the conscious efforts of the National Education Commission to expand the university's collections into the Congress Kingdom. During his professorship Lelewel completed a two-volume study of the history of libraries and printing in Poland, inspired by Christian Gottlob Heyne, a professor of classical philology and director of the University Library in Göttingen whose catalogue system was widely used throughout Europe.[38] In addition, Lelewel volunteered to deliver lectures on the history of the sixteenth and seventeenth centuries, as well as the comparative history of Poland and Spain. Lelewel's poverty in emigration was due to his unwillingness to obtain permanent employment. To that end, in 1834 he was offered a professorship at the newly established Université Libre de Bruxelles, but turned it down on the grounds that the Polish Constitution (of 1815) stipulated that Poles entering foreign service would forfeit their citizenship.[39] Subsequently, he accepted the commission to catalogue Brussels' municipal collection of coins, although he expected only nominal payment for his efforts.

---

[36] Mickiewicz's poem was titled *Do Joachima Lelewela* (1822).

[37] On the University of Warsaw see Józef Bieliński, *Królewski Uniwersytet Warszawski 1816–31*, 2 vols. (Warsaw, 1907–11).

[38] Irena Treichel, *Pierwszy polski podręcznik bibliotekarski* (Wrocław, 1957), 23.

[39] In reality, the constitution did not contain such a clause.

The Romanian Universities of Iaşi and Bucharest were established, following the unification of the two principalities, in 1860 and 1864 respectively, and their inauguration was a symbolic confirmation of newly acquired statehood.[40] Their forerunners were princely academies founded in Bucharest in the late seventeenth, and in Iaşi in the early eighteenth, century, renowned centres of Byzantine learning. Of these, Kogălniceanu was briefly associated with the academy in Iaşi, re-established in 1835 as Academia Mihăileană (Mihailean Academy, named after the prince), with the intention of introducing practical subjects such as agriculture into the curriculum. The initial grandiose plans may create the impression that the Academy resembled a modern university; however, subsequently only a very limited part of the curriculum was realized and its social effects were also restricted.[41] In 1843 Kogălniceanu launched an introductory course to modern history at the Mihailean Academy. His inaugural discourse, *Cuvânt pentru deschiderea cursului de istorie naţională în Academia Mihăileană* (Discourse to open a course on national history in the Mihailean Academy), offered an interpretation of the milestones in Romanian history. However, just a few weeks after it began, the course was abruptly terminated and its tutor arrested.

Kogălniceanu's involvement in laying the foundations of the University of Iaşi is also remarkable. He hoped that an institution embracing a variety of disciplines could be created, but the limited financial resources only allowed for three faculties: philosophy (including natural sciences), law and theology (with medicine added in 1879). Kogălniceanu always referred to his time at the University of Berlin with warmth and gratitude, but Romanian institutions primarily drew on the French educational tradition and, in particular, the Napoleonic model of higher education.[42]

Palacký remained absent from the university scene. At first sight, especially in light of Prague University's reputation as the oldest in Central Europe, and Palacký's reputation as an outstanding historian, this may seem puzzling. Yet, although universal history acquired an independent chair within the Philosophical Faculty in 1783, on

[40] Jean Livescu, 'Die Entstehung der Rumänischen Universitäten im Zusammenhang der europäischen Kulturbeziehungen (1850–1870)', in Richard Georg Plaschka and Karlheinz Mack (eds.), *Wegenetz Europäischen Geistes, Wissenschaftszentren und geistige Wechselbeziehungen vom Ende des 18. Jahrhunderts bis zum ersten Weltkrieg* (Munich, 1983), 34.

[41] Keith Hitchins, *The Romanians 1774–1855* (Oxford, 1996), 196.

[42] Jan Sadlak, *Higher Education in Romania, 1860–1990: Between Academic Mission, Economic Demands and Political Control* (Buffalo, New York, 1990), 4, 11.

the whole, in this epoch the University was not known for its high standards and its mission remained the training of loyal bureaucrats.[43] Nevertheless, the years 1848 to 1850 saw an attempt to introduce reforms, based on Humboldt's ideas. In our epoch, Prague University was a German-speaking institution, ideologically opposed to Palacký's interpretation of Czech history. For example, Josef Linhart Knoll, the Professor of General and Austrian History, was a passionate defender of a centralized and Germanized Austrian Empire and vigorously and publicly attacked the first volume of Palacký's *Geschichte*, demanding that it be suppressed before it inflamed 'thirteen million Slavs burning with national fanaticism and hatred against the Germans'.[44] However, attempts were made to integrate Palacký into the university, at least on a symbolic level. To coincide with the University's 500th anniversary, he was decorated with an honorary doctorate by the faculties of philosophy and law. Ironically, the planned festivities did not take place in the revolutionary year of 1848 and the document was sent to him by post. In 1849, discussions commenced about the establishment of a second professorship in history, with the responsibility for undertaking teaching in the Czech language. Though Palacký would have been an obvious candidate for such a position, Felix von Schwarzenberg and the entire Ministerial Council categorically rejected his appointment.[45]

Like the Academy from which the University of Vilna evolved, Hungary's University was originally a Jesuit foundation, established in 1635 and located first in Nagyszombat (today Trnava), later in Buda and then, after 1784, in Pest. The majority of professors in the late eighteenth to early nineteenth century were members of ecclesiastical orders. The year 1774 marked a watershed in the study of history, whereby it was reclassified as an independent discipline, rather than affiliated with aesthetics as a branch of rhetoric.[46] It was not until 1844, however, when Hungarian became the official language, that it was also designated as the medium of university teaching. In 1847, the Chair of History became vacant and Horváth was considered a strong candidate.

---

[43] On the history of the university see František Kavka, *The Caroline University of Prague: A Short History* (Prague, 1962).

[44] Zacek, *Palacký*, 55.

[45] Jan Havránek, 'František Palacký a Univerzita Karlova', *Acta Universitatis Carolinae—Historica Universitatis Carolinae Pragensis* 21 (1981), 78.

[46] Erzsébet Muszka, *A történelem és a történeti segédtudományok oktatása egyetemünkön, 1770–1848* (Budapest, 1974), 7.

Regrettably, his modesty and lack of personal connections hindered his application; as soon as he discovered that his more ambitious friend, who was an excellent literary scholar but not a historian, had announced his candidature, he withdrew.[47]

PUBLICATION OF PRIMARY SOURCES

The creation of a systematic collection of historical documents involved a tedious, time-consuming and financially demanding process. As part of this systematization, and in line with the unifying tendencies of scholars attempting to promote national cultures, a demand for the foundation of national archives emerged. In Hungary Horváth was the first scholar to instigate the establishment of the National Archives during the revolution in 1848; Palacký propounded the idea of an official Archive of the Kingdom of Bohemia in 1862, and Kogălniceanu was the driving force behind the initiation of the Romanian national archives.

With varying frequency, all five historians visited domestic and foreign archives. Daukantas's position was unfortunate: ironically, although in St Petersburg he was working literally next door to the pivotal sources of Lithuanian history, the archive of the former Grand Duchy of Lithuania known as *Metrika*, he was denied access to these documents. As we have seen, his opportunities were restricted to a visit to the Teutonic Order's archive in Königsberg, and his intention to publish a collection of archival sources, the *Acta Lithuanorum*, remained an unfulfilled aspiration.[48] Horváth and Lelewel made imaginative and resourceful use of their years in exile, when, prevented from consulting sources in their home countries, they explored foreign libraries with the intention of extracting sources relevant to national history. Kogălniceanu studied primary sources in Vienna and, in 1849, travelled to Cracow, where he compared notes with the editor of a periodical specializing in Polish historical and literary monuments.

Palacký's attainments in the field were so extensive that they merit separate consideration. He undertook numerous library and archival visits at home and also in Germany, Austria-Hungary and France; a particularly spectacular enterprise was his research trip to the archives of

---

[47] Várkonyi, *Pozitivista szemlélet*, II. 95.   [48] Daukantas, *Raštai*, II. 731.

the Vatican in 1837, where he examined thousands of documents. Prior to this, almost without exception, only close allies of the papacy were granted access to the repositories and then only to consult individual sources. Extraordinarily, Palacký, despite being a Protestant, gained permission to use the archives in their entirety, an honour only the founder of *Monumenta Germaniae Historica*, Georg Heinrich Pertz, had enjoyed before him. It seems likely that the successful outcome of Palacký's application was due to the diplomatic skills of his negotiators, Count Kaspar Sternberg and Count Rudolf Lützow, the imperial envoy to the papal court. Such assistance was particularly vital because, as Palacký himself lamented, ever since historians, including the Protestant Ranke, had utilized their findings in a manner that could be perceived as hostile to the papal cause, visitors had been treated with great suspicion.[49]

At some point the young Horváth contemplated abandoning historical writing and directing his efforts towards source collecting and editing. In a letter addressed to a friend he posed the following question: 'What will be more advantageous: the collection of sources or the pursuit of research, in spite of the inadequate material available, which will necessarily render the result rather poor?'[50] Even at a later stage, the publication of primary sources remained an essential task for Horváth, because he believed that these allowed historians to correct the distorted 'comfortable second-hand' views of the national past.[51] His four-volume collection of *Hungarica* from the libraries of Brussels launched the *Monumenta Hungariae Historica*, an initiative of the Hungarian Academy, in 1857.[52] Horváth also sought to instil the spirit of archival research into the next generation and, in the 1870s, he conducted trips for young people to various archives in the country. Palacký published six volumes of *Archiv český* (Czech Archive), a collection of various documents on Bohemia and Moravia up to 1526. He also initiated *Scriptores Rerum Bohemicarum*, while Kogălniceanu launched its Romanian equivalent, the *Scriptores Rerum Rumaniarum* (1845–52), alongside *Archiva Românească* (Romanian Archive). Conceived in 1840, Kogălniceanu's intention with the latter journal, which, in the event, only ran to a few issues due to financial difficulties, was to preserve

[49] Palacký, *Zur Böhmischen Geschichtschreibung* (Prague, 1871), 73.
[50] Horváth's letter to his friend Ferenc Toldy, 14 March 1847, in Várkonyi, *Pozitivista szemlélet*, II. 56.
[51] 'Horváth Mihály beszéde', 6.
[52] Horváth Mihály, *Magyar történelmi okmánytár, a brüsseli országos levéltárból és a burgundi könyvtárból*, 4 vols. (Pest, 1857–9).

valuable manuscripts. To varying extents, the impact of *Monumenta Germaniae Historica* (and also that of the *Monumenta Austriae Historica*) was discernible on all these ventures.

Whilst Horváth registered the paradoxical nature of historical research in the absence of satisfactory primary sources, such realization, coupled with time constraints, compelled Kogălniceanu to abandon his intention to produce a comprehensive national history altogether. He chose, instead, to refocus his energies on the publication of primary sources. In this respect, his edition of Moldavian and Wallachian chronicles of the seventeenth and eighteenth centuries was a particularly momentous initiative. Authored by eminent scholars such as Miron Costin, Constantin Cantacuzino and Dimitirie Cantemir, these sources had previously been available only in manuscript form. Hoping to stimulate interest abroad, Kogălniceanu also prepared a selection of these sources in a French version, *Fragments tirés des chroniques Moldaves et Valaques*. On the whole, he fostered the cause of these chronicles in the belief that they would serve as substitutes until a large-scale national history was completed: 'The time will come when Romania possesses a national history, until that book appears, the comprehensive publication of the chronicles written by our ancestors—with all their defects and imperfections—will remain the most valuable and interesting history of Romania.'[53]

JOURNALS

Literary and scholarly journals proved instrumental in forging cultural unity, and promulgating knowledge to the reading public, as well as in expanding the audience they reached. Lelewel undertook editorial activities in Vilna and Warsaw: in 1815 he assisted in launching the journal *Tygodnik Wileński* (The Vilna Weekly), where his inaugural lecture was also published.[54] In the years of emigration his articles, primarily on the Polish cause, frequently appeared in the journals of various émigré societies. Daukantas was deprived of the opportunity to contribute to periodicals, but his practical booklets on subjects as

---

[53] Kogălniceanu, *Opere*, II. 392.
[54] Other titles included the *Dziennik Wileński* (The Vilna Daily), *Gazeta Literacka* (The Literary Gazette) and the liberal periodical affiliated with Freemasonry, *Pamiętnik Warszawski* (The Warsaw Journal).

diverse as bee-keeping and brandy-distilling served a similar purpose to my other protagonists' journal articles. He published these items under various names, in order to create the illusion that he was not a solitary activist embarking on the education of Lithuanians. Horváth supplied articles, both original and translated, for the two foremost periodicals of the Reform era, the *Athenaeum* and *Tudománytár* (Repository of Knowledge). Following his return to Hungary from emigration he also became a founder of a new professional historical periodical, *Századok*. Palacký and Kogălniceanu held prominent positions as editors, and the two innovative journals which appeared under their auspices, *Časopis českého Muzea* and *Dacia Literară*, are eminently comparable.

As Chapter 1 has revealed, Palacký's friends were sceptical about his suggestion that the journal of the Bohemian Museum should appear not only in a German but also in a Czech version, because they believed that it was too late to breathe new life into the Czech nation. Palacký (at least according to his own account) reprimanded them by declaring: 'Even if I were of gypsy birth and the last of my clan, I should still consider it my duty to strive with all my might in order to preserve an honourable memory of it in the history of mankind.'[55] Moved by such persistence and dedication, Count Kaspar Sternberg agreed to sponsor the twofold enterprise. The objective of the two variants diverged inasmuch as the German monthly version was to contain scholarly contributions, whilst the quarterly Czech variant aimed at popularizing scholarly achievements and maintaining and cultivating the Czech language.

In both cases, advancing knowledge and interest in *Vaterlandskunde* among the Bohemians and identifying potential contributors and offering them space comprised fundamental aims for their founders.[56] The symbolic integration of diverse territories constituted another important mission. The scope of the journal encompassed all lands that, at any stage, had belonged to the Bohemian crown, including Silesia, Lusatia and, to some extent, Brandenburg and Luxembourg. The thematic range embraced legal, cultural and historical aspects, with special attention devoted to a critical examination of sources, coins and inscriptions. Furthermore, the editors wished to demonstrate the potential benefits of national-academic activities to the foreign public, as well as addressing misconceptions about their country. Both periodicals were inaugurated in 1827 under Palacký's editorship, but subsequently followed different trajectories. The German version, despite considerable publicity,

[55] Palacký, *Dílo* (Prague, 1941), I. 43.   [56] Palacký, *Gedenkblätter*, 47.

including an enthusiastic review from Goethe in the Berliner journal *Blätter für Wissenschaftliche Kritik*, proved unpopular and folded in 1831–2. Initially the editors encountered similar difficulties with the Czech version: the target of disseminating 200–250 copies was difficult to achieve, and the censor's interventions did not help the cause. Nonetheless, in the longer term, these obstacles were overcome and the journal, albeit in a different form, has survived until the present day. At a later stage of his career, in the 1860s Palacký launched further journals, including titles such as *Národ* (The Nation), *Národní listy* (National Papers) and *Pokrok* (Progress).

Uniquely, Kogălniceanu distinguished himself not only by his contribution to journals but also in the modernization of printing. In 1830 he succeeded in challenging existing monopolies in Moldavia and secured a number of state publishing contracts. As well as the first printed editions of Moldavian chronicles, numerous innovative literary and historical journals, he also produced translations of Russian, Spanish and French literature and even Romania's first cookery book. *Dacia Literară* (Literary Dacia) strove to fuse disparate strands of thought on history, language and literature into a coherent cultural doctrine.[57] Kogălniceanu sought to publish writers from Moldavia and Wallachia and also reproduced articles from a Transylvanian paper. By doing so he hoped that 'our journal is also becoming the general repository of Romanian literature, in which, as in a mirror, we are going to see the writers of Moldavia, Wallachia, Transylvania, Banat, Bukovina, each of them with their own thoughts, language and form'.[58]

Kogălniceanu's intention with his innovative enterprise to transcend regional identities and foster the unity of Romanian language and literature was also apparent in the use of the word *Dacia* in the journal's title, as this term symbolically embraced all Romanian territories. His cross-regional approach dovetailed with an anti-political stance and a preference for an authentic national taste. Overall, this agenda constituted a major theoretical contribution towards the idea of national literature. Kogălniceanu insisted that his was a literary enterprise; in that context 'literature' became synonymous with intellectual superiority and integrity: unlike politics, a state business, literature belonged to the nation.[59] His message proved so formidable that the Moldavian prince,

---

[57] Hitchins, *The Romanians*, 193.   [58] Kogălniceanu, *Opere*, I. 223.
[59] Alex Drace Francis, *The Making of Romanian Culture: Literacy and the Development of National Identity* (London, 2006), 133.

Mihail Sturdza, banned the journal after three issues. Three years later my protagonist and his collaborators tried again, and the result of their efforts was another short-lived journal, *Propaşirea* (Progress). Nevertheless, the connotations of the word 'progress' attracted the censure of the authorities; therefore the title was subsequently altered to the safer *Foaia sătească* (Village Broadsheet).

Only 250 copies of *Časopis* were printed initially and most journals published in the Romanian lands rarely achieved a print-run of more than 500 whilst many had even smaller readerships: Kogălniceanu's *Propaşirea* (Progress) circulated in just 40 copies. Nevertheless, the modest print-run and readership of these often short-lived journals should not be seen as an indicator of their importance. Paradoxically, the state imbued these enterprises with a great deal more significance than they actually merited, as shown by its repressive actions, which only resulted in the enhancement of their symbolic status.[60] Moreover, it appears that, to some extent, the editors deliberately addressed their work to an imaginary, anticipated audience, one which they hoped to create precisely through their efforts. One might wonder, for example, about the purpose of the numerous translated pieces in Hungarian periodicals, including those of Horváth, when educated members of the public were usually in a position to access the originals. In that context, founders of the Hungarian journal, *Athenaeum*, justified the abundance of translated pieces with the claim that many readers possessed the knowledge and intellect to appreciate such works, but lacked the financial resources to purchase foreign books. But perhaps cultural wish-fulfilment provides the most satisfying explanation, as the targeted social stratum must have been quite insignificant at the time.

The Hungarian *Századok*, which has survived until the present day, merits special mention because it represents a different genre of professional historical journals. In this capacity, its equivalents are not *Časopis českého Muzea* and *Dacia Literară*, but the *Český časopis historický* (Czech Historical Journal) established in 1895 in Prague, and the Polish *Kwartalnik Historyczny* (Historical Quarterly), founded in 1887 in Lwów. Its counterparts on the international scene are the *Historische Zeitschrift* (1859) the *Revue Historique* (1876) and the *English Historical Review* (1886). Compared with the foundation dates of these pre-eminent ventures, *Századok*, inaugurated in 1867, appears to be a remarkably early manifestation of professionalization, especially because

[60] Ibid., 133.

the first attempt to establish a professional medium was made somewhat earlier, in 1865. Although the intended readership was initially comprised of both scholars and non-educated people, over time the journal evolved into a forum for professional historians. The first article to appear in *Századok* was Horváth's inaugural lecture at the introductory meeting of the Historical Society in 1867. The text was also published, in complete or shortened form, by every leading daily paper of the time, exemplifying the cultural and political significance of the occasion. In addition, the second volume of the journal was launched with Horváth's contribution, a study on the era of early Christianity in Hungary.

AUXILIARY SCIENCES

Proficiency in auxiliary sciences was deemed an essential prerequisite for professional scholarship as well as being useful in the study of national history. Kogălniceanu promoted archaeology, especially in the province of Dobrogea, which, as we shall see later, originally did not fall within the national borders, but had been offered by Russia in compensation for the loss of Bessarabia, a Romanian territory. Kogălniceanu hoped that archaeological findings might facilitate the symbolical integration of Dobrogea into Romania.[61] Palacký ventured into a range of auxiliary disciplines, including the publication of essays and manuals in the field of genealogy, topography, chronology and diplomatics. In the latter domain, his recognition of the value of medieval formularies for historical research was especially notable.[62]

Lelewel held a position of supremacy, even in terms of international comparison, in the fields of numismatics and geography. In addition to minor essays in his youth, his publications included a two-volume book on Celtic numismatics and a collection of essays entitled *Études Numismatiques et Archéologiques*, published in Brussels in 1841. His innovative method of classifying coins provided a framework for modern numismatics. The Polish scholar also excelled in the study of geography. His minor but inventive work, *Examen géographique des voyages de Benjamin de Tudèle* (Brussels, 1852), attempted to locate the itinerary of Rabbi Benjamin Tudela, a celebrated traveller in the twelfth century. Lelewel's *Géographie des Arabes* (1851) was followed by

---

[61] Zub, *Kogălniceanu, istoric*, 796.   [62] Zacek, *Palacký*, 50.

Géographie du moyen Age (Brussels, 1852–7). This monumental opus, which also contained an atlas of fifty plates engraved by the author, brought him international acclaim. As with Edward Freeman, whose *Historical Geography of Europe* (1881) attracted more attention than his book on the Norman Conquest, Lelewel's international reputation was founded on his research into geography, rather than his service to Polish historiography. Not only did geography have a more widespread appeal, but it also represented a highly prestigious occupation in our epoch, enjoying a reputation as a complex subject that occupied a place in the dominion of knowledge 'where students of physical and moral science came together'.[63] A long list of subscribers to Lelewel's book, comprising mainly professors such as Henry Hallam, prominent publishing houses and booksellers, such as Brockhaus and Avenarius, as well as, surprisingly, the king of Belgium, testifies to its impact.

The establishment of mass schooling in a national framework created a demand not just for textbooks, but also for atlases which could also be used to express territorial demands and to confirm the desired unity of the nation. For example, German and French maps produced at the time of the Franco-Prussian War (1870–1), showing the position of Alsace, were a manifestation of such motivations.[64] Lelewel published two atlases with educational intentions: one of these dealt with the ancient world, while the other provided an overview of Polish history from 850 to the period of the partitions with the help of twelve maps.[65] On the one hand, these maps potently exemplified the decline of the Polish state. On the other, the representation of former historical frontiers served as a reminder of an independent national existence before the partitions and also directed attention to present aspirations.[66]

CENSORSHIP

In his younger days Horváth took the view that censorship could be justified because it prevented the evolution of 'misleading' ideas. As a junior priest confined to a small village, he dreamt about moving to

[63] Arnold, *Introductory Lectures on Modern History*, 124–5.

[64] Jeremy Black, *Maps and History: Constructing Images of the Past* (New Haven, 1997), 52.

[65] *Atlas do Historyi i geografii starożytnej* (Warsaw, 1828); *Atlas do Dziejów polskich z dwunastu krajobrazów złożony* (Warsaw, 1829).

[66] Black, *Maps and History*, 82.

the capital and he even coveted the job of the censor.[67] Unsurprisingly, this attitude changed radically once he started to publish. From this it can also be seen that censorship was a widespread phenomenon in the majority of European countries during the first half of the nineteenth century, and typically involved state, as well as ecclesiastical, surveillance.[68] Yet, the ever increasing number of publications made it impossible to control the influx of ideas, and prohibition could be counter-productive: it served as advertisement, because it drew people's attention to publications about whose existence they might otherwise never have known. Scholars also devised imaginative ways to ameliorate the effect of control, or to avoid it entirely, and consequently censorship did not succeed in its purpose during our epoch.

The severity of censorship was contingent upon the prevailing political situation, the subject of the publication in question, the censor's personality, and possibly also his mood. School textbooks received especially close scrutiny because of their unusually broad impact, and writings addressing the history of the recent past or present were also notoriously prone to censorial intervention. Apart from time constraints, this was one reason for Kogălniceanu's abandonment of the plan to continue his national history. At some point Horváth also withdrew from examining a topic relevant to the recent past for the same reason. The publication of Lelewel's lectures on the comparative history of Poland and Spain, on which his *Historyczna paralela* (A Historical Parallel) was based, was banned by the censor 'to protect the students from the negative examples of foreign institutions where unrest and religious indifference characterized the atmosphere at universities'.[69] In particular, Lelewel's approval of revolutionary means irritated the censor and, as a result, his manuscript was only published after the relaxation of censorship during the revolution in 1831.[70]

Not only were the decisions of the censors often capricious and inconsistent, but the same work could produce different verdicts at different times. Daukantas's only historical book which he saw published, *Būdas*, did not initially cause any concern and was granted permission for

[67] Márki, *Horváth Mihály*, 49; for more on censorship in Hungary see Várkonyi, *Pozitivista szemlélet*, II. 74–8.

[68] On censorship in the nineteenth century see Robert Justin Goldstein, *Political Censorship of the Arts and the Press in Nineteenth Century Europe* (New York, 1989).

[69] Bieliński, *Królewski Uniwersytet Warszawski 1816–31*, I. 14–15.

[70] Subsequently, it was published in the *Stuttgart Annalen für die Geschichte und Politik* 1834, and in the *Revue du Nord* in 1835.

publication in 1845. Incidentally, the anti-Polish biases in his work were not far removed from the Russian imperial intention to de-Polonize the newly acquired lands after Poland's partitions. Nevertheless, ten years later, when the political climate had altered radically, some statements suddenly acquired deeper resonance. In the course of the Crimean War, the French and English navies appeared in Baltic harbours and the Russian authorities feared an eventual uprising. In 1855 the following letter was sent to the Governor-General of Vilna:

A Lithuanian book is being circulated in this country. It is entitled 'Character' and chronicles the customs of ancient Lithuanians. The book was published in St Petersburg by Hintz and passed by the Vilnius censor Vaškevičius. Even now it is accessible to the public, although in my opinion it should be, as your excellency can see from the parts I have attached, banned.[71]

The sentences picked out by the censor included: 'the Lithuanians have never shied away from confronting their enemies' and 'every pious man is responsible to God and not to a ruler who inflicts suffering on him'.[72] The Russian authorities harboured suspicions about the author's identity, hiding behind the name 'Lankys': 'The book must have been written by a certain Kontantas who enjoyed the hospitality of bishop Volonczewski (= Valančius) and researched Lithuanian history.'[73] In the end, the book was not banned but a secret decision was made not to sell it in public and also to alert the governor should another edition appear.

Another instance of whimsy is provided by the censoring history of Horváth's multi-volume *Magyarország történelme* (History of Hungary), a version of which was also widely used in schools. Horváth assumed that the arbitrariness was partly due to the vague guidelines that censors had to observe; and the fear of losing their job also helped to explain the often extreme measures.[74] In Horváth's case, the ecclesiastical censor, who was his former teacher at the seminary, raised several objections about chapters concerning the recent past and intervened in the text to such an extent that it completely lost its integrity. Following that, however, the censorial committee overruled the censor's deletions and pronounced the work decent and trustworthy; in fact it should not have attracted the attention of the censor in the first place.[75] On the other hand, Horváth anticipated that a different version of this textbook,

---

[71] Merkys, *Simonas Daukantas*, 162–3.   [72] Ibid., 163.   [73] Ibid., 164.
[74] Horváth, *Magyarország történelme*, VIII. 502.   [75] Márki, *Horváth Mihály*, 69.

from which 'sensitive' issues were largely absent, would pass without major objections. Yet, it was returned in a mutilated condition, with one-quarter of the text cancelled. Revealingly, most of the deleted passages concerned Horváth's views on the Catholic Church, whilst his treatment of the Habsburg dynasty was rarely questioned.

Palacký's experiences provide yet another testament to the severity of theological censorship. As one of the most prolific authors in Bohemia, his confrontations with the imperial censors were especially frequent, although he himself acknowledged that not all were malevolent. At times he was even consulted before final decisions were made, and occasionally, his complaints were taken into account.[76] The publication of the volume of the *Dějiny* containing Palacký's contentious interpretation of the role of the Hussite movement, and the magnitude of John Hus, caused bitter conflicts. As will be shown in Chapter 8, for Palacký, Hus was a martyr for freedom of expression as well as the founder of the Reformation. This standpoint was seen as injurious to Catholicism, and the author was even warned by Count Sedlnitzky, head of the *Polizei- und Zensurhofstelle* in Vienna, that the Austrian government could not tolerate interpretations deemed hostile towards the ruling religion. Under these circumstances Palacký feared that the next volume of his work, which tackled even more controversial issues, would reach the public only 'in a castrated form' and a 'whole army of Jesuit-friends' would attack him.[77] Rumours circulated that the *Dějiny* had been banned and even that Palacký was going to be forced into exile. Yet, these negative effects proved short-lived and in fact the controversy drew public attention to his work. Surprisingly, after this insulting episode in 1844, Palacký's publications did not attract much further censorship, even during the years of absolutism after 1848.

My historians employed various strategies to mitigate the interference of censorship. Sometimes a careful choice of words could solve the problem. Censors' aversion to phrases such as 'revolution', 'responsible government' 'democracy' and 'progress' was common knowledge. This is why the editor of *Athenaeum* recommended that in the proposed title of Horváth's article, *A demokrácia kifejlődése honunkban* (The Development of Democracy in our Country), 'democracy' should be altered

---

[76] For Palacký's encounters with censorship see his two notes of 1834 and 1839 to the censor in *Gedenkblätter*, 103–4, as well as Josef Zacek's article 'Metternich's Censors: The Case of Palacky', in Brock and Skilling (eds.), *The Czech Renascence in the Nineteenth Century*, 95–112.

[77] Jirí Kořalka, 'Bavorská a saská korespondence Františka Palackého 1836–1846', *Husitský Tábor* 5 (1982), 240.

to 'peoples' rule'. With hindsight, such caution proved unnecessary, because even the original title passed censorship without difficulty.[78] On the other hand, as we have seen, the title of Kogălniceanu's journal *Propașirea* (Progress) proved unacceptable to the censors. But not every publication was exposed to the same degree of scrutiny. For example, in the Reform Era certain Hungarian periodicals qualified as 'literary' ones and these received more lenient treatment from censors, thereby becoming hiding-places for publications containing potentially subversive political messages. As has been illustrated by Daukantas's case, pseudonyms were also employed by my historians. Kogălniceanu's writings appeared under the guise of 'a Russian man', 'a philosopher', and 'an old warrior'.[79] Whilst he was in emigration Horváth's writings were published under the pseudonym 'Mihály Hatvani', despite the fact that his identity must have been perfectly obvious to the authorities, particularly so because of the allusion to Hatvan, the town where he formerly resided and also because his first name remained unaltered.[80]

Publishing abroad presented another escape route from censorial intervention. Horváth's account of the War of Independence of 1848–9, *Magyarország függetlenségi harcának története 1848 és 1849-ben*, became a 'sacred' text in the mid-1860s. Printed in Geneva, and banned in Hungary, it was smuggled into the country and sold in a bookstore under a false cover. As a contemporary observer noted:

One fine day, in Mór Ráth's bookstore, a book was passed around to people sitting on his red sofa, Alzog's *Katolische Moraltheologie*, a thick volume. It was circulating in silence; afterwards everyone bought a copy, and some even had tears in their eyes. No one would have guessed what a deeply moving effect Catholic morals exercise on elderly men. When they returned home, they locked Alzog's book carefully away. There was something else concealed behind the cover. A sacred book.[81]

CONCLUSION

Our epoch saw the contours of the historical discipline thrown into sharp relief. This was a slow and gradual process that continued

---

[78] Horváth, *Magyarország történelme*, VIII. 502.

[79] For a comprehensive list of these pseudonyms see Zub, *Michail Kogălniceanu, 1817–1891: Biobibliografie*, 568.

[80] Márki, *Horváth Mihály*, 186.   [81] Ibid. 277.

throughout my protagonists' entire lifetimes. In the first half of the nineteenth century, the relationship between history and other disciplines, such as law and philology, was not yet clearly defined. Therefore, my historians cannot be considered as 'professional' historians, at least not in the strict sense of the word which associates professionalization with the Rankean 'shift'. In this context, William Keylor's statement about their French contemporaries is equally applicable to them:

Guizot, Thiers, Lamartine, Thierry, Mignet, Quinet, Michelet and other contributors to this period of prolific historical production who straddled the worlds of politics, journalism and higher learning could hardly be described as professional historians. Attracted to a variety of callings, these successful authors of general histories were understandably ill-suited to the time-consuming drudgery of archival organisation, textual criticism, and monographic scholarship.[82]

On the other hand, on the basis of the knowledge and skills that these scholars possessed it would also be an injustice to classify them as amateurs. Considering that, as the previous chapter argued, their standards of historical writing were shaped by the Enlightenment tradition and not by the Rankean paradigm, it seems more appropriate to assess the nature of their work with reference to the word 'pre-scientific' (*vorwissentschaftlich*), denoting a stage when historical writing was undergoing a transformation into a *Wissenschaft*.[83]

The foundation of new institutions and periodicals was often motivated not only by professional incentives but also by a sense of rivalry. The *Revue Historique*, established in 1876 as a counterpoint to the rival *Historische Zeitschrift* of 1859, provides a good illustration of this.[84] By the same token, a healthy sense of regional rivalry among scholars in East-Central Europe could be as much an inspirational source as the innovative developments in 'Western' countries. In this region the task of institutionalization was primarily undertaken by private scholarly societies. These institutions' principal motivation was the fostering of national culture and reinforcing of cultural integrity, irrespective of borders. Within that scheme the study of national history represented a prestigious activity. Another important intention of these scholarly societies, the collection and publication of sources, was informed by an aspect

---

[82] William R. Keylor, *Academy and Community: Foundation of the French Historical Profession* (Cambridge, MA, 1975), 28.

[83] Horst Walter Blanke, *Historiographiegeschichte als Historik* (Stuttgart, 1991), 55.

[84] Michael Bentley, *Modern Historiography: an Introduction* (London, 1999), 77.

of democratization, thereby increasing the visibility and accessibility of the historical documents for the national educated public.

Because the dominant state exercised less control in the cultural field than in the political arena, the cultural setting was frequently employed to disguise political demands. Newly founded universities, such as Vilna and Warsaw, were often better equipped to implement innovative ideas than older, rigidly structured, establishments. On the whole, however, universities, ancient and new, usually experienced more intrusive state interference than private organizations. Inconsistent as censorship often was, it could still be a thorn in the side of my historians. Yet, in the long term, its effects were surprisingly inconsequential. For example, political reasons prevented Palacký from obtaining a professorship at Prague University, but he succeeded in exerting much greater influence on national scholarship as the Historiographer of the Bohemian Estates and author of *Dějiny* than any university professor of his time could have done.

Institutionalization and professionalization showed remarkably early manifestations in East-Central Europe, as the case of the Hungarian Historical Society and its periodical, *Századok*, indicates. This phenomenon confirms a general trend in the history of this process on the European scale: 'peripheral' and non-dominant national cultures usually led the way, turning the absence of established or even rigid structures to their advantage. For example, the Danish *Historisk Tidsskrift* (Historical Journal) was also founded before its more famous counterparts were called into being, in 1839. On the other hand, the 'belatedness of the centre' can be observed in dominant academic cultures, such as those of Austria and Britain. In the latter case, the slower pace was also due to the distinctive patterns of British academic life, in particular the singular relationship between class structure and educational opportunity which, to a greater extent than in continental Europe, prevented unprivileged people from accessing the system.[85] All in all, the expeditious nature of institutionalization in East-Central Europe can best be viewed as a phenomenon capable of accelerating the process of nation-building, an especially favourable development for the purposes of emancipatory nations.

[85] Michael Bentley, *Modern Historiography: an Introduction* (London, 1999), 78.

4

Intellectual Background

ENLIGHTENMENT IN NATIONAL CONTEXTS

An insight into my historians' intellectual world may help to contextualize their achievements in the field of national history and beyond. It also enables an appreciation of their endeavours from the diachronic perspective that characterizes enquiries into intellectual transfers, complementing the predominantly synchronic approach of the comparative method.[1] No attempt at a comprehensive analysis is undertaken; this would be unnecessary in light of the extensive existing literature which reconstructs (and on occasion even over-reconstructs) the five historians' intellectual mindsets in individual contexts. Instead, in accordance with the comparative perspective of my enquiry, I seek to unravel shared directions that provide common denominators and offer interesting instances of transmission as well as parallels without necessarily implying a direct relationship. Admittedly, even such a conditional appraisal has limitations, as it invariably entails a strong element of speculation.

Born in the late eighteenth and early nineteenth centuries, my historians first encountered the intellectual milieu of the late Enlightenment in their respective national contexts, which explains my choice of this era as the point of departure. That they subsequently emerged as 'national historians' constitutes no paradox; the compatibility of cosmopolitanism with patriotism—the patriotic incentives of Enlightenment scholars and their contribution to the development of national identities—has been widely acknowledged.[2] Until recent decades, the Enlightenment in East-Central Europe (and, in more general terms, Eastern Europe)

---

[1] Werner and Zimmermann, 'Beyond Comparison: Histoire Croisée and the Challenge of Reflexivity', 35.

[2] It was first pointed out by Franco Venturi in his book *Italy and the Enlightenment: Studies in a Cosmopolitan Century* (New York, 1972), 18–19 and subsequently became common knowledge.

received moderate attention and was primarily perceived in terms of Westernization. Such an approach overlooked the unique dynamic of the region's own cultural and intellectual life and implied that these territories had previously languished in torpor before illumination from the West transformed them.[3] Recent debates resulted in the revision of the traditionally favoured view of predominantly francophone Enlightenment, and a more pluralistic, even fragmented, definition of the movement has allowed more scope for the exploration of 'peripheries'. Local Enlightenments are no longer regarded as feeble reflections of the European mainstream, but in terms of their own unique configurations.[4]

Nonetheless, studies into 'peripheral' Enlightenments have not yet entirely overcome methodological difficulties. The spectre of backwardness, in particular, continues to haunt discourses, whereby the Enlightenment in our region is perceived in terms of a superficial or distorted reception of foreign ideas in the course of a unilateral transfer. This is not to suggest that backwardness should be completely discarded: my historians were acutely aware of their societies' shortcomings and were prepared to acknowledge that some of these could be tackled by adopting 'Western' ideas. However, the assertion that provincial settings were incompatible with creativity and, consequently, reception was identical with the passive and repetitive import of ideas, is no longer tenable.

The Enlightenment's legacy for my historians was manifold and sufficiently powerful to make them successors to, rather than antagonists of, an earlier scholarly generation. As I have indicated, although historians in the Romantic era wanted to overcome the inadequacies of Enlightenment-style general histories, they remained greatly indebted to the accounts which they aimed to supersede. They accommodated national history within the history of a common humanity and revisited Enlightenment scholars' pertinent preoccupations in the individualist setting of national history. In addition, the fundamental ideals of Enlightenment scholarship, including political liberty and social justice, and in particular, the belief that feudalism must be abolished, strongly resonate in their writings.

[3] Keith Hitchins makes this claim for Romania in *The Romanians 1774–1866*, 129.
[4] Roy Porter and Mikuláš Teich (eds.), *Enlightenment in National Context* (Cambridge, 1981); Teodora Shek Brnardic,'Intellectual Movements and Geopolitical Regionalization: The Case of the East European Enlightenment', *East Central Europe* 32:1–2 (2005), 147–78; Richard Butterwick, Simon Davies and Gabriel Sánchez Espinosa, *Peripheries of the Enlightenment*, Studies on Voltaire and the Eighteenth Century, 2008:1 (Oxford, 2008).

Depending on their national heritage and their own propensities, the historians evoked and amalgamated to varying extents some constituents of the political languages of early modern European scholarship. The language of classical *republicanism* emphasized active participation in affairs of state, which was regarded as the embodiment of true liberty. Republican rhetoric could often be informed by a cyclical political sociology that associated private property and the money-based economy with luxury and corruption: the root of all evil. Adherents to republicanism frequently contemplated the decay of states and loss of liberty; in particular, they discerned in the fate of Rome history's greatest cautionary lesson.[5] Lelewel's and Daukantas's writings were suffused with this style of thought, although in incarnations that occasionally diverged from the mainstream tradition of classical republicanism. On the other hand, the language of *political economy and commercial society* was of great relevance to Horváth's endeavours. Unlike republicans, purveyors of this tradition believed that the pursuit of private interest could also be of public benefit (and consequently they considered it the citizen's duty to pursue this).[6] Accordingly, rather than encouraging participation, they stressed the absence of restraint upon the individual. Importantly, irrespective of the intricacies of their individual lines of argument, my historians were united in their belief that it would have been anachronistic to base modern society on the restoration of ancient liberty.

The form and extent of these intellectual traditions depended not just on individual preferences, but also on the characteristic traits of respective national scholarly conventions. It should be kept in mind that scholarly achievements in my historians' countries were inherently diverse.[7] Furthermore, not all similitude was due to local peculiarities; on the other hand, individual traditions could occasionally display more parallels with 'mainstream' developments than with regional variations. Enlightenment in the Bohemian Lands and Hungary exhibited some similar tendencies.[8] Here, in addition to the *Zeitgeist*, the impact of the French Revolution and the reforms initiated by Maria Theresa

---

[5] Burrow, *A Liberal Descent*, 29–30.

[6] Antony Pagden, 'Introduction', in Pagden (ed.), *The Languages of Political Theory in Early Modern Europe* (Cambridge, 1987), 11–12.

[7] Teodora Shek Brnardic: 'The Enlightenment in Eastern Europe: Between Regional Typology and Particular Micro-History', *European Review of History* 13:3 (2006), 413.

[8] For an overview see R. J. W. Evans, 'The Origins of Enlightenment in the Habsburg Lands', in Evans, *Austria, Hungary and the Habsburgs* (Oxford, 2006), 36–55.

and Joseph II were of great significance. The two rulers' centralizing and homogenizing incentives threatened the political and economic interests of the Czech and Hungarian nobility and acted as impetus for the growth of territorial estate patriotism. Moreover, Germanization intensified national sentiment and contributed to the renewal of national languages. Importantly for our purposes, it also promoted studies into the national past because, in order to challenge the state's attempts at centralization, representatives of the local nobility felt compelled to demonstrate the ancient nature of their liberties. The young Palacký was inspired by the initiator of critical analysis in historical research in the Bohemian lands, and also that of source editions, the Piarist Gelasius Dobner (1719–90). He was also fortunate enough to be mentored by the two greatest figures of the Bohemian Enlightenment, Abbé Dobrovský (1753–1829), the founder of Slavonic philology, and Josef Jungmann, who instigated the Czech linguistic renewal. As we shall see, Horváth's ideological mindset was not only formed by Enlightenment, but through his oeuvre this heritage was preserved and transmitted into the second half of the nineteenth century, rendering him a late representative of the Josephinist tradition.

The intricate landscape of the Polish Enlightenment, and even that of later epochs, has usually been studied alongside antinomies of monarchy versus republic, state versus nation and universalism versus national uniqueness.[9] The monarchic-state-universal argument typically represented a Westernizer attitude in its criticism of the *szlachta* democracy, ascribing its downfall to inadequate political structures. By contrast, the republican-national-unique viewpoint was mainly (but not exclusively) Slavophile in orientation, being harshly critical of the Enlightenment heritage and admiring the ancient *szlachta* democracy which it associated with the authentic spirit of Polish history.[10] In his youth, at the Piarist boarding school, and later at the University in Vilna, Lelewel had been exposed to some of the most eminent scholars of the Polish Enlightenment. As we shall see, his avowed

---

[9] See especially Andrzej Feliks Grabski, *Myśl historyczna polskiego oświecenia* (Warsaw, 1976); Jan Adamus, *Monarchizm i republikanizm w syntezie dziejów Polski* (Łódź, 1961); Marian Henryk Serejski, *Naród a państwo w polskiej myśli historycznej* (Warsaw, 1973); *Swojskość a cudzoziemszczyzna w dziejach kultury polskiej* (Warsaw, 1973); Jerzy Kłoczowski (ed.), *Uniwersalizm i swoitość kultury polskiej*, 2 vols. (Lublin, 1989–90).

[10] Andrzej Walicki, *Poland Between East and West: The Controversies of Self-Definition and Modernization in Partitioned Poland* (Cambridge, MA, 1994), 17. A useful survey is Piotr P. Wandycz, 'Historiography of the Countries of Eastern Europe: Poland', *American Historical Review* 97:4 (1992), 1011–25.

republican tendencies dovetailed with the Enlightenment legacy. In particular, his demand to 'ennoble' the people, by bestowing political rights upon them which formerly the nobility enjoyed, resonated with the aims of radical Polish Enlightenment thinkers.[11] Within the field of historical scholarship, whilst disparaging the monarchist conviction of the foremost Enlightenment historian, Adam Naruszewicz, Lelewel appreciated and was indebted to his scholarly attainments.

An intriguing example of Enlightenment in a local milieu, which is not restricted to one specific national context, is provided by the case of Vilna.[12] This is because the multicultural and multireligious atmosphere of this thriving town, with its university and numerous publishing houses, hosted representatives of the Polish, Lithuanian and Jewish Enlightenment and also contributed to their respective national revivals. Other centres of Enlightenment and the subsequent national revival in Lithuania were Daukantas's home region, Samogitia, where Polish cultural influence remained less marked, and Lithuania Minor (East Prussia), especially the University of Königsberg. It was in Königsberg that the Prussian cantor Christian Gottlieb Mielcke published a Lithuanian–German and German–Lithuanian dictionary in 1800, containing a page-long appreciative foreword, entitled 'Nachschrift eines Freundes' (Postscript of a Friend), asserting that:

the particular character, as well as the purity of the language, of Prussian Lithuanian deserves to be preserved in both school and church classes, because language is a superior means of forming and preserving this character. I would also add that the Lithuanian is used to conversing with his superiors on an equal footing and with a trusting openheartedness, and is less inclined to servile behaviour than his neighbouring peoples. (. . .) It is important for the education of every 'small people' (*Völklein*) in a country—for example, in Prussian Poland—to teach and spread the language in schools and churches using the purest form of that language, even if the language is spoken only outside the country. Through this the language becomes more suited to the particular characteristics of the people, and thereby the people grow more enlightened.[13]

---

[11] Walicki, *Poland Between East and West*, 12.

[12] See Daniel Beauvois, *Lumières et société en Europe de l'Est: l'Université de Vilna et les écoles polonaises de L'Empire Russe (1803–1832)*, 2 vols. (Lille, 1977).

[13] Translation taken from J. D. Mininger, '*Nachschrift eines Freundes*: Kant, Lithuania, and the Praxis of Enlightenment', *Studies in East European Thought* 57 (2005), 2–3; the original German text appeared in Christian Gottlieb Mielcke, *Littauisch–deutsches und deutsch–littauisches Wörterbuch* (Königsberg, 1800), 16.

The *Nachschrift*'s author was a no less eminent scholar than Immanuel Kant, whose services Mielcke engaged to defend Lithuanian language and culture against the increasing encroachment of German education in the region.[14] Another instance of educators who valued contact with celebrated savants of the age is the eminent Polish statesman Ignacy Potocki. He was responsible for national education and textbooks and commissioned Étienne Bonnot de Condillac to write his *La Logique ou les premiers développements de l'art de penser* for Polish and Lithuanian schools, which was published in 1780, the year after the author's death.[15]

The term 'Romanian Enlightenment' may be an anachronism, as developments in the Danubian principalities diverged from those in Transylvania, which formed part of the Habsburg realm. In the principalities, the Phanariot regime severely curtailed contacts with Europe, leading to Greek cultural domination and the increasing isolation and impoverishment of native culture in the first half of the eighteenth century.[16] This does not mean, however, that no attempts at reform were made: especially noteworthy are those introduced by Constantin Mavrocordat in the 1740s. Inspired by the spirit of Enlightened absolutism, these reforms sought to create fiscal stability and also abolished serfdom. Nevertheless, they had no staying power and came to be abolished soon after their installation.

In Transylvania, which benefited from established contacts with Austrian and Hungarian culture, the activity of scholars known as representatives of the Transylvanian school is especially remarkable.[17] Around 1700, in the hope of obtaining the same privileges as the Catholic clergy, part of the Roman Orthodox Church in Transylvania accepted the leadership of the Pope and founded the Greek-Catholic (Uniate) Church. Unlike their Orthodox counterparts, whose spiritual centre was in Constantinople, eminent members of the Uniate clergy studied in Vienna and Rome, where encounters with classical antiquity prompted them to reconceptualize the theory of Roman origin (of the Romanians), which had previously been advanced by seventeenth-century representatives of the chronicle tradition.

---

[14] Mininger, '*Nachschrift*', 6–7.

[15] Bronius Genzelis, *Švietėjai ir jų idėjos Lietuvoje (XIX a.)* (Vilnius, 1972), 188.

[16] Vlad Georgescu, *Political Ideas and the Enlightenment in the Romanian Principalities (1750–1831)*, (New York, 1971), 108.

[17] Keith Hitchins, *A Nation Rediscovered: Romanian Intellectuals in Transylvania and the Idea of the Nation 1700–1848* (Bucharest, 1999).

According to this hypothesis, which later became canonical, Romanians were direct descendants of the Roman colonists who had settled in Dacia after its conquest in the early second century AD. Transylvanian Romanian scholars supported this theory by appeals to philology, such as the Latinization of the language and the replacement of the medieval Cyrillic alphabet with Latin characters. All these developments represented a reorientation of Romanian culture towards the West.

HERDER'S LEGACY

If scholars were to single out one intellectual authority who exercised an indelible influence on the scholarship of Central and Eastern Europe in the late eighteenth and early nineteenth centuries, they would undoubtedly choose Johann Gottfried von Herder (1744–1803). The German scholar's firm and undisputed primacy within the intellectual landscape of the region leads us to consider whether his dominance was also reflected in my protagonists' scholarly ventures. Two strands of Herder's thought appear to be paramount for my historians' purposes: the attractive and empowering aspects of Herder's concept of nationhood for nations seeking emancipation, and Herder's familiarity with the region, which was aligned with a fresh and sympathetic approach to the future potential of these largely unknown nations within European culture.

For Herder, nations were not just a collection of individuals, but organisms, comparable to plants or the diverse flowers in the garden of humanity, whilst simultaneously showing affinity with humans through their dynamism and morphology: they grew, had a spirit and a lifespan.[18] Herder understood history as a benevolent process and firmly believed that it had a divine purpose. Nonetheless, his assumption of national uniqueness was not (yet) identified with a divine mission corresponding to the messianic tradition of chosen people.[19] Herder's views were formulated within the context of enlightened cosmopolitanism and incorporated a profoundly humanitarian dimension, evident in the assumption that nobility and dignity were inherent in seed form in every man. This was epitomized in Herder's *Humanitätsideal*, his belief

[18] Iggers, *The German Conception of History*, 35 and 45.
[19] Frederick M. Barnard, *Herder on Nationality, Humanity and History* (Montreal, London and Ithaca, 2003), 40–1.

that 'the purpose of our existence is to develop this incipient element of humanity fully within us.'[20]

Herder emphasized that each nation contributed to the richness of human life and that the national sentiment joined nations together rather than dividing them. Far from being apolitical, this conviction was informed by a strong antipathy towards the status quo and a demand for a redefinition of politics, which was apparent in the assumption that 'backward' societies possessed creative energies which could enable them to eclipse the outdated practices of more advanced cultures.[21] Furthermore, the high value that Herder attached to language and folksongs implied more than the celebration of ethnic characteristics; it demonstrated his provocative assertion that belonging to the nation was not identical with membership of the state.[22]

Herder developed familiarity with the cultures of Slavic and Baltic people, in particular, during his stay in Riga (then part of the Russian Empire), where he held his first position as a clergyman during the 1760s after completing his studies at Königsberg. His celebrated *Slavenkapitel* (chapter on the Slavs) states that:

the Slavic people occupy more space on earth than they do in history (. . .) Despite their accomplishments, they were never an enterprising race of warriors or adventurers like the Germans; they simply followed after the latter and peacefully occupied the sites and countries vacated by them (. . .) They settled on land abandoned by other peoples, to cultivate and colonize it as herdsmen or ploughmen. Thus, after earlier destruction, migration and evacuation countries would benefit from their tranquil, industrious presence. (. . .) They were charitable, excessively hospitable, fond of free country ways, yet submissive and obedient, averse to pillage and robbery. None of this, however, enabled them to withstand oppression, rather, it invited subjugation.[23]

Herder also predicted that this people, 'once happy and industrious', would finally rise from their long slumber, cast off their chains and

---

[20] Iggers, *The German Conception of History*, 38.
[21] Johann Gottfried Herder, *Auch eine Philosophie der Geschichte zur Bildung der Menschheit* (1774), in Herder, *Werke in Zwei Bänden*, ed. Karl Gustav Gerold (Munich, 1953), II. 9–97, quoted in Fania Oz-Salzberger, *Translating the Enlightenment* (Oxford, 1995), 13.
[22] Barnard, *Herder on Nationality, Humanity and History*, 38.
[23] Johann Gottfried von Herder, *Geschichte der Europäischen Völker* (Berlin, 1952), 482–3. My translation is based on, but is not identical with, the excerpt in Hans Kohn, *Nationalism: Its Meaning and History* (Princeton, 1955), 106–7.

repossess their lands.[24] Undoubtedly this sympathetic attitude was in accord with the aims of scholars in Central and East Europe, and contributed to the high regard in which Herder's ideas were held among the Slavs. Nevertheless, the aspiration to promote the mother tongue had already existed in the region before scholars became familiar with Herder's ideas; consequently, he did not 'awaken' the national sentiment in them, but instead enabled non-dominant ethnic groups to clearly perceive their inferior status.[25]

Whilst there is no doubt that Lelewel and Palacký were indebted to Herder, some caveats are necessary when assessing the extent of his influence. As Chapter 6 will reveal, their portrayal of the early Slavs clearly reverberated with Herder's ideas, but it diverged from the German scholar's argument on a crucial point: they both claimed that the early Slavs were outstanding representatives of civic freedom, political engagement and democratic spirit, and this emphasis on political consciousness did not feature in Herder's works. It is also worth noting that Herder's main line of argument—that belatedness corresponds to rejuvenation—was initially advanced in the context of German culture.[26] Furthermore, several scholars have noted that the more general characteristics in Herder's description: a love of agriculture and domestic work and a quiet, industrious, peace-loving nature, were archetypical traits that could be attributed to any peasant group.[27]

Herder can be credited, however, with inspiring the young Lelewel's fascination with oriental civilizations, especially ancient India,[28] whilst Palacký's categorical appeals to humanity, his conviction that humanity possessed innate nobility and dignity, clearly resonated with Herder's *Humanitätsideal*. A central pillar of Palacký's theory of history, *božnost* (*Gottartigkeit*, deiformity), 'the final though unattainable goal of human

---

[24] Herder, *Geschichte der Europäischen Völker*, 484.

[25] Holm Sundhaussen, *Der Einfluß der Herderschen Ideen auf die Nationsbildung bei den Völkern der Habsburger Monarchie* (Munich, 1973), 23.

[26] Ulrich Muhlack, 'Universal History and National History, Eighteenth and Nineteenth Century German Historians and the Scholarly Community', in Benedikt Stuchtey and Peter Wende (eds.) *British and German History 1750–1950. Traditions, Perceptions, Transfers* (London 2000), 29.

[27] Robert Pynsent, *Questions of Identity. Czech and Slovak Ideas of Nationality and Personality* (London and Budapest, 1995), 75.

[28] Jan Tuczyński, *Herder i herderyzm w Polsce* (Gdańsk, 1999), 86.

life', 'the highest humanity' and 'kinship and likeness to God', can also be associated with this idea.[29] Nonetheless, the precise origins of the *Humanitätsideal* are difficult to grasp, because its tenets also feature in the work of other eminent thinkers, including Goethe, Winckelmann, Schiller and Wilhelm von Humboldt.[30] Two fundamental elements in Daukantas's views testify to Herder's impact: the association between nation and nature, and the emphasis on the inherently noble character of early Lithuanians, untainted by the evils of civilization. Likewise, Lithuanian scholars' appeals to folklore are reminiscent of Herder. Yet, Daukantas makes only one direct reference to such influence, drawing upon it to support his own postulation about the unique values of the Lithuanian language.[31] Herder was but one of the numerous scholars whom Kogălniceanu encountered in his youth, and his legacy remained largely irrelevant for Horváth, as was the case for many others in Hungary: whilst the German thinker's famous (and misinterpreted) prediction about the extinction of the Hungarians in a sea of Slavic people had found a resounding echo among Hungarians in the early nineteenth century, by the 1830s to 1840s, Herder's pre-eminence had been superseded by other authors.[32]

My handful of cases would not be sufficient to reach a more general conclusion about Herder's legacy; nevertheless, they tend to confirm an earlier suspicion that Herder's impact on national cultures in the region may have been overestimated. One reason for this is that it is impossible to distinguish between stimulus, exhortation, direct and in-direct influence, the intensification of an already existing autochthonous or borrowed idea and a combination of multifarious influences, when assessing Herder's impact.[33] A further difficulty is that some ideals that have become associated with his name had already been formu-lated by earlier scholars, whilst some arguably original elements in his thought (for example, regarding national character) became com-mon knowledge so rapidly that their true origin could not be clearly identified.[34] This is not to diminish Herder's contribution to schol-arship, it simply appears to be advisable to confine his popularity to distinct periods and individual authors rather than to consider it universal.

[29] On this theme see Josef Fischer, *Myšlenka a dílo Františka Palackého*, I. 77–8.
[30] Iggers, *The German Conception of History*, 37.
[31] Daukantas, *Raštai*, II. 739.   [32] Várkonyi, *Pozitivista szemlélet*, II. 43.
[33] Sundhaussen, *Der Einfluß der Herderschen Ideen*, 21.   [34] Ibid., 21.

THE IMPACT OF THE SCOTTISH
ENLIGHTENMENT

British scholarship played a less intense role in my historians' work than German or French and its impact could be direct as well as indirect. Palacký and Lelewel possessed the linguistic skills to read British authors in the original, whilst the other three scholars availed themselves of German and French translations. To some extent their familiarity with the intellectual mindset of British scholars, in particular those of the Scottish Enlightenment, was derived not from original accounts, but through indirect encounters. In this context, as the next section will reveal, the mediating role of scholars associated with the University of Göttingen, a focal point of entry for British ideas, is especially noteworthy. Of the various patterns of transmission, I shall primarily focus on the reaction to William Robertson's two pivotal studies, the *History of Scotland During the Reigns of Queen Mary and of King James VI till His Accession to the Crown of England* (1759) and *History of the Reign of Charles V* (1769).

In their youth, Lelewel and Palacký became familiar with several British authors, and they particularly appreciated the new horizons which these scholars opened up in the study of history and aesthetics. Lelewel's *Historyka* offered a critical assessment of the historiographical attainments of an array of scholars, among them Adam Ferguson, Bolingbroke, Robertson and Hugh Blair. Both my Polish and Czech scholars praised Bolingbroke's *Letters on the Study and Use of History*, with Lelewel hailing the 'pragmatic didacticism' that permeated the book.[35] They admired Hugh Blair equally, especially his *Lectures on Rhetoric and Belles Lettres* (1759), the first study to assess the role of rhetoric in shaping culture. Lelewel acclaimed Robertson, Hume and Gibbon for combining a broader philosophical background with extensive research and the impartial stance they adopted in their scholarly endeavours.[36]

As has been hinted above, the postulates of commercial language, first championed by representatives of the Scottish Enlightenment, diverged significantly from the republican tradition with regard to the assessment of material wealth. It was no longer considered the root of corruption, but a force to be embraced for the advancement of

[35] Lelewel, *Dzieła*, II/1. 398.   [36] Ibid., II/1. 826.

society. Moreover, contrary to the cyclical and pessimistic nature of the republican interpretation of European history, scholars who subscribed to commercial language elucidated European history in terms of the transition from feudal, medieval to modern, commercial social systems. Their main concern was to explain how feudalism, a system characterized by the absence of (all but aristocratic) liberty, was eroded by numerous developments, including the incorporation of cities, the development of new technologies, the expansion of domestic and overseas markets and the relative decline of aristocratic wealth.[37] In the commercial tradition, the Crusades, the discovery of America and the Reformation constituted watersheds in European history. Scholars also identified a final, modern stage of development, in which the expansion of commercial activity would facilitate greater access to property, and hence liberty, for an ever increasing number of people.[38]

My historians' familiarity with commercial language was just as likely to be traceable to the influence of Göttingen scholars, rather than directly coming from Hume, Robertson, Gibbon or Voltaire. Nonetheless, Horváth's essay, *Párhuzam* (Parallel), in which he contrasts the semi-nomadic Hungarians' way of life in the ninth century to the civilization of European people, contains numerous direct references to William Robertson's *History of the Reign of Charles V*. Like the majority of the Hungarian learned public, Horváth gained access to Robertson's work through the German translation of the Göttingen historian Julius August Remer. In addition, *Tudománytár* (Repository of Knowledge), a leading scholarly journal to which Horváth contributed articles, published the first sections of Robertson's *History of Charles V* in Hungarian between 1834 and 1836, on the basis of Remer's translation.

In the *Párhuzam* Horváth's assessment of the system of vassalage in feudal Europe is supported entirely by the information that he gleaned from Robertson's book. He also relies on Robertson's account for the discussion of minor details, such as the relationship between early German aristocracy and the king, which he contrasts to the view expounded in the relevant volume of the Guthrie-Gray *Weltgeschichte* (of which more below).[39] Interestingly, the ten references to Robertson's *History of Charles V* in Horváth's footnotes are cited in three different ways: the first variant is 'Remer (!), *Geschichte K Karl des V*'; the second appears as 'Robertson and Remer's *Geschichte K. Karl des V.*' and the

---

[37] O'Brien, *Narratives of Enlightenment*, 11.   [38] Ibid., 11–12.
[39] *Horváth Mihály kisebb történelmi munkái*, I. 46.

final version is 'Robertson's *Geschichte K. Karl des V*'.[40] These variations indicate the amorphous relationship between authors and translators in our era, through which authorship, to some degree, could be conferred on the translator, as the next chapter will reveal.

Robertson's works championed the strengths of a new Scottish historiography, which was especially admired for the spirit of synthesis that animated his long introductory essay to the *History of Charles V*, 'A View of the Progress of Society in Europe', together with its sophisticated relation of the origins of the modern state system, the rise and fall of feudalism.[41] This was despite the fact that Robertson's rationale for the growth of European civilization was not particularly original, but owed a huge debt to Montesquieu, Adam Smith and David Hume's *History of England*, as he acknowledged himself.[42] Depending on the compatibility between his message and the culture it was received by, Robertson's ideological mindset could either increase his popularity or act as a hindrance. Thus, Robertson's Protestant credentials facilitated his entry into German academic circles, whilst in Catholic Italy, translators were compelled to publish his books under false imprints and places of publication.[43] However, Robertson did not only inspire translations; his works, in particular the much-emulated *View of Progress*, were also considered exemplary for the pursuit of universal and national history. Julius August Remer, the above-mentioned translator of the *History of Charles V*, nurtured ambitions to produce an account of the post-Reformation period in a Robertsonian vein, and Friedrich Schiller represented only one of several scholars who wanted to write histories taking Robertson's books as templates.[44]

In Polish circles, Robertson's work was usually translated from the French version, rather than the English original. Lelewel's students, inspired by their teacher's high regard for the Scottish scholar, translated

---

[40] The first variant can be found in *Horváth Mihály kisebb történelmi munkái*, I. 14, 22 and 78, the second variant ibid., 25 and 27, the third variant ibid., 34, 45, 46, 49 and 54.

[41] Nicholas Phillipson, 'Providence and Progress: An Introduction to the Historical Thought of William Robertson', in Stewart Brown (ed.), *Robertson and the Expansion of Empire* (Cambridge, 1997), 60.

[42] Phillipson, 'Providence and Progress', 60.

[43] Franco Venturi, 'Scottish Echoes in Eighteenth Century Italy', in Istvan Hont and Michael Ignatieff (eds.), *Wealth and Virtue: The Shaping of Political Economy in the Scottish Enlightenment* (Cambridge, 1986), 355.

[44] For example Thomas Abbt intended to write a history of Braunschweig taking Robertson's *History* as a template. See Franz X. Wegele, *Geschichte der deutschen Historiografie seit dem Auftreten des Humanismus* (Munich, 1885), 768.

some parts of the *History of Charles V* for the *Dziennik Wileński*, a journal that appeared under Lelewel's editorship (1824). Further testament to Robertson's popularity among Polish intellectuals is provided by an episode from the history of the foremost learned society of the age, Towarzystwo Przyjaciól Nauk. When discussing the parameters of an envisaged new history of Poland in 1812, an eminent member of the society, Stanisław Potocki, recommended that this work should ideally be written in the vein of Robertson and Hume and should be introduced with an essay emulating the 'View of Progress'.[45] He concluded by expressing a hope that a suitable candidate for this task could be found, who would become the 'Polish Hume or Robertson'.[46] Thirteen years later a Hungarian scholar expressed a similar wish: 'What distinction it would bring to our nation, if finally, the Hungarian Gibbon, Hume, Robertson or John Millar came to the attention of the world!'[47]

Lelewel, who regularly attended the Society's meetings, greatly admired these scholars, and the preface to his first, fragmentary, national history reveals that he endeavoured to follow in their footsteps, expressing a wish to write an impartial national history, 'in the style of Gibbon and Robertson, but by a Pole, who belongs to the Roman Catholic Church . . . and to write it in a way that Poles and foreigners, Christians and non-Christians, friends and enemies would all consider impartial and truthful'.[48] He also recommended the translation of foreign books to be used in Polish schools and among the recommended titles was Robertson's *History of Charles V*.[49]

According to Palacký's diary, he became fond of historical learning after 'having read Robertson's writings and Bolingbroke's meditation on history'.[50] Furthermore, as the previous chapter demonstrated, his youthful ambition lay in writing 'a history of Bohemia in the fifteenth century à la William Robertson'; his characterization of Robertson, as a scholar who became a great historian despite representing a smaller nation, provides a further instance of the Scottish historiographer's

---

[45] Marian Henryk Serejski, *Historycy o historii*, 68–9.

[46] Paweł Komorowski, *Bolingbroke, Robertson, Gibbon: Znajmość i recepcja ich dzieł w Rzeczypospolitej doby Oświecenia (1761–1820)* (Warsaw, 2003), 28.

[47] Imre Bethlen, *II. Rákóczi György ideje* (Nagyenyed, 1829), Introduction, without page numbers.

[48] Lelewel, *Dzieła*, VI. 47.   [49] Lelewel, *Dzieła*, VII. 307.

[50] Palacký, *Korrespondence a zápisky*, I. 59. On British influences on Palacký see Otakar Vočadlo, 'English Influences upon Palacký', *Slavonic Review* 3:9 (1925), 547–53; Simeon Potter, 'Palacký a anglické písemnictví', *Časopis Matice Moravské* 53 (1929), 87–141.

role as a trendsetter in the region.[51] Palacký's choice of Scotland as a point of reference could have been due to the obvious parallels that it displayed with his homeland: both were small and marginal members of composite states, enjoying little international prestige. Yet, Robertson's predicament diverges from Palacký's emancipatory motives in several ways. The Scottish scholar showed scepticism towards the antiquity of the Scottish kingdom and the distinctive Gaelic legacy of its constitution; he also remained unconvinced about the unique heritage of the Scottish Reformed Church. Robertson accepted that the ideas of the Reformers instilled in the people of Scotland a new spirit of liberty, but for him, John Knox, the leader of the Scottish Reformation, represented an anachronism, and in his ferocious exploits, he perceived the conduct of an earlier more brutal age.[52] He advocated Scotland's Union with England, and reimagined it as a North British province because he believed that would be conducive to the cause of progress and liberty.[53] By contrast, although he did not pursue the idea of national independence, Palacký's stance was centrifugal; he pleaded for a greater degree of autonomy from the dominant Habsburg state. As will be expounded in Chapter 8, his argument was postulated on a firm belief in the antiquity of the nation, the unique legacy of its ancient democratic institutions and the Hussite movement's significant contribution to the cause of European civilization. Whether the young Palacký was aware of the implications of Robertson's message, in particular his confident puncturing of Scotland's pride as a historic free nation, remains questionable.

Daukantas and Kogălniceanu did not engage with Robertson's legacy to the same extent as the other three historians, but the occasional reference in their writings reveals a familiarity with his *History of Charles V*, in both cases via French translation. Robertson attributed a pivotal, if collateral, role to the Crusades in the dismantling of feudalism. According to his famous description, these were 'wild expeditions, the effect of superstition and folly', which nevertheless confronted Europeans with their unrefined manners and encouraged commerce and the development of towns.[54] The Lithuanian scholar's only cursory

[51] Kořalka, *František Palacký (1798–1876): Životopis*, 46.
[52] Colin Kidd, 'The Ideological Significance of Robertson's *History of Scotland*', in Brown (ed.), *William Robertson and the Expansion of Empire*, 140–1.
[53] Ibid., 123.
[54] William Robertson, *The History of the Reign of Emperor Charles V* (New York, 1836), 18.

reference to Robertson's *View of Progress* appears in a minor detail about the Teutonic Knights' move to Venice during the Crusades.[55] Nonetheless, it will be explained later that Daukantas viewed the Crusades as a detrimental episode, associated with forced Christianization. Lastly, Kogălniceanu extensively consulted the *History of Charles V* during his sojourn in Spain, to familiarize himself with the history of the country, even incorporating five pages from the book into his own travel notes, *Notes sur L'Espagne*.[56]

THE *SPÄTAUFKLÄRUNG* IN GÖTTINGEN

My historians were influenced in myriad ways by a generation of German scholars who succeeded Herder's contemporaries and preceded the representatives of the German historical school, such as Ranke, Droysen and Dahlmann. They were active primarily between 1770 and 1850, an era associated with the late Enlightenment, the *Spätaufklärung* in German scholarship and culture. Since the mainstream current of German Enlightenment, the *Aufklärung* occurred after its French and British counterparts, and the *Spätaufklärung* emerged even later, representatives of the latter were able to benefit from the heritage of earlier generations. However, it would be incorrect to assume that receptivity to foreign ideas and models was purely imitative, when in fact it was selective and purposeful. The critical and creative rethinking of foreign schemata not only instigated new directions in scholarship but helped scholars to engage with already existing problems in German intellectual life.[57] This era was undoubtedly characterized by an unusually syncretic intellectual world; no other epoch in German culture could boast such diversity: the *Sturm und Drang*, Classicism, early and late Romanticism.[58] It was also a time of political turbulence: the French Revolution, the ensuing Jacobin terror, the revolutionary wars, and the intensification of national sentiment all challenged the ideals of the *Aufklärung*. This accounted

[55] Daukantas, *Raštai*, I. 148.

[56] These five pages were omitted from the published version of Kogălniceanu's *Notes sur L'Espagne*, and I was not in a position to check the barely legible manuscript (which was written on a coach). Thus, unfortunately I was unable to identify the passage in question.

[57] Reill, *The German Enlightenment*, 31.

[58] Christopher Becker-Schaum, *Arnold Hermann Ludwig Heeren: Ein Beitrag zur Geschichte der Geschichtswissenschaft zwischen Aufklärung und Historismus* (Frankfurt am Main, 1993), 291.

for a further peculiarity of the epoch; the simultaneous presence of ideals traditionally considered to be in agreement with and in opposition to ideals inherent in the *Aufklärung*.[59]

Göttingen University was founded in 1734 under the auspices of the Elector of Hanover, who was then George II of England, and in the eighteenth century the town became a flourishing site of German scholarship, and a major gateway for the reception of British ideas.[60] Here, a group of talented scholars, including Johann Christian Gatterer (1729–99), August Ludwig Schlözer (1735–1809), Christian Gottlob Heyne (1729–1812) and Arnold Heeren (1740–1840), often referred to as the 'Göttingen school', initiated new avenues of historical enquiry.[61] Representing a variety of disciplines, such as philology, German and international law and *Staatswissenschaften* (political science), diversities among these scholars were significant. Yet, they were linked by their essentially historical approach to human developments and a critical examination of the past. They also endeavoured to establish a firm factual basis for their analysis, and their writings successfully integrated several distinct trains of thought in eighteenth-century scholarship.[62] A crucial ambition of Göttingen scholars resided in laying the foundations for a new type of history that they called *Universalhistorie*, as advocated (albeit not fulfilled) by Gatterer, which pursued an innovative approach whereby historical writing was not simply reduced to the narration of events and the unrelated summary of national histories. World history was to be endowed with a philosophical framework, and the historian was expected to consider cause and effect carefully, as well as relate his narrative to the broad areas of social and economic life.[63]

Göttingen scholars did not regard the classical heritage as an outdated relic of a bygone age, rather, in the spirit of neohumanism, they distinguished themselves by inventing a new pedagogical purpose for

---

[59] Ibid., 291.

[60] Hermann Wellenreuther, 'Göttingen und England im achzehnten Jahrhundert', in *250 Jahre Vorlesungen an der Georgia Augusta 1734–1984* (Göttingen, 1985), 30–63; Michael Maurer, *Aufklärung und Anglophilie in Deutschland* (Göttingen and Zurich, 1987).

[61] Marino, *Praeceptores Germaniae: Göttingen 1770–1820*; Rudolf Vierhaus, 'Die Universität Göttingen und die Anfänge der modernen Geschichtswissenschaft im 18. Jahrhundert', in Hartmut Boockmann und Hermann Wellenreuther (eds.), *Geschichtwissenschaft in Göttingen, eine Vorlesungsreihe* (Göttingen, 1987), 9–29.

[62] Iggers, 'The University of Göttingen 1760–1800 and the Transformation of Historical Scholarship', *Storia della Storiografia* 2 (1982), 18.

[63] Ibid., 27.

studying it.[64] As I have explored in the previous chapter, the institutional framework of the university provided a blueprint for the foundation or re-establishment of several universities in the region, including those of Warsaw, Vilna, Moscow and Tartu. Neo-humanist ideas infiltrated the University of Vilna when the Göttingen scholar Ernest Grodek became professor there, and Lelewel and Daukantas were strongly influenced by the currents of neohumanism. In addition to the institutional framework, methodological innovations introduced by German historians, especially their standards of source criticism, were also deemed exemplary by my historians, as illustrated by Lelewel's *Historyka*. It is also worth recapitulating that a ground-breaking venture associated with the University, *Monumenta Germaniae Historica*, became the epitome of source editions, providing a template that was emulated throughout Europe. Scholars in Bohemia counted Göttingen scholars as a major influence, benefiting from contacts with them; to that end, Palacký's article, *Geschichte der schönen Redekünste bei den Böhmen (für Eichhorn's Literaturgeschichte in Göttingen bestimmt)* was produced, as the title indicates, at the request of the Göttingen scholar Johann Gottfried Eichhorn.[65]

As well as the conceptual framework, the substance of my five historians' work was also indebted to Göttingen scholars, whose pioneering research into the history of Central and Eastern Europe helped to gradually improve the status of the region within the European intellectual landscape. In this context, the achievements of August von Schlözer (1735–1809), though less spectacular than those of Herder but equally significant, cannot be ignored. Schlözer, who promoted Locke's and Montesquieu's ideas in Germany, admired the genre of universal history and earned recognition for his *Vorstellung einer Universalgeschichte* (1772), and its successor, *Weltgeschichte nach ihren Haupttheilen im Auszug und Zusammenhange*.[66]

[64] On the study of philology see 'Ulrich Muhlack, Klassische Philologie zwischen Humanismus und Neuhumanismus', in Rudolf Vierhaus (ed.), *Wissenschaftler im Zeitalter der Aufklärung* (Göttingen, 1985), 93–119.

[65] On scholarly contacts between Bohemian scholars and Göttingen, see Walter Schamschula, *Die Anfänge der tschechischen Erneuerung und das deutsche Geistesleben (1740–1800)* (Munich, 1973), especially 94–116.

[66] On Schlözer's activities in general: Ursula A. J. Becher, 'August Ludwig v. Schlözer', in Hans Ulrich Wehler (ed.), *Deutsche Historiker* (Göttingen, 1989), VII. 7–22; on Schlözer in Eastern Europe see Helmut Neubauer, 'August Ludwig Schlözer (1735–1809) und die Geschichte Osteuropas', *Jahrbücher für Geschichte Osteuropas* 18 (1970), 205–30.

Schlözer spent several years in St Petersburg, undertaking innovative research into Russian history, culminating in a translation of the famous *Nestor Chronicle*. His familiarity with Eastern Europe found further expression in the *Allgemeine Nordische Geschichte* (1771), which included a detailed and favourable account of the history of the Slavs. He claimed that: 'apart from the Arabs, who once reigned from Malacha to Lisbon, I do not know of any people in the entire world, who spread themselves, their language, their rule and their colonies so unusually extensively'.[67] Interestingly, Schlözer declared that the Slavs were undoubtedly Northern people, even if they inhabited lands with Southern 'air and climate',[68] although he admitted the term 'Northern' was highly arbitrary and relativistic. For his purposes the Elbe and the Danube acted as the dividing lines between the ancient 'Southern' and the modern 'Northern' world.[69] Both Lelewel and Palacký were thoroughly acquainted with and relied on Schlözer's achievements and drew upon them in their work. Furthermore, the *Nordische Geschichte* was one of the first scholarly accounts to dispute the Turkish ancestry of the Hungarians in favour of the Finno-Ugrian, an argument that Horváth incorporated into his own discussion of their origins, although he retained some scepticism towards it. Daukantas relied heavily on Schlözer's and Ludwig August Gebhardi's account of Baltic history, *Geschichte von Littauen, Kurland and Liefland* (Halle, 1785), whilst Kogălniceanu consulted his *Zur Geschichte der Deutschen in Siebenbürgen*.

The widely read journals and magazines produced at Göttingen revealed a keen interest in Northern and Eastern European and, more specifically, Slavonic history and culture.[70] As early as the 1740s, lectures were offered at the university on Russian and Polish history, whilst connections with the eastern and northern parts of Europe were also forged through the considerable number of students from those regions.[71] Schlözer's path was followed by subsequent 'minor' scholars who embarked on the study of East European history. The

---

[67] August Ludwig Schlözer, *Allgemeine Nordische Geschichte*, 2 vols. (Halle, 1771), I. 221.
[68] Ibid., I. 2–3.   [69] Ibid., I. 2.
[70] Manfred Hildermeier, 'Von der Nordischen Geschichte zur Ostgeschichte: Osteuropa im Göttinger Horizont', in Boockmann and Wellenreuter (eds.), *Geschichtswissenschaft in Göttingen*, 115.
[71] Hildermeier, 'Von der Nordischen Geschichte zur Ostgeschichte', 115; Ulrich Schindel, 'Christian Gottlieb Heyne und Göttingen as Mittler europäischer Aufklärung in Ungarn', *Ural-Altaistische Jahrbücher* 10 (1991), 53–70.

multi-volume *Allgemeine Weltgeschichte*, a translation and adaptation of the venture of two British scholars, William Guthrie's and John Gray's *A General History of the World*, was particularly useful to them.[72] The substantially revised German version was produced under the editorship of Heyne, and its German contributors acknowledged the accomplishments of the English original, but also highlighted its abundant mistakes, misunderstandings and overall unreliability, which they tried to rectify as far as possible.[73] To that end, new volumes were adjoined to the original, in order to cover the history of regions that had been neglected in the English version, such as Eastern and Northern Europe.

The *Guthrie-Gray Allgemeine Geschichte* included the history of Hungary, Wallachia, Moldavia, Transylvania, Lithuania (and also Norway and Denmark). All these were addressed by Ludwig August Gebhardi, a professor at Lüneburg and member of the Historical Institute in Göttingen.[74] These volumes enjoyed considerable popularity in Eastern and Northern Europe and were frequently consulted by local historians for reference purposes, including my historians. Individual parts were also translated into local languages, such as Greek, Serbian, Hungarian and Danish, and became trendsetters for national histories. Horváth and Kogălniceanu relied on Gebhardi's *Geschichte des Reichs Hungarn und der damit verbundenen Staaten* (1778), which formed part XV of the *Guthrie-Gray Weltgeschichte*. The first two of Gebhardi's four volumes concentrated on the history of the Hungarian Empire, whilst the third discussed the history of Transylvania, Galicia, Dalmatia, Croatia and Slavonia and the fourth dealt with the history of Serbia, Bosnia, Bulgaria, Wallachia and Moldavia. Daukantas's histories drew extensively on Gebhardi's other contribution to this series, *Geschichte von Lithauen, Preussen, Ostlichen Preussen und Liefland* (1789)[75]. Not only were these valuable to my historians as secondary sources, they also familiarized them with central themes in European history, as Horváth's discussion of vassalage has demonstrated.

[72] Guthrie's and Gray's venture was itself an adaptation, an abridged version of a monumental historical enterprise entitled *Universal History from the Earliest Account of Time to the Present*.

[73] Johann August Ernesti, 'Vorrede', *Allgemeine Weltgeschichte ausgefertigt von Guthrie Gray und anderen in diesen Theilen der Wissenschaften berühmten Gelehrten* (Leipzig, 1765), I. viii–ix.

[74] Apart from Gebhardi, another Göttingen historian, Johann Christian Engel (1770–1814), was equally significant for my protagonists.

[75] This work was co-authored with August Schlözer.

It was largely through the mediation of Göttingen scholars that my historians came to understand the main tenets of 'commercial language'. In this context, the role of an eminent philologist and historian, Arnold Hermann Ludwig Heeren, is especially remarkable. Heeren's intellectual mindset was typical of the syncretism of the *Spätaufklärung*. His focus on the individual character of nations testified to the influence of Romanticism, but the systematic, comparative and typifying tendencies of his work run counter to the Romantic worldview.[76] Politically, Heeren aligned himself with constitutional liberalism, although he preferred to conceal this commitment. His writings were aimed at academics and the informed public alike and, of his rich oeuvre, two books were especially appreciated by my historians.[77] The first one, *Ideen über die Politik, den Verkehr und den Handel der vornehmsten Völker der alten Welt*, continued the tradition of universal histories as expounded by Schlözer and Gatterer. Nevertheless, Heeren relinquished his predecessors' totalizing approach, focusing instead on underlying issues, hence the title of his work, *Ideen*. His comparative approach and geographical backdrop recalled Montesquieu's principles, whilst the scholarly analysis of economic life resonated with Adam Smith's style of thought.[78] Heeren was also influenced by, though not always in agreement with, William Robertson, and the resemblance in their arguments can probably be explained by shared theoretical assumptions.[79] Heeren's other celebrated volume, *Handbuch der Geschichte des Europäischen Staatensystems und seiner Colonien* (1809) was translated into English and French soon after its publication. It was primarily concerned with the study of constitutions and political institutions, and was one of the first studies to attend to aspects of colonial history.

Horváth's arguments and preoccupations were hugely indebted to Heeren, who was, in all likelihood, his favourite author. As the next chapter will reveal, the Hungarian scholar translated his major article *Az államelméleti theóriák eredete, kifejlése és befolyása, Heeren után* (The Origins, Development and Influence of State Theories in Modern

---

[76] Becker-Schaum, *Arnold Herrmann Ludwig Heeren*, 291–9.

[77] Importantly, Heeren saw his work as part of literary studies: for him historical science (*Geschichtswissenschaft*) only served as an auxiliary discipline (*Hilfswissenschaft*); see Becker-Schaum, *Arnold Herrmann Ludwig Heeren*, 296.

[78] Horst Walter Blanke, 'Verfassungen, die nicht rechtlich, aber wirklich sind: A. H. L. Heeren und das Ende der Aufklärungshistorie', *Berichte zur Wissenschaftsgeschichte* 6 (1983), 147.

[79] Heeren reviewed Robertson's *Historical Disquisition on India* in *Bibliothek der Alten Litteratur und Kunst* (which he himself edited) 9 (1792), 120.

Europe, after Heeren, 1842) into Hungarian, and quoted extensively from his other writings. He hailed Heeren's prize-winning essay on the Crusades, *Versuch einer Entwicklung der Folgen der Kreuzzüge für Europa*, for 'elucidating the causes and consequences of the Crusades in a brilliant way'.[80] Horváth's two volumes on the history of commerce and trade in Hungary, inspired mainly by Heeren's work, 'nationalized' the standard Enlightenment postulate about the beneficial role of the growth of towns in the dismantling of feudalism, by adapting it to the Hungarian context.

As has been explained in Chapter 1, Lelewel studied the profession of librarianship drawing upon Heeren's biography of Heyne, whose innovative cataloguing system was widely employed in Europe. Lelewel's early book, *Dzieje starożytne Indii* (1820), which assessed the literature, philosophy, legal system and geography of ancient India, and its relationship with other civilizations, drew heavily on Heeren's *Ideen*.[81] Furthermore, his lectures on European history at the University of Vilna, especially those relating to the more recent and contemporary period, were almost entirely based on Heeren's *Handbuch*, portraying the Crusades, the Reformation and America's discovery as the crucial junctures of European history.[82] Daukantas relied on Heeren's *Ideen* for his reconstruction of the trading routes of ancient Lithuanians.[83] Palacký's diaries and Kogălniceanu's library also provide evidence that they had encountered Heeren's works, but his impact remained perfunctory.

ENCOUNTERS WITH NIKOLAI KARAMZIN

Nikolai Karamzin (1766–1826), a foremost Russian author, enjoyed considerable popularity on a European scale, as well as among four of my historians. In his homeland, he edited numerous journals and magazines and his contribution to the renewal of the Russian language attracted much praise, whilst his sentimental stories were well-received abroad. Karamzin's major historical achievement, *Istorija gosudarstva rossijskago* (1818–29, History of the Russian State) was a twelve-volume

---

[80] *Horváth Mihály kisebb történelmi munkái*, II. 21.

[81] Jan Tuczyński, *Herder i herderyzm w Polsce* (Gdańsk, 1999), 86.

[82] The lectures appeared as *Dzieła*, Vol. III. (Warsaw 1959), under the title *Wykłady kursowe z historii powszechnej w uniwersytecie wileńskim 1822–24*.

[83] Daukantas, *Raštai*, II. 17.

opus which related the history of the Russians until 1611, and prompted Alexander Pushkin to herald him as the Colombus of ancient Russia. Also available in French and German translations, the *Istorija* contributed to the awakening of international interest in Russia, especially after the victories over Napoleon brought the Tsar's empire into the limelight. In a similar vein to Robertson's celebrated introduction to the *History of Charles V*, the 'View of Progress', Karamzin's preface, enunciating his philosophy of history and containing a précis of his interpretation of Russian history, became the most widely read part of his work.

Karamzin divided Russian history into three distinct stages: pre-political, monarchical and autocratic. He structured developments around the fluctuation between anarchy and authority, and he found that the scale of anarchy was in inverse proportion to the extent of the prince's power and his concern for the welfare of the people. He traced Russia's greatness to benevolent autocracy, and the *Istorija*, an extended 'statesman's handbook', sought to unravel the development of autocratic rule and how it could be most effectively sustained.[84] At the same time, Karamzin maintained that the rule of the prince was not absolute; it was challenged by the Slavic libertarian tradition, especially the early Slavs' public assemblies. He took pride in Russia's oriental heritage, in which he located the unique genius of the Russian people and also asserted that his nation was on a par with other European countries. On the ideological front, not only was Karamzin a conservative representative of the hereditary nobility, fiercely critical of liberalism and the occidental culture of the West, but he also defended autocracy and serfdom because he thought these could save Russia from foreign invasion.[85]

Karamzin provided inspiration for several members of the Slavic *res publica litteraria*. In G. P. Gooch's general survey on nineteenth-century historical writing, Palacký is characterized as 'an avid reader of Karamzin and Johannes von Müller', but it would be a gross exaggeration to assign primacy to the Russian author in Palacký's very complex intellectual world. His diary exhibits familiarity with Karamzin, but Lelewel appears to have been more decisively influenced by the Russian scholar. In 1822 Lelewel published a review article on Karamzin's *Istrorija* in the Russian

[84] R. E. McGrew, 'Notes on the Princely Role in Karamzin's *Istorija Gosudarstva Rossijskago*', *American Slavic and East European Review* 18:1 (1959), 13–14.

[85] Vladimir Rhyzkov, 'Enlightenment, Freedom, and Civic Society in Nikolai Karamzin's Political Thought', MA thesis (Budapest, Central European University, 2004), 13.

journal *Severny Archiv* (Northern Archive), in which he favourably contrasted the achievements of the Polish Enlightenment historian Adam Naruszewicz with those of Karamzin.[86] Carefully disguised under historiographical criticism, this was nevertheless an ideological polemic against the Russian scholar.[87] Lelewel began with the claim that 'several writers aspire to be historians but only very few can achieve that aim. It is not difficult to find talented historians, but few display real maturity': the four scholars who met that criterion were Thucydides, Tacitus, Robertson and Hume.[88] With this declaration my protagonist implied that it was unwise for Karamzin to venture into historical writing; he should have simply remained an author.[89]

Lelewel was also dismayed that Karamzin's ambition to teach politicians and lawmakers how to govern Russia prompted him to focus on the history of rulers and the state, to the detriment of the history of the people. The impact of the new, professional standards of historical writing was revealed in Lelewel's dismissive attitude towards Karamzin's admired narrative skills; he declared that these were of secondary importance. While the review brought Lelewel popularity, Karamzin himself did not take it seriously, declaring that his opponent's nationality would be defence enough. In response to criticism of his conservatism and authoritarian tendencies, he added ironically that 'at least I am liberal, I allow them (i.e. his critiques) to say and to write what they wish'.[90] Despite this critical attitude and their fundamentally different political stances, Lelewel's arguments reveal similarities with Karamzin's; especially noteworthy are their shared views on the unique democracy of early Slavic communities, except that for Karamzin the ancient Russians, and for Lelewel the early Poles, were seen as the foremost representatives of democracy and equality. A further parallel is that, like Karamzin, Lelewel also refuted occidentalism, the belief in the superiority and exemplary nature of Western European values.

Daukantas's view of Karamzin's work was unaffected by the discrepancy between his democratic tendencies and the Russian scholar's approval of authoritarianism.

---

[86] The revised version of his article was published as 'Porównanie Karamzina z Naruszewiczem', in *Dzieła*, II/2. 588–628.

[87] Frank Mocha, 'The Karamzin–Lelewel Controversy', *Slavic Review* 31:3 (1972), 600.

[88] Lelewel, *Dzieła*, II/2. 589.

[89] Mocha, 'The Karamzin–Lelewel Controversy', 600.

[90] J. L. Black, *Nicholas Karamzin and Russian Society in the Nineteenth Century* (Toronto, 1975), 143.

Karamzin's *Istorija* assumed twofold relevance for Daukantas: he employed it as a sourcebook whenever his narrative benefited from reference to Russian history, and secondly, Karamzin's anti-Polish tendencies rendered his arguments especially attractive for the Lithuanian scholar. Daukantas was often inclined to ignore more obvious sources, especially Polish ones, if he found them unsympathetic to the cause of Lithuania. Karamzin's verdict on Lithuanian history represented a more appealing alternative; for example, his account was more favourable towards the ancient pagan Lithuanians than were Polish chronicles, emphasizing their bravery in warfare, and he also tended to be more appreciative of Lithuanian rulers. Karamzin's impact on Daukantas was so great that the preface of *Pasakojimas* contained an acknowledgement to him.[91]

Kogălniceanu's obvious fascination with Karamzin's intellectual world was evident in his inaugural lecture at the Mihailean Academy in 1843 in Iaşi, *Cuvânt pentru deschiderea cursului de istorie naţională în Academia Mihăileană*. This piece, an introduction to a lecture series on Romanian history, extensively relied on the preface to Karamzin's *Istorija*. Kogălniceanu read the Russian scholar's *opus magnum* in French translation. *L'histoire de l'empire de la Russie* was published in Paris simultaneously with the Russian original, initially under Karamzin's supervision. It is worth noting that a Romanian translation of the *Istorija* was also published in 1833.[92] The first part of Karamzin's preface contained a meditation on the meaning and purpose of history, paying tribute to conventional topoi, in particular the *magistra vitae*, whilst the second part highlighted the most crucial junctures in Russian history. Kogălniceanu adopted this twofold structure for his own lecture. The first section was in fact a word-for-word translation of the first passages from Karamzin's preface. Kogălniceanu's text indicated the source of inspiration, although not the depth of his involvement with Karamzin's text:

After the contemplation of the world, after the wonders of nature, nothing is more interesting, more noble or more worthy of our attention than History. History, gentlemen, — as some of the most respected authors have remarked — is the true account and presentation of the accomplishments of humankind; it is the accumulation of ages and experiences. Therefore, it can legitimately be called the voice of our predecessors and the icon of past times. Karamzin calls

[91] Daukantas, *Raštai*, Vol. II., 8.
[92] Drace Francis, *The Making of Romanian Culture*, 119.

(history) the testament left by our ancestors to their grandchildren, to serve as an interpretation of the present time and as a guide for the future.[93]

Like Karamzin, Kogălniceanu devotes the second part of his text to an assessment of the key turning-points in Romanian history, in which he necessarily departs from the Russian version to some extent. He adopts some archetypal rhetorical devices from the Russian scholars' work. For example, Karamzin writes:

My heart beats quicker upon hearing the names of the boyars than on hearing the name of Themistocles or Scipio and venerates the deeds of Sviatoslav, Dmitri Donskoi, Oleg, Dimitiri Pozharski in Russian history.[94]

Similarly, Kogălniceanu declares:

My heart beats when I hear the names of (the Romanian rulers) Alexander the Good, Stefan the Great, Michael the Brave. I am not ashamed to tell you that these men are more important for me than Alexander the Great, Hannibal or Caesar. Their battles are of greater interest because they were won by Romanians.[95]

Lastly, Horváth's lack of familiarity with the Russian scholar testifies to a cultural barrier; in nineteenth-century Hungary no significant cultural ties were forged with Russia, and the Hungarian liberals' generally ambivalent feelings towards the Russian Empire, and their fear of Panslavism, could have also contributed to that apathy.

CONTEMPORARY RESONANCES: THE FRENCH LIBERAL SCHOOL

A study of foreign intellectual influences needs to take into account that these can have a delayed effect, because, for example, censorship hindered the circulation of foreign books and translation could often take a long time. On the basis of hitherto assessed authors, it would be tempting to conclude that my historians were primarily influenced

---

[93] Kogălniceanu, *Opere*, II. 386. My translation relies on but is not identical with the excerpt in Balázs Trencsényi and Michal Kopeček (eds.), *Discourses of Collective Identity in Central and Southeast Europe (1770–1945)*, Vol. II: *National Romanticism—The Formation of National Movements* (Budapest and New York, 2007), 46.

[94] Karamzin, *Istorija Gosudarstva Rossijskago* (Moscow, 1989), I. 4; and the French verison, trans. Jauffret [sic], *Histoire de L'Empire Russie* (Paris, 1819), I. xix.

[95] Kogălniceanu, *Opere*, II. 389.

by the mindset of earlier generations, because ideas travelled to their countries with significant delay, preventing them from becoming fully conversant with the intellectual world of their contemporaries. This was far from being the case; they were strongly influenced by contemporary currents of thought. Of these, their engagement with the ideas of the French liberal school testifies to an almost immediate pattern of reception, although the direct traces of this transmission are relatively scarce.

On a superficial level, French historians of the Restoration period, such as Thierry, Guizot and Michelet may not appear to be obvious sources of inspiration, given that the legacy of the French Revolution, their main preoccupation, rendered some of their insights unique. Yet, in a wider context, some of the French scholars' fundamental concerns, as well as their elevated position in society, offer useful comparisons and help to explain why they could be inspirational to my historians. Because of the role it played in public life, history was perhaps valued even more highly in France than in Germany, and historians' greater willingness to engage with social issues and reform resonated particularly deeply with my protagonists.[96] The majority of Enlightenment scholars as well as contemporary historians, irrespective of their nationality, believed that historical writing should be accompanied by action, and thus, their vision of progress was essentially reformist; they saw change as fundamental.[97] Moreover, whereas English liberal thought was not fashioned as a means of political reform, French theories of social change were designed to explore political issues or to try to resolve pressing political problems of the time.[98] As Chapter 7 will reveal, the French scholars' preoccupations with feudalism provided a common denominator in this context. As well, Guizot's *Histoire générale de la civilisation en Europe*, a major contribution to the study of the concept and history of European civilization, received widespread support and acclaim in most European countries, including East-Central Europe.

To varying degrees, my historians were all conversant with French historians of the Restoration period. I have not found allusions to their works in Daukantas's writings, but this does not mean that he never encountered them. Daukantas's home library contained Guizot's

[96] Iggers, 'Nationalism and Historiography', 19.
[97] Reill, *The German Enlightenment*, 72.
[98] Larry Siedentop, 'Two Liberal Traditions', in Alan Ryan (ed.), *The Idea of Freedom: Essays in Honour of Isaiah Berlin* (Oxford, 1979), 174.

Conseils de morale (1829), Michelet's *Précis d'histoire moderne* and his essay on Vico, and it is likely that, towards the end of his life (by which time he had already completed his histories), he familiarized himself with Thierry's works.[99] Kogălniceanu encountered the intellectual world of several scholars in his youth, especially during his stay in France. Subsequently, as editor of the journal *Archiva Românească*, he introduced the first volume by adapting a trope from Thierry's *Lettres sur l'Histoire de France*; according to this, history provided the criteria to ascertain which nations were progressing and which were lagging behind.[100]

Horváth's texts offer scant evidence of the direct impact of French scholars upon his thought. On one occasion he establishes a parallel between the Hungarian politician Ferenc Deák (the main agent behind the Compromise) and George Washington, declaring that Guizot's characterization of the American statesman is equally applicable to his Hungarian counterpart.[101] Nevertheless, Horváth's familiarity with Thierry and Guizot is unquestionable, as both scholars enjoyed considerable popularity in nineteenth-century Hungary; their writings were widely read both in the original and in translation and were reviewed and discussed in well-known journals.[102] Horváth's interest in the English Revolution is likely to have been aroused upon reading Thierry's works, rather than those of English scholars. Moreover, Horváth's fellow prominent historian László Szalay saw Guizot as a role model, visiting him in Paris and subsequently embarking on correspondence with him.[103]

It is probable that the French scholars' arguments were 'internalized' to such an extent that they became common knowledge. For instance, the periodicals in which Horváth's articles appeared (*Tudománytár, Athenaeum*) published reviews of Guizot's *Histoire générale de la civilisation en Europe* (1841) and Michelet's *Histoire de France* (1840). Interestingly, neither of these was based on the original work; the review of Guizot's book was adapted from the journal *Göttingsche Gelehrte Anzeigen*, whilst Michelet's came from the *Journal des Savants*. Thierry's books were also sold in large numbers and received generous coverage in Hungarian journals, despite the fact some of them were

99 J. Lebedys, 'Simano [*sic*] Daukanto Biblioteka', in *Lietuvių Literatūros Instituto Darbai*, vol. I (Vilnius, 1947), 60.

100 Kogălniceanu, *Opere*, II. 404.

101 Horváth, *Huszonöt év Magyarország történetéből*, I. 345.

102 Várkonyi, *Pozitivista szemlélet*, II. 44–5.   103 Ibid., II. 170.

officially banned.[104] Analogies between the French scholars' outlook and Horváth's perspective were highlighted by two prominent Hungarian scholars in the early twentieth century, independently of each other. One of them compared Horváth to Thiers, Guizot, Thierry and Macaulay because of his anti-feudal stance and interest in the 'third estate',[105] while the other claimed that Horváth transplanted the historical concept of French liberalism to Hungarian soil.[106]

Palacký's Protestant interpretation of Czech history and debt to the tradition of the Bohemian Brethren has been likened to Guizot's Huguenot background and austere Calvinism.[107] He first ventured into Guizot's intellectual world of European society and civilization in the 1840s, during his sojourn in Nice. Subsequently, he warmly recommended Guizot and Thierry to his friends and also embarked on the translation of *Histoire générale de la civilisation en Europe* with his son; their Czech version was published in 1851.[108] Yet, as with Horváth, direct references to the French historians are few and far between. One instance is Palacký's appeal to Guizot to reinforce his assessment of early German history and, possibly also his characterization of the Germans as *Räubervolk* (aggressors).[109] Palacký's son, a Francophile, sent a copy of his father's book to Thierry, whilst Palacký himself established contacts with editors of the *Revue des deux Mondes*, and in 1855, Saint-René Taillandier published an article entitled *Histoire et historien de Bohême: Franz Palacky*. This publication gradually introduced the Czech question into the international political arena.

Lelewel was well acquainted with representatives of the French liberal school, even composing an article which engaged in a virtual dialogue with Guizot, intended to correct the French scholar's hypotheses on Polish history, as Chapter 7 will reveal.[110] However, Lelewel's real French 'counterpart' is undoubtedly Jules Michelet; both scholars epitomize a

[104] Ibid., II. 76.

[105] Henrik Marczali, 'Horváth Mihály emlékezete', *Budapesti Szemle* 141 (1910), 176.

[106] Bálint Hóman, 'A történelem útja', in Bálint Hóman (ed.), *A Magyar történetírás új útjai* (Budapest, 1931), 31.

[107] This is the main claim in Josef Válka, 'Palacký a francouzská liberální historiografie', *Sborník prací filozofické fakulty brněnské univerzity* C 33 (1986), 101–9.

[108] Josef Válka, 'La théorie de l'histoire chez Palacký', *Sborník prací filozofické fakulty brněnské univerzity* 14 (1967), 99.

[109] Palacký, *Die Geschichte des Hussitenthums und Prof. Konstantin Höfler: kritische Studien* (Prague, 1868), 76.

[110] Lelewel's response was published in Polish as *Joachima Lelewela odpowiedź na ankietę historyczną François Guizota*, transl. Marian Heryk Serejski (Wrocław, 1962).

genre of Romantic historiography which carried messianistic overtones, and the intellectual exchange between the two scholars was informed by a degree of reciprocity. Michelet showed a keen interest in Polish history, especially the life of the freedom fighter Tadeusz Kościuszko and the Revolution of 1830. He refers to Poland as the Christ of nations and his footnotes reveal that his understanding of Polish history was partly derived from his acquaintence with Lelewel's writings.[111] At the same time, Michelet made recourse to Kogălniceanu's *Histoire* when referring to episodes of Romanian history, proving that my historians were not entirely unknown to contemporary Western scholars.[112]

CONCLUSION

Of the diverse sources of inspiration in my historians' work, the relevance of domestic scholarship, the Scottish and German variations of Enlightenment, as well as the impact of Nikolai Karamzin and the French liberal school have been assessed. My analysis has also highlighted the fundamental pitfalls that underline the study of intellectual transfer. In particular, it has emerged that, more often than not, the genesis of an idea may not be identifiable with a single source or author, nor may it be possible to detect, especially on the basis of tacit hints, whose ideas my historians originally appropriated when they advanced a claim which had widespread appeal at the time. To that end, the impact of the *Zeitgeist* should not be underestimated. No sharp clear line may be drawn between *influence* and *similarity*: the common framework, the prevalent dilemmas which informed a given epoch often rested on shared assumptions and thus provoked analogous responses. A further complexity lies in the academic conventions of the age, which allowed for a more extensive incorporation of other scholars' arguments than would be the case today. Furthermore, the intellectual worlds of the authors whose ideas this chapter is concerned with were not independent, but intricately entwined. For example, Herder provided inspiration for representatives of the Scottish Enlightenment and also influenced Arnold Heeren, although the appropriation of that

---

[111] For Michelet's reference to Lelewel's *Geschichte Polens* see Jules Michelet, *Légendes démocratiques du Nord*, ed. Michel Cadot (Paris, 1968), 40 and 282.

[112] For Michelet's reference to Kogălniceanu's *Histoire* see Michelet, *Légendes démocratiques du Nord*, 241.

heritage necessarily resulted in deviations from the original message.[113] Additionally, Heeren's and the French historians' evocation of commercial language and, to some extent, their concept of civilization was influenced by Scottish scholars, such as Adam Ferguson and William Robertson.[114]

The reliance of my historians on foreign authors and concepts should be approached with caution. On a superficial level an extensive absorption may imply lack of originality and even cultural dependency. It may also presuppose a tendency towards a heterogeneous mindset. Yet, such *syncretism* can be viewed in terms of intellectual vibrancy, all the more so, because my historians made a conscious effort to acquaint themselves with a variety of intellectual traditions. The key to accessing another culture was language, and in that respect, they were better equipped that many of their contemporaries, especially Palacký, who could read some fourteen languages.

Romantic-liberal historiography absorbed numerous tenets of Enlightenment scholarship. My protagonists were profoundly indebted not only to the political ideals and conceptual framework of the Enlightenment, but also to the information which their predecessors discovered about the history of their nation. This legacy has also been observed in other national contexts; for instance, Macaulay is deemed a direct inheritor of the Enlightenment, in addition to benefiting from the intense influence of literary Romanticism and his commitment to political science.[115] My findings have confirmed common knowledge about the prominent role of the Göttingen academic community as a mediator in the intellectual encounters between Britain and Germany. They have also testified to established views on Göttingen's position as a major gateway for the exploration of the history of Eastern and Northern Europe and also its significant impact on local scholarship. In addition, as a side-effect, another link has emerged, one which unites those two directions of interchange: the route that ideas followed from Britain to Göttingen and *then* from there to Central and Eastern Europe.

[113] Roy Pascal, 'Herder and the Scottish Historical School', *Publications of the English Goethe Society* 14 (1938–9), 23–42.

[114] Friedrich Engel-Janosi, *Four Studies in French Romantic Historical Writing* (Baltimore, 1955), 99. For the impact of British scholarship on Heeren see Hellmut Seier, 'Heeren und England', in Lothar Kettenacker, Manfred Schlenke and Hellmut Seier (eds.), *Studien zur Geschichte Englands und der deutsch–britischen Beziehungen: Festschrift für Paul Kluke* (Munich, 1981), 48–78.

[115] Peter Ghosh, 'Macaulay and the Heritage of the Enlightenment', *English Historical Review* 112:446 (1997), 359.

Nikolai Karamzin's reception testifies to a pattern of transmission which defied the traditional 'centre to periphery' route. Instead, it exemplifies intellectual transfer between 'peripheries', without necessarily traversing the 'centre'.

As my historians' encounters with the French historians of the Restoration period indicate, influence does not necessarily translate into obvious signs, such as references and footnotes. The paucity of direct traits may also signify the popularity of certain authors, as it may suggest that their views became part of common knowledge and thus did not incur specific mention. The unrepresentative nature of my sample may be partially responsible for the absence or weak impact of some prominent intellectual trends and individual authors. For example, only relatively moderate evidence points to Macaulay's influence in my historians' writings, although Lelewel and Palacký were undoubtedly well-acquainted with his oeuvre. Yet, the English scholar's overall popularity in East-Central Europe, evident from numerous reviews, translations and discussions of his celebrated essays and *History of England*, is undisputed. Also, a prominent Hungarian scholar who assessed Horváth's legacy in an obituary suggested that his studies on significant and fascinating Hungarian historical figures might have endeavoured to domesticate a genre which came to be associated with Macaulay's essays. This could have been driven by Horváth's intention to convince the reading public that outstanding heroes were not only to be found in foreign books: Hungarian history also yielded remarkable characters.[116]

It is noteworthy that the five historians were inspired by *one* distinct generation of German scholarship—Gatterer, Schlözer, Heeren—the last representatives of a universalist tradition. In that context, the silencing of Heeren, 'the last German proponent of a broad Enlightenment vision of world history' by a chorus of vicious critics in 1832 marked a symbolic caesura in German historiography.[117] The next generation embarked on a different trajectory. Their faith in universally applicable values was now shattered and (apart from a few isolated thinkers who, like the Freiburg historian Karl von Rotteck, remained faithful to the principles of 1789), historians came to believe that alien concepts and

---

[116] Marczali, 'Horváth Mihály emlékezete', 181.

[117] Jürgen Osterhammel, 'Peoples without History in British and German Historical Thought', in Benedikt Stuchtey and Peter Wende (eds.), *British and German Historiography, 1750–1950: Traditions, Perceptions and transfers* (Oxford and London, 2000), 266–7.

traditions could not be transplanted to German soil.[118] Scholars who exemplified this new trend, including Barthold Niebuhr, Georg Gottfried Gervinus, Friedrich Christoph Dahlmann and Gustav Droysen, exerted virtually no impact on my protagonists' writings.[119] Nor were my historians, as we have seen, influenced by the new Rankean 'paradigm'. Like their methodological desiderata, their intellectual world also seems to have represented a critical moment of transition; their fundamental engagement with the national past dovetailed with a great debt to the Enlightenment legacy.

[118] Iggers, *The German Conception of History*, 40–1.

[119] Although Palacký had scholarly contacts with some of these scholars, for example he met Friedrich Christoph Dahlmann, Karl Theodor Welcker, Georg Gottfried Gervinus and Ludwig Häusser in 1859 in Heidelberg, and Dahlmann read parts of his *Geschichte von Böhmen*, there is little evidence of the significant influence of these scholars in his own work.

5

Language as Medium, Language as Message

THE FECUNDITY OF INFERIORITY COMPLEXES

Linguistic change is often assessed in teleological terms, such as the 'triumph' and 'evolution' of language or national 'awakening'. Whilst it would be inadvisable to dismiss an element of 'development' altogether, neither should it be equated with linear progress, rather, with a constant conflict between centripetal and centrifugal forces, convergence and divergence, and continuous readjustment to contemporary realities.[1] Motivation for the enrichment of European languages was characteristically informed by an 'anxiety of deficit'; concerns about the poverty of the vernacular in comparison to other tongues.[2] During the Middle Ages Latin seemed limited in capacity when compared to Greek, subsequently vernacular languages sought liberation from Latin and in the Orthodox world from Church Slavonic.[3] In the sixteenth century French scholars lamented that their mother tongue was not as elaborate as Greek and Latin, whilst their English counterparts also perceived their language as imperfect and unsophisticated.[4] Additionally, in accordance with Herder's assertion that dominant nations based their rule less on military might than on 'the use of a more cultivated language', cultures under foreign domain attempted to emancipate themselves linguistically.[5]

---

[1] Peter Burke, *Languages and Communities in Early Modern Europe* (Cambridge, 2004), 13.

[2] Ibid., 17.

[3] Thorsten Fögen, *Patrii sermonis egestas: Einstellungen lateinischer Autoren zu ihrer Muttersprache, Ein Beitrag zum Sprachbewußtsein in der römischen Antike* (Munich and Leipzig, 2000), 41.

[4] Richard Foster Jones, *The Triumph of the English Language: A Survey of Opinions Concerning the Vernacular from the Introduction of Printing* (Stanford, 1953), 10.

[5] Burke, *Languages and Communities*, 164.

Scholars embarked on linguistic standardization on pragmatic as well as on ideological grounds; in order to promote communication between various regions and to endow their language with the prestige and dignity associated with Latin. This entailed the publication of grammars, the regulation of orthography and the purification of the language from foreign influences. The second half of the eighteenth century marked a turning-point in these developments: whilst earlier linguistic pursuits revolved around variety, in this epoch scholars grew increasingly preoccupied with unity. Language and nationality became more closely entwined and this phenomenon was enshrined in the conviction that nations, like individuals, had ideas unique to them which were manifested in the genius of language.[6] From this it followed that the pinnacles of language corresponded perfectly to the pinnacles of the literary and political tradition; conversely, political decline exposed language to corruption and decay.[7] The forging of links between language and nation was often animated by ideological aims.[8] For example in Britain in the second half of the eighteenth century, the establishment of a common language was seen as essential for cementing the amalgam of four distinct nations, England, Scotland, Ireland and Wales.[9]

The inferiority complex, a result of confrontation with the standards of other languages, supplied a powerful dynamic for elevating respective vernaculars to the status enjoyed by other tongues. Opportunities for enrichment included the reintroduction of old words, borrowing words from dialects, the creation of new expressions from native roots as well as translations of foreign terms. Confidence in the eloquential power of European vernaculars gradually began to increase and the notes of self-disparagement grew much fainter. No longer was the elegance of Latin seen as unattainable, and vernacular languages evolved into the media of instruction, as illustrated by John Locke's statement: 'if a gentleman be to study any language, it ought to be that of his own country'.[10] 'Topoi of humility' were thus superseded by

---

[6] This idea has traditionally been associated with Herder, but can be traced back to earlier times.

[7] Tony Crowley, *Language in History: Theories and Texts* (London and New York, 1996), 64.

[8] The nexus between language and state-building is discussed in R. J. W. Evans, 'Language and State Building: The Case of the Habsburg Monarchy', *Austrian History Yearbook* 35 (2004), 1–24.

[9] Crowley, *Language in History*, 68.   [10] Ibid., 66.

'topoi of pride'. In his *Briefe zur Beförderung der Humanität* Herder asserted that German was a language of reason, power and truth which uniquely allowed the imitation of foreign idioms in every expression, in every translation.[11] French scholars celebrated the elegance, unique rational transparency and pleasing expression of their tongue, whilst self-congratulatory comments on the English language encompassed characteristics such as freedom of thought, independence and ability to engage in rational discussion, in contrast to the 'flimsiness' and 'arbitrariness' of French, the 'graveness' of Spanish and the 'hoarseness' of Teutonic tongues.[12] Another archetypal manifestation of these 'topoi of pride' lay in the equation of one's own tongue with Adam's language, the pre-Babel language of Eden.[13]

Linguistic concerns in my protagonists' cultures followed a similar trajectory: they were initially conditioned by lamentations on the poverty of language.[14] In that context, Jan Kollár, Palacký's (Slovak) friend, evocatively likened attempts at using the language for sophisticated purposes to 'playing a piano which has no strings'.[15] The cultivation of the mother tongue was informed by an emancipatory desire and appeared to be, as the following quotation from Palacký illustrates, a requirement of the *Zeitgeist*:

The national language is undeniably the most fundamental and dearest aspect of our Bohemian ancestors' legacy to future generations. It was through this medium that the Czechs were able to form an independent nation and acquire a history which shall forever occupy an illustrious place in the annals of the world . . . It is therefore crucial for our generation to preserve this language . . . In an era when nearly all lesser European nations are, as it were, competing to *return* to their previously neglected national languages, the most sacred symbol of their existence . . . (think of the Poles, Hungarians, the Dutch, Danes and Finns), it would be inappropriate for the Czechs to fall behind.[16]

---

[11] Muhlback, 'Universal History and National History', 29.

[12] Crowley, *Language in History*, 62 and 71.

[13] Medieval views on the origins of languages are discussed in Arno Borst, *Der Turmbau von Babel: Geschichte der Meinungen über Ursprung und Vielfalt der Sprachen und Völker*, 4 vols. (Stuttgart, 1957–63).

[14] For a monumental study of linguistic developments in the region see Tomasz Kamusella, *The Politics of Language and Nationalisms in Central Europe during the Nineteenth and Twentieth Centuries* (Basingstoke, 2008).

[15] For a comparison between the Czech and Hungarian linguistic renewal see Henrik Becker, *Zwei Sprachanschlüsse* (Leipzig and Berlin, 1948).

[16] Palacký, *Gedenkblätter*, 62.

Polish was already employed as a literary language and used for the production of legal and social documents during the Renaissance, whilst Latin terminology was preserved in scholarship where precision was required.[17] Latin was favoured by the Polish nobility in the early modern period and the Jesuits' influence further strengthened its hold. Lelewel portrayed the Enlightenment era as one of linguistic improvement, when Polish infiltrated political life and yielded literary gems.[18] As we shall see, the disappearance of the state facilitated the rise in status of language within Polish culture.

In the Hungarian context, the linguistic renewal in the eighteenth and nineteenth centuries was triggered by Herder's misunderstood prediction about the extinction of Hungarian.[19] In Horváth's time, efforts were made to iron out some of the extremities which emerged from the rapid introduction of radical linguistic novelties. Nevertheless, Latin, which had become increasingly associated with pedantry elsewhere, survived as the official language of the state until as late as 1844, providing both a means of defence against German influence and a neutral lingua franca which could be shared by the subjects of a multinational empire irrespective of their own mother tongue. Although the suppression of the War of Independence of 1848–9 had a detrimental effect on Hungarian intellectual life, it stimulated language reform. As a reaction to the Germanizing efforts of Habsburg neoabsolutism, extreme Hungarianizing neologisms came to proliferate, followed by a period of consolidation.[20]

Intensified scholarly interest in the Lithuanian language, especially on the part of foreign scholars, was motivated by the threat of extinction. The precedent set by the loss of another member of the Baltic language family, Old Prussian, in the seventeenth century, might have exacerbated this concern, together with some peculiarities of Lithuanian culture, especially the absence of written language before the adoption of Christianity in 1387. Furthermore, although the Reformation in the sixteenth century was conducive to the promotion of Lithuanian

---

[17] Janusz Tazbir, 'Polish National Consciousness in the Sixteenth to Eighteenth Century', *Harvard Ukrainian Studies* (1986), 320.

[18] Lelewel, *Dzieła*, VIII. 354–5; *Geschichte Polens unter Stanislaus August* (Braunschweig, 1831), 60.

[19] On Herder's prediction see János Rathmann, *Herder eszméi—a historizmus útján* (Budapest, 1983), 123–37.

[20] István Fodor, 'Hungarian: Evolution—Stagnation—Reform—Further Development', in István Fodor and Claude Hagège (eds.), *Language Reform: History and Future*, 5 vols., Vol. II (1983–84), 61–2.

culture within the ecclesiastical sphere, the vernacular was not elevated to a medium of literature and state. Instead, official affairs in the Grand Duchy of Lithuania were conducted in a Slavonic language which bore closest resemblance to Byelorussian.[21] As we have seen in the previous chapter, foreign academics, such as Immanuel Kant, helped local scholars to improve the standing of their language. In the nineteenth century, the emergence of comparative linguistics, a new scholarly discipline, served to raise the status of Lithuanian. As a member of the Indo-European language family, its prestige was also enhanced by the growing reputation of the Indo-European language theory.

The well-cultivated language of Czech humanism, as represented by the classical tradition of the Bible originating in the religious sect of the Bohemian Brethren, underwent a decline after the Battle of White Mountain in 1620, when Bohemia was incorporated into the Habsburg Monarchy: it gradually disappeared from the public sphere into private life.[22] The modern literary language was resuscitated after long neglect, and codified by the eminent Enlightenment scholar Josef Dobrovský, in the late eighteenth century. Nonetheless, numerous grammatical and orthographical issues remained to be settled in the following decades and Czech only gradually penetrated every area of life. In the Romanian principalities the late eighteenth and early nineteenth centuries were characterized by attempts at cultural unification. Uniquely, whilst in other countries scholars typically strove to liberate their tongues from the legacy of Latin, Romanians were inspired, even at the risk of artificiality, to accentuate parallels by borrowing neologisms from Latin and Italian and by replacing the Cyrillic alphabet with its Latin counterpart. Kogălniceanu wished to improve Romanian's reputation as an insignificant and inflexible language.[23] He noted that during his sojourn in Berlin he was referred to as 'der schwarze Grieche' (the 'black Greek'), in the absence of words to denote Romanians. To that end, Kogălniceanu claimed to have been the first person to use the words *roumain* and *Roumanie* in the French language.[24]

[21] See Jerzy Ochmański, 'The National Idea in Lithuania from the 16th to the First Half of the 19th Century: The Problem of Cultural-Linguistic Identification', *Harvard Ukrainian Studies* (1986), 301–15.

[22] This phenomenon is elucidated in David Crystal, *Language Death* (Cambridge, 2002), 22 and 83.

[23] Kogălniceanu, *Opere*, I. 239.   [24] Ibid., II. 606.

LANGUAGE AS A BRIDGE: IN THE SERVICE OF UNITY

Language possessed twofold potential for underpinning national unity: horizontal and vertical. Transcending regional and state boundaries, it acted as a bridge between members of the envisaged national community who had been scattered over separate realms. In this vein Kogălniceanu declared that 'I regard as my fatherland all territories where Romanian is spoken, and as national history the history of all Moldavia, before its partition, that of Wallachia and that of the brothers in Transylvania.'[25] This potential took on extra significance in Polish culture following the disappearance of the state. Citizenship (of the noble classes) and a common fatherland could no longer be regarded as appropriate criteria for nationhood; such correlation would have turned nineteenth-century Poles, having fallen under German and Russian rule, into Germans and Russians, a prospect that Polish patriots found abhorrent.[26] From this precarious situation Polish residents of three different empires could appeal to language as a common denominator, leading Lelewel to define language and national history as the two strongholds of nationality.[27]

The vertical dimension of promoting social cohesion through language could be pursued by taking popular speech as a model, rather than the high or formal variant. Like his counterparts in Finland, Norway and Serbia, Daukantas, who created the first broad conception of a standard written language during the entire history of the Lithuanian language, followed popular usage.[28] This was in accordance with an already mentioned intention that his writings should be read not only by learned people but also by 'the Lithuanian mothers, who would like to tell their children the deeds of the ancient ancestors, but, without having written texts, often make mistakes'.[29] At the same time, Daukantas utilized the horizontal dimension of the unifying potentials

---

[25] Ibid., II. 394.   [26] Walicki, *Philosophy and Romantic Nationalism*, 64.

[27] Lelewel, 'Prawność narodu polskiego', in Andrzej Walicki and Jan Garewicz (eds.), *700 lat myśli polskiej: Filozofia i myśl społeczna w latach 1831–1864* (Warsaw, 1977), 779; in English version 'Legitimacy of the Polish Nation', in Trencsényi and Kopeček (eds.), *Discourses of Collective Identity*, II. 36.

[28] Giedrus Subačius, 'Three Models of Standard Written Lithuanian Language in the 19th Century: J. A. Pabrėža, J. Ciulda, S. Daukantas', *Lituanus* 43:1 (Spring 1997), 13–26. Daukantas's linguistic achievements are discussed in Zigmas Zinkevičius, *Lietuvių kalba XVIII–XIX a* (Vilnius, 1990), 146–56, 13–25, 20–3.

[29] Daukantas, *Raštai*, I. 39.

of language, as he sought to produce a written version which would appeal to all ethnic Lithuanians. In light of the significant local variations, he feared that it might prove impossible to forge a standard spoken variant. Hence, he abandoned any attempt to formulate rules: 'I pray you dear Lithuanian reader, not to be annoyed with me for not using the language of your parish. After you have read it once, you will be able to read it again pronouncing the words as people in your parish would speak.'[30]

If this twofold unifying motivation constituted one driving force behind Daukantas's Polish–Lithuanian and Lithuanian–Latin dictionaries, another one was his collection of folk songs, tales and proverbs. This provided a parallel with his German contemporary, the poet Achim von Arnim, whose anthology of folksongs was similarly inspired by the belief that they united the dispersed people of the German-speaking area.[31] Daukantas's confidence in the suitability of Lithuanian to every sphere of life is especially noteworthy against the backdrop of the succeeding generation's inability to engage with the language fully, as demonstrated by their preference for Polish in correspondence and communication. Palacký contributed to the resolution of undetermined grammatical and orthographical issues. Overall, he took a moderate stance regarding the process of linguistic codification, which acted as a brake on the wheels of sometimes unnecessary reforms. On the whole, his views on linguistic matters became more conservative as he reached maturity; in particular, he strongly opposed the development of a separate Slovak literary language.[32] In 1829 he devised a scheme for a Czech encyclopaedia with the primary intention of uniting and stabilizing professional terminology and gradually introducing it into practice.[33]

The correlation between language and nationhood was powerfully shown in Palacký's choice of languages, as was the paradox that underlay efforts to achieve national unity: that these were bound to entail a degree of exclusion. In his youth my historian considered the Bohemians to be bilingual and therefore wrote in both German and Czech.[34] His *magnum opus* was commissioned by the Bohemian Estates, who expected it to be composed in German; however, in the 1840s, Palacký started working

---

[30] Daukantas, *Raštai*, II. 790–1.   [31] Burke, *Languages and Communities*, 170.

[32] For Palacký's views on language see: Jaromír Bělič, 'Zásady Palackého v otázkách jazykové kultury', in František Kutnar (ed.), *Tři studie o Františku Palackém*, Acta Universitatis Palackianae Olomucensis, 1 (Olomouc, 1949), 166–237.

[33] This scheme did not materialize and a new attempt in 1850 was also postponed.

[34] Palacký, *Spisy drobné*, II. 60.

simultaneously on a Czech version. Nonetheless, following attacks by German scholars after his refusal to attend the Frankfurt Parliament in 1848, an episode addressed in Chapter 8, he declared that 'because of this offensive situation and the subsequent acceptance of the principle of the equality of nationalities [within the Empire], I have resolved to leave the ranks of German historians forever and henceforth can only compose my work in the Czech language'.[35]

Through the abandonment of German, Palacký's narrative became detached from the Bohemian identity of the upper classes; at the same time, it accentuated his association with the common people. But there was more to this metamorphosis than a symbolic gesture. According to a universal trope in European culture (in Horváth's words) 'the spirit, morals and customs of a people are expressed in the language, which acts as a mirror of their character' and 'language is the moral and spiritual force of a nation'.[36] This assertion implied that it would be impossible for a foreign language accurately to convey the message of the national historian because, however unintentionally, it would always be bound by foreign concepts and attitudes. Consequently, the German and Czech versions were not identical, although the content itself was not substantially altered, because the vast scope of the work would have rendered this unfeasible. However, the grand narratives diverged significantly. The German version commences with a geographical description of the Bohemian lands and the Czech one with a philosophical musing about the meaning of Czech history. The portrayal of the life, religion and character of the ancient Slavs takes on a new 'Romanticized' glow. Moreover, throughout the Czech text, Palacký attempts to replace foreign words (denoting, for example, oligarchy, republicanism and civilization) with newly coined Czech equivalents.[37]

The contrast between the two versions is perhaps most explicit in the titles. *Geschichte von Böhmen* (History of Bohemia) refers to a historical-territorial entity, that of the Bohemian lands. The Czech variant, *Dějiny národu českého v Čechách a v Moravě* (the History of the Czech nation in Bohemia and Moravia), addresses the history of

[35] Palacký, *Zur Böhmischer Geschichtschreibung*, 123,

[36] *Horváth Mihály kisebb történelmi munkái*, I. 103.

[37] On the differences between the two versions see: Josef Válka, 'Německá a česká verse Palackého Dějin', *Sborník prací filosofické fakulty brněnské univerzity* C 15 (1968), 79–91; Olga Svejkovska, 'The Relationship Between the German and Czech Versions of Palacký's *History of the Czech Nation*', *East European Quarterly* 15:1 (1981), 65–84.

an ethnic group, the Czech-speaking people. In the Czech version, the integrity of Bohemia and Moravia is underlined not just through the appearance of the latter province in the title, but also by arguments that reveal the author's dismissive stance towards some Moravian patriots' struggle for autonomy. Displacing the territorial with an ethnic concept results in the marginalization, or even exclusion, of the German-speaking population from the narrative. Lastly, some alterations in the Czech text are due to the difference in audience: whilst the German version appeals to a small circle of learned men, the Czech text addresses the national public.

The aim of linguistic homogenization characterized Hungarian politicians' and scholars' ambitions in the first half of the nineteenth century. The use of three languages—Latin in law, political life and the Church; German by the Viennese administration; and Hungarian by the dominant nationality—became increasingly untenable.[38] Accordingly, the promotion of Hungarian was seen as a cultural and political necessity and thus a major objective of Hungarian liberals. The non-Hungarian subjects of the multinational and multilingual kingdom were understandably agitated by this prioritization of Hungarian at the expense of other languages. As will be seen in Chapter 9, Horváth showed a sympathetic attitude towards some of the nationalities' complaints and supported their right to promote their language. Nevertheless, he retained the conviction that, regardless of how many languages were spoken in the country, only one constitution was effective, from which it followed that there could only be one political nation.[39]

LANGUAGE AS EVERGREEN COWBERRY: REPRESENTING CONTINUITY

In the Preface to *Būdas* Daukantas asserts that Lithuanian, being purer and clearer than all other tongues spoken in his time, represents an unparalleled phenomenon and that in the past rulers, princes and bishops mastered this language. He notes, with a touch of melancholy:

All that is now gone. The Lithuanian nation is flooded by foreign nations, her lords, kings, dukes and even the priests already speak in a foreign tongue, are

---

[38] Miklós Molnár, *A Concise History of Hungary* (Cambridge, 2001).
[39] Horváth, *Huszonöt év*, II. 116.

dressed in foreign apparel, and spread foreign truths. In short, Lithuania has already lost its spring-green leaves and merely recalls her deeds from ancient writings, just as a forest displays its twigs in winter. *Among these, language alone remains like a green cowberry,* protected from frost until spring arrives as a sign of all that was.[40]

The cowberry is a popular berry in Lithuania and has a unique attribute of not freezing under the snow, instead remaining green and vibrant during the harsh winter. Thus, Daukantas's metaphor offers a powerful image of the capacity of language as bearer of continuity, irrespective of the destiny of the state. Through the community of its speakers, language represents a more constant factor in the history of the nation than any other constituent, one which may remain dormant, but can never be extinguished, not even under foreign domination. In a similar vein, language also epitomized the continuous existence of the Polish cultural and historical heritage during an era when the Polish state lay in the grave. Although not engaged in linguistic pursuits himself, Lelewel contributed to remoulding the Polish tradition, adhering to the proposal of the Enlightenment scholar Hugo Kołłątaj: 'Poles, if we cannot harm our neighbours who are devouring us, let us try to be indigestible!'[41] Lelewel and his generation could not succeed in restoring Poland's lost statehood, but the 'indigestion' that they created through their contribution to national culture and scholarship promoted the nation's continuing existence.

The search for evidence of continuity in Romanian culture was markedly fashioned by philological arguments. As Alexandru Zub put it: 'As a pivot of nationality, its dearest "gem", the language represented both a clear expression of it and a guarantee for the future: as long as there was a Romanian language of obvious Latin origin—evidence of a distinct ethnic origin—future developments could be accepted without existential fears; such developments could only embody the conclusions of *many centuries of evolution*'.[42] The connection between Romanians and Romans, which was embedded in the humanist chronicle tradition in the second half of the seventeenth century, proved fundamental to the gradual reorientation of Romanian culture. Kogălniceanu's contribution

---

[40] Daukantas, *Raštai*, I. 408. My translation draws on (but is not identical with) Trumpa, 'Simonas Daukantas, Historian and Pioneer of Lithuanian Rebirth', 16.

[41] John Stanley, 'Towards a New Nation: The Enlightenment and National Revival in Poland', *Revue Canadienne des Etudes sur le Nationalisme—Canadian Review of Studies in Nationalism* 10:1 (1983), 106.

[42] Zub, *A scrie și a face istorie*, 344.

to the promotion of language represented a continuation of the work of the activists of the Transylvanian school, whose main efforts lay in improving the prestige of language by *restoring* its original Latin qualities and thus enhancing its noble character.

To that end, representatives of the Transylvanian school professed that the Cyrillic alphabet had found its way into Romanian as a consequence of contestation, in particular the influence of the Church Slavonic language, and that Latin must have been the original version. Among these scholars was Petru Maior, who compiled the first Romanian dictionary and also *Istoria pentru începutul Românilor în Dachia* (History of the Origins of the Romanians in Dacia, 1812), an inspirational volume for Kogălniceanu. Maior derived Romanian from vulgar Latin. He composed an essay *Dialogu pentru începutul limbii române între nepot și unchiu* (Dialogue Between a Nephew and his Uncle on the Origins of the Romanian language, 1825), for educational purposes, in which an uncle explains to his nephew the distinction between classical and vulgar Latin.[43] In response to the nephew's confusion about the differences between French and Romanian, the uncle claims that the Slavic influence, though superficial, disguises the true nature of Romanian: 'How often this has happened to me, that whenever I was in doubt about whether a word was Latin, I would write it with Latin letters, and at once its gleaming Latin face would appear and would seem to smile at me for having freed it from slavery and from its poor Cyrillic rags.'[44]

Due to the efforts of the Transylvanian scholars, the Slavonic alphabet was gradually replaced by the Latin in their own homeland. However, in Moldavia and Wallachia the Slavonic variant prevailed until the unification of the principalities. Kogălniceanu published the chronicles of Moldavian princes in two editions; the first version, employing the Cyrillic alphabet, appeared prior to unification and the second edition, using the Latin alphabet, following unification.[45] As with Palacký's two versions of his History, the significance of this change went far beyond

---

[43] The essay appeared in Maior's *Lexicon Valachico-Hungarico-Germanicum* (Buda, 1825), see Keith Hitchins, *A Nation Discovered: Romanian Intellectuals in Transylvania and the Idea of Nation, 1700–1848* (Bucharest, 1999), 125. A modern edition of the *Dialogu* can be found in Petru Maior, *Scrieri* (Bucharest, 1976), II. 302–33.

[44] Maior, *Lexicon Valachico–Hungarico–Germanicum*, 72–3, quoted in Hitchins, *A Nation Discovered*, 126.

[45] The first version, the preface to *Letopisețile Țării Moldovii*, can be found in Kogălniceanu, *Opere*, II. 448–52, the second version, the preface to *Cronicele României sau Letopisețele [sic] Moldaviei și Valachiei*, ibid., 501–11.

the replacement of one set of characters by another. The titles of the two editions provide powerful hints about this transformation. The Cyrillic version was entitled *Letopiseţele Moldaviei (şi Valahiei)* (1860), 'Annals of Moldavia (and Wallachia)', whilst the Latin (1872) bore the name, *Chronicele României*, 'the Chronicles of Romania'. Thus, Latinization was indicated not only through the new alphabet, but also by the replacement of the Slavic word *letopis* (annals) with its Latin equivalent, *chronica*. Furthermore, Moldavia and Wallachia, the latter of which was initially in parenthesis to indicate its subordinate position from Kogălniceanu's perspective, was replaced by the name of the new, unified state: *România*. In the preface to the second edition Kogălniceanu explains the symbolic meaning of this shift: in the twelve years which had elapsed between the two editions, his country underwent a substantial transformation: 'the desire of our ancestors has been fulfilled: today, we have a Romania!'[46]

THE UNIQUE LANGUAGE: ANTIQUITY AND OTHER VIRTUES

Language provided excellent opportunities through which the idea of uniqueness, a fundamental theme of national historiography, could be promoted. To that end, Kogălniceanu's and Daukantas's narratives were particularly embellished by proud declarations about antiquity. As we have seen, in the Romanian context this encompassed the hypothesis of Latinity. By contrast, Daukantas's plea exploited the potential of Indo-European linguistic theory. According to him, the cradle of the Lithuanians lay in ancient India, an assertion indebted to the discovery that the common ancestor of European languages had not been biblical Hebrew, as scholars had long maintained. Instead, by the late eighteenth century, the focus of linguistic scrutiny had shifted to the assumption of a common Indo-European language. Such a hypothesis had been formulated earlier, but gained widespread popularity after the publication of William Jones's celebrated discourse *On the Hindus*, in 1786, which emphasized the affinity of Greek, Latin and Sanskrit:

The Sanskrit language, whatever may be its antiquity, is of a wonderful structure; more perfect than the Greek, more copious than the Latin, and more exquisitely

---

[46] Kogălniceanu, *Opere*, II. 501.

refined than either; yet bearing to both of them a stronger affinity, both in the roots of verbs and in the forms of grammar, than could have been produced by accident; so strong that no philologer could examine the Sanskrit, Greek and Latin, without believing them to have sprung from some common source, which, perhaps, no longer exists.[47]

From this time onwards, 'Indo-European', which was believed to closely resemble the sacred language of India (Sanskrit), was usually employed as the main vehicle for explaining the origins and transformations of European languages.[48] The new theory also helped to create the discipline of comparative linguistics, which transformed William Jones's intuitive approach into a more scientific method. When the German linguist Franz Bopp (1791–1867) published his *Vergleichende Grammatik des Sanskrit, Zend, Griechischen, Lateinischen, Litauischen, Alt-Slawischen, Gotischen und Deutschen*, his work was generally acknowledged to have inaugurated a new era.[49] Bopp's conclusions were primarily influenced by Jacob Grimm, Friedrich von Schlegel and Herder's presupposition of the *Ursprache* as being expressive of the *Urvolk*.[50]

Daukantas's works contain references to Bopp's master, the Dane Rasmus Rask (1787–1832), in particular to his book *Über den Ursprung der altnordischen Sprache*. His thesis also benefited from the proximity of the (German) university of Königsberg, where prominent scholars were among the first to engage in the study of comparative linguistics. In addition to Immanuel Kant's foreword to a Lithuanian dictionary, cited in the previous chapter, the most important impulse for Daukantas was the essay written by the Königsberg scholar Peter von Bohlen, *Ueber die Verwandtschaft zwischen der Lithauischen und Sanskritsprache*.[51] Bohlen claimed that it would be no exaggeration to refer to Lithuanian as the

[47] R. H. Robins, *A Short History of Linguistics* (London, 1976), 134.

[48] Maurice Olender, 'Europe, or How to Escape Babel', *History and Theory* Beiheft 33 (1994), 21.

[49] In the preface to the second English edition, a fellow linguist praised it with the following words: 'it may be justly assigned a place in that department of study corresponding to that of Newton's *Principia* in mathematics, Bacon's *Novum Organum* in mental science or Blumenbach in physiology'. Franz Bopp, *A Comparative Grammar of the Sanscrit, Zend, Greek, Latin, Lithuanian, Gothic, German and Sclavonic Languages* (London, 1854), without page numbers.

[50] P. A. Verbung, 'The Background to the Linguistic Concepts of Bopp', *Lingua* 2:4 (1949–50), 443. Schegel's famous book was entitled *Über die Sprache und Weisheit der Inder*.

[51] For a brief discussion of Bohlen's career see Götz von Selle, *Geschichte der Albertus-Universität zu Königsberg in Preussen*, 2nd edn. (Würzburg, 1956), 293–4.

'Nordic (dialect of) Sanskrit'. His article proved crucial for Daukantas because it collated and systematized arguments in support of the antiquity of the Lithuanian language, among which were Herder's and Wilhelm von Humboldt's views. Bohlen refers to Herder when noting the peculiar character of Lithuanians and Latvians, likening them to 'daughters of an ancient mother' who probably originated from remote territories.[52] He also quotes Humboldt, who found the Latvian and Lithuanian languages to be significantly more refined than the cultural standards of their speakers and implied that therefore these languages must be survivors of an ancient and highly sophisticated language: Sanskrit.[53] As the German scholar put it: 'Lithuanian . . . with far more fortune than others of its sisters has stayed loyal to the Sanscrit [*sic*] stock it descends from'.[54]

Finally, another significant aspect emerges from Bohlen's article: the suggestion that the striking similarities between the Sanskrit and Lithuanian languages on the one hand, and between the ancient Indian religion and ancient Baltic religion on the other, are due to the common fatherland of the two nations.[55] Daukantas draws on Bohlen's examples when assessing the similarities between Sanskrit and Lithuanian, for instance the Lithuanian sentence 'Dewas dadau dantas, dewas dasyati eva danas' (God has given us teeth, God will give us bread), which is nearly identical to its Sanskrit equivalent.[56] He also discusses parallels between Greek, Latin, Thracian and Lithuanian river names and place names,[57] as well as evoking a traditional means of revealing analogies between languages: the comparison of the Lord's Prayer in several versions.[58]

Moralizing deductions from grammatical forms was an omnipresent phenomenon in this epoch and antiquity constituted only one criterion of prestige. For example, according to an implicit and consensual

[52] Peter von Bohlen, 'Ueber die Werwandtschaft zwischen der Lithauischen und Sanskritsprache, vorgetragen am 6. November 1828', *Historische und Literarische Abhandlungen der Königlichen Deutschen Gesellschaft zu Königsberg* (1830), 120.

[53] Ibid., 134.

[54] Wilhelm von Humboldt, *On Language: The Diversity of Human Language-Structure and its Influence on the Mental Development of Mankind*, trans. Peter Heath (Cambridge, 1988), 203–4.

[55] Peter von Bohlen, 'Ueber die Werwandtschaft zwischen der Lithauischen und Sanskritsprache, 136.

[56] Ibid., 122. The modern Lithuanian variant of this sentence is: 'Dievas davė dantis, Dievas duos ir duonos.'

[57] Daukantas, *Raštai*, I. 54.   [58] Ibid., I. 53–4.

hierarchy of languages, monosyllabic, uninflected languages, such as Chinese, were believed to be the most primitive of all. Agglutinative languages fared slightly better, but were still considered inferior to inflexional ones. Palacký found that Czech did not belong to the 'pragmatic' and 'accentuating' Romance languages, but to the 'imaginative' and 'quantitative' (*quantitierend*) antique languages.[59] He not only asserted that Czech was the most ancient (after Old Slavonic) and most comprehensive of all the East-European languages, but with reference to scholars such as Adelung and Dobrovský, found the Czech language to be even richer in basic words (*Stammworte*) than German. Despite lacking a genuine form for passive structures, and a perfect ration of vowels and consonants, these minor shortcomings did not affect its overall advanced nature—its 'happy combination of measure and melody'—which elevated Czech above numerous other contemporary languages.[60]

Another intriguing exemplification of the 'uniqueness argument' is found in an essay which the young Palacký composed with his friend Pavel Josef Šafářík, *Počátkové českého básnictví, obzvláště prozódie* (Elements of Czech Versification, especially Prosody; published in Pressburg in 1818). In this piece, which consists of six 'letters' with accompanying poems, the two authors subscribe to the Indo-European theory and advocate a quantitative prosodic system based on vowel length (*časomíra*) to replace the prevailing system based on stressed and unstressed syllables (*přízvuk*). They acknowledge with pride that theirs is among the few languages able to accommodate the allegedly more ancient and superior prosodic system based on vowel length. Furthermore, they are delighted to discover that the German language lacks that attribute. Thus, beneath the surface of the discourse on these highly technical issues lay an ideological attack on German culture, as the essay was underpinned by a plea to free Slav culture from German tutelage. Nonetheless, providing yet another instance of the negative and analogous nature of the authors' attitude towards German culture, their efforts were inspired by and imitated Friedrich Gottlieb Klopstock, the founder of Classicist poetics in the German language, who attempted to introduce ancient prosodic forms into German.[61]

Like Daukantas, the Czech scholars use the Indo-European hypothesis to position their culture in a wider framework, although they are

---

[59] Palacký, *Gedenkblätter*, 39.   [60] Ibid., 39.

[61] Palacký and Pavel Jozef Šafárik, *Počátkové českého básnictví, obzvláště prozódie* (Bratislava, 1961), 39.

primarily concerned with the origins of the metric system. Following the ideas of the eminent Enlightenment scholar Josef Jungmann, they forge a link between Slavonic and ancient Indian prosody. This is based on an argument that appears in the book of the celebrated orientalist Henry Thomas Colebrooke (1765–1837), *Essays on the Religion and Philosophy of Hindus*. According to this, the Slavonic languages retained the merits of ancient Greek, Latin and Sanskrit and show greater similarity with those ancient languages than with the more modern Germanic languages. In this hierarchical structure the Slavonic languages represent the closest heirs not only of antique languages but also of the proto-European (i.e. ancient Indian) civilization.[62] This is echoed in Palacký's later statement which singles out the prosodic system in order to demonstrate the links between Indian and Czech: 'A truly remarkable triumph, to which other contemporary nations aspire in vain, has already been demonstrated in our language: the survival of the Indian prosodic system based on vowel length.'[63] In accordance with one of the key aims of national scholarship to free the language from 'contestation', Palacký and Šafářík recommend that the phonic structure of the language should be altered by replacing sounds lacking euphony with euphonious ones or by inserting vowels into cacophonous consonant groups, thereby endowing them with the traits that typify the structure of the ancient language.

The appropriateness of one's own language for metric verse was professed by representatives of other nations, such as the Hungarians. Four years after publication of the Czech scholars' account, an essay appeared in a Hungarian journal on 'the greater suitability of the Hungarian language to metric verse than that of other languages, advancing the claim that Hungarian was better suited to metric verse than German, Greek, English, French, Polish, Italian or any other language.[64] The fascination with the metrical system is indicative of a European-wide phenomenon. For example, in England debates about the translation of dactylic hexameter, the metrical form associated with classical epic, revealed more than a comparison of different systems

---

[62] Vladimír Macura, *Znamení zrodu. České obrození jako kulturní typ*, 2nd edn. (Prague, 1995), 48.

[63] Palacký, *Korrespondence a zápisky*, Vol. III (Prague, 1911), 56, quoted in Macura, *Znamení zrodu. České obrození jako kulturní typ*, 38.

[64] Gábor Sebestyén, 'A magyar nyelvnek a mértékes versekre minden más nyelvek felett való alkalmatos volta', *Tudományos Gyűjtemény* 5 (1822), 50–8.

of versification; they were intimately associated with the formation of national literary culture.[65]

ENRICHING THE NATIONAL CULTURE THROUGH TRANSLATIONS

Translations, whether from Latin and Greek into vernacular languages or, increasingly, from the eighteenth century onwards, from one vernacular into another, possessed great potential for enriching and expanding the national language and helping to transform literary standards. Sometimes it proved impossible to find direct equivalents to foreign words, which led to the widening of vocabulary, whilst the foreign values incorporated through translation inspired deliberations about the virtues and vices of the impact of foreign cultures. Only Palacký nurtured a theoretical interest in translation, emphasizing the accuracy of the meaning over word-for-word reproduction.[66] Nonetheless, all my historians were aware of the twofold dimension of translation; that it could both enrich and impoverish national culture. Typically, the enthusiasm for the transmission of foreign ideas and scholarship was eventually superseded by an emphasis on the necessity of autochthonous culture, expressive of the nation's peculiar character.

Conditions of authorship have been viewed differently in various ages, and translations typically bore the imprint of both the environment and the predilections of the author. In our era it was generally accepted that the translator would take liberties with syntax, vocabulary and structure, omit and add passages, whilst commercial incentives could also prompt changes.[67] Some degree of transformation, taking into account the translators' domestic context, was considered not only permissible but even essential. From this vantage point, translation has sometimes been viewed as occupying a position on the borderline between reproduction and original creation, as illuminated by a

[65] Yopie Prins, 'Metrical Translation: Nineteenth Century Homers and the Hexameter Mania', in Sandra Bermann and Michael Wood (eds.), *Nation, Language and the Ethics of Translation* (Princeton and Oxford, 2005), 229–56.

[66] For a discussion of Palacký's views see Jiří Levý, *České teorie překladu* (Prague, 1957), 65–145 and 357–66 and Lumír Klimeš, 'K Palackého překladu Dialogu Jana z Rabštejna', *Slovo a slovesnost* 22:3 (1961), 181–6.

[67] Fania Oz-Salzberger, 'Translation', in Alan Charles Kors et al. (eds.), *Encyclopedia of Enlightenment* (Oxford, 2003), IV. 183.

metaphor which compares the translator's task of 'transfusing' his own innovative spirit in the *caput mortum* of the original to that of an alchemist.[68] A certain amount of creative freedom was necessary for my historians to rise to the challenge of transmitting complex ideas into languages with inadequate terminology and no established academic conventions. This input sometimes rendered it acceptable for them (and, in general, for their contemporaries) to suppress the original author's name.

In our region, translation was widely employed as a short-cut, a suitable device for the rapid transformation of the national culture, which could temporarily fill the gap between aspirations and realities.[69] As has been noted earlier, the source culture from which scholars derived inspiration was often identical to the one from whose vestiges they sought to emancipate their own traditions. Translations necessarily involved the loss of certain aspects of the original meaning and even misunderstanding or misconstrual. This was even more the case in our context, where my historians' native languages might have been unsuitable for conveying a sophisticated discourse. Without doubting that their translations contained inaccuracies, it is worth remembering that their intention was not necessarily to provide a 'faithful translation'. Rather, through an admittedly selective reading of the text, they focused on a specific agenda which was of primary interest to them. In other words, translation was not their ultimate *goal*, but a *tool* for the enrichment of national culture, thereby reducing the relevance of the concept of equivalence as a primary requisite of translation.[70] Translations formed a modest, but not negligible, part in my historians' lifework. In addition to the texts discussed below, they included Lelewel's rendering of the *Edda* into Polish, Palacký's translation of two songs from Ossian, as well as agricultural advice books by Daukantas. Moreover, as Chapter 7 will reveal, Horváth's biographical sketch on the life of Roger Williams, the founder of Rhode Island, was a translation of the relevant chapters from the Swiss Jean Frédéric Astie's (1822–94), *Histoire de la république des États-Unis*.

---

[68] Theo Hermans, 'Literary Translation: The Birth of a Concept', *New Comparison* 1 (1986), 34–8; Martin Procházka, 'Cultural Invention and Cultural Awareness: Translational Activities and Author's Subjectivity in the Culture of the Czech National Revival', *New Comparison* 8 (1989), 57; Levý, *České teorie překladu*, 83.

[69] Vladimír Macura, 'Problems and Paradoxes of the National Revival', in Mikuláš Teich (ed.), *Bohemia in History* (Cambridge, 1998), 190.

[70] Procházka, 'Cultural Invention and Cultural Awareness', 57.

THE LITHUANIAN ROBINSON

Education understandably occupied a prominent place on the national historians' agenda and, in addition to schoolbooks and textbooks, translations and adaptations specifically addressing young people could effectively fulfil that mission. In his educational works Daukantas repeatedly stresses: 'I hope that my book will awaken the longing for virtue and goodness in my readers and that it will also initiate the love of righteousness.'[71] Daukantas's translations included Cornelius Nepos's *De viris illustribus*, and some of the fables of Aesop and Phaedrus. He compiled a Latin textbook *Epitomae historiae Sacrae* (with comments in Lithuanian) and also adapted the German author Joachim Heinrich Campe's novel, *Robinson der Jüngere* into Lithuanian.[72] Campe's *Robinson der Jüngere* (1779) was itself an adaptation of Defoe's *Robinson Crusoe*. Daukantas's Lithuanian Robinson, *Rubinaičio Peliūzės gyvenimas*, was written around 1846 but only published in 1984.[73]

Campe's *Robinson der Jüngere* enjoyed immense popularity and soon became an *allgemeines Kulturgut*, appearing in over one hundred editions by the end of the nineteenth century (Daukantas's version was based on the twelfth) and inspiring a plethora of translations and adaptations into the majority of European languages (including three Latin versions) as well as numerous non-European languages. In several countries these translations marked turning-points in the linguistic revival and they also inaugurated the new genre of national literature for children. This happened in accordance with the increasing role of children's and young people's literature from the second half of the eighteenth century, a phenomenon animated by social changes, especially the formation of a bourgeois society which opened up new markets.[74]

Unlike Defoe, Campe intended to produce a novel primarily for educational purposes. In this effort he was motivated by Rousseau's

---

[71] Daukantas, *Vertimai ir sekimai* (Vilnius, 1986), 86.

[72] Campe was also author of a five-volume dictionary of the German language and winner of a prize question set by the Berlin Academy on the purity of the German language.

[73] Ibid., 12–13. Daukantas also prepared another version of the translation, *Palangos Petris i jo vargai* (1855). It was granted permission by the censor but his expectation to publish it failed and subsequently the manuscript vanished. In all probability it was not significantly different from the version discussed here.

[74] Angelika Reinhardt, *Die Karriere des Robinson Crusoe vom literarischen zum pädagogischen Helden* (Frankfurt am Main, 1994), 113–14.

claim in *Emile* that *Robinson Crusoe* was the only suitable book for children under the age of twelve. Faithful to the principles of philanthropic education, his aim was 'to entertain in a pleasant manner, because I know that the hearts of children are more receptive to useful knowledge when they are being amused at the same time'.[75] Campe makes some significant changes to Defoe's original.[76] For instance, he embeds the novel in a narrative structure whereby a father recounts the story to his children over the course of twenty-one nights. Furthermore, the nature of the relationship between Crusoe and Friday also undergoes an important transformation: in the original, it is a strictly hierarchical one between master and his subject, whilst the German Friday becomes Crusoe's 'assistant', revealing that companionship can improve the human condition. Another indication of Campe's differing ideological mindset is that, unlike Defoe, he vigorously condemns slavery.

Some translations of Campe's *Robinson* displayed only minor changes, while others involved greater intervention. Daukantas's version falls into the first category: he did not alter the text significantly, but merely finetuned the book to Lithuanian circumstances. Adaptations typically domesticated the plot and characters. In Daukantas's book Robinson becomes *Peliūze Rubinaitis*, Hamburg is changed to Palanga, London to Königsberg and the river Thames to the river Nemen (Niemūnas). Thus, Campe's original:

Once upon a time, there lived a man in the city of *Hamburg*, whose name was *Robinson*. He had three sons. The eldest chose the profession of a soldier, and was shot in a battle against the *French* . . .[77]

becomes in Daukantas's version:

Once upon a time, there lived a man in the city of *Palanga* whose name was *Rubinas*. He had three sons. The eldest one became a soldier and was shot in the battle against the *Swedes* . . .[78]

In the Lithuanian variant the character Lotte becomes Onelė, Gotlieb is renamed Pilė, (from the Latin form of Gotlieb—Theophil) and the Lithuanian Friday is called Nedėldienis (from the Lithuanian word for

---

[75] Joachim Heinrich Campe, *Robinson der Jüngere* (Stuttgart, 2000), 5.

[76] These are discussed in Leah Garrett, 'The Jewish Robinson Crusoe', *Comparative Literature* 54:3 (2002), 216, and Reinhardt, *Die Karriere des Robinson Crusoe*, 135–7.

[77] Campe, *Robinson der Jüngere*, 21.

[78] Daukantas, *Vertimai ir sekimai* (Vilnius, 1984), 216.

Friday).[79] Nevertheless, on occasion, Daukantas forgets about these self-imposed changes, which leads to minor inconsistencies. Domestications could also alter the religious context of Campe's text, which championed religious toleration but nevertheless remained faithful to Protestant and Pietist values.[80] Tailoring the religious backdrop of his account to the Lithuanian context, Daukantas's Robinson becomes Catholic. This causes some discrepancies in the story. In Campe's original, when the Protestant Robinson encounters a Catholic Spaniard on the island, he uses this opportunity to teach Friday about the differences between the Protestant and Catholic faiths. In order for this episode to make sense, Daukantas is forced to render the Spaniard a Protestant. Another intriguing instance of religious domestication in the Lithuanian text occurs when Robinson interrogates Friday about his own religion, asking him to name the God to whom his people pray and the chief priest of his religion. Friday's God is *Toupan* (a God worshipped by the Tupis, Brazil's aboriginal inhabitants) and he calls the priest *Owoka-kee*. Daukantas replaces the South-American God and priest with the principal deity of ancient pagan Lithuanians, *Perūnas* and their priest, the *Krivė*.[81]

The nature of *Robinson Crusoe's* reception, and the numerous *Robinsonades* it inspired, depended significantly upon the political and geographical status of the receiving culture.[82] Therefore, the story evoked different resonances in those countries which possessed colonies or, at least, bordered the sea and those which did not. Daukantas's text betrayed his home region's proximity to the sea, evident in the ease with which he accommodated naval terminology. Moreover, as Chapter 8 will explain, he incorporated the colononization of Tobago by the Duchy of Courland, a fief to the Polish-Lithuanian Commonwealth in the seventeenth century, into his narrative of Lithuanian history.[83]

---

[79] Daukantas, *Vertimai ir sekimai* (Vilnius, 1984), 18–19.

[80] An especially remarkable conversion takes place in a Yiddish adaptation which was composed by a Galician scholar some twenty-five years before the Lithuanian version. In *Robinzon die geshikhte fun Alter-Leb*, Robinson Crusoe is renamed Reb Alter-Leb; he is a Jew from Hamburg who eats Kosher on the island and his friend Friday is also renamed Shabes.

[81] Campe, *Robinson der Jüngere*, 233; Daukantas, *Vertimai ir sekimai*, 373.

[82] Another highly successful adaptation was Johann David Wyss, *Der schweizerische Robinson* (Zurich, 1812).

[83] Incidentally, Tobago, a small island of the Lesser Antilles, provided inspiration for Defoe, as he visited the island before embarking on his novel.

PROMOTING ACADEMIC LANGUAGE
IN HUNGARY

In the early nineteenth century, Horváth's most admired author, Arnold Heeren, lamented that despite its strengths in terms of historical research, German scholarship remained deficient in historical writing. He diagnosed the cause of this discrepancy in the persistent usage of Latin in all academic fields: it was only in the final quarter of the eighteenth century that the mother tongue gained ground in historical writing, by which time England, France and Spain had long since produced their Clarendon, Mezeray and Ferrera.[84] In an assessment of his immediate predecessors' achievements, Horváth likewise bemoans the shortcomings that stem from the employment of foreign languages in academic writing. Books produced in Latin failed to reach a wider audience, whilst German and Austrian accounts of Hungarian history were permeated with foreign concepts and thus, 'either through false national competition, or not understanding the essence of our national institutions, distorted our history'.[85] My protagonist praised the achievements of scholars who pioneered the chronicling of history in Hungarian, but expressed disappointment that they used the outdated version of the language at a time when other scholars chose the more sophisticated variant that followed the principles of the linguistic renewal.[86] Horváth contributed to the creation of an academic language which gradually acquired the capacity to address complex problems. Occasionally he experimented with the invention of new words; for example, he coined the Hungarian equivalent of the German word *volkstümlich*. However, translation went a lot deeper than simply finding suitable words. In the process fundamental concepts penetrated the local academic discourse, for instance those of democracy and Hegelian dialectics.

An especially demanding text was Arnold Heeren's major article, *Über die Entstehung, die Ausbildung und den praktischen Einfluß der politischen Theorien und die Enthaltung des monarchischen Prinzips in dem neueren Europa*.[87] Horváth's version, *Az országtani theóriák eredete, kifejlése és gyakorlati befolyása az újabb Európában, Heeren után* (On

---

[84] Arnold Ludwig Heeren, *Historische Werke*, 15 vols. (Göttingen, 1821–6), VI. 441.

[85] Horváth here alludes to Ignaz Aurelius Fessler (1756–1839) and Johann Christian Engel (1770–1814), *Horváth Mihály kisebb történelmi munkái*, I. v (preface).

[86] Horváth, *Huszonöt év*, I. 50.   [87] Heeren, *Historische Werke*, I. 365–451.

the Origins, Development and Influence of State Theories in Modern
Europe, inspired by Heeren, 1842) first appeared in the leading journal
of the Reform Period, *Athenaeum*. Although the title acknowledges
that Horváth drew upon Heeren's work, it conceals the depth of
his engagement with the German scholar's text; in particular that he
faithfully adheres to the original, to an extent which today would be
considered 'word-for-word' translation. The essay evaluates the political
ideas of Machiavelli, Grotius, Bodin, Hobbes, Locke, Montesquieu
and Rousseau, focusing primarily on contractual theories and problems
connected with the division of power. The article identifies various
state forms, located between the two poles of autocracy and democracy,
in line with a mainstream conviction of the *Aufklärer*, who criticized
absolute monarchy but did not entirely favour democracy. At the same
time, by appealing to a powerful metaphor, the Heeren–Horváth essay
denies the existence of an ideal state form: 'What is every constitutional
form if not an empty form? What is it, if it is not a track upon which
a wagon travels? Naturally, it is not unimportant how the track is
constructed . . . but no matter how excellent the construction, does it
follow that the wagon will remain in the track? Can the track alone
force the wagon to remain in it? That depends upon the team of horses
and the driver.'[88] In this spirit, author and translator conclude that:

> Neither democracy, nor aristocracy or absolute monarchy are preferable and
> the true key to political understanding lies in grasping the nature of the
> unique conjunction of spiritual, moral, and structural elements that animated
> a specific historical entity at a specific time . . . To establish a form of state
> which includes the guarantees of its permanence in itself is more absurd than to
> invent the perpetuum mobile, which is permanently in motion without external
> influence.[89]

Another essay on the theory of history, *Gondolatok a történetírás
theóriájából* (Reflections on the Theory of Historiography) (1839)
a word-for-word translation of Wilhelm Wachsmuth's work, appeared without indicating the original source. Horváth translated
the introductory chapter (entitled *Die Aufgabe*) from Wachsmuth's
five-volume *Europäische Sittengeschichte*. Besides Heeren, this Leipzig
professor exercised the greatest influence on Horváth's historiographical

---

[88] Heeren, *Historische Werke*, I. 450–1. I have used the translation which can be found in
Reill, *The German Enlightenment*, 137–8.
[89] Horváth, *Polgárosodás, liberalizmus, függetlenségi harc*, 102.

views.[90] The lack of reference to the author of the text may appear puzzling at first sight, but, as has already been noted, standards of authorship in our era diverged significantly from those of our times and translators habitually masqueraded their pieces as originals.

The Wachsmuth–Horváth article advocates a programme that is founded on two pillars. Firstly, historiography should not exclusively concentrate on the deeds of the ruling elite, but also investigate the life of the unprivileged classes. Secondly, the descriptive historical method should be succeeded by a pragmatic-analytical approach adhering to the principles of Hegelian dialectics.[91] As we have seen, the first point was an omnipresent, perhaps even the most frequently voiced, historiographical desideratum of the age. The relevance of the second criterion may be illuminated by contextualization. Horváth's article appeared at a time when an ardent controversy about the virtues and vices of Hegel's ideology permeated Hungarian cultural life, marking a crucial stage in the reception of German idealism.[92] Attacks on Hegelians were based on their allegedly anti-religious and revolutionary views and because they championed an ideology which anti-Hegelians believed to be incongruous with the 'national spirit'. In turn Hegelians sought to prove the compatibility of the German philosopher's system of thought with religious morals and the preservation of the existing political order. This debate, which at times raged viciously, ultimately served to enliven Hungarian cultural and academic life, because the relevant publications in academic journals engaged a uniquely wide range of readers in active participation. Another positive side-effect was the impetus which the development of specific philosophical vocabulary received through the attempts to convert Hegelian terms into Hungarian.

Nevertheless, it would be erroneous to conclude that Horváth was an enthusiastic Hegelian. He might have been impressed by Hegel's theory in his youth, but only sporadic references pertaining to the relationship between reason and spirit and arts and sciences testify to his familiarity with the German philosopher. Nor did he become involved in the controversy. At a more mature age, when writing the history of the Reform Period, he seems to have denounced Hegel's ideals, stating that 'some of our thinkers, having completed their studies at

---

[90] Horváth was also inspired by Wachsmuth's *Entwurf einer Theorie der Geschichte* (Halle, 1820), which also influenced Lelewel; for a reference see *Dzieła*, II/2. 402.

[91] Horváth, *Polgárosodás, liberalizmus, függetlenségi harc*, 20.

[92] Béla Pukánszky, *Hegel és magyar közönsége* (Budapest, 1932).

German universities, became the apostles of a hair-splitting speculative philosophy, especially that of the extremely obscure system of Hegel.'[93]

THE BIRTH OF MODERN POLITICAL LANGUAGE IN ROMANIA

Kogălniceanu's two short essays, *Despre Civilisaţie* (On Civilization, a translation) and *Despre Pauperism* (On Pauperism, an adaptation, both 1845) provide illuminating instances of the ways in which these concepts infiltrated Romanian political vocabulary.[94] The original version of the piece on civilization was composed by Élias Regnault and appeared in the *Dictionnaire Politique: encyclopédie du langage et de la science politiques* (first edition Paris, 1842), which was edited by a group of French publicists and journalists. Whilst not one of the most prominent scholars of his generation, Regnault's name clearly resonated with Kogălniceanu because he had shown a keen interest in the Romanian principalities, culminating in the book *Histoire politique et sociale des principautés danubiennes* (Paris, 1855). In his account Regnault drew attention to the unresolved diplomatic problem of the 'Eastern question'. The ambitions of *Dictionnaire Politique* were addressed in the publisher's and chief editor's forewords. These express regret that whilst the natural sciences had acquired well-defined linguistic conventions, in the political sciences this was not yet the case. Parliamentary discourses, political debates in the press, as well as public discussions, desperately needed precise and universally accepted definitions, and hence the dictionary's aim lay in contributing to that goal.[95] The editor in chief warned:

the lack of consensus presents a grave danger. If Buffon and Cuvier failed to provide a perfect anatomical description of an elephant or a cheese mite, such an oversight did not, in any way, influence the destiny of the world. Nevertheless, in the political, and also in the moral sciences, (such) uncertainty about the meaning of words can lead to regrettable consequences. From the confusion of language stems the confusion of ideas. The spirit stagnates in a milieu where diverse interpretations reign.[96]

---

[93] Horváth, *Huszonöt év*, II. 25.   [94] Kogălniceanu, *Opere*, I. 558–661 and 572–7.
[95] Garnier-Pagès's foreword in *Dictionnaire Politique: encyclopédie du langage et de la science politiques* ed. *Garnier-Pagès Étienne* (Paris, 1855), x.
[96] Laurent Pagnerre's introduction in *Dictionnaire Politique: encyclopédie du langage et de la science politiques*, vii–viii.

Thus, the authors concluded that only the use of a consensual political language was deemed capable of eliminating ignorance, the source of prejudices, errors and sophisms.[97]

As we have seen in the previous chapter, *civilization* evolved into a leitmotiv of political and cultural thought in the first half of the nineteenth century. Originally associated with the late-Enlightenment paradigm of civility and *politesse*, it gradually acquired new connotations. François Guizot, who made one of the most enduring contributions to the definition of the concept, found that 'civilization essentially consists of two principles: the improvement of the exterior and general condition of man, and that of his inward and personal nature; in a word, in the improvement of both society and humanity'.[98] Regnault's entry in *Dictionnaire Politique* ascribes meanings to civilization which correspond to this canonical French interpretation, in particular to the conviction that the true history of humanity equates to the constant expansion of civilization, also known as progress.[99] By affiliating the concept with freedom and equality, the Regnault–Kogălinceanu article endows it with a democratic aspect. Furthermore, civilization is also associated with *emancipation*, which is defined as a twofold battle: between man and nature on the one hand, and between humans themselves on the other.

The 1840s represented seminal years in the formation of modern Romanian political and social vocabulary, testifying to the gradual erosion of feudal structures through 'modernization'. By translating and publishing this article in the *Calendar pentru poporul românesc* (Calendar for the Romanian People) in 1845 (and on two further occasions), Kogălniceanu contributed to the redefinition of the word *civilizaţie* in the Romanian language. In this epoch, civilization evolved into a cornerstone of Romanian political thought, to which every prominent scholar had recourse. Diverse as their concepts might have been, material progress was perhaps less important than a strong moral-political component.[100]

---

[97] *Dictionnaire Politique* proved succesful in its intention to establish conventions, even creating new expressions in the process. For example, the terms 'extreme right' and 'extreme left' were inaugurated on its pages.

[98] Guizot, *Historical Essays and Lectures*, 269.

[99] Karol Weintraub, *Visions of Culture* (Chicago, 1966), 86.

[100] See Simeon Marcovici's entry 'Civilizaţia' in Paul Cornea and Mihai Zamfir (eds.), *Gîndirea românească în epoca paşoptistă*, 2 vols. (Bucharest, 1968), I. 230–9.

This extension of the meaning of the word reflected a shift that occurred in social theory in the 1840s.[101] Until that period, in accordance with the prevailing Enlightenment concept of civilization, it denoted knowledge and moral education (as a synonym of *cultură*) and also reflected the status of material culture. From the 1840s, civic freedom and equality became the semantic foci of the word and it also acquired an association with *sociabilité*, civilized social conduct. (As antonym, *barbarie* was used.)

The article *Despre Pauperism* (On Pauperism—a neologism in the Romanian language) first appeared in 1845 in the *Calendar pentru poporul românesc*. Kogălniceanu was inspired by a minor French economist, Adolphe Gustave Blaise (1811–86), who also contributed articles to the above-mentioned *Dictionnaire Politique*. Blaise's essay on pauperism appeared in a French popular magazine.[102] Kogălniceanu's essay commenced with a lengthy quotation from Blaise's text, and went on to reconsider the problem of pauperism in the Romanian context.[103] The message of the article was reinforced by an illustration of a beggar. The long and presumably direct quotation from Blaise's text emphasizes the two elements that operate in any society: those of necessity and liberty. The right to work is defined as a cornerstone of every society, and also an equalizing factor. Kogălniceanu reminds his readers that pauperism represents a problem for underdeveloped and prosperous societies alike: nowhere else is it more conspicuous than in the industrially advanced nation of England. He emphasizes the individual's responsibility for his own affairs, but also acknowledges that, under certain circumstances, the state has to intervene. Therefore he proposes the establishment of orphanages, a hospital for the terminally ill, and measures to curb alcoholism. Additionally he suggests setting up a *depozit de cerşători (depôt de mendicité)*, which he describes as a 'place which accepts the sick, old and poor people and offers them work according to their capacities'. The other establishment which he promotes is the *casă de păstrare (maison d'épargne)*: 'an institution where the diligent worker can deposit his money in good times and can have guaranteed access to it in hard times (earning interest)'.[104] The fact that the French version of these organizations is indicated in parentheses

[101] Klaus Bochmann, *Der politisch-soziale Wortschatz des Rumänischen (1821–1850)*, (Berlin, 1979), 115.
[102] Unfortunately, I was unable to trace the original French article, nor could I find a clue in the secondary literature about its location.
[103] Kogălniceanu, *Opere*, I. 572.   [104] Ibid., 576.

may indicate that Kogălniceanu himself coined the Romanian terms and thus the French originals had to be maintained as points of reference.

TOWARDS CREATING 'ORIGINAL' SCHOLARSHIP

Whilst acknowledging that no clear line may be drawn between 'original' production and 'imitation', Palacký's pursuits in aesthetics and Lelewel's studies in the theory of historiography merit separate attention. These incorporated achievements in foreign scholarship, but in such a way that allowed them to draw imaginative conclusions about their chosen subjects. Palacký's fascination with aesthetics is reflected in several essays along with his unfulfilled ambition to construct an aesthetic system.[105] An early piece, *Přehled dějin krásovědy a její literatury* (A Historical Survey of the Science of Beauty and the Literature on the Subject) appeared in 1823, in the journal *Krok* (Step), the oldest multidisciplinary publication in the Czech language. The author's intention was to devise a philosophical terminology in the Czech language, as illustrated by his avoidance of the term *estetika* to designate reflections of beauty and art in Czech; instead, he coined the neologism *krásověda*.[106]

Palacký's essay is primarily a critical assessment of aesthetic theories from the time of classical antiquity. The main impulse for his analysis was provided by Göttingen scholars, in particular by Friedrich Bouterwek's *Geschichte der Poesie und Beredsamkeit seit dem Ende des dreizehnten Jahrhunderts* (1801). Both the Czech and German scholars employ a particular trope when likening the development of modern aesthetics to a continuous movement, a relay-race, in the course of which new nations emerge on the scene and take the lead from earlier ones. Another Göttingen scholar, the historian Ludwig Wachler, applied this motif to the history of European historiography and the same tendency informed Guizot's scheme of civilizational progress, according to which 'the civilization of the Egyptians and Phoenicians prepared the way for that of the Greeks; while that of the Romans was not lost to the barbarians who established themselves upon the ruins of the empire (and so forth)'.[107]

---

[105] Palacký, *A Historical Survey on the Science of Beauty and the Literature on the Subject*, ed. Tomáš Hlobil, trans. Derek and Marzia Paton (Olomouc, 2001).

[106] Ibid., xi.

[107] Blanke, *Historiographiegeschichte als Historik*, 268; Guizot, *Historical Essays and Lectures*, 8.

Both Bouterwek and Palacký locate the birth of aesthetics in ancient Greece and argue that the field emerged due to the favourable natural conditions and political freedom, a constellation particularly conducive to independent thinking. The modern period is then divided into an Italian era (from the early sixteenth century), a French (from the mid-seventeenth century), a British (from the mid-eighteenth) and a German period (from the end of the eighteenth century). Palacký accepts some of Bouterwek's conclusions (without indicating his source), as shown by his assessment of Samuel Johnson's work and his dismissive stance towards Edmund Burke's aesthetics.[108] On other occasions, however, he presents his individual judgements, rejecting the aesthetic visions of the revolutionary Encyclopaedists such as Diderot, Voltaire and Helvetius, whilst revering Montesquieu, Rousseau and, in particular, Madame de Staël. Lastly, Palacký adjoins a new, anticipated Slavonic-Czech phase to the relay race and expresses the hope that in the future Czech aesthetics would be liberated from its dependence on German cultural dominance and ultimately achieve its individual style.[109]

Lelewel's enquiry into the theory of history and especially his attempt to systematize his thoughts on the subject mark a unique scholarly venture in early nineteenth-century East-Central Europe.[110] In *Historyka* (a term coined by himself) the analysis encompasses three categories. The first one, *Krytyka* (Criticism), relates to the truth content of events and addresses sources and source criticism. The second component, *Etiologika* (Aetiology), revolves around the causal relationship between circumstances of time, places and events. Among the elementary and auxiliary subjects in this field are politics, ethnography and *Statistik* (also known as *Staatskunde*, a discipline describing the internal situation of the state). Lastly, the third component, *Historiografia* (Historiography), concerns the manner of presentation.

Lelewel's system can be described as truly original, yet it also reveals a debt to contemporary scholarship, which he assesses critically. This includes a loosely but meaningfully edited compilation of numerous historians' ideas about 'the art and methods of history', such as Voltaire, Bonnot de Mably, Lenglet du Fresnoy, Karl von Rotteck, Bolingbroke,

---

108 Palacký, *A Historical Survey on the Science of Beauty*, xlviii.

109 Ibid., 20–1, 68–9.

110 For an analysis of Lelewel's ideas see Nina Assorodobraj's introduction 'Wstęp' to *Dzieła*, Vol. II/1: *Pisma Metodologiczne* (Warsaw, 1964), 7–93.

Hugh Blair, Wilhelm Wachsmuth and Johann Christoph Gatterer.[111] The emphasis on source criticism as well as the belief in the indispensability of auxiliary sciences indicates a degree of 'professionalization'. Nonetheless, Lelewel's interpretation of sources stands on a par with that of his contemporaries, rather than with the definition of modern professional scholarship. Accordingly, epic poetry and myths are also classified as primary sources, rendering his views comparable to those of scholars such as Schlözer, Niebuhr and Michelet. They all believed that myths, legends and epic poetry were phenomena meriting serious study, as they were unique fountainheads for the historians of antiquity, especially in relation to the period before the emergence of literacy.

The emphasis on critical research also manifests itself in the author's orientation towards historiographical desiderata which no longer revolve around rhetoric and are no longer confined to the art of writing.[112] This becomes obvious in Lelewel's comments, for example, on the standards of English historiography: he praises the pragmatic didacticism represented by Bolingbroke (demonstrating another appeal to the *magistra vitae* tradition), but criticizes Bolingbroke's contemporaries—including the lesser-known John Hill and Jonathan Richardson—for being overly concerned with style and composition: 'about critical research, they displayed very little'.[113]

CONCLUSION

The prolonged emphasis on, sometimes bordering on an obsession with, language has frequently been seen as an attribute indicative of the development of national cultures in Central and Eastern Europe. Nevertheless, language did not necessarily represent a pivotal, and certainly not the sole criterion of nationhood for my protagonists. Moreover, an approach which confines the predominance of linguistic involvement to distinct regions obfuscates the parallels in the development of European vernacular cultures, which appear to be far more fundamental than

---

[111] See his overview of historical-methodological literature given in *Dzieła*, II/1. 393–470.

[112] Violeta Julkowska, *Retoryka w narracji historycznej Joachima Lelewela* (Poznań, 1998), 43.

[113] In this context he refers to John Hill's *Essays on the Principle of Historical Composition* and Jonathan Richardson's *Morning Thoughts or Poetical Meditations, Dzieła*, II/1. 398.

individual and regional variations. Linguistic consolidation was necessary to enable scholars to conduct academic writing in the vernacular, a process which appears to have consisted of similar stages in the majority of European languages. The vernacularization of national culture corresponded with scholars' attempts to appeal to a wider audience and thereby democratize not only historical writing, but also academic culture in a more general sense.

My historians employed their native tongues innovatively: Lelewel wrote the first textbook on ancient history in the Polish language for students, as well as the first geographical treatise in Polish.[114] His accounts of bibliography and historiography were landmark developments in Polish culture. Palacký's essays on aesthetics represented the first attempts to use the Czech language for philosophical discourse since the seventeenth century. Kogălniceanu authored two plays, *Două femei împotriva unui bărbat* (Two Women Against One Man) and *Orbul fericit* (The Happy Blind Man), as well as an unfinished autobiographical novel, *Tainele inimei* (Mysteries of the Heart). In addition to the topicality of language as a medium, it also assumed relevance as the conveyor of national identity. As we have seen, language could be utilized to buttress arguments highlighting the unity and continuity of the nation as well as its antiquity and uniqueness.

My historians' encounters with translation reveal that this activity presented an effective vehicle for enriching their language. In the process, they often had to modify the premises of the source culture, in the light of the demands of different linguistic, cultural, political or economic circumstances. In a more general context, the character of the origins of 'cultural invention' among small nations undergoing a 'revival' has also been described as translation-like. As Palacký's attitude to German culture in his studies into the prosodic system has revealed, this process typically exhibited a twofold attitude towards the source culture: analogy and negation.[115] Linguistic pursuits thus required my protagonists to manoeuvre between transmitting new philosophical and political concepts and acting as guardians of the values of their native culture.

---

[114] Lelewel, *Historia geografii i odkryć* (Warsaw, 1814).
[115] Procházka, 'Cultural Invention and Cultural Awareness', 57.

6

National Antiquities

THE INTEREST IN ORIGINS AND EARLY SOCIETIES

The search for origins, whether in a universal or particular setting, represented a perennially popular theme in European history. Its prevalence was to a large extent due to the powerful capacity that myths of origins possess to enable people to position themselves in time and space. Another reason for the omnipresent nature of such myths in national historiography lay in their potential to provide a foundation for ideologies which contribute to the creation of a sense of community and cohesion within societies.[1] In medieval chronicles and humanist writing such pursuits addressed the genealogies of ruling dynasties. In addition to attributing biblical descent to the royal family, under the widespread impact of Italian humanism in the European historiographical tradition almost every nation cherished a classical version of national antiquity, which originated the rulers from a Greek or Roman mythological figure. Thematizations of antiquity were inherently tied to cultural legitimization, and classical variants often represented a competing alternative to theories asserting Germanic descent. For example, in English historiography, the Romanist interpretation associated Brutus, the great-grandson of Aeneas, with the forefather of the nation and endowed English institutions with Roman lineage. However, later, the strong Protestant component in English national consciousness envisioned the Romans as 'foreign' and the Anglo-Saxon tradition subsequently gained more popularity.[2] Correspondingly, in the French tradition the pursuit of antiquity was

---

[1] Hugh A. MacDougall, *Racial Myth in English History* (Montreal, 1982), 1.

[2] For an account of origins in English historiography, in addition to MacDougall's above-mentioned book see Reginald Horsman, 'Origins of Racial Anglo-Saxonism in Great Britain before 1850', *Journal of the History of Ideas* 37:3 (1976), 387–410.

informed by the rivalry between Gallo-Roman and Franco-Germanic interpretations.[3]

As has been argued in the previous chapter, the quest for ancestries often dovetailed with the search for the common ancestors of European languages. In the early modern period the theory of biblical origins, and by extension the derivation of European languages from Hebrew, gradually lost credibility. An alternative tradition evolved, one which originated European peoples and languages from the barbarian Scythians (or Goths). Ever since the period of late antiquity, the Scythians had enjoyed the reputation of being Noah's sons and, therefore, the most ancient people in Europe. Opposed to the excess, avarice and decadence of the Hellenes, they were also cast in the role of the noble savage and thus were portrayed as simple, generous, hospitable, frugal and highly virtuous people of the North.[4] Initially, the Scythian lineage featured not so much as a fixed point of reference, but as abstract prototype in scholarly accounts seeking to elucidate the origins and transformations of European languages.[5] However, these attractive traits also meant that the Scythians became prime candidates for ancestries in individual contexts. Among the array of nations associated with Scythian lineage were the Franks, Celts, Bulgarians, Swedes, Poles and Hungarians.

The Scythians also played a major role in the Nordic renaissance of the eighteenth century, when Nordic poetry and myth evolved into a viable alternative inspiration to Greek and Roman antiquity. Historians expressed admiration for the allegedly uncorrupted liberties of the 'barbarians' and asserted that their love of freedom, unspoiled independence and civic virtues were necessary for the regeneration of Europe. It was in this vein that a prominent author of the Nordic revival, the Swiss Paul-Henri Mallet, published his two epoch-defining books, *Introduction à l' Histoire de Dannemarc* (1755) and *Monuments de la mythologie et de la poésie des Celts et particulièrement des anciens Scandinaves* (1756), which introduced the learned public to portions of the Icelandic Eddas in French translation. Interestingly, Mallet himself did not hold myths in high regard but, as historiographer of the Danish king, he felt obliged to promulgate a favourable opinion of the Nordic people, in particular

---

[3] See Krzysztof Pomian, 'Franks and Gauls', in Lawrence D. Kritzman (ed.), *Realms of Memory: Rethinking the French Past* (New York, 1982), 27–76.

[4] James William Johnson, 'The Scythian: His Rise and Fall', *Journal of the History of Ideas* 20:2 (1959), 252.

[5] Maurice Olender, 'Europe or How to Escape Babel', 18.

the Danes.[6] Nonetheless, his volumes ignited an interest in primitive peoples and contributed to the adoration of the *bon sauvage*.[7] Mallet's writings achieved European-wide recognition through the vehicle of numerous translations. For example, an enormously popular adaptation by Bishop Percy, entitled *Northern Antiquities* (1770), was instrumental in the dissemination of the Nordic vogue on English soil.[8]

From the 1760s onwards, Macpherson's discovery of what was claimed to be the ancient poetry of a third-century Highland Scottish bard named Ossian added further impetus to the veneration of Nordic antiquity. Macpherson provided the gloomy scenery and melancholy mood and Mallet supplied the themes of crude heroic life and adventures. In their fusion they rendered Norse poetry unpolished but more exhilarating than the time-honoured rigorous poetic rules of classical antiquity and French classicism.[9] Ossian also catalysed an interest in the discovery of alleged ancient specimens of literature in Europe, which often served to bolster the self-image of 'peripheral' societies. Some of these forgeries proved so convincing that even eminent and critically-minded scholars of the age were deceived by them.

Another hypothesis of origins, chronologically preceding the classical and Nordic variant, associated the Orient with the cradle of modern civilizations, with 'mankind's great mother bosom'.[10] To the subscribers of this theory belonged Herder, who had originally assumed that the birthplace of nations lay in the North, but later expressed a strong belief in the oriental cradle.[11] Nonetheless, the oriental theory and the Northern variant were not mutually exclusive. On the contrary, with the help of the popular peregrination myth it was possible to reconcile Scandinavism (*ex Septentrione Lux*) and Orientalism (*ex Oriente Lux*). To that end, the eighteenth-century interest in the origins of modern nations was characterized by a powerful appeal to a medieval tradition about the migration of a savage chieftain, Odin, and his followers from Asia to Scandinavia and his subsequent defeat of the Roman eagles.[12] In fact, several scholars simply took it for granted that the earliest Scandinavian monuments and traditions were of oriental lineage. As has been discussed earlier, a dominant variant of the oriental descent

---

[6] Thor J. Beck, *Northern Antiquities in French Learning and Literature: A Study in Preromantic Ideas*, 2 vols. (New York, 1934–5), I. 15.

[7] M. Seliger, 'Race-Thinking During the Restoration', *Journal of the History of Ideas* 19:2 (1958), 273.

[8] Burrow, *A Liberal Descent*, 114.   [9] Beck, *Northern Antiquities*, I. 10.

[10] Ibid., II. 19.   [11] Ibid., I. 71 and II. 20.   [12] Ibid., II. 5.

was expounded by supporters of the Indo-European theory, who traced association with the ancient Indians in several nations' ethnogenesis through the web of language and, to some extent, religion. Although this hypothesis later incorporated premises based on the racial superiority of the Indo-European peoples, in the first part of the nineteenth century the racial element was still largely absent.

As these instances reveal, the humanist and Enlightenment scholars' attraction to the *origines gentium* was informed by a degree of continuity. Yet, Enlightenment scholars applied a different conceptual framework which enabled them to relate to the genesis of humanity, language and civilization in conjectural ways. Their interest resided in the origins of the state, beginnings of speech, first occupancy and the emergence of property.[13] Furthermore, it was in the Enlightenment era that mythological foundations gradually became discredited. Such a mindset was evident in the proclamation of Lord Bolingbroke that 'we have . . . neither in profane nor in sacred authors such authentic, clear, distinct, and full accounts of the originals of ancient nations . . . as deserve to go by the name of history'.[14] In a similar vein, Schlözer complained that

the superstition and ignorance of past centuries have spoiled the history of every nation; they have also spoiled ours. There was a time when we searched for our ancestors in the land of the Tower of Babel; the Slavs were found at the siege of Troy . . . There was a time when it was believed that the town of Moscow took its name from Mosoch, grandson of Noah . . . Ignorance, I emphasise, has devised its own miseries.[15]

In the course of the nineteenth century, approaches to ethnogenesis underwent a further transformation, whereby philosophical and conjectural aspects were replaced with an empirical, individual and national framework. The focus now shifted to the study of native laws and customs, which were considered the pivotal manifestations of national characteristics, expressions of the *Volksgeist*. Romantic scholars historicized the Enlightenment myth of the 'state of nature' by attempting to reconstruct 'original' institutions.[16]

When defining their stance on national antiquity, my protagonists were naturally confronted with their respective medieval and early

---

[13] Donald Kelley, 'Ancient Verses on New Ideas: Legal Tradition and the French Historical School', *History and Theory* 26:3 (1987), 325.

[14] Henry Bolingbroke, *Historical Writings*, ed. Isaac Kramnick (Chicago, 1972), 48.

[15] August Schlözer, *Tableau de l'histoire de Russie* (Gotha, 1769), 13, quoted in Reill, *The German Enlightenment*, 88.

[16] Donald Kelley, 'Ancient verses on New Ideas', 325.

modern traditions. Humanist authors traditionally associated the Hungarians with the Huns, a people regarded as a Scythian tribe in classical scholarship.[17] The equivalent Polish convention traced the genesis of the nation to legendary Sarmatia, a land which was likewise associated with Scythia. Both Horváth and Lelewel rebutted these theories, partly because they proved unacceptable in terms of scholarly verification, but also for the reason that the Sarmatian and Scythian explanations were confined to the origins of the premodern *natio*, the nobility, a convention that conflicted with the two scholars' political persuasions. Kogălniceanu's vision of antiquity drew upon the mainstream contemporary theory about Roman ancestry, but, as we shall see, he disapproved of the extremist version of this amorphous hypothesis. Daukantas's speculations about the early days of the Lithuanians blended layers of the classical Romanist tradition with a newly emerging speculation about the Indian descent of the Lithuanians.

Historians pursuing the study of antiquity usually recognized a distinction between history and 'prehistory', whilst showing awareness that the relationship between the two always proved elusive. In the context of universal history, such a division could include an 'obscure' and a 'historical' period, the former associated with the age of superstition and fable, the latter with human knowledge and historical accuracy.[18] As for national history, Guizot delineated the initial period of French history as a chaotic era, that of Gauls, Franks and Romans. It was only thereafter, he maintained, that the historian could speak of 'Frenchmen' and was able to study France itself.[19] In my protagonists' accounts the 'ancient' period typically extended to the era before the foundation of the state and the adoption of Christianity. In Polish and Czech historiography this involved the period between the arrival of the Slav tribes in Central Europe in the fourth century and the establishment of the state in the late tenth century. In the Hungarian case the long migration from the Hungarians' original homeland near the Ural mountains to Central Europe, and then the epoch between their arrival in the Carpathian basin in the late ninth century and state foundation and Christianization a century later, were considered to form a prequel to 'proper' history. The Lithuanians were the last nation in Europe to adopt

[17] Johnson, 'The Scythian: Its Rise and Fall', 255–6.

[18] Such a scheme was applied in Johann Christoph Gatterer's *Versuch einer allgemeinen Weltgeschichte bis zur Entdeckung Amerikens* (Göttingen, 1792).

[19] Guizot, *Historical Essays and Lectures*, 347.

Christianity in the fifteenth century, and consequently the veneration of the pagan past played a pivotal role in Daukantas's narrative. As has been hinted in previous chapters, the contours of Romanian antiquity were marked by ambiguities because of the virtually missing links between the Roman period in ancient Dacia and the foundation of the medieval principalities in Moldavia and Wallachia, a gap which represented more than a thousand years.

THE VANTAGE POINT: TACITUS

The inadequate and scattered nature of sources that could provide reliable hints about the early days of the nation heavily circumscribed the pursuit of national antiquity. In my protagonists' contexts the majority of such documents were produced by foreigners, contained only perfunctory clues and were typically imbued with an unsympathetic tone, exacerbating matters further. It is therefore unsurprising that historians fabricated their portrait of national antiquity by resorting to universal topoi. Given the generally prescriptive nature of national historiography in this epoch, perhaps to an even greater extent than usual, the emphasis was placed on the ideal rather than the actual, and statements on antiquity echoed contemporary political demands. In other words, the prehistoric stage of society, as depicted by Romantic historians, resembled a laboratory in which elements of a desired society were to be detected.

The depth with which a historian delved into the past varied in individual cases, but a general consensus existed on the most crucial aspect of primordial society: unalienable liberty, dating from time immemorial. ' "What is ancient is liberty, what is modern is despotism", said Madame de Staël. With this one saying she recounted our history and the history of all Europe,' wrote Augustin Thierry in his *Dix ans d'études historiques*.[20] This ostensibly unexceptional remark provided a valuable asset for the purposes of emancipatory nations because it implied that liberty was not granted by someone else but had always belonged to them. Consequently, if they had been deprived of their liberty, that could only have happened in an illegitimate way.[21] Such

---

[20] Thierry, *Dix ans d'études historiques*, 345.
[21] John Pocock, *The Ancient Constitution and Feudal Law: A Study of English Historical Thought in the Seventeenth Century*, 2nd edn. (Cambridge, 1987), 16.

a line of argument can be observed in my historians' mission to de-legitimize foreign domination in their countries and justify their claims for national independence.

Liberty since time immemorial represented the major but certainly not the only archetypical postulation employed to elucidate national characteristics in ancient times. Additional traits commonly associated with primordial societies have often been termed 'Tacitean' liberties. This is because, before the sciences of linguistics and archaeology gained access into the new territory which nineteenth-century scholars began to call prehistory, (*Vorgeschichte*), for many scholars Tacitus and to some extent Caesar indicated the starting-point of national history.[22] Tacitus characterized the government of ancient Germans as a democracy tempered by the power of the prince and the chieftains. He and his followers, the Tacitists, bestowed upon the ancient Germans a variety of (mainly positive) features, a tendency towards drink and violence notwithstanding: racial and moral purity, piety and integrity, constancy and fortitude, opposition to usury, natural nobility, and especially a love of liberty.[23] Other tropes addressed the rule of German kings which Tacitus deemed to be consensual and elected by a 'grand assembly', and the enduring distaste of the Germans for written laws: it was assumed that they did not commemorate their deeds or keep their laws through written records but rather through traditional songs.[24]

The Tacitean attributes provided a universal toolbox for historians attempting to reconstruct the earliest days of national life. For example, Mallet, who could find no trace of the desired 'democratic spirit' in modern Danish institutions, nor in the sparse material which was accessible on the ancient Scandinavians, appropriated all the essential traits from Tacitus and amalgamated them with Montesquieu's doctrine of liberty emerging from the woods of the North.[25] The evocation of Tacitus' *Germania* held a lasting and dominant appeal for Englishmen as an account of their ancestors: it remained present even in high-Victorian scholarship.[26] Following Montesquieu's argument it was generally assumed that the roots of the British political system were brought to the shores of England by Germanic tribes from the forests of Germany. The Anglo-Saxons were viewed as a freedom-loving people,

---

[22] Kelley, *Fortunes of History*, 184.   [23] Ibid.

[24] Donald Kelley, 'Tacitus Noster: The Germania in the Renaissance and the Reformation', in T. J. Luce, A J. Woodman (eds.), *Tacitus and the Tacitean Tradition* (Princeton, 1993), 161.

[25] Thor Beck, *Northern Antiquities*, I. 71.   [26] John Burrow, *A Liberal Descent*, 109.

enjoying representative institutions and flourishing primitive democracy which was crushed by the Norman conquest.[27]

These qualities constituted essential components of the humanist and early modern historiographical tradition and found their way into national historiographies in the nineteenth century. They evolved into a universal skeleton in the representation of antiquity, regardless of whether historians endowed their nations with Germanic ancestry or not. As will be apparent in the following sections, my historians also appealed to the theme of the noble savage. By making recourse to the Northern, Eastern and Latin traditions of antiquity, they dressed Tacitean themes in distinctive national garbs. On the one hand, the variants described below attest to the extremely widespread applicability of those archetypes. On the other, they also indicate that although extremely flexible, such topoi were not always universally applicable. To that end, Hungarian antiquity as discerned by Horváth, devoid of straightforward references to the mainstream variants, represents an exception. Last but not least, it is important to emphasize that the categories which I employ below were devised for the purposes of thematization and in reality appeals to antiquity rarely crystallized around one tradition. Far more typical was the amalgamation of different, and often seemingly incongruous, variants into a coherent vision.

NORDIC ANTIQUITY

Lelewel's first attempts at historical study were characterized by his fascination with the barbarian mythologies and epic literature of Northern Europe, whilst his work addressed the standard themes of the Nordic repertoire. They also mirrored the intellectual milieu at the university in Vilna, informed by the stimulus of the *Spätaufklärung*. In his student years Lelewel composed an essay on the origins of the Lithuanians, which later appeared under the title *Rzut oka na dawność litewskich narodów i związki ich z Herulami* (A Glance at the Antiquity of the Lithuanian Nations and their Relations with the Heruli). In this early piece he vehemently attacked Schlözer's theory on the Germanic origins of the Lithuanians. He also anonymously published a book entitled *Edda, czyli księga religii dawnych Skandynawii mięszkańców* (Edda: Or the Book of

---

[27] Reginald Horsman, 'Origins of Racial Anglo-Saxonism in Great Britain before 1850', 388.

Religion of the Ancient Inhabitants of Scandinavia). This was in fact the revised Polish translation of Paul-Henri Mallet's *Introduction à l'Histoire de Dannemarc*. As such, it epitomized the dissemination of Northern themes to various outposts of the European intellectual scene through the medium of translation. In addition to making the *Edda* accessible in national languages, such ventures often contained a foreword, in which the translators voiced their own theories about the origins of the Scandinavians. Of such speculations on the translator's part, Thomas Percy's introduction to his above-mentioned *Northern Antiquities* held most sway. Percy notably pointed out that Mallet erroneously related the Scandinavians to the Celts and ascertained that they in fact belonged to different ethnic stocks.[28] Lelewel's introduction to the Polish version of the *Edda* exemplified the tradition which invited the translator to enter into a dialogue with the original work. Like Percy, he refuted Mallet's hypothesis and also expounded his own (fallacious) theory which asserted that the Scandinavians originated from the Scythians.[29] His avid interest in the Scythians was aroused on reading another 'classic' of the Nordic repertoire, John Pinkerton's *Dissertation on the Origin of Scythians or Goths* (1787), in a French translation.

Lelewel's interpretation of early Polish history reveals an obvious debt to the Nordic heritage. As has been explained above, he renounced the Sarmatian tradition along with the assumption that the Polish nobility retained an ethnic character different from the rest of the population. Positing his nation's history within a European framework, Lelewel complies with the axiomatic theory resting on the supposed authority of Mallet and Montesquieu which located the *vagina gentium* and the cradle of freedom in the North.[30] Subscribing to this 'liberty myth' and postulating climate theory, Lelewel discerns two different paths of development inherent in the course of European history, a Nordic and a Southern variant. Not only does he designate the Nordic people as the foremost representatives of freedom, but he also bestows upon them the attributes of political activity and a sense of communal responsibility. By contrast, he diagnoses the conditions of the people of south-western Europe, whose society emerged from the foundation of the old Roman empire, as more advanced but ultimately tarnished by the rigid hierarchy

---

[28] Ibid., 391.

[29] Lelewel, *Edda, czyli księga religii dawnych Skandynawii mieszkańców* (Wilno, 1807), introduction, 5.

[30] Montesquieu, *The Spirit of Laws*, ed. Anne Cohler, Basia Miller and Harold Stone (Cambridge, 1981), 282.

of the feudal system.[31] My other historians' narratives were similarly informed by this binary opposition between national antiquity and feudalism, as we shall discover.

In Montesquieu's and other classical accounts the Germans and Scandinavians were associated with the virile Nordic people. Their 'human deluge' was considered to have destroyed the morally and physically decadent Roman empire. In a different way, Lelewel links the Slavs and Scandinavians, who fell beyond the influence of the old Roman empire, with the population of the North.[32] Although this view may have deviated from the 'mainstream' perceptions of the Nordic people, it was on the whole not unprecedented: Russia and Poland were commonly identified as Northern lands in historical literature, at least until the mid-nineteenth century, particularly when the term 'Nordic' was employed as a geographical marker, rather than in relation to ethnogenesis. Such an understanding was indebted to the tradition of classical antiquity.[33] According to this, the Poles resided in a territory which lay north of the ancient civilized world, both the West-Roman 'Occident' and the East-Roman 'Orient'. This Southern–Northern divide remained undisputed at least until the rearrangement of Europe at the Congress of Vienna (1815).[34] Therefore, as Chapter 9 will reveal, influential books of the age, such as Schlözer's *Allgemeine Nordische Geschichte*, regarded the Slavs as a Nordic populace, and for a number of contemporary scholars the perception of Slavs as Northern Europeans likewise comprised an essential element of the myth of 'Slavness'.[35]

Lelewel insists that the values associated with the Northern people were most fully developed in the egalitarian community of the early Poles, which he terms *gminowładztwo*, an expression originating from the word *gmino*, i.e. people or community.[36] In addition to their independence and political commitment, other virtues of the ancient Poles included their aversion to luxuries, their bravery without recklessness and their warm-heartedness without being quick to anger.[37] With regard to the economic structure of these early societies, Lelewel argues that in

---

[31] Lelewel, *Dzieła*, II. 589–628.   [32] Ibid.

[33] Hans Lemberg, 'Zur Entstehung des Osteuropabegriffs im 19. Jahrhundert. Vom "Norden" zum "Osten" Europas', *Jahrbücher für Geschichte Osteuropas* 33 (1985), 58.

[34] Ibid., 63.   [35] Pynsent, *Questions of Identity*, 76.

[36] A detailed analysis of this concept is given in Franciszek Bronowski, *Idea gminowładztwa w polskiej historiografii* (Łódź, 1969). Bronowski argues that Lelewel was inspired by French republicanism when devising this theory, which was also present in his predecessor's Naruszewicz's writings, but in a negative connotation.

[37] Lelewel, *Polska, dzieje a rzeczy jej*, III. 278; *Betrachtungen*, 188.

pagan times the Slavs lived under a system of collective land-ownership, another element which set them apart from the rigid hierarchy of the feudal system in Southern Europe. As for their religion, the Polish scholar maintains that idolatry, which he associated with the religion of the early Slavs, had Indo-German roots.[38] To that end, he exploited August Schleicher's theory of the Indo-German relationship and various etymologies in order to prove the antiquity of the early Slavs' religion.

Lelewel's portrayal of early Polish society, especially the emphasis on the democratic principles inherent in ancient Polish communalism, bears traces of his republican conviction as well as his appeal to the heritage of Panslavism. Some elements of the *gminowładztwo* concept, especially Lelewel's attribution of political awareness to the ancient Slavs, and in particular the Poles, defied traditional images. Not only were the Slavs deemed to be lacking in political dynamism, but it was believed that they were a *Taubenvolk* and that theirs was a *Lammesgeschichte*. As has been pointed out in Chapter 4, not even Herder, whose sympathetic account of the Slavs provided them with immense symbolic capital, viewed the Slavs or Poles as outstanding representatives of civic freedom or the democratic spirit. Thus, Lelewel's account was founded on other, 'native' theories; the most important single incentive was provided for him by the writings of the greatest contemporary authority in Slavonic law, Wacław Maciejowski (1793–1883), who also exerted an influence on Palacký. Whilst the young Lelewel originated Polish law in Norman sources, under Maciejowski's influence he went on to argue for the indigenous nature of Slavic law.[39] Lelewel's main postulate that the early Slavs, and especially the Poles, enjoyed unmatched democracy and legal equality was originally voiced by Maciejowski, and both scholars' verdicts displayed a critical attitude towards the influence of German individualism and German law in the Slavic legal tradition.[40]

This was because they maintained that the two legal systems were incompatible, an opinion also expressed by Palacký, Nikolai Karamzin and the Serbian scholar Vuk Karadzić.[41] At the same time, somewhat paradoxically, Lelewel's representation of early Polish society, especially his emphasis on self-government and the common ownership of lands,

[38] Lelewel, *Cześć bałwochwalcza Sławian i Polski* (Poznań, 1857), 26–7.
[39] Bronowski, *Idea gminowładztwa w polskiej historiografii*, 40.
[40] Wacław Maciejowski, *Historya prawodawstw słowiańskich*, 2 vols. (Warsaw and Leipzig, 1832), I. 2, see also in the German version *Slavische Rechtsgeschichte*, 4 parts (Stuttgart and Leipzig, 1835–9), 2.
[41] Josef Pekář, 'K sporu o zádruhu staroslavanskou', *Český časopis historický* 6 (1900), 244.

bears some resemblance to the *Mark*-community, the Germanic village communes as epitomized in the accounts of Romantic historians. Such free village communities were deemed by several scholars to have formed the core of ancient German, Anglo-Saxon and Scandinavian societies. Nevertheless, the more precise contours of such society, as with Lelewel's *gminowładztwo*, remained ambiguous. The *Mark*-community, by its very vagueness, could be accorded the most varied meanings.

INDO-EUROPEAN ANTIQUITY

Daukantas's portrayal of the ancient Lithuanians both endorsed and challenged earlier traditions. The earliest reference to the Baltic peoples was made in Tacitus's writings, which featured as a major point of orientation in the Lithuanian historian's narrative. Chroniclers alluded to the Lithuanians in the ninth and tenth centuries, but the first more accurate sources became available only from the late thirteenth century. In addition, Daukantas relied on authors commonly associated with the Nordic renaissance. These included Mallet's and Pinkerton's writings, Schlözer's *Nordische Geschichte* as well as Lelewel's essay on the origins of the Lithuanians. Humanist chronicles endowed the Lithuanians with Roman descent and accounted for their origins by availing themselves of one of the most prevalent foundation myths, the trope of peregrination. According to the story, Prince Palemonius, who was related to Nero, escaped from the violence of the emperor and settled at the bay of the river Nemen in Samogitia, thus becoming the forefather of the Lithuanians.[42] Daukantas denounced this legend on the grounds of unreliability; nonetheless the Roman connection continued to remain a constituent of his explanation, albeit integrated in a more ambitious hypothesis about the Indian cradle of the Lithuanians.

As has been revealed in the previous chapter, Daukantas primarily utilized linguistic arguments when advancing the hypothesis according to which the ancestral homeland of the Lithuanians lay in India. It has also been noted that his assertion that Lithuanian revealed the closest resemblance to Sanskrit among the living languages was indebted to theories put forward by prominent scholars, including Herder and Wilhelm von Humboldt. Such arguments were commonly reiterated

[42] Žukas, *Simonas Daukantas*, 110.

in the context of religion. For example, Rasmus Rask, the Danish linguist who exerted significant influence upon Daukantas, drew on comparisons between Buddha and the Northern chieftain, Odin, as well as identifying analogies between the Edda and the Zend-Avesta.[43] Like Lelewel, who affiliated idolatry, which he considered to be the religion of the ancient Slavs, with Indo-European lineage, Daukantas established parallels between the ancient Indian and Baltic-Lithuanian deities.[44]

In the light of the unusually extensive pagan heritage in Lithuanian culture, a corollary of late Christianization, it is not surprising that Daukantas paid significant attention to the study of Baltic deities: an entire chapter in his *Būdas* amplifies the religious life of ancient Lithuanians. His reconstruction of the Baltic pantheon was grounded in the humanist tradition, which knitted together scholarly books, folk customs and chronicles.[45] He also exploited his friend Tadeusz Narbutt's gargantuan volume on the history of Lithuanian (Baltic) mythology. Narbutt was the last scholar to enrich the Lithuanian-Baltic pantheon with new figures. Following contemporary fashion, unlike earlier scholars who endowed the Lithuanians with Graeco-Roman gods, he planted the gods of India into the Baltic soil.[46] This was emulated in Daukantas's hypothesis according to which the Lithuanian principal deity, Perūnas, was the incarnation of the Indian god Wisnu. Additionally, Daukantas endorsed a medieval tradition originating from Peter of Duisburg's *Chronica Terrae Prussiae* which held that the ancient Lithuanians were commanded by a mythical high priest, the *Krivė*, who represented an approximate equivalent of the Pope.[47] As will be shown below, Daukantas assumed that the *Krivė* possessed an authority comparable to that of the secular ruler, the Grand Duke.

A peculiarity of Daukantas's narrative lies in his powerful appeal to nature. He turns natural into national history, a process whereby 'popular myths, memories and supposed national virtues are projected onto a significant landscape in an attempt to lend more continuity and distinctiveness to national identity'.[48] In the course of this 'nationalization of nature' he shapes the impenetrable forests into principal 'agents' of the Lithuanian past. The veneration of natural history has often been seen

---

[43] Beck, *Northern Antiquities*, II. 155. [44] Daukantas, *Raštai*, I. 495.
[45] Endre Bojtár, *Foreword to the Past: A Cultural History of the Baltic People* (Budapest, 1999), 316.
[46] Ibid., 317. [47] Krapauskas, *Nationalism and Historiography*, 40.
[48] Oliver Zimmer, 'In Search of Natural Identity: Alpine Landscape and the Reconstruction of the Swiss Nation', *Comparative Studies in Society and History* 40:4 (1998), 643.

as a substitute nurtured by nations deprived of any more direct means of political self-expression.[49] Nevertheless, albeit to varying degrees, most national traditions adopted a reverent approach to natural phenomena, such as mountains, forests and seas. Therefore, perhaps Daukantas's admiration of nature can be better accommodated within the context of the Romantic cult of nature, whilst also noting that the theme of the forest, a 'sylvan Arcadia', represented an ancient and universal topos of European culture. Last but not least, the reverence for the forest can also be linked to Tacitism: following Tacitus's *Germania*, antiquarians looked for the traditions of liberty and the roots of parliamentary democracy in the Hercynian forest where the ancient Germans supposedly frolicked.[50]

Daukantas argues that whilst other nations enjoyed the protection of castles, mountains and seas, Lithuanians were sheltered by forests, which also served as the 'granaries of all their wealth'. They were impenetrable and so deep that the sun, the moon and the stars were concealed by the leaves, so eternal night reigned there.[51] These attributes which Daukantas bestows upon the forests represent typical appeals to nature, and in that capacity correspond to the role attached to the mountains in Swiss historiography; both natural phenomena were regarded as purifying and unifying forces and as defensive castles.[52] In the protection of the forest, according to Daukantas, the ancient Lithuanians enjoyed a blissful existence. In this idyllic epoch a perfect harmony existed between nature and the people, and lands were common property.[53] The ancient Lithuanians were virtuous and loved freedom; serfdom and immorality were unknown to them. Rulers were elected with the consent of the people, and acted in their interest, adhering to the popular will: 'It is known that until the most recent epoch, the world was free, and without the consent of the people neither the Grand Duke nor the *Krivė* dared to interfere in state affairs, which is just, because whosoever carries the burden should know why he is carrying it.'[54] Beyond the material benefits which the forests conferred, they also possessed a sacral quality, and in this respect, similarities are apparent with Tacitus's Germans, who adored natural phenomena such as great oaks:

Entire forests were preserved and designated as holy; without permission from the Lithuanian forest priest, no one was allowed to break off a single green shoot

[49] Simon Schama, *Landscape and Memory* (London, 1996), 48.
[50] Kelley, 'Tacitus Noster', 164.   [51] Daukantas, *Raštai*, I. 424.
[52] Oliver Zimmer, 'In Search of Natural Identity', 643.   [53] Daukantas, *Raštai*, I. 572.
[54] Ibid., I. 578, quoted in Krapauskas, *Nationalism and Historiography*, 76.

or even to step into the forest unless they were seeking protection from death in the sacred place . . . holy trees could be felled only by the priests themselves with their holy axes . . .[55]

In Daukantas's account the impenetrable forests are 'humanized': a parallel is drawn between the gradual felling of the trees and the degeneration of national life. This trope of decline was also employed in Herder's writings: he argued that the ancient Germans had lost their character in the course of their interaction with Rome, and, with their forests, their freedom had been hollowed out.[56] In Daukantas's narrative the disappearance of the forests is symbolically associated with the arrival of foreigners imposing foreign mores on the ancient Lithuanians. The invasion of the Germans, and the resulting introduction of Christianity, disrupted the primordial harmonious epoch, as did the subsequent influx of the Poles, in the course of which Lithuanian society was compelled to succumb to the influence of the feudal system.

PUTATIVE CZECH ANTIQUITY

As illustrated in the previous chapter, similarly to Daukantas, Palacký cherished the Indo-European heritage in terms of linguistic comparison. His association of the Czech metrical system with the sophisticated patterns of ancient Sanskrit versification attested to the high prestige of poetry in the Romantic era, rendering it more ancient than prose and, in that respect, 'the mother tongue' of the human race, a theory expounded in Herder's celebrated essay, *Über die Wirkung der Dichtkunst auf die Sitten der Völker* (1778).[57] In addition to the veneration of oral poetic traditions, inspiration for the study of antiquities in Palacký's youth was provided by the supposedly ancient Gaelic poetry translated by James Macpherson, which represented an important catalyst to the production of Norse-themed poetry. It may be significant that Palacký's

[55] Ibid., I. 426.
[56] Stefan Berger and Peter Lambert, 'Intellectual Transfers and Mental Blockades: Anglo-American Dialogues in Historiography', in Stefan Berger, Peter Lambert and Peter Schumann, *Geschichte, Mythos und Gedächtnis in deutsch–britischen kulturellen Austausch 1750–2000* (Göttingen, 2003), 18.
[57] Andrew Lass, 'Romantic Documents and Political Monuments: The Meaning-Fulfillment of History in 19th-Century Czech Nationalism', *American Ethnologist* 15:3 (1988), 464.

first scholarly endeavour comprised a translation of two songs from *Ossian*, which at that stage he still believed to be original.

Nevertheless, the predominant plot employed by the Czech historian represents another cluster of variants, one which underscored the Czechs' embeddedness in the Slavic community and insisted on the reconstruction of 'Slav antiquity'. Remarkable in the young Palacký's vision of antiquity is that his postulate did not subscribe to the tendency to over-inflate the virtues that supposedly informed the ancient Slav society. In that vein, Palacký rebutted Jan Kollár's popular etymology which derived the word 'Slav' from that of *sláva* (glory). Asked Palacký: 'On what was that glory based before the fifth century? The Germans conquered world-ruling Rome; our Slavs could not resist the Huns or Germans, nor did they conquer the Byzantines.'[58] Subsequently, Palacký's assessment underwent a major transformation, in the course of which his image of national antiquity was rendered strikingly reminiscent of Lelewel's interpretation, except for the fact that the virtues which Lelewel reserved for the Poles were appropriated by him for the Czechs. In its new incarnation, Palacký's portrayal of antiquity came to profess constituents which had been 'traditionally' ascribed to the Slavs: he envisaged his ancestors as peaceful, industrious, charitable, almost extravagantly hospitable people, devoted to their rustic independence. A further analogy with Lelewel's interpretation can be traced in the attribution of political activity to the early Czechs. Given the archetypal nature of visions of national antiquity, another reason for this similitude lies in the parallel directions of the two scholars' enquiry: they both nurtured an interest in the legal and constitutional history of the ancient Slavs. To this end, the common denominator between Lelewel's and Palacký's reconstruction of the primeval national tradition was the above-mentioned Maciejowski's assessment of the 'constitutional history' of the ancient Slavs.

Correspondingly, in Palacký's *magnum opus* the portrayal of the early days of the Czech nation, which constitutes a rather brief episode in the grand narrative, is informed by his adjusted vision of the Czechs. Similarly to the other four historians, his depiction resonates with the postulates of nineteenth-century liberalism:

Not without feelings of pride will a descendant understand that his Slavic ancestors preserved and defended among themselves for ages those things for

[58] Zacek, *Palacký*, 78.

which even the greatest and most cultivated nations of our age strive and aspire, not always successfully: general liberty of all in the land, equality before the law and justice, the government both hereditary, and elected and responsible to the assembly, free elections of local offices and representatives of the nation, and other such institutions, even including the praiseworthy shield of all general liberties, trial by jury.[59]

Palacký attempted to amplify the early nations of national history by drawing upon casual references to the Slavs in the works of Roman and Byzantine writers and he also utilized legends and the chronicles of his predecessors which dated back to the tenth century. More conspicuous was his reliance on two sensational and much debated manuscripts which were 'discovered' in 1817 and 1818 respectively. Of these two documents, the *Rukopis* (manuscript) *Zelenohorský* was dated by the discoverers to the ninth or tenth century, and the *Rukopis Královédvorský* to the late thirteenth century. If accepted as authentic, the former would have constituted the oldest specimen of Czech literature in existence.[60]

It is worth noting that in the context of contemporary European forgeries the two discoveries represented remarkable examples, inasmuch as they were available for scholarly investigation as physical objects. In contrast, Macpherson's *Ossian*, which, despite the halo of its Gaelic origin, was offered to the reading public in English 'translation', and the majority of other textual forgeries, were never 'discovered' and were thus presented to the public as concrete items, as written texts involving the actual use of parchment, ink and medieval orthography.[61] The discovery of the manuscripts ignited one of the most resounding polemics during the national revival and Palacký himself became a major agent in the debate.[62] The aesthetic beauty of the manuscripts captured the attention of several foreign scholars, most notably Goethe. However, the documents aroused suspicion soon after they were brought to light, especially because the Pan-Slavist poet and librarian of the newly founded Royal Museum of Bohemia, Vacláv Hanka, seemed to be involved in

---

[59] Palacký, *Dějiny národu českého v Čechách a v Moravě* (1939), I. 12, and *Gedenkblätter*, 137; my translation is based on the excerpt in Agnew, 'Czechs, Germans, Bohemians?' 69.

[60] The manuscripts were published in numerous editions. An important one is *Rukopisy Královédvorský a Zelenohorský*, ed. J. Karlik (Prague, 1936).

[61] Lass, 'Romantic Documents and Political Monuments', 463.

[62] See R. J. W. Evans, ' "The Manuscripts": The Culture and Politics of Forgery in Central Europe', in Geraint H. Jenkins (ed.), *A Ratteskull Genius: The Many Faces of Iolo Morganwg* (Cardiff, 2005), 51–68.

all such discoveries. By the late nineteenth century most scholars had discredited the documents and named Hanka as their forger, and as a corollary, the manuscripts became redefined as literary masterpieces of little historical value.[63]

It is against the backdrop of the emerging consensus on the forged nature of the manuscripts that Palacký's stubborn vindication of their authenticity needs to be assessed. As the most authoritative historian of his age, and possessed of excellent palaeographical skills, he did not hesitate to put his scholarly reputation at risk in the academic battlefield by disregarding the evidence and even trying to explain away some discrepancies in his argument by concocting a hypothesis about the existence of an independent Czech orthographical tradition dating from the late ninth century.[64] One reason for Palacký's attitude arguably had to do with his own reliance on the manuscripts in the *Dějiny*: had he denounced them, the prestige of his scholarly work would have been compromised, but it is difficult to comprehend his stance unless we attend to its broader political context. The mature Palacký's portrayal of antiquity underwent changes in response to the new realities of contemporary politics, and illustrated his own unhappy impressions of the contemporary Germans in the Habsburg Empire and the German lands.[65] His reverence for Czech antiquity is best interpreted as a dialogue and contest with German culture, the purported values of which his narrative both mimetically reciprocated and countered. By making recourse to the manuscripts, his intention was to refute the dismissive slurs of German commentators. He also sought to inject the Czech past with the historical longevity needed to partake in the founding of European culture and also with the required state-generative potency.

Furthermore, the two discoveries enabled the Czechs to argue that they possessed an epic tradition, a folk genre that would compare with German, Russian and Balkan epic cycles and which was thought to be lacking for the Western Slavs.[66] To that effect, the manuscripts purportedly predated the famous *Nibelungenlied* and rendered the ancient Czechs the primeval inhabitants of the Bohemian lands. In addition, they remedied the image of the ancient Czechs refracted

---

[63] Lass, 'Romantic Documents', 460.

[64] Orthographical questions are discussed in Franz Palacky and Paul Joseph Šafařik, *Die ältesten Denkmäler der böhmischen Sprache* (Prague, 1840), 63–72. See also Milan Otáhal, 'The Manuscript Controversy in the Czech National Revival', *Cross Currents: A Yearbook of Central European Culture* 5 (1986), 247–77.

[65] Zacek, *Palacký*, 74.   [66] Lass, 'Romantic Documents', 460.

through the eyes of German chroniclers, which portrayed them as a people whose submissive society was characterized by intrigues and treachery and proved too immature for political organization.[67] Instead, these documents celebrated the early Czechs for their love of equality and justice, in much the same tone as Palacký's above-quoted description. Perhaps the most celebrated passage in the *Rukopis Zelenohorský*, the fragment of the poem 'The verdict of Libuša', was often cited to that effect in order to demonstrate the sophisticated nature of early Czech civilization. It contained a reference to a primeval parliament, from which Palacký concluded that the Czechs could not have been a lawless, wild horde even before the foundation of the state.[68] Palacký's reading of the same fragment also testified to the legal superiority of Czech society: whilst in German law inheritance followed the convention of primogeniture, under Slavic law the first born offspring was not entitled to undue advantages, and children inherited equally, irrespective of gender.[69] Such claims about the just and exemplary nature of primeval society were opposed to the feudal system, based on the principle of subjection and represented by the Germans. Last but not least, the manuscripts redefined the German chroniclers' account of the military proficiency of the early Germans as aggressiveness, by presenting them as cruel but cowardly invaders fighting for plunder and booty.[70]

As well as attempting to preserve the reputation of his own work, another reason for Palacký's endorsement of the manuscripts could have been his awareness of the potential which the manuscripts offered for fuelling the Czech national revival. As they testified to advanced cultural and civic conditions among the Czechs far earlier than had been imagined, they entirely recast the picture of the Czech past. Thus, irrespective of their forged nature and thus failure in scholarly terms, they gave a significant impetus to Czech culture by providing it with a confidence boost and inspiring many artistic pieces. However, it would be misleading to single out the forged manuscripts as portentous for Palacký's vision of Czech antiquity. His interpretation did not solely rest on the manuscripts, and as we have seen, it contained archetypal elements which were omnipresent in national historiography. Nor was he alone in his approval of forgeries. James Macpherson's *Ossian* was

[67] Agnew, 'Czechs, Germans, Bohemians?,' 68.
[68] Palacký and Šafařik, *Die ältesten Denkmäler der böhmischen Sprache*, 102.
[69] Ibid., 99–100.   [70] Ibid.

promoted by two pre-eminent intellectuals of the age, Hugh Blair and Adam Ferguson.[71] Moreover, Herder used Macpherson's work as a model, which he incorporated in his own search for German cultural origins, and the greatest mediator of the Scottish epic was Goethe, whose literary hero, the young Werther, famously declared that *Ossian* had replaced Homer in his heart.[72] Last but not least, the forgeries themselves can be interpreted as 'aids' assisting cultural wish-fulfilment. In this context, Hugh Trevor-Roper's claim that the inventors of manuscripts were *fantaisistes* rather than forgers, genuine in the sense that they lived their own fantasies, seems especially valid.[73]

ROMAN ANTIQUITY

Discourses on ethnogenesis were typically infused with layers of classical thought and, as a result, Roman ethnogenesis was esteemed by several historiographical traditions. The Romanians' appeal to Latin antiquity represented a distinctive national variation of this convention. When Romanian scholars sought to improve their nation's prestige by portraying it as a sole representative of Latinity in the 'Slav sea' of the Balkans, their argument also revolved around territorial legacies. Just as the Czech manuscripts strove to demonstrate that the first inhabitants of the region had been the ancestors of the Bohemians, the Romanian arguments were likewise directed against competing claims of other nations. The debate around the province of Transylvania was a major source of contention, as will be explained in Chapter 9, because both Romanian and Hungarian scholars needed to justify first occupancy and then the uninterrupted presence of their respective nations, in order to assume the legitimate ownership of this province.

As has been shown earlier, the theory of Roman continuity first emerged in the humanist chronicle tradition in the second half of the seventeenth century and gained full elaboration a century later. According to the standard hypothesis, as expounded by the representatives of the Transylvanian school, the Romanians were direct descendants

---

[71] Fiona Stafford, *The Sublime Savage: A Study of James Macpherson and the Poems of Ossian* (Edinburgh, 1988), 79.

[72] Nicholas Boyle, *Goethe* (Oxford, 1991), 174–8.

[73] Hugh Trevor-Roper, 'The Invention of Tradition: The Highland Tradition of Scotland', in Eric Hobsbawm and Terence Ranger (eds.), *The Invention of Tradition* (Cambridge, 1983), 41.

of the Romans who had settled in Dacia after their victory over the Dacians in AD 106. In addition, the Transylvanian scholars asserted that Christianity had been introduced to ancient Dacia by the Roman colonists. A fault in this grand theory lay in the denial of any association with the primeval inhabitants of Dacia itself. The Dacians were perceived as a burdensome barbarian element and, in that capacity, as disrupting the scheme of Latinity.[74] Thus, in order to allow for the Romanians' pure Roman descent, Romanian scholars were compelled to assume that the Dacians were entirely exterminated in their wars against the Romans, whilst not denying the survival of other ethnic groups.

The young Kogălniceanu was confronted with this canonical interpretation and, as with my other historians, the scant historical and archaeological evidence only allowed for speculations on his part. In the *Histoire*, he endows the Dacians with Scythian lineage and Tacitean attributes.[75] They are portrayed as the bravest, most bellicose and the most independent people of their time who elected their leaders in a democratic way. They favoured death over subjugation to foreign nations, and as such, Kogălniceanu notes, they were rather different from contemporary Moldavians and Wallachians. This analogy inherent in the latent criticism of contemporary Romanian society hints at the acceptance of some affiliation with the Dacians. Nevertheless, in his lecture at the Mihailean Academy in 1843, Kogălniceanu invoked the Dacians as the people whose soil the Romanians had taken over, but who were not ethnically identical with them.[76]

Thus, Kogălniceanu endorsed the theory of Roman descent and even identified Roman elements in Romanian folklore: 'Our peasants have preserved a multitude of Roman superstitions, their weddings include ceremonies practiced by the citizens of Rome.'[77] In addition, he argued that the Romanians preserved undiluted ethnic purity, a Tacitean claim originally made in the context of the peoples of Germany who were deemed to have remained untainted by intermarriage with other races, 'a nation peculiar and pure, like no one but themselves'.[78] Emulated in the Romanian context, in Kogălniceanu's words, 'The Romanians never wanted to take in marriage women of another folk . . . They always remained a nation apart, preserving their ways and customs of

---

[74] Boia, *History and Myth*, 89.   [75] Kogălniceanu, *Opere*, II. 51.
[76] Ibid., II. 67.   [77] Ibid., II. 67, quoted in Boia, *History and Myth*, 88.
[78] Horsman, 'Origins of Racial Anglo-Saxonism', 389.

their ancestors, without losing anything of the daring and courage of the citizens of Rome.'[79] To confirm this, Kogălniceanu cited Gibbon's *Decline and Fall* in the English original: 'The Wallachians are surrounded by, but not mixed with the Barbarians.'[80] In his early work, the *Histoire*, an interesting episode reveals that the historian also forged a link with Roman culture on a territorial basis, recounting a local legend: 'In the year 8 AD from the border of the Tiber (i.e. from Rome) an extraordinary man arrived, who had the sweetness of a child and the kindness of a father. He sighed constantly and sometimes talked to himself, but when he spoke to others, honey seemed to flow from his mouth.'[81] Association of this kind with Ovid was professed not only in Romanian historiography but also in Russian and Polish scholarship. This is because the poet's place of exile remained somewhat enigmatic. In his *Tristia* and *Ex Ponto* he made references to Tomis, located on the icy, wind-swept western shores of the Black Sea.[82] Alternatively, in Romanian, Polish and Russian chronicles, Ovid's place of exile was often positioned in Bessarabia, on the shores of the estuary of the river Dniester. Following that tradition Kogălniceanu also transferred Ovid from Tomis to Bessarabia and claimed that he died in the latter place.

Thus, Kogălniceanu adhered to the mainstream interpretation which did not allow for concessions in terms of purity. It was only towards the second half of the nineteenth century, once Romanian independence was achieved, that concerns of purity and nobility assumed a less pivotal role, and the Dacians were gradually endowed with a greater stake in Romanian ethnogenesis. Nevertheless, in the 1840s Kogălniceanu became increasingly critical of extremist Romanist interpretation of his age, which identified the starting-point of Romanian history with the foundation of Rome in 753 BC, rendering Romans and Romanians identical. He disparaged the prevalent 'Romanomania' among contemporary scholars and called for the necessity of distinguishing between Romanians and Romans:

Only bankrupt nations refer constantly to their ancestors . . . Even if we are descended from Hercules, if we are rogues the world will know us as such; on the contrary, if we get rid of demoralization and civic discord, which drive us to

[79] Kogălniceanu, *Opere*, II. 67.   [80] Zub, *Mihail Kogălniceanu istoric*, 293.
[81] J. P. Trapp, 'Ovid's Tomb: The Growth of a Legend from Eusebius to Laurence Sterne, Chateaubriand and George Richmond', *Journal of the Warburg and Courtald Institutes* 36 (1973), 53.
[82] Ibid., 53.

peril, we shall approach with more determined steps the path of brotherhood, of patriotism, of a sound, not superficial civilization, as we have it; then Europe will respect us, even if we are descended from the hordes of Genghis Khan. Therefore, gentlemen, I will not hide from you that our laws, customs and language and beginnings stretch back to the Romans; history asserts these truths with firmness, but let me tell you once again that I am far from gratifying a ridiculous mania by talking to you about the deeds of the Romans as if they were ours. I am going to do something more useful, though; if you really want to be known as true sons of the Romans, I will urge you to do what resembles the deeds of the ruling people of the world.[83]

In addition to the role of the Dacian element in Romanian ethnogenesis, another contested chapter lay in the definition of the contours of Romanian antiquity, in particular the inscrutable dark millennium that extended between the withdrawal of the Romans from Dacia in the third century and the foundation of the medieval principalities in the fourteenth century. In that context, Kogălniceanu approved the mainstream argument which asserted that a majority of the Roman population remained in place and, in the following centuries, seeking refuge from the attack of barbaric tribes, withdrew to the mountains. Thus, when the Hungarians entered Transylvania in the tenth century, they found these descendants organized in small state-like entities.

SEMI-NOMADIC ANTIQUITY

Ethnogenesis constituted an enigmatic episode in Hungarian historiography as it remained unravelled for an unusually long period. The myth of Hunnic ancestry, introduced by a medieval chronicler, endured virtually unchallenged until the second half of the nineteenth century, when scholars demonstrated that the story had been adopted from German chronicles. By this time new research into linguistics suggested a connection to the Finns and the Finno-Ugrian language family. The first book which asserted the common origins of the Hungarian and Finno-Ugrian languages appeared in 1770.[84] Following that discovery the new hypothesis gradually gained recognition, not least because Schlözer's approval of the Finno-Ugrian theory in his *Nordische Geschichte* lent

---

[83] Kogălniceanu, *Opere*, II. 393, my translation relies on the excerpt in Trencsényi and Kopeček (eds.), *Discourses of Collective Identity*, II. 49.

[84] János Sajnovics, *Demonstratio Idioma Ungarorum et Lapponum Idem Esse* (Copenhagen, 1770).

international support to it. Paradoxically, whereas new linguistic evidence hinted at the Finno-Ugrian ancestry, the physical appearance of Hungarians and their customs indicated Turkish background, which only served to intensify the perplexity surrounding origins. Scholars in the first half of the nineteenth century conducted fierce debates on this problem, which were animated by issues of identity, prestige and pride: the Finnish ancestry created embarrassment for some Hungarian patriots as they were reluctant to grant it any recognition, decrying it as 'smelling of fish'. It is against this backdrop that Horváth's demonstrative indifference to origins and, in more general terms, to the period *prior* to the adoption of Christianity calls for explanation.

One motive behind Horváth's apathy was undoubtedly related to the scarcity of relevant documents, which encumbered the study of early Hungarian history. He revealed little affinity for addressing the epoch in which, as he put it, 'myths turned into history', and to which references were disconcertingly sparing. At a later stage, as an already established scholar and successful contestant in two academic competitions, his participation was requested in another competition to write a 'Hungarian Mythology', the religious history of the pagan Hungarians. He declined the invitation asserting that the dearth of reliable sources made such a venture impossible.[85] Horváth's personal predilection also played an important role. Even in the fledging stages of his scholarly career, whilst still at the seminary where theology and classics featured as pinnacles of the curriculum, he was principally attracted to contemporary history. The impressive achievements of the reform era, the stimulating intellectual atmosphere and later the prospect of partaking in political life, offered a more appealing route for him than the opportunity to contribute to nebulous academic debates. Last but not least, Horváth did not succumb to promises of gratification which the veneration of the national past potentially offered. In the *Párhuzam* he proclaimed that: 'Culpable is the nation which has such great need for laudation and glory that it considers the antiquity and fame of its predecessors to be its most significant merit.'[86]

The need to commence the story somewhere meant that he gave brief consideration to this era in the opening pages of the various versions of his *Magyarország történelme*, expounding both contested theories about origins, but showing reluctance to further elaborate on the issue in the

---

[85] Várkonyi, *Pozitivista szemlélet*, II. 63.
[86] *Horváth Mihály kisebb történelmi munkái*, I. 80.

absence of reliable evidence. Not entirely convinced by either variant, he assigned the Turkish version somewhat more credibility. He noted, with a hint of gentle irony, that 'ever since Schlözer approved the Finno-Ugrian theory, it has become fashionable to relate Hungarian and Finnish'.[87] To this end, Horváth asserted that linguistic similarities could not in themselves replace proofs of origins and advocated that the study of language should be accompanied by ethnographical research. Whilst revealing no great fascination with origins, the crucial period of the Hungarians' settlement in the Carpathian basin and their state foundation captured the historian's imagination. He offered the most detailed account of the deeds and disposition of early Hungarians in his first major piece of work, the *Párhuzam*. Nevertheless, in his mature writing, whilst again refraining from embarking on a nuanced study of the problem, Horváth revised his initial verdict, admitting that his original portrayal had been rose-tinted.

The relatively late influx of the nomadic Hungarians into what later became their homeland was widely recorded in foreign sources, but such records did not assist Horváth's cause. On the contrary, those early documents, which were mainly German, conveyed a very unflattering view of the Hungarians. Otto of Freising depicted them as cruel, disgusting, inhuman beings, who would not baulk at devouring the hearts of the people they had killed. So powerful and persistent was this image that Horváth had difficulty trying to flesh out a respectable picture of the ancient Hungarians. Rather than exploding those stereotypes, he recast the traditional image by ameliorating those alleged dreadful dispositions. Thus, he did not deny the Hungarians a degree of wildness but confined such conduct to exceptional situations. In the young Horváth's account, the Hungarians led a peaceful life of equality, simplicity and independence upon entering the Carpathian basin. The primeval inhabitants of the land were permitted to retain their freedom, but were compelled to adopt Hungarian customs. It was only when the Hungarians embarked on military adventures in the neighbouring territories that the truth-loving, peaceful shepherds turned into cruel, grasping robbers and war evolved into the organizing principle of their life. Domestic work was sneered at by the Hungarians as something servile, and instead they idled away most of their day in *dolce far niente*. This period saw the emergence of selfishness and greed, as a consequence of the material enrichment which resulted from the military adventures.

[87] Horváth, *Magyarország történelme*, I. 21.

With these qualities, argues Horváth, the ancient Hungarians recalled Caesar's Gauls and Tacitus' Germans: 'they were disgusted by acquiring things by the sweat of their brow if they could have been obtained by violence and blood'.[88] What makes this direct reference to Tacitus and Caesar notable is that, unusually in the context of national historiography, Horváth makes recourse to this trope in its negative incarnation. Nevertheless, another appeal to the Tacitean 'toolbox' seeks to attach some prestige to the Hungarians: Horváth diagnosed a virtuous disposition in what he saw as his ancestors' respect for women and monogamy. Although still considered the property of their husbands, they were not treated as slaves or objects. Hungarian men were faithful and showed respect towards them.[89] The episode which the young scholar cites to provide support for his assertion illustrates the charming quality of his effort to offer a judicious, yet not unsympathetic view of the early Hungarians. According to his argument, the consideration for women manifested itself in 938 when Prince Zoltán and his army angrily wreaked havoc in Saxony after an unsuccessful military adventure, destroying, among other things, a nunnery. Although all the nuns were butchered, their virtue remained intact.[90] Horváth also quotes Spittler's *Geschichte Europas* to the effect that the history of humanity showed few precedents for such a 'gradual ennoblement' as happened in the case of the Hungarians.[91]

As with my other protagonists, Horváth's verdict on early Hungarian society was directed against the precepts of the feudal system and carried liberal overtones. Horváth maintains that whilst feudalism, with its organizing principle of serfdom, killed freedom at its roots, early Hungarian society was informed by the limited authority of the prince, derived from a rightful contract. He interprets the legendary tradition of the blood contract of the seven chieftains as a primitive but democratic constitution, and in a similar vein, the legendary meeting of the chieftains at Pusztaszer in the ninth century as a primitive form of parliament, a Hungarian Witenagemot. On the whole, Horváth finds that the Hungarian legal system was necessarily less advanced than the established (albeit arbitrarily formed) laws of feudal Europe, but better suited to its purpose.[92] Thus, early Hungarian society echoed several claims of the Reform era, including the more equitable distribution of public burdens, the emancipation of

---

[88] *Horváth Mihály kisebb történelmi munkái*, I. 115.   [89] Ibid., I. 112.
[90] Ibid., I. 113.   [91] Ibid., II. 64.   [92] Ibid., I. 126.

serfs and the harmonization of the interests of different segments of society:

Because civilization is not to be found where the legal system is rigidly established, but where the constitution fits its purpose, where social relations are defined by rightful laws and where the prince has sufficient authority to advocate the implementation of those laws, where the contribution to public good is in proportion to the advantages drawn from it, where the constitution serves not just a few privileged individuals, but the entire nation.[93]

CONCLUSION

Origins provide a cornerstone of every nation's self-legitimization and consequently historians have shown a keen dedication to this theme, although the intensity of the engagement was contingent upon the preferences of individual authors and often remained confined to distinct epochs in historiography. Furthermore, as national history was typically produced in a chronological order, the early phase of history naturally affected the vantage point of the grand narrative, irrespective of whether the historian preferred to linger on that subject or not. Historians' efforts to unravel the earliest stages of national history were hampered by the scarcity of available sources. Among these were occasional references in medieval chronicles, linguistic phenomena, artificial legal comparison and even forgeries. Out of these clues emerged typically sympathetic accounts of the early days of national history, which were often informed by self-gratification.

It is certain that antiquity, inextricably linked with concerns about prestige, provided valuable symbolic resources for scholars with 'emancipatory needs'. My historians' emphasis on the common origins of the privileged and unprivileged members of society implied that people had an equal stake in national history irrespective of their political and legal status. Furthermore, my historians' claims about adequate historical longevity were animated by an intent to attest their nations' rightful and undisputed membership of European civilization. Nevertheless, as we have seen, excesses in the veneration of the past were not omnipresent, but contingent upon the stances of individual scholars and the general political atmosphere. It would also not be appropriate to consider the

---

[93] Ibid., I. 125.

'idealization of the past' as peculiar to historians in East-Central Europe and contemptuously to regard the vested interest in antiquity as a sort of compensation on the part of 'non-historical' nations for the absence of a proper statehood. Furthermore, it was not necessarily the deliberate intention 'to idealize' or 'to falsify' history, but rather it was the historians' efforts to fill the lacunas that induced them to strain slender evidence. As the eminent Danish historian Barthold Niebuhr declared: 'I am a historian, thus, I know how to construct a total picture from individual pieces . . . and if pieces are missing, I also know how to render them complete.'[94]

Although my five protagonists' vantage points were somewhat diverse, they discerned a similar landscape of antiquity. Just as with other Romantic historians, they exploited universal tropes, such as the theme of the noble savage and Tacitean topoi. As a consequence, representations of early societies in European historiography, whether of the Anglo-Saxons, the Franks, the Czechs or the Lithuanians, were marked by striking resemblances, drawing on some prominent themes which appeared in countless variations. In that context, it was of little relevance what kind of sources were employed, what methodologies historians exploited and whether and to what extent the historian 'idealized' the past.

As we have seen, the qualities which historians reserved for their own nation comprised freedom since time immemorial, a sort of primitive democracy in which rulers were endowed with limited power and were compelled to observe the popular will. Other virtues included bravery and justice, hospitality and respect for women. Additionally, most historians typically professed the existence of a legislative body which could be associated with an earlier form of the constitution. As has become most manifest in Lelewel's typology, with particular references to the assertion that the early Poles were warm-hearted but not hot-blooded and revealed bravery but not recklessness, the alleged national virtues were often posited in the middle of two extremes, one's own nation representing the 'golden middle way'. Furthermore, antiquity was *relational* and *competitive*, as claims about seniority and other virtues were made in relation to equivalent assertions about other nations, typically a neighbour with overlapping interests or the dominant state from which emancipation was sought. Scholars substantiated the view that their own nation held more ancient lineage and harboured more virtuous qualities than those 'rivals'. Taking pride in the virtues reserved for one's own nation

---

[94] Wegele, *Geschichte der deutschen Historiographie*, 1005.

sought to boost the confidence of the national community and was intended—whether deliberately or not—as cultural wish-fulfilment.

Nevertheless, universal topoi and canonical traditions were dressed in 'individual colours'. By availing themselves of the great conventions of Nordic, Eastern and Latin variations of antiquity, historians infused traditional premises with layers peculiar to their own national heritage and also to their own political-ideological preferences. As we have seen, slight differences also prevailed in the nature of 'evidence' on the basis of which scholars construed their astonishingly analogous interpretations of national history. In some instances legal documents were deemed to provide the most reliable access to the past; in others linguistic phenomena and traces in religion and folklore were endowed with more significance. Thus, perceptions of national antiquity were simultaneously *multiple* and *shared*. In addition, although the tropes exploited by the portrayal of the national past revealed extreme flexibility, they nevertheless had limitations. For example, it would hardly have been possible for Horváth to devise a convincing narrative about the peaceful, gentle nature of Hungarians against the evidence of German sources which attested to their brutality.

Images of national antiquity were imbued with explicit political overtones and need to be set against the backdrop of contemporary political and social problems. Importantly, national antiquity was not discerned as a paradise lost, nor did historians advocate the return to primitive primeval conditions, although they might have lamented the loss of certain values, such as a sense of communal belonging. Even in those instances when the restoration of allegedly lost liberties was initiated, as exemplified by claims to bestow political citizenship upon the common people, such demands were formulated in the context of a modernizing discourse, whereby the contemporary wish-list of liberals was projected into the remote past in order to endow it with more justification. To the pivotal political concerns especially relevant to antiquity belonged foreign domination and the survival of feudal structures within society. Just as a consensus existed about the nature of national antiquity, informed by freedom and prosperity, my historians were in accord when accounting for the vanishing of that primeval liberty. As I shall demonstrate in the next chapter, they related the disappearance of original conditions to the introduction of the feudal system in their countries, a development that they interpreted in the context of foreign colonization.

7

Feudalism and the National Past

THE STUDY OF FEUDALISM IN HISTORICAL SCHOLARSHIP

My historians' keen and astringently critical interest in feudalism accompanied their political agenda which launched a fierce attack against the prevailing outdated structures of their societies and proposed to transform them into modern ones. Nonetheless, as with antiquity, scholarly pursuits in feudalism can be accommodated within a much wider spatial and temporal framework. Historical debates about its origins and nature dated back to the sixteenth century and gained new impetus two centuries later, a motivation which emerged from contemporary needs.[1] Although vassals, fiefs, vassalage and feudal tenure featured in the writings of early modern scholars, they did not contextualize those concepts within a broad feudal theory. Out of medieval collections and provincial customs jurists constructed the 'feudal law' and they placed primary significance on the twelfth-century description of Lombard laws, the *Libri Feudorum*, which was for a long time perceived as the archetype of feudal principles. The concept of 'feudalism' constituted a larger fiction, which was used by scholars to account for centuries of social relationships since the early Middle Ages.[2] The fabricated nature of the concept has been famously illuminated in the English context by John Pocock, who demonstrated that, until the middle of the seventeenth century, English scholars showed no awareness of a radical break between pre-feudal, feudal and post-feudal stages in their history; it was only in the seventeenth century that, due to the emerging

---

[1] Kelley, 'Ancient Verses on New Ideas', 328.
[2] Carl Stephenson, 'The Origin and Significance of Feudalism', *American Historical Review* 46:4 (1941), 797.

acquaintance with the continental legal system, such a division arose in scholarly literature.[3]

By the Enlightenment period feudalism was one of the pivotal concerns of historical studies, and a consensual understanding of at least its main tenets generated meaningful scholarly debate. Even in countries where the feudal system had been moribund and was subsequently abolished, it became a target of considerable deliberation. As J. Mackrell said of France: 'when the "sleep of reason brought forth monsters" one of the first to appear was feudalism. . . . The hysterical tone of some of the writings on "feudalism" itself betrays the limits of eighteenth-century rationalism.'[4] In the nineteenth century, fear of the resurgence of feudal institutions, for example, that of the corvée, imbued scholarly accounts with a tone of neurotic anxiety.[5] According to an evocative analogy in a contemporary French dictionary, feudalism might appear to be dead but, like a vampire, still wished to gorge itself on blood.[6] A further indication of the haunting spectre of feudalism, this time in the German context, can be traced in a text that has already featured in Chapter 3: the inaugural editorial of the *Historische Zeitschrift*. As late as 1859, the editors felt compelled to stress that for them feudalism exemplified an unconscionable ideology because 'it imposed lifeless elements on progressive life'.[7]

A common denominator between authors who criticized feudalism was their reinterpretation of the concept of liberty. In the traditional standpoint, famously enshrined in Montesquieu's *De l'esprit des lois*, liberty corresponded to the rights that distinguished one person or group from others, i.e. what the modern world calls 'privilege'. In contrast, for the revolutionaries of 1789 and their adherents, liberty was conditional upon equality before the law, and consequently feudal rights represented the antithesis.[8] Adversaries of feudalism invoked humanitarianism and common sense to dissociate historical arguments from tradition. The mere fact that a harmful system had prevailed for centuries did not constitute a legitimate ground for its survival. On the contrary, the

---

[3] Pocock, *The Ancient Constitution and the Feudal Law*, 119.

[4] J. Q. C. Mackrell, *The Attack on Feudalism in Eighteenth Century France* (London, 1973), 1.

[5] Ibid., 187.   [6] Ibid., 188.

[7] Heinrich von Sybel, 'Vorwort', *Historische Zeitschrift* 1 (1859), iii.

[8] Fredric L. Cheylette, 'Feudalism', in Maryanne Cline Horowitz (ed.), *New Dictionary of the History of Ideas*, II. 829–30.

longer an unjust system had survived, the more urgent was the need to eliminate it. Humanitarian arguments appealed to freedom and equality, although inequality itself was not condemned (as it was seen as 'natural'); rather, inequality based on privilege was seen as preventing the rise of talents and thus hindering providential intentions.[9] Because private property was considered an essential precondition for the existence of every society and also for full citizenship, feudal and seigniorial privileges were also rejected on the grounds that they interfered with the rights of the holders of private property.[10] In addition, opponents of feudalism resorted to utilitarian lines of reasoning; in particular, by arguing that feudal and seigniorial 'rights' do not benefit their owners but, in reality, run counter to their interests.[11]

The prolific accounts of feudalism in the eighteenth and nineteenth centuries ushered in new perspectives in historical writing; they animated the study of social, legal and institutional aspects of history, which in turn emphasized the dependence of political institutions on social conditions. Those scholars who had the deepest impact on the formation of my historians' views, such as Eichhorn, Tocqueville, Rotteck, Guizot, Thierry, Heeren and Robertson, approached the subject from a disapproving perspective. According to Guizot, feudalism represented 'a first step out of barbarism', but it was otherwise granted little recognition, and was even characterized as politically ruinous, a 'cancerous growth' within the state.[12] Whilst portrayals of national antiquity frequently paid homage to rural freedom, opponents of feudalism buttressed their arguments by extolling urban liberties. In contrast to the Rousseauian republican rhetoric, which perceived servitude as a product of civilization and luxury, in the new 'commercial' language servitude was perceived as the product of old barbaric and warlike ages. It was assumed that political progress only became possible when, as a corollary of emerging industry and commerce, feudalism began to decline in medieval towns and consequently the inhabitants of those towns were released from servitude.[13] Accordingly, towns were imbued with qualities which rendered them different from villages not only in their physical appearance but also in moral condition, because the town-dwellers' free status was considered superior to the social organization of feudal

---

[9] Gruner, 'Political Historiography in Restoration France', 361.

[10] Mackrell, *The Attack on Feudalism*, 139.   [11] Ibid., 144–5.

[12] Stephenson, 'The Origin and Significance of Feudalism', 791 and 809.

[13] O'Brien, *Narratives of Enlightenment*, 12.

structures.[14] Thierry was hardly the only historian in this era who believed that 'our distant predecessors in our quest for political freedom were the medieval townsmen'.[15]

In this vein, historians who wanted to discredit the feudal system habitually suffused their narratives with the language of freedom, equality and the democratic spirit in the ancient period; and inequality, hierarchy and political privileges by birth at the feudal stage. It followed that the qualities exemplified by feudalism were not only construed as the direct opposites of freedom and modern society, but also as the antitheses of the desiderata of national historiography. The grand design of national history demanded antiquity, yet, feudalism was evidently not an ancient, let alone a perennial phenomenon. National historians showed eagerness to emphasize unity and continuity, but feudalism exacerbated the social division of the national community, and consequently represented discontinuity with the alleged egalitarian system of antiquity. Finally, whilst national history was deemed to profess constituents unique to the respective nation's tradition, feudalism was perceived as a genuinely foreign development, inimical to the national spirit.

In keeping with this anti-feudal stance, my protagonists' narratives revealed no affinity with the conservative-Romantic-nostalgic celebration of monarchy, hierarchy and feudal institutions. They reviled the adulation of the feudal tradition as exemplified by Walter Scott, although it is necessary to note that Scott's fascination with feudalism was based on entirely different, nostalgic premises, recognizing that feudalism was dead and beyond retrieval and accepting the inevitability of its demise.[16] Furthermore, as I shall demonstrate in the following chapter, there was a lot more to my protagonists' accounts of the medieval period (a political epoch) than their condemnation of feudalism (a legal system).[17] It is true that they perceived the foreign invasions and political turmoil associated with the influence of feudalism as phenomena that ruptured the national existence. Nevertheless, this embodied only part of their story. The medieval epoch could also host successful national dynasties, and bear witness to the expansion of the state and the advent of movements

[14] Reill, *The German Enlightenment*, 157.

[15] Thierry, 'Letters from the History of France', in Stern, *Varieties of History*, 70.

[16] R. J. Smith, *The Gothic Bequest: Medieval Institutions in British Thought 1688–1863* (Cambridge, 2002), 134.

[17] Josef Válka, 'František Palacký—historik', in Milan Myška (ed.), *Památník Palackého 1798–1968* (Ostrava, 1968), 45.

that proved crucial to national self-understanding, such as Hussitism in Bohemia. The Middle Ages were often perceived as the link between old and new eras, the locus of national identity, in which the desire for national unity emerged.[18]

CONQUEST AND COLONIZATION

'Open history wherever you will, if you find a people . . . living under a regime of servitude, you can be sure that earlier on you will find a conquest.'[19] Augustin Thierry's words represent an approach that scholars have often adopted when exploring the origins of oppression and social inequalities, the most disparaged tenets of the feudal system: they widely contended that the emergence of privileged groups was rooted in conquest. Furthermore, they habitually identified the alleged conquerors and conquered with two different ethnic stocks or races and assumed that over the centuries the original racial distinctions gradually faded away; only the division between oppressors and oppressed survived. For example, in French history these elements were traced in the ancient Franks and Gauls, through the Frankish conquest of Gaul in the early Middle Ages, which provided a conceptual framework for scholarly arguments.[20] In English historical writing, the theory of the Norman yoke, the Normans' overrunning of the Anglo-Saxons in the eleventh century, featured as the equivalent explanatory strategy for social differentiation.[21]

The idea of conquest was also of some relevance to my historians. Nonetheless, their appeal to this theme deviated from the common trajectory, which explained the source of inequalities in terms of one ethnic group's subordination of another, whilst both subsequently merged into the same nation. In contrast, my historians perceived conquest not as a conflict between two elements *within* the (future) national community, but as one between the national community and a conquering foreign nation. Such a divergence can be discerned in

---

[18] Effi Gazi, *'Scientific' National History: The Greek Case in Comparative Perspective* (Frankfurt am Main, 2000), 66.

[19] Thierry, *Dix ans d'études historiques*, 255, quoted in Shirley M. Gruner, 'Political Historiography in Restoration France', 354.

[20] Pomian, 'Franks and Gauls', 27–76.

[21] See Christopher Hill, 'The Norman Yoke', in Hill, *Puritanism and Revolution: Studies in Interpretation of the English Revolution of the 17th Century* (London, 1965), 50–122.

the incongruous interpretations of the emergence of inequalities in Polish history, as advanced by Guizot and Lelewel. In his lectures delivered on the history of Poland at the Sorbonne in 1828–9 Guizot ascribed a crucial role to the competing influence of two racially different groups, in other words, he searched for the 'Norman conquest' in Polish history.[22] Such a contention was not uncommon in Polish historiography. Especially adherents of the monarchist tradition asserted that the Sarmatian nobility represented a racially distinct entity from the Slavic peasantry. In his voluntary comment of 1829, *Réponse à des questions faites sur l'histoire ancienne de la Pologne* (which probably never reached Guizot), Lelewel fiercely disputed the French historian's point that class differences in Poland were the outcome of a conquest, and that the alleged conquerors and the conquered belonged to two ethnically distinct groups. Instead, he professed that the native nobility (*szlachta*) had vanquished the people during the course of a long historical process and not as invaders of an ethnically foreign element.[23] The denial of the foreign nature of conquest carried an important implication for national historiography, because it reasserted the common provenance of the nobility and the rest of the nation. If these two strata had been alienated, this could only have happened at a later stage. This line of argument proved crucial to my historians' efforts to support the harmonization of the interests of the various social groups in their countries. Despite their disapproval of the excesses of the nobility, they nevertheless attributed to them a pivotal role in sustaining and defending the nation's independence.

Whilst often contradictory in their accounts of the origins of social divisions, my protagonists were unanimous in their belief that the imposition of the feudal system, the result of a foreign conquest, represented an illegitimate phenomenon. Kogălniceanu ascribed the emergence of feudalism in the Romanian principalities to Hungarian and Polish influence.[24] Palacký and Lelewel diagnosed the principal trauma of medieval history in German colonizing tendencies, a process posing a hazard to national existence and ultimately responsible for

---

[22] Such interpretation was also traceable in Polish historiography. See Zygmunt J. Gasiorowski, 'The "Conquest" Theory of the Genesis of the Polish State', *Speculum* 30:4 (1955), 550–60.

[23] This was the main argument of Lelewel's essay, *Stracone obywatelstwo stanu kmiecego* (Brussels, 1846), which was later republished in his *Polska wieków średnich*, Vol. IV (Poznań, 1851), 5–25.

[24] Kogălniceanu, *Opere*, III/1. 174.

the destruction of ancient Slavic democracy. Lelewel impugned the foreign presence in Polish cities while Palacký regretfully eschewed the Germanization of towns and borderlands, even declaring that German feudalism was 'the mutual insurance company with which the stolen goods are insured'.[25] Furthermore, both Lelewel and Palacký aligned the advance of feudalism and the ensuing repression with Western Europe's conversion to Christianity; and in broader terms, with the close alliance between the Church and Emperor. They also maintained that the Slavs resisted Christianity for fear of the loss of their independence, and once it was imposed on them, the Church purged old Slavic customs and thereby smoothed the way to feudalization.[26]

Daukantas's argument stressed that those Germans who forced Christianity on the Lithuanians, the Teutonic Knights and Sword Bearers, were misusing the Christian mission in order to justify their expansion into Lithuania. Instead of teaching the pagan Lithuanians Christian love and virtue, they forced them to abandon their own religion, deprived them of their properties and did not respect them as human beings.[27] On the other hand, Horváth's identification of feudalism as foreign in origin dovetailed with the assumption that Christianity performed a fundamental role in the moral and material advancement of European civilization and that it paved the way for the early Hungarians to adopt Western European civilization.[28] Such a favourable stance needs to be assessed in the context both of Horváth's mindset and of the peculiarities of the Hungarians' history: only the foundation of the state and conversion to Christianity could guarantee their survival in the Carpathian basin.

Most historians subscribing to a version of the conquest theory nevertheless would have conceded some benefits of colonization, in particular that contact with foreigners somehow enhanced the national culture or stimulated political development. That the Norman Conquest had proved in some measure favourable to England was postulated by several historians of the Victorian era; they contended that it instituted the

---

[25] Lelewel, *Polska, dzieje a rzeczy jej*, III. 128–9; *Betrachtungen*, 65-7; Palacký, *Geschichte des Hussitenthums*, 76. For the elucidation of the general context of colonization see two essays, Jan M. Piskorski, 'Medieval "Colonization of the East" in Polish Historiography' and Josef Zemlicka, 'Die Deutschen und die deutschrechtliche Kolonisation Böhmens und Mährens im Mittelalter', both in Jan M. Piskorski (ed.), *Historiographical Approaches to Medieval Colonization of East-Central Europe* (New York, 2002), 96–106 and 107–44 respectively.

[26] Lelewel, *Dzieła*, III. 280–8 and Palacký, *Dějiny*, I. 137–40.

[27] Daukantas, *Raštai*, I. 98, quoted in Žukas, *Simonas Daukantas*, 52.

[28] *Horváth Mihály kisebb történelmi munkái*, II. 8.

capacity for ordered self-government and effective self-organization.[29] My historians, in addition to dwelling on the negative effects of colonization, occasionally acknowledged the positive consequences of contact with foreigners. Palacký admitted that, under certain conditions, German laws guaranteed greater security to the inhabitants than Czech customary law. Throughout his accounts of the history of Hungarian history and commerce, Horváth highlighted the contribution of foreign settlers to the advancement of handicrafts, trade and mining in Hungary.[30]

THE LATE ARRIVAL OF FEUDALISM AND ITS ILLEGITIMATE NATURE

While scholars may have differed in their assessment of the exact coordinates of the expansion of the feudal system throughout Europe, they generally agreed that it did not extend to every corner of the continent; the intensity of its impact varied from country to country, and some territories escaped it altogether. To that end, historians who disapproved of the feudal system eagerly appropriated this line of enquiry for their own context, asserting either that feudalism did not exhibit itself in its classical incarnation and hence did not constitute an integral part of national history, or that it never found its way to their countries. Such assertions existed even in historiographical traditions that were deemed to belong to the 'European core'; for instance, a number of English historians in the eighteenth and nineteenth centuries argued that the feudal polity represented a late occurrence which only gradually crept into their country. Additionally, they insisted that Norman feudalization did not completely extinguish the original freedom, and that not all society was organized in a feudal structure.[31]

My protagonists also believed that in their countries feudalism occurred much later than in other areas and never matured into

[29] Burrow, *A Liberal Descent*, 143–4.

[30] Jiří Štaif, 'The Image of the Other in the Nineteenth Century: Historical Scholarship in the Bohemian Lands', in Nancy M. Wingfield (ed.), *Creating the Other: Ethnic Conflict and Nationalism in The Habsburg Empire* (New York and Oxford, 2003), 88; *Horváth Mihály kisebb történelmi munkái*, II. 56.

[31] Such arguments were expounded by William Blackstone, see Paul Vinogradoff, *Villainage in England* (Oxford, 1892), 9 and by Edward Freeman, see M. De Sanctis, *Freeman and European History* (Farnborough, 1990), 31.

a full-blown system and never entirely penetrated society. Palacký's article, *Zur Geschichte der Unterthänigkeit und Leibeigenschaft in Böhmen*, initially banned for fear of providing Bohemian subjects with ideas that could be used against the authorities, (erroneously) asserts that serfdom had been imposed on Bohemia after the Hussite wars in the late fifteenth and sixteenth centuries, rather than in the thirteenth century, as contemporary scholars maintained.[32] Kogălniceanu also stresses the irrelevance of feudalism and in particular the inimical nature of serfdom in the Romanian lands, ascribing its imposition to Polish and Hungarian conquests. Lelewel purveyed the argument that feudalism in Poland never gained ground.[33] Among other sources, he availed himself of Henry Hallam's *View of the State of Europe during the Middle Ages* (1818), an eminent book which articulated the idea that fully-fledged feudalism only evolved in France, Great Britain and in some Norman-Frankish colonies, whereas Scotland, Poland and Russia escaped it altogether.[34] In Daukantas's view, the first attempt to enslave the Lithuanians was undertaken by the Teutonic Knights in the twelfth to thirteenth centuries, but the local population defended itself with the sword. Thus, feudalization was finally established by Polish rulers after the Union of Lublin of 1569, when Lithuanians became 'like a bull permanently mired in its own manure'. Yet, even on that occasion, the Lithuanians mounted strenuous resistance and therefore never fully succumbed to this foreign system.[35]

Thus, Daukantas's and Lelewel's explanations are mutually exclusive: whilst Daukantas censured the Poles for introducing feudalism to Lithuania, Lelewel professed not only that classical feudal structures did not arise in Poland but also that it was precisely due to Polish influence after the Union of Lublin that the Lithuanians were liberated from the vestiges of feudalism.[36] According to Lelewel, in Lithuania (and also in Bohemia) feudalism, serfdom and personal interdependence resulted from German colonization in the fourteenth century.[37] The discrepancy between these two scholars' standpoints exemplifies a typical

---

[32] His original intention was to publish this essay in the journal of the Bohemian Museum. But the censor would not give his consent to this, because 'it offered the Bohemian subjects a lot of harmful material which could be misused against the authorities', see Palacký's comment on this in *Gedenkblätter*, 93.

[33] Lelewel, *Polska, dzieje a rzeczy jej*, III. 120–7; *Betrachtungen*, 58–69.

[34] Kelley, *Fortunes of History*, 101.   [35] Daukantas, *Raštai*, II. 645.

[36] Lelewel, *Polska, dzieje a rzeczy jej*, III. 129; *Betrachtungen*, 66.

[37] Lelewel, *Histoire de la Lithuanie et de la Ruthénie jusqu'à leur union définitive avec la Pologne conclue à Lublin en 1549*, trans. E. Rykaczewski (Paris and Leipzig, 1861), 13.

incongruence of the argumentative strategies employed by historians representing overlapping histories: what one party perceived as a *process of colonization*, the other viewed as an *act of civilizing*.

These tropes are frequently entwined with assertions which cast further doubt on the legitimacy of feudalism. Historians saw, in the uprisings and revolts of peasants, proof that the feudal order had never penetrated their societies, for when circumstances allowed, rebels stood up against the unjust system. In this way, uprisings came to symbolize the inextinguishable spirit of ancient freedom. Horváth's marked interest in the causes and consequences of the (Dózsa) peasant uprising in 1514 in Hungary was ignited by this conviction, as was Palacký's fascination with the Hussite movement of the fifteenth century, which he construed as a democratic reaction to the feudal-foreign influences in Bohemia.[38]

Furthermore, in keeping with the assumption that the essence of national history is reflected in language, the purported absence or foreign origin of linguistic terminology associated with the feudal system was likewise invoked in order to demonstrate its extraneous nature. Daukantas detected the etymology of the Lithuanian word for corvée—*baudža*—in a Polish expression.[39] Kogălniceanu concluded that, in the Romanian language, the words that signified the various stages of serfdom were of foreign—Hungarian and Slavic—origin.[40] In the same way, Lelewel stated that the ancient Polish language remained free of feudal terminology and contained no equivalent to express the word 'aristocracy'. Furthermore, foreign words (*allodium, feudum*), in the absence of native ones, were employed in an idiosyncratic and confusing way because the concept remained so alien to the Poles.[41]

HUMANITARIANISM, COMMON SENSE AND URBAN LIBERTIES

Though not, perhaps, believing conversion to Christianity to be favourable to the national interests in the past, all my protagonists accepted the importance of leading ideals of Christianity in their own times. In line with the views of many contemporary historians, they reserved their most vehement criticism for serfdom. They believed that

---

[38] Palacký's portrayal of the Hussite movement is considered at length in the next chapter.
[39] Daukantas, *Raštai*, II. 756.   [40] Kogălniceanu, *Opere*, I. 592.
[41] Lelewel, *Polska, dzieje a rzeczy jej*, III. 123; *Betrachtungen*, 71.

this institution was wholly incompatible with the commandment 'love your neighbour as yourself'; and that it violated the ideals of Christianity by degrading social existence for the majority of the population.[42] It is noteworthy that Kogălniceanu's study *Sclăvie, vecinătate, boieresc* (On Slavery, Serfdom and Statute Labour, 1853) was initially published as a foreword to the Romanian translation of Harriet Beecher-Stowe's *Uncle Tom's Cabin*. The Romanian version appeared in 1853, one year after the publication of the original. Kogălniceanu introduced his article by making recourse to Beecher-Stowe's renowned association of slavery with sacrilege, the violation of human dignity, and ultimately the principles of Christianity.[43]

My five historians recognized that repression manifested itself in various forms throughout history and Kogălniceanu himself distinguished between slavery in the ancient world and in the contemporary Americas on the one hand, and the serfdom of the peasants in the Romanian lands on the other; the latter of which he regarded as a 'milder form' of ancient slavery. Conversely, in an intriguing comment on the worsened condition of the Hungary peasantry, following the brutal suppression of the uprising of 1514, Horváth developed an uncommon line of reasoning. After the uprising, peasants were deprived of the last remnant of their liberty, the freedom of migration, which provided them with the sole protection against oppression and abuse of power. From this Horváth concluded that the new condition of the Hungarian peasantry was to an extent even more shameful than the institution of slavery in the ancient world, because, while slaves were deprived of freedom on an individual basis, in Hungary an entire social stratum was communally robbed of liberty.[44]

In addition to highlighting the illegitimate and foreign nature of feudalism, and also its incompatibility with the principles of humanitarianism, my historians invoked common sense and utility, thereby raising further doubts about the justifying power of tradition and the allegedly ancient or perennial elements of feudalism. 'Slavery is as old as is the world,' quotes Kogălniceanu, one of its defenders. By contrast, he proclaims that, although slavery is old, it only occurred when people became able to produce more than was absolutely necessary for their survival.[45] Horváth strengthens his plea for the abolition of serfdom

---

[42] Kogălniceanu, *Opere*, I. 594.   [43] Ibid., I. 592.
[44] Horváth, *Az 1514-es pórlázadás, annak okai es következményei* (Budapest, 1986), 35.
[45] Kogălniceanu, *Opere*, I. 593.

by incorporating a Hungarian reformer's eloquent argument into his narrative. Emulating the conservative postulate that 'if (the) people have survived in the status of serfdom for eight centuries, they will survive for a few more years', the Hungarian politician stated at the diet: 'Our ancestors were pagans for centuries, but we do not condemn them for adopting Christianity. For eight centuries the peasants were compelled to live without civil rights, but it is nevertheless just to endow them with those rights.'[46]

Further appeals to common sense were characterized by demands for the revision of ancient laws, the relevance and validity of which had diminished by the nineteenth century. In pre-revolutionary France, when advocates of feudalism attempted to justify serfdom through reference to Roman law, Voltaire famously declared that Roman law on slaves was as relevant to serfdom in France as the decree relating to the Vestal Virgins.[47] Besides the issue of slavery, my protagonists' arguments addressed, first and foremost, the anachronistic tradition which, as in many other European countries, ensured the nobility's immunity from taxation in return for their defence of the country. In an article dedicated to the history of the Hungarian army, Horváth exposed the anachronistic and paradoxical nature of this ancient tradition: whilst the nobility's exemption from taxation remained in force in the nineteenth century, through the establishment of professional armies their ancient obligation had become redundant.[48]

Last but not least, the historians considered serfdom incompatible with economic development and modernization. Daukantas surmised that, after serfdom had been imposed on Lithuania, people were no longer willing to manufacture goods and conduct trade, and consequently Lithuanian trade suffered dramatically.[49] His agricultural books sought to encourage the development of local industry and help remedy that deficiency. In his accounts of economic history, Horváth named industry and commerce as the two phenomena which, second to the adoption of Christianity, contributed most substantially to the advancement of civilization, both on the European continent and in his country.[50] He asserted that the sobering impact of industry and

[46] Horváth, *Huszonöt év Magyarország történetéből*, I. 391.
[47] Mackrell, *The Attack on Feudalism*, 108.
[48] *Horváth Mihály kisebb történelmi munkái*, I. 244.
[49] A separate chapter in *Raštai*, I. 617–646, assesses the role of trade in the early days of the Lithuanians.
[50] *Horváth Mihály kisebb történelmi munkái*, II. 8–9 and 160–1.

commerce, and the material well-being which resulted from the prosperity of those activities, gradually aroused civil liberty in Hungarian towns starting in the thirteenth century.

In that way, Horváth accepted, without reservation, the idea that the role of emerging trade and commerce and the emboldening of the *tiers état* in medieval towns contributed to the dismantling of feudalism. He remained unreflective of the circumstances in Hungarian history which impeded the applicability of this argument to the Hungarian context, above all the weakness of towns and of the middle classes and predominantly foreign — mostly German — urban population. Nor did he consider another peculiarity that Hungarian towns became incorporated into the feudal system and thus could hardly represent an alternative to it. But these shortcomings have to be evaluated in light of the wish-list of contemporary liberals in the Reform Period, who sought to offer a programmatic agenda for the future and whose agenda Horváth's scholarship buttressed. To these demands belonged the evolution of a powerful middle class in Hungary, because: 'where a diligent middle class is non-existent, where the overwhelming majority of the people belong to a servant class, how can bourgeois civilization arise, how can the flowers of a nobler humanity blossom?'[51]

The young Lelewel, under the influence of Arnold Heeren, similarly postulated that, in the period of the Crusades, the growth of trade and the development of towns were principal factors in the advancement of culture and the decline of feudalism.[52] Nevertheless, his belief that Poland followed a genuinely different route from Western Europe did not allow for the appropriation of this argument for the Polish context in his later works. Instead, he linked the prosperity of towns with decay in national history. This was because, for Lelewel, towns represented foreign colonies which imported new customs alien to the character of Polish legal tradition, and were likened to the 'exotic plant' of Teutonic law. This placed national unity at a grave disadvantage and threatened the national existence.[53] Lelewel's point of departure is identical to that of Horváth: the absence of a proper middle class (*Dritter Stand*) in his country. But whilst Horváth lamented this, Lelewel disagreed with foreign scholars who detected in this phenomenon one of the reasons for the grave situation of the Polish peasantry.[54] He maintained that if

---

[51] *Horváth Mihály kisebb történelmi munkái*, I. 57.   [52] Lelewel, *Dzieła*, III. 338–40.

[53] Lelewel, *Polska, dzieje a rzeczy jej*, III. 88–9; *Betrachtungen*, 36.

[54] Lelewel, *Polska, dzieje a rzeczy jej*, III. 434; *Betrachtungen*, 319.

a comparison was to be ever meaningful, Poland should be juxtaposed with ancient Rome and Athens. In that context he asked: 'has someone ever put forward the argument that in Rome and Athens the existence of a middle class could have been beneficial for the plebeians and for the slaves?'[55]

FEUDAL INSTITUTIONS AS NATIONAL INSTITUTIONS

The generally anti-feudal tone of liberal historiography was obviously paralleled with a critical stance towards the stratum who enjoyed privileges within that system. By asserting that the origins of the nobility's privileges lay in usurpation, historians questioned their legitimacy. Representatives of the nobility were condemned for their egoism, their apathy about their country's welfare and their willingness to capitulate to foreign powers. The historians also lamented the nobility's resistance to come to terms with the 'spirit of the age', their reluctance to understand the necessity of social consensus and to share their anachronistic privileges with other people. When a Hungarian nobleman, in a letter addressed to Horváth, disapproved of the Hungarian scholar's critical stance towards the glorious ancestors, Horváth reminded him of the humanitarian implication of the nobility's 'sacrifice' with the following words: 'In order to achieve its intended purpose, historical writing must rise up from the small-minded views of nationality (of the noble *natio*) to the condition of humanity.'[56] But such views were not always unanimous. In particular, as we shall see, Palacký's amiable relations with Bohemian and Hungarian aristocrats, whose patronage he enjoyed, resulted in a more sympathetic attitude than that of his colleagues. He remained convinced that the nobility and the intelligentsia were best qualified for political leadership, and demanded the abolition of feudal rights, and that the nobility cease to be 'feudal' and become more 'national' in character.[57]

Furthermore, my historians tended to distinguish between aristocracy and the lesser nobility, and their criticism was more frequently levelled at the former group. Lelewel held the aristocracy to some extent responsible for the decline of Poland, whilst Palacký blamed them for

---

[55] Lelewel, *Polska, dzieje a rzeczy jej*, III. 435; *Betrachtungen*, 321.
[56] Horváth, *Polgárosodás, liberalizmus, függetlenségi harc*, 24.   [57] Zacek, *Palacký*, 24.

adopting German habits, contributing to the cementation of feudal structures and ultimately the defeat at White Mountain in 1620 which resulted in the incorporation of the Bohemian lands into the Habsburg Empire. On the other hand, my historians endowed the lesser nobility with virtues which in 'Western' liberal historiographies were ascribed to the *tiers état*. In particular, they perceived this class as crucial for sustaining national identity. For example, for Lelewel, the *szlachta* was the inheritor and transmitter of the original democratic values of the ancient *gminowładztwo* to the Commonwealth (*Rzeczpospolita*). Besides, the glorious moments of national history were often associated with the accomplishments of the representatives of the upper classes.

The same twofold attitude informed my protagonists' approach to the historical institutions of the nobility, the diets and the constitutions. On the one hand, the difference between constitutional and effectual liberty was recognized and these institutions were seen as crucial to the nobility in perpetuating their privileges. On the other, they were deemed indispensable to the maintenance of national independence and identity. Horváth's and Lelewel's narratives, ascribing crucial roles to these institutions, resembled a persistent and widespread trope in historiography, appealing to the 'ancient constitution'. The rationale behind such myth was to seek to prove that the ancient and immemorial nature of the constitution prevented the king from altering or annulling it.[58] In early modern French tradition, Hotman's *Francogallia* asserted the antiquity of the assembly of the nation; Coke, in England, repeated the argument for the parliament and common law; in Sicily, the antiquity of baronial privilege and the *parlamento* was emphasized; in the Netherlands, that of the sovereign and independent Dutch towns; in Sweden that of the nobles in their *riksrad*. By 1600 or thereabouts there was hardly any constitutional movement without its accompanying historical myth.[59] In the eighteenth century, the argument lost its potency in several historiographical traditions, because its aristocratic biases were irreconcilable with the tenets of modern liberalism.[60] However, as we shall see, in my historians' contexts, it proved possible to overcome that difficulty and integrate the originally aristocratic tradition into the liberal national debate.

---

[58] Pocock, *The Ancient Constitution and the Feudal Law*, 16–17.   [59] Ibid., 16.

[60] See Colin Kidd's argument in the British context, 'The Ideological Significance of Robertson's History of Scotland', 126.

The belief in the vital importance of these institutions naturally contributed to my historians' keen interest in the study of constitutions and diets and, in broader terms, legal history. Lelewel found the ultimate expression of Polish national spirit in the constitution; Horváth in the diets. In the *Historyka*, Lelewel declared that the examination of constitutions was an important task of the historian, as it contributed to a better understanding of a society's nature.[61] His keen interest in constitutional history manifested itself in the study *Trzy konstytucje polskie* (Three Constitutions of Poland), which analysed the constitutions of (i) the Commonwealth, (ii) the small, autonomous Duchy created by Napoleon in 1806 and (iii) the Polish Kingdom established by the Congress of Vienna in 1815, and paid attention to the social as well as political implications of these three documents.[62]

Horváth not only assigned a prominent role to the Hungarian Diet and the local self-governments in national history, but also maintained that the local county gatherings were unique in Europe in that their sphere of authority surpassed their English, German, French and Spanish counterparts. These were real decision-making bodies, not just forums for expressing opinion.[63] As for the Diet, Horváth declared that 'no part of our nation's history is as interesting and instructive as the history of our diets. The diets are the arteries of national life, they mirror the standards of civilization, they indicate the level of social conditions'.[64] In the constitution, Horváth detected the guarding bastion of the country's independence. He argued that it resisted foreign influences and maintained its original nature, which meant that in all periods the Hungarian constitution remained hostile to the system of vassalage.[65]

CREATING MODERN SOCIETY: THE EMANCIPATION OF THE PEASANTRY

The five historians insisted that a fundamental transformation of their societies was necessary in order to cast off the 'shackles' of feudalism and modernize their countries. There was also agreement about the most

---

[61] Lelewel, *Dzieła*, II. 191. [62] Ibid., VIII. 467–539.
[63] Horváth, *Huszonöt év*, II. 3–4.
[64] *Horváth Mihály kisebb történelmi munkái*, I. 377.
[65] Horváth, *A magyarok története rövid előadásban*, 6th edn. (Budapest, 1887), 274.

urgent aspect of that change; as Kogălniceanu put it, 'the improvement of the situation of the peasantry means improving the foundations of our national existence'.[66] Such demands were justified by appeals to both historical precedence and common sense. The emphasis on the freedom of the entire population in the ancient period of national history carried the assumption that emancipation epitomized a return to an appropriate condition and not a genuinely novel occurrence. But Kogălniceanu also had recourse to utilitarian grounds when warning his contemporaries that, without being offered any motivation to turn into loyal citizens, peasants would become foreigners in their own country, unwilling to defend their ancient land against invasion. In their desperation, Kogălniceanu added, they would even engage in 'some terrible form of opposition'.[67] Lelewel argued along similar lines, resorting to humanitarianism as well as to national interests, when pointing out that the restoration of Polish independence was doomed to failure if no adequate remedy was to be found for the problems of the peasantry, because they constituted more than half of the population, and thus the core of the nation. He supported enfranchisement because 'the future fate of Poland lies not in diplomacy and the assistance of governments but in insurrection and the emancipation of the peoples'.[68]

With this conviction, my protagonists undertook pioneering research into the history of the peasantry, genuinely believing that those responsible for the reforms would benefit from their historical insights. Horváth asserted that, 'in the history of mankind there hardly exists a more important issue than the relationship between the different social strata',[69] This observation motivated him to study the legal situation of the Hungarian peasantry in meticulous detail. Kogălniceanu's dedication to the problem gained exposure in scholarly articles, and his parliamentary speeches on the subject likewise benefited from this thorough knowledge of the historical context. Lelewel's most mature work, *Uwagi nad dziejami Polski i ludu jej* (Obvservations on the History of Poland and its People), offered the first social history of Poland, with his narrative primarily focusing on the conditions of the Polish peasantry. Given this sympathetic attitude, it is not surprising that

---

[66] Kogălniceanu, *Opere*, III/I. 162.   [67] Ibid, III/I. 194.

[68] Lelewel, *Dzieła*, Vol. VIII (Warsaw, 1961), 166, quoted in John D. Stanley, 'Joachim Lelewel', 64. For more on Lelewel's attitude towards the peasantry see Elżbieta Cesarz, *Chłopi w polskiej myśli historycznej doby porozbiorowej 1795–1864* (Rzeszów, 1999), 116–33, 159–61.

[69] Horváth, *Polgárosodás, liberalizmus, függetlenségi harc*, 42.

the historians expressed appreciation towards those rulers who showed consideration for the plight of the lower classes. To that end, both Palacký and Horváth wrote highly of Maria Theresa's and Joseph II's reform incentives.[70]

Although the chief and immediate concern of liberal historians in East-Central Europe remained the abolition of serfdom, this represented only the first stage of the desired modernization. Other requisites included equality before the law through the termination of the feudal justice system, granting of property rights to peasants as well as the right of representation, the promotion of trade and commerce, and secularization. At the same time, it was pointed out that people could only take advantage of those proposed entitlements if they obtained education, enabling them to become useful citizens. It is true that, by 1848, with the exception of Romania, serfdom was *de jure* abolished in my historians' countries, but regional variations remained considerable and the new laws were often not enforced.[71] Furthermore, emancipation only addressed personal freedom and equality before the law and did not deal with property ownership. To that end, it was not so much the abolition of serfdom which animated historical analysis, as its necessity was taken for granted, but the regulation of the condition of the peasantry after emancipation. In particular, a serious dilemma revolved around the question of whether they should receive ownership of the land which they had cultivated for centuries and, if that happened, what compensation, if any, should be offered to the land-owning classes for relinquishing their estates.

Horváth addressed the conditions of the peasantry in Hungary in three studies, which covered the period from the Turkish occupation of the country in the fifteenth century until the rule of Joseph II in the late eighteenth century.[72] Another major article scrutinized the causes and consequences of the Hungarian peasant uprising of 1514. Maintaining that people deprived of their rights were not in a position to form a community, Horváth's stated mission was to advocate the inclusion of non-privileged classes into the political nation. Accordingly, his study advocated the restoration of the principle of harmony between rights

---

[70] Palacký, *Gedenkblätter*, 273 and 292; *Horváth Mihály kisebb történelmi munkái*, II. 120, 220–1, 255.

[71] For a regional overview see Emil Niederhauser, *The Emancipation of the Serfs in Eastern Europe*, trans. Paul Body (Boulder, 2004).

[72] 'Vázlatok a magyar népiség történetéből', in *Horváth Mihály kisebb történelmi munkái*, III. 389–432.

and obligations in society and stipulated a sympathetic attitude to the peasants' problems: 'Let us offer to this stratum which carries a heavy burden every compensation for the sufferings of the past, all the more so because the welfare of the country, our industry and commerce is dependent on them.'[73]

Kogălniceanu's accounts of the vicissitudes of unprivileged classes were clear indicators of his social sensitivity. Given his active engagement with agrarian reform in Romania, the contemporary resonances of his research are hardly surprising. He firmly believed that emancipation in itself would only create millions of homeless people and therefore it ought only to be undertaken by granting the lands to the people who had cultivated them.[74] Consequently, crucial to this analysis was the arrangement of the land reform which was to be undertaken after the peasants had been freed from feudal burdens. Kogălniceanu also contemplated the means of compensation that was to be offered to the land-owners for the transfer of the land to the peasants. He highlighted the peculiarities of land ownership in the Romanian territories which were to be taken into account by the executors of the reform, in particular that the conditions of private property originated in Slavic and not Western European models. Kogălniceanu partook in the creation and enactment of the Rural Law of 1864, which attempted a compromise, a partial transfer of ownership to the peasants, resulting in the coexistence of great estates with small properties.[75]

The Romanian scholar's interest in the history of Gypsies was sparked in his youth. Whilst a student at the University of Berlin, he wrote an essay on the origins, language and legal condition of the Gypsies, allegedly upon the encouragement of Wilhelm von Humboldt, to whom he was introduced in the salons of Savigny.[76] He also combined scholarly interest with political action and played an instrumental role in the abolition of the slavery of the Gypsies who, bound to the landowner and not to the land, were possessions of their masters. Although liberated in 1856, they were excluded from the Rural Law of 1864. Towards the end of his life, in a discourse which commemorated the twenty-fifth anniversary of the foundation of the Romanian Academy, *Dezrobirea ţiganilor, ştergerea privilegiilor boiereşti, emanciparea ţăranilor* (The Liberation of the Gypsies, the Abolition of Boyar Privileges and

[73] Horváth, *Polgárosodás, liberalizmus, függetlenségi harc*, 30.
[74] Kogălniceanu, *Opere*, III/I. 173.   [75] Boia, *History and Myth*, 35.
[76] Kogălniceanu, *Opere*, I. 606.

the Emancipation of the Peasantry), Kogălniceanu repeatedly pointed to the grave situation of the Gypsies and expressed his conviction that, as musicians, tradesmen, etc., they could provide a useful service to society.[77]

Education was deemed to be as crucial to improved living standards among the peasantry as legal regulations. In addition to Lelewel's, Horváth's and Palacký's national histories and Daukantas's textbooks which doubled as schoolbooks, another remarkable and related achievement included Horvath's enthusiastic backing of the establishment of one of Hungary's first kindergartens in the town where he served as a parish priest in 1841.[78] Daukantas's booklets on bee-keeping, and on the growing of tobacco and hops, were intended to promote local industry. As we have seen, Kogălniceanu was engaged in editorial activities on an entrepreneurial basis and edited *Calendar pentru Poporul Românesc* (Almanac for the Romanian People), a pragmatic magazine aimed at the local population. Among other things, he contributed to the magazine with an article on alcoholism. Quoting Cassius from Shakespeare's play *Othello*, he warns against the dire consequences of excessive alcohol consumption: 'every inordinate cup is unblessed and the ingredient is a devil'.[79] As Chapter 5 revealed, his article on pauperism, whilst maintaining that every able person had a duty to work in society, promoted the establishment of special institutions to support orphans as well as infirm and elderly people.

LIBERALISM VERSUS DEMOCRACY

Romantic historiography, especially before 1848, was intimately associated with (moderately) liberal aspirations and values, primarily with the conviction that inequality, hierarchy and political privileges by birth violated the principles of liberal constitutionalism. In post-revolutionary France, historians supported the intentions of the liberal bourgeoisie to re-establish French and European politics on a national, rather than dynastic basis.[80] British scholars' narratives reinforced the progressive constitutional and electoral reform of the nineteenth century which culminated in the extension of the franchise in 1832 and 1867.[81] Even

---

[77] Ibid., I. 612.   [78] Márki, *Horváth Mihály*, 49.
[79] Kogălniceanu, *Opere*, I. 562.   [80] Gossman, *Between History and Literature*, 153.
[81] Berger, 'Apologies for the Nation State', 7.

several German historians of the era defined themselves as liberals, although the absence of a unified German state meant that their conception of liberty was different from that of the French and British liberals.[82] For classical liberals, the notion of political participation was secondary to legal and economic aims such as equality before the law and the free use of private property.[83] This is because they disapproved of democracy in the form of universal or manhood suffrage with immediate effect, although they foresaw it as an acceptable development in the distant future.[84] Liberals of the era usually defined themselves in opposition to *both* the aristocracy and the lower classes, to feudalism and socialism; all afraid of despotism exercised either from above or from below.[85] Even Jules Michelet, who considered himself a democrat, identified with the cause of the peasantry and the artisans of pre-industrial France and not with the modern urban proletariat, whom he regarded with trepidation.[86]

My historians' aspirations were genuinely indebted to the European tradition of liberalism; nevertheless it would be a mistake to construe their liberalism as homogeneous landscape. Some reservations are also necessary in assessing their ideological horizons, as the term 'liberalism' may not be entirely applicable, in its classical meaning, to their contexts. This is because political agendas in East-Central Europe followed some distinct trajectories, as manifested in the special emphasis on modernization and in the significance of debates on centralization versus autonomy, and, in more general terms, in the relationship of non-dominant nations to the dominant empire.[87] Furthermore, it is also necessary to note that some aspects of Palacký's and Kogălniceanu's political thought revealed affinities with conservative ideals.

All my historians believed that the world was progressing inevitably towards the growth of liberty. Kogălniceanu eloquently voiced his liberal convictions in his *Profesie de credință* (Political Credo) of 1860, which also resonated with the other historians' views.[88] In this short

---

[82] Iggers, *The German Conception of History*, 92–3.

[83] Alan S. Kagan, *Aristocratic Liberalism: The Social and Political Thought of Jacob Burchhardt, John Stuart Mill, and Alexis de Tocqueville* (New Brunswick and London, 2001), 141.

[84] Ibid., 140.   [85] Ibid., 142.

[86] Gossman, *Between History and Literature*, 157.

[87] For an overview of the conceptual problems of liberalism in East-Central Europe see Maciej Janowski, 'Kozy i jiesoty', *Roczniki Dziejów: Społeczych i Gospodarczych* 56–67 (1996–7), 69–92.

[88] Kogălniceanu, *Opere*, I. 368–70.

manifesto, the Romanian historian listed his principles in fourteen points, the first of which addressed the unification of the Romanian principalities. The rest included, among other things, the emancipation of serfs, the reform of the electoral system, a constitutional representative government, as Kogălniceanu put it 'representative in the strictest and widest sense'. Furthermore, the Credo included classical liberal demands, such as the freedom of expression and press, a fair tax system, the support of local self-government, and the improvement of education. Secularization was stipulated by Kogălniceanu, as well as the other scholars, because the separation of Church and State constituted one of the prerequisites of de-feudalization and modernization.

Episodes from the national past were invoked to support the case for this process: Lelewel advanced the claim that the prosperity of the Polish-Lithuanian Commonwealth lay in its neutrality in religious issues and the distinction between matters of religion and those of politics and citizenship.[89] As the next chapter will reveal, Palacký postulated that the moderate Hussite king, Jiří of Poděbrady (1458–71), championed the principle of modern state sovereignty, in the face of medieval papal intervention into the affairs of the state. Horváth promoted the emancipation of non-Catholic denominations in Hungary as well as the introduction of civic marriage. His biographical sketch on Roger Williams, *Williams Roger, „a szabad egyház a szabad államban" elv megteremtője, s megtestesítője* (Roger Williams, the Initiator and Representative of the 'Free Church in a Free State' Principle') saw in Roger Williams, the creator of the principle of having a 'free church in a free state', a model he found suitable for the regulation of the relationship between the Church and State in Hungary. Horváth's concern was put to a practical test whilst serving as Minister of Religion and Education during the revolution of 1848. His ecclesiastical politics corresponded to the principle that he advocated: he denounced the existence of a state religion in Hungary and tried to promote proportional representation of various denominations.

Palacký thought of himself as a liberal and asserted that inequality, hierarchy and political privileges by birth were against liberal constitutionalism and against the democratic spirit of the Slavs. At the same time, he was no democrat. Czech, as well as foreign radicals, including Karl

---

[89] Lelewel, *Polska, dzieje a rzeczy jej*, III. 308; *Betrachtungen*, 214.

Marx, often lambasted him for his attitude, and he became stigmatized as a supporter of conservative forces.[90] Nevertheless, his aversion to revolution, socialism, communism and popular democracy was very much along the lines of classical liberalism. In his essay *O demokratii* (On Democracy, 1864) Palacký commented ironically on the extremely fashionable nature of that word in his time, and made recourse to Plato, according to whom democracy was not necessarily identical to the 'rule of the people', but rather the rule of 'enlightened people'.[91] Like 'classical' liberals of the age, Palacký maintained that not everyone was endowed with the same talents by nature, and therefore the complete equality of the people represented a utopia. He made a clear distinction between natural rights and political rights. In that context, Palacký noted that the emancipation of peasants in 1848 restored their natural rights which they had enjoyed in the early times, but of which they were subsequently deprived by force. On the other hand, voting represented a political right, a 'public office', and was limited to those competent enough to make meaningful use of it.[92]

Although Daukantas's democratic tendencies are evident, he remained absent from political life and his narrative did not employ a modern political vocabulary. Horváth defines 'democratic freedom' as the guiding principle of the age, and in his article *A demokrácia kifejlése korunkban* (The Development of Democracy in Our Age, 1841) introduces the Hungarian reading public to the main premises of Tocqueville's *Democracy in America*. He expresses the conviction that Tocqueville's main principle, that society was progressing towards (greater) equality, was applicable to Hungary. In his *Huszonöt Év* (Twenty-Five Years), he comments on the counterproductive nature of the government's strategy in the 1830s, which withheld concessions from the peasantry for fear of the 'nightmare of democracy' in the country, an attitude which ultimately proved untenable because it became impossible to act against the direction of the *Zeitgeist*.[93]

Kogălniceanu's political credo was indebted to the agenda of the Prussian politician Count Hardenberg (1750–1822), 'democratic principles in a monarchic government'. Although he supported the extension of political participation, similarly to Palacký, he subscribed to the maxim

---

[90] Otakar Odložilík, 'A Czech Plan for a Danubian Federation', *Journal of Central European Affairs* 1:3 (1941), 259–60.

[91] Palacký, *Spisy drobné*, I. 190.

[92] Palacký, *Politisches Vermächtnis*, 20; *Poslední mé slovo*, 49.

[93] Horváth, *Huszonöt év*, II. 66.

according to which 'the gun and the vote are powerful weapons': if used unwisely, they can pose a danger to society.[94] As the Romanian scholar's life and political career extended into the 1870s and 1880s, he lived to see the reform of the electoral system in his country, whereby the peasants were granted the right of political participation, and a constitutional representative government was created. Whilst democracy and liberalism became easier to reconcile towards the late nineteenth century, the peaceful coexistence of liberalism and nationalism proved more and more difficult. In this context, 1848 marked a watershed in the history of European liberalism. The demise of classical liberal thought, and the increased emphasis on collective, rather than individual values, can be observed in the shift which marked Kogălniceanu's way of thinking evident in his declared support for prioritizing national principles over liberal ones during the 1880s, as the next chapter will show.

WAYS OF CHANGE: REFORM VERSUS REVOLUTION

In addition to the requisites of modernization, scholars also debated the forms and strategies in which those changes were to be achieved. In that context, representatives of 'classical' liberalism had to confront with the problem of creating a society different from the one in which they lived, but not through revolutionary means.[95] For English Whig historians, the distinctive aspect of the Glorious Revolution of 1688, the zenith of a libertarian parliamentary tradition stretching back to the Magna Carta, was its non-revolutionary nature. Chartism and the 1848 European revolutions taught a lesson to English scholars, who concluded that reform at the right time could prevent a revolution and therefore promote national stability.[96] At the other end of the scale, for French historians, the vantage point was understandably the French Revolution, which consciously rejected the past and intended to remove any associations with it through recasting social, political and economic

---

[94] Diana Mishkova, 'The Interesting Anomaly of Balkan Nationalism', in Zoltán Iván Dénes (ed.), *Liberty and the Search for National Identity: Liberal Nationalisms and the Legacy of Empires* (Budapest and New York, 2006), 451–2.

[95] Kagan, *Aristocratic Liberalism*, 142.

[96] John Burrow, Stefan Collini and Donald Winch, *That Noble Science of Politics* (Cambridge, 1984), 196–7.

conditions.[97] Nevertheless, in the nineteenth century, the benefit of hindsight enabled French historians of the liberal school to apprehend that, like all upheavals, the French Revolution had precursors. They also acknowledged that the revolutions had been too indiscriminate in their denunciation of the past. My historians were usually appreciative of the achievements, if not necessarily the methods, of the French Revolution. Kogălniceanu was more approving of the Girondist than the Jacobin tradition. In an article inspired by Wachsmuth, *Európa belviszonyai a francia forradalom idejétől fogva* (Europe's Internal Conditions from the French Revolution Onwards, 1839), Horváth gave a very positive assessment of the fundamental changes which the revolution brought about. His overall judgement was that the revolution had given a new direction to the human spirit.[98]

Given that historical writing and political participation were inextricably linked for my historians, their own participation in revolutions as an influence on their views cannot be ignored. Importantly, none of them initiated these movements; rather, they found themselves in the midst of revolutionary upheavals. In his youth, Palacký concluded in his diary that revolutions were horrific developments in the life of humanity, but they were a 'regenerative necessity' because they introduced novel and powerful elements into nature as well as society. Moreover, Palacký argued that revolutions expressed the people's will and nations were entitled to break out of their chains by force if the authorities did not understand the *Zeitgeist*.[99] On the other hand, Palacký came to loathe revolutions in his later years, especially as he associated them with socialism and anarchy. The historian's abhorrence of unlawful action triggered a compromising episode of his life: the betrayal to the authorities of a planned student-led uprising in Prague in May 1849. The young Palacký's article on the Polish revolutionary hero Kościuszko already foreshadowed his future attitude to abrupt change: he praised the Polish hero as a man of temperate ideas, who only liked true liberty, believed in law and order, and 'detested anarchist radicalism as much as aristocratic presumption and despotic violence'.[100]

Horváth and Kogălniceanu emphasized the necessity of striking a balance between the content and the form of changes. This was

---

[97] Vinogradoff, *Villainage in England*, 10.
[98] The article can be found in *Horváth Mihály kisebb történelmi munkái*, II. 475–91. A similar statement is made in Horváth, *Magyarország története*, VII. 466.
[99] Palacký, *Korrespondence a zápisky*, I. 58.   [100] Palacký, *Spisy drobné*, II. 5.

a crucial issue for my protagonists, because they often found that, in relation to Kogălniceanu's assessment of the grave situation of Romanian Gypsies, the requisite changes would be so intense that they would normally qualify as revolutionary.[101] Kogălniceanu finds the ideal way in Hardenberg's reforms and quotes the memoirs of the Prussian politician: 'Lucky is the state which can follow universal developments without the need for violent actions.'[102] Therefore, the revolution should ideally be initiated by the wisdom of the government and not by major convulsions. Moreover, Kogălniceanu warns opponents of the reform that radical solutions were always born when the necessary changes were not implemented in time. Arguing for the necessity of giving lands to the emancipated peasants, he refers to Odilon Barrot, the conservative minister who claimed that 'Communist and subversive ideas' were born in and spread nowhere quicker than in countries where the peasantry and workers were poverty-stricken or live in colonial oppression.[103] Likewise, Horváth considers the brutal suppression of revolutionary principles as an insane method of prevention, as prohibition only promoted revolutionary ideals by introducing them to the wider public.[104]

Lelewel represents something of an anomaly among my historians because the discrepancy between the realities in his country and the desires of Polish patriots could only be overcome by radical change. Hence his conviction that the restoration of the partitioned Poland—the creation of a free, independent country where people enjoy legal equality—necessitated a revolution or uprising.[105] He also emphasized that the success of such uprising depended on the regulation of the conditions of the peasantry. Nevertheless, this stance did not render Lelewel a radical in the Polish political arena; indeed, he represented the most moderate Left and was often accused of being a 'man of palliatives'.[106]

CONCLUSION

Scholarly deliberations on feudalism emerged from my historians' firm conviction of the need to eliminate what they perceived as an unjust

---

[101] Kogălniceanu, *Opere*, I. 611.   [102] Ibid., I. 607.
[103] Kogălniceanu, *Opere*, III/I. 194.   [104] Horváth, *Huszonöt év*, I. 81.
[105] Lelewel, *Dzieła*, VIII. 114–15; *Geschichte Polens*, 481–2.
[106] Walicki, *Philosophy and Romantic Nationalism*, 34–5.

and impractical system. They sought to distance feudalism from the heart of the national past: it was seen as an illegitimate and abortive development; a result of foreign conquest which never took root in their countries. Inimical to the national spirit, colonization disrupted the coherence and continuity of national history, and, by triggering the emergence of social inequalities, also disturbed unity. In short, feudality was defined in terms of the negation of the essence of national history. Just as the theme of 'rural freedom' in the ancient history of the nation corresponded to the antithesis of the feudal system, the modern, urban version of liberties was also considered incompatible with, and socially and morally superior to, the feudal era.[107] The five scholars were at slight variance in their preferences for the new political landscape, but on the whole they advocated a society in which the anachronistic remnants of feudalism were abolished, political participation was no longer based on privileges and, if not universal, was extended to a wider range of the population. Furthermore, in their ideal society, which their historical accounts underpinned, political rights and obligations were to be in parity.

Evaluating the legacy of my protagonists' arguments in both a broad context and a contemporary setting reveals that many of their observations are in keeping with current perspectives on feudalism. Classical definitions, associated primarily with fiefs and vassalage (such as those by François-Louis Ganshof and Marc Bloch) have been discredited as anachronistic constructs and it has been pointed out that the label 'feudalism' itself imparted a false sense of unity to a concept employed to describe the most varied conditions.[108] The document which was earlier seen as the quintessential manifestation of the feudal system, the *Libri Feudorum*, is no longer believed to represent the state of European society as a whole. In a book which marked a watershed in the study of feudalism, Susan Reynolds has concluded that by conflating a variety of experiences, historians ended up creating a feudal world which was, in fact, non-existent, or which at best applied only to parts of France for short periods.[109]

---

[107] Gossman, *Between History and Literature*, 106.

[108] F. L. Ganshof, *Feudalism*, trans. Philip Grierson (New York, 1964); Marc Bloch, *Feudal Society: The Growth of Ties and Dependences* (Chicago, 1964). Their theses were criticized in E. A. R. Brown, 'The Tyranny of a Construct: Feudalism and Historians of Medieval Europe', *American Historical Review* 79 (1974), 1063–88.

[109] This is the main thesis of Susan Reynolds in *Fiefs and Vassals: The Medieval Evidence Reinterpreted* (New York and Oxford, 1994).

As for the manifestations of feudalism in East-Central Europe, scholars' approaches are informed by analogous attitudes. Sławomir Gawlas has argued that in Poland and East-Central Europe feudalism represented a 'developmental anomaly', a phenomenon emerging from the accelerated transition and modernization which was imposed on society from above as a corollary of German colonization.[110] Another formulation of this thesis in the Polish context is that feudalism only existed for a short time in the fourteenth and fifteenth centuries and even then 'as an influence and not a system'.[111] Thus, in light of contemporary evidence, my historians' overall verdict about the inimical nature of feudalism in their countries, while exaggerated, was not completely fictional. Whilst they negated this system's relevance for their national histories, in the 'golden age', the theme of the next chapter, they saw the quintessential manifestation of the national spirit.

---

[110] Sławomir Gawlas 'Die Probleme des Lehnswesens und des Feudalismus aus polnischer Sicht', in Michael Borgolte (ed.), *Das europäische Mittelalter im Spannungsbogen des Vergleiches* (Berlin, 2001), 97–123.

[111] Norman Davies, *God's Playground*, 2 vols. (Oxford, 1981), I. 214.

8

The Golden Age

THE EVOLUTION OF MASTER NARRATIVES

The nineteenth century witnessed the crystallization of grand schemes in national history. Out of various and often competing versions, master narratives gradually emerged and became canonized as the 'valid' interpretations of the past. Historians envisaged their nation's history as a continuum, in which conflict and reconciliation, crisis and triumph; glorious and tragic epochs alternated with each other. Even if those monumental histories remained unfinished, their narrative typically unfolded, in a teleological way, towards an ultimate goal, often encompassing national independence, liberation from foreign powers or simply prosperity, civilization and 'progress'. Within that overall scheme, the zenith of the national past, the point at which quintessential national virtues were most clearly manifest, occupied a privileged place. Like the portrayals of national antiquity, representations of the golden era were wishful in nature and resonated with contemporary concerns.

Greek and Italian historians eagerly plundered the legacy of ancient civilizations. The Romantic period also saw the rehabilitation of the Middle Ages, an era generally treated with contempt by Enlightenment scholars, because of its perceived association with superstition and crude barbarian customs. Beneath the surface of the reviled feudal system and foreign occupation, historians detected noble strivings for liberty. A further reason for focusing on this previously neglected epoch lay in its capacity to reinforce arguments about the continuous nature of national history. One of the simplest and most effective schemes of periodization was comprised of ancient, medieval and modern epochs. Even the legacy of less tangible continuities could be exploited in this way; for example, the Holy Roman Empire offered a potential blueprint for a future German state, whilst proponents of Italian unification evoked the medieval Italian city-states as paradigms. Furthermore, as has been demonstrated in earlier chapters, aspects of continuity were detected not just in the history of the state and political institutions but also in language and folklore.

Due to their personal involvement in the state-building process, historians contributed to the creation of the national territory, the anticipation and validation of national borders, as well as to the justification of subsequent border changes. Representations of the Golden Age were also employed, particularly in those historiographies that sought to redress the status quo, in order to articulate the geographical dimensions of the (desired) state. Thus, the epoch in which the nation reached its territorial peak was almost invariably cast as the most triumphant period of national history. Historical narratives characteristically echoed the homogenizing and centralizing propensities of the age, by providing historical validation for the unification of provinces that were deemed to belong to the national territory. The unique traits of the nation's past could be found in outstanding heroes, glorious battles, the ancient constitution and unparalleled ideological orientations, such as an unmatched striving for liberty. In addition to traditional figures—rulers, saints and great warriors—a new mould of unconventional heroes emerged on the scene; peasant leaders and heretics featured among them. Uniqueness could also involve a religious dimension, illustrated by the British representation of themselves as a non-sectarian Protestant country, whilst Catholicism constituted an indispensable tenet of Spanish national historiography.

The counterpoint to those glorious eras was typically identified with a rupture in continuity and unity, especially as a corollary of foreign domination. As the previous chapter has shown, feudalization was typically perceived in such terms. Although occasionally these episodes were glossed over or neutralized, disturbances were in fact necessary in order to provide the 'rhythm' of the narrative, by incurring a tension between prosperous eras and times of adversity. Even traumatic events reflected wishful tendencies: causes of failure were often seen as synonymous with the absence of the desired attributes of the national past. In that context nineteenth-century German historians directly evoked the contemporary German situation to argue that ancient Greece deserved its fall due to a lack of unity.[1] Although subsequent

---

[1] Arnaldo Momigliano, 'J. A. Droysen between Greeks and Jews', *History and Theory* 9 (1970).

generations revised or even refuted these grand schemes by emphasizing other aspects, the legacy of the Romantic era has lasted until the present day.

VIRTUE IN THE FOREST: PAGAN LITHUANIA

Daukantas's narrative extends from ancient times to 1569, the year which marks the Union of the Lithuanian Grand Duchy with the Kingdom of Poland, and consequently the end of his nation's history as an independent entity. As has been previously explained, his postulate of antiquity and uniqueness was based on the association between Lithuanian and the Indo-European language family, and the assertion that Lithuanian was the most archaic of all living Indo-European languages, bearing the closest resemblance to Sanskrit. Daukantas's account dedicates special attention to the epoch prior to the adoption of Christianity in the late fourteenth century. In his portrayal of everyday life, of the religion and customs of early Lithuanians, he extensively avails himself of folklore—the songs, tales and proverbs which he amassed during visits to the countryside.[2] His writings also invoke classical precedents, abounding in allusions to Tacitus, Pliny, Ptolemy and Herodotus. In addition, his frequent use of symbols, metaphors and other literary devices betrays a large debt to the humanist tradition, an influence which probably owed as much to the intellectual climate of the University of Vilna as to his predilections. The extensive pagan heritage which earned Lithuanians the nickname 'Saracens of the North' inspired my protagonist to draw parallels between the exploits of early Lithuanians and those of ancient Greeks and Romans. This type of analogy is a common feature of national historiographies, as writers eagerly appropriate the classical heritage to enhance their own nation's prestige. Daukantas was particularly keen to emphasize the compatibility of paganism and virtue: 'Readers may disapprove of my reverence towards the Lithuanians, whilst I denounce the immorality and aggression of Christians. Yet, if the virtue of pagan Romans and Greeks is admired by the Christian world to this day, why should the honourable Lithuanians not be venerated?'[3]

---

[2] Daukantas, *Žemaičių tautosaka*, 2 vols. (Vilnius, 1984–5).
[3] Daukantas, *Raštai*, I. 39.

Daukantas's text is imbued with republican overtones, as exemplified by the importance which he attributes to *virtue* and *knowledge*. His *Darbai* (Deeds) begins with the following statement: 'Oh, Virtue! Empty is this word in our times.'[4] He repeatedly asserts that honour comes from knowledge and understanding, rather than military achievement, and bemoans that early Lithuanians were skilled in warfare but lacked education. This equal weighting of virtue and education epitomizes Daukantas's eclectic approach to the humanist tradition. Recourse to the former reveals the influence of civic humanism, transmitted directly by the classics; his appeal to the latter resonates with the tenets of 'modern humanism'—the Enlightenment scholars' displacement of virtue with education and cyclical views of history with historicism.[5]

Daukantas shows his unreserved admiration for the pagan era, which he presents as a kind of Rousseauian dream of natural efflorescence, before corruption emerged as a corollary of modern civilization. Freedom and agriculture provided the Lithuanians with a virtuous way of life and moral strength in war. They were simple people, but hospitable to foreigners; for example, the Jews, having suffered expulsion from other countries, were readily welcomed in their land.[6] In keeping with the republican tradition, Daukantas depicts early Lithuanians as 'people in arms'. He claims that every freeman and landowner was obligated to take up arms, under the leadership of an elected military commander. He also endows Lithuanians with exceptional bravery, using the universal trope of preferring death to capture by the enemy.[7]

Daukantas believes that the authority and prestige enjoyed by pagan priests regulated the power of rulers. He also emphasizes that during this era, political institutions (such as the diet, which was responsible for the election of rulers), were independent and free of Polish influence.[8] To this end, his familiarity with the work of Grotius, Pufendorf and Algernon Sidney, which is evident from his footnotes, may have contributed to his appeals to natural law and ideas about sovereignty, non-alienable freedom and the social contract.

Daukantas's lively and imaginative portrayal of early life is accompanied by a more systematic account of episodes in Lithuanian statehood. He relates the deeds of rulers in chronological order, adopting a traditional humanist approach to periodization. Legendary, as well as

[4] Ibid., I. 403.   [5] Kagan, *Aristocratic Liberalism*, 5.
[6] Daukantas, *Raštai*, II. 639.   [7] Ibid., I. 174 and 609.   [8] Ibid., I. 640.

historical, figures feature in his stories. Of the episodes in Lithuanian statehood, Daukantas gives extensive consideration to Grand Duke Vytautas, whose reign (1401–30) came within the Christian era. In Vytautas he sees an exceptionally gifted, though not infallible, military leader. Under his rule in the early fifteenth century the Grand Duchy of Lithuania grew into the largest and most powerful state in the region, stretching from the Baltic to the Black Sea and far into the East. Vytautas's death represents one of the most poignant moments in Daukantas's narrative; he believed that, from that point on, when the title and power of the grand duke was transferred to the king of Poland, Lithuanian independence gradually began to diminish. It may be significant that two versions of Daukantas's national history are concluded with an appeal to Nikolai Karamzin's statement that 'if Vytautas' successors had been as wise as he was, today the Russian state would not exist'.[9]

As explained in the previous chapter, Daukantas, despite being a devout Catholic, blames the adoption of Christianity for the demise of the Lithuanian state and the ensuing foreign conquest. The initial expansion of the Teutonic Knights and Sword Bearers was subsequently exacerbated by Polish feudalization. Parallel to this account of external forces, Daukantas relays a story of moral corruption and inner debasement, ascribing the onset of decay to the felling of the impenetrable forests, which provided early Lithuanians with protection and shelter. According to Daukantas, this was a consequence of the discovery of America, where increasing numbers of people were enticed in order to seek wealth by digging for gold. The felling resulted from the need to build ships: 'All were desirous of wealth, which was not available to them. Therefore, *they felled the forests which, from the times of their ancestors, were held sacred*. They exported wood to foreign countries as timber for ship building, and wood was burned to ashes in the forests and sold to foreign glass manufacturers.'[10]

Daukantas claims that the discovery of America also increased the amount of crops exported from Lithuania, which facilitated an uneven distribution of its assets. A minority within society developed an appetite for possessions, enslaved the rest of the people, and ordered the expansion of arable lands at the expense of the forests. The rich considered the ancestors' old traditions as inappropriate and outdated, and instead developed extravagant habits of eating, drinking and dressing, which were catered for by an influx of foreign merchants (notably German),

---

[9] Daukantas, *Raštai*, II. 706.   [10] Ibid., I. 428–9.

who supplied them with luxurious items on which to spend their wealth.[11] The characteristic feature of Daukantas's narrative lies in the juxtaposition of seemingly incompatible arguments, belonging to the republican and commercial traditions, to account for the impact of the discovery of the New World and the material enrichment it generated for some European societies. As explained earlier, republicans associated the acquisition of wealth through trade with corruption. In contrast, for Scottish Enlightenment thinkers and their disciples in Germany, the discovery of America marked a beneficial development in the history of European civilization, by contributing significantly to the rise of European trade. These two apparently irreconcilable ideas were amalgamated and rendered compatible in Daukantas's account.

He assigns a villainous role to the discovery of America in national history, condemning the overindulgence of the corrupt elites by drawing upon republican attitudes to 'luxury', which equated indulgence in material wealth with debauchery. On another occasion, however, Daukantas's fascination with America follows the commercial tradition. He enthusiastically reports the colonizing ambitions of Prince Jacob of Courland (1610–81), for the sake of which he even ventures beyond his self-imposed terminus of 1569.[12] The Duchy of Courland, although autonomous, was fief to the Polish-Lithuanian Commonwealth, hence Daukantas's appropriation of this territory for the purposes of national history, which is not in the least self-explanatory. Prince Jacob, who was of German origin, purchased lands from the king of Spain in Tobago in the seventeenth century and later traded in slaves using the colony. Daukantas's enthusiasm stems from his conviction that the acquisition of colonies was beneficial and he maintains that through the settlement of Jacob's subjects in Tobago, Lithuanians succeeded in establishing a foothold in the New World.[13]

Moreover, centring on the rhetoric of vice and virtue, Daukantas emphasizes the usefulness of trade throughout his history, dedicating a whole chapter to the subject in his book, *Būdas*.[14] In addition to wax, honey, linen, leather, salt, fish and crops, he specifically focuses on amber (a luxury item), which has since become a Lithuanian treasure and national symbol. In tracing various trading routes he draws on classical authors, including Ovid, whose beautiful explanation of the origins of amber: 'tears turned into stone', he also adopted. Among

[11] Ibid., I. 429.   [12] Ibid., I. 644.   [13] Ibid.
[14] In *Būdas* a separate chapter is dedicated to trade: *Raštai*, I. 403–654.

contemporary authors, Arnold Heeren's writing features prominently in my historian's account of trade and commerce.[15] Daukantas's insistence on the incompatibility of trade and serfdom, as well as his emphasis on the importance of local production, also reflects his affinity with the commercial tradition.

A scarcity of primary sources impeded Daukantas's work, forcing him to rely instead on humanist chronicles and secondary sources. Yet, having read much of the same material as his predecessors, he arrives at fundamentally different conclusions. His ethno-linguistic perspective on the national community overlooks an earlier tradition in which the nobility constituted the political nation and sees the peasantry as the core of the national community. His account of the Lithuanian past is correspondingly more socially and geographically integrated than that of his predecessors. His emphasis on language incorporates every territory where Lithuanian was spoken, though the geographical contours of his vision of Lithuanian history are not as well-defined as those of the other historians. Daukantas's narrative includes regional variations, in particular, the distinct episodes in the history of his homeland, Samogitia. This territory was considered the most authentic of Lithuanian regions, escaping foreign influence to a greater extent than the other territories. It was also, in 1413, the last area in Europe to convert to Christianity, even later than other parts of Lithuania; serfdom was also much less widespread and less severe than elsewhere in the country.

Daukantas's determination to celebrate and redeem Lithuania's medieval pagan heritage necessitated his exaggeration of the rather tenuous connection that existed between the medieval principality and his own era on the one hand, and the undermining of more tangible continuities with the early modern tradition, extending from the year of the Union to Poland's third partition in 1795 on the other. Although he was not the first scholar to portray his homeland's history as an independent entity, rather than a mere constituent of a Polish federal state, he lent the hitherto vague concept clearer definition.[16] Another breakthrough in Daukantas's narrative is the identification of Polish influence with oppression and the destruction of a more advanced local culture. He locates the origins of oppression in the medieval period, and argues that, in the early fifteenth century, when Great Vytautas attempted to become

---

[15] Daukantas, *Raštai*, II. 17.
[16] Vicent Trumpa, 'Simonas Daukantas, Historian and Pioneer of National Rebirth', 13.

king, with the support of the Holy Roman Emperor, Sigismund, the bishop of Cracow verbally attacked the Lithuanians. Daukantas laments the fact that, according to the sources, the Lithuanians did not retaliate. Thus, he composed a reply of his own to the bishop:

The Lithuanians remained silent. *No one among them dared to say to the Bishop:*

we want to have equal rights with the Poles and not to be their slaves . . . Although the Lithuanians swore to fight the enemy, they never took an oath to become Poles, or read and write in Polish instead of Lithuanian, to give up their historical rights or to obey Polish laws.[17]

POLAND: A TRUE REPUBLIC

Lelewel's historical landscape was shaped by his determination to redress what he saw as the injustice of the partitions and his arguments resound with his republican conviction. Understandably, he focuses significantly on the reasons for Poland's tragic fate, as well as speculating about his homeland's future. His early historical writings deal extensively with the ancient Slavs, whom he regards as freedom-loving people, skilled in agriculture. In addition, he asserts that early Polish society (*gminowładztwo*) was characterized by its democratic nature, civic spirit and level of active political engagement. For Lelewel, the essence of Polish history was created from the friction between two forces: national principles and foreign principles. The former were inherent in republican ideals, an elective monarchy, religious toleration and the freedom of the nobility. The latter was characterized by the influx of monarchism and ultramontanism, and the persecution of non-Catholic denominations led by the Jesuits. Lelewel repeatedly contends that whenever national principles were betrayed in Poland, the nation's fortunes suffered.[18]

My historian devised two chronologies. The first version, following a pattern familiar to periodizations of universal history, identifies various stages of eclipse and decline in the Polish past, distinguishing between 'Conquering', 'Divided', 'Flourishing' and 'Declining' phases, to which Lelewel later added the contemporary era: 'Poland in the Throes of Rebirth'. The second variant defines historical epochs in terms of political structures: absolutism (860–1139); aristocracy (1139–1374); *szlachta*

---

[17] Daukantas, *Raštai*, I. 393–94, quoted in Žukas, *Simonas Daukantas*, 62–63.
[18] Lelewel, *Polska, dzieje a rzeczy jej*, III. 308; *Betrachtungen*, 214.

(noble) democracy (1374–1607 or 1333–1607); and interruptions of the *szlachta* democracy.[19] Of these, *szlachta* democracy was supposedly the most distinguished one, characterized by economic and political success, rapid military expansion and imperial grandeur. He especially admired the Jagellonian dynasty, who were at the height of their power in the sixteenth century, extolling their social and political justice and religious toleration, as well as their equitable treatment of the peasantry. This epoch, which saw the revival of the unique character of the ancient Polish community—its freedom, public spirit and political commitment—is believed to represent the apex of Polish history:

> The nation, united with Lithuania, exerted daily influence on the Kingdom of Prussia, took Livonia under its protection, influenced the Danube, the Don, and the Narva . . . Without doubt the Polish nation was distinctive, prosperous, and politically active, but only in an effectively benign manner. While the other European countries were gripped by anarchy and drenched in blood to the detriment of their liberty, Poland alone was the envy of all.[20]

The republican nature of gentry democracy, the origins of which Lelewel traced to the thirteenth century, exemplified quintessential traits from the Polish past. Lelewel prides himself on the Polish republican tradition, refuting contemporary beliefs that a republican system only suited small realms. He maintains that Poland uniquely constituted a large republic, whereas the ancient Greek and Roman states and medieval federations of towns and cantons were all small entities.[21] He also highlights that, unlike the French hereditary system, in Poland the king was a civil servant, an elected head of state.[22] The histories of Greece and Rome not only provided insight into the nature of virtue, as we have seen, but also helped to explain the reasons for the rise and decline of empires and states. Roman history was a guiding light throughout the eighteenth century, but, in the first half of the nineteenth century, the emergence of democratic principles and the potential dangers associated with those ideals transformed political thinking and shifted scholars' attention to Athens.[23] Lelewel evoked both Roman and Greek analogies; in particular he made a powerful case

[19] The first pattern of chronology was applied in *Dzieje Polski potocznym sposobem opowiedziane*, the second in *Uwagi nad dziejami Polski i ludu jej*.

[20] Lelewel, *Dzieła*, VIII. 263–4; my translation draws on but is not identical with Skurnewicz, *Romantic Nationalism*, 107.

[21] Lelewel, *Polska, dzieje a rzeczy jej*, III. 173; *Betrachtungen*, 105.

[22] Lelewel, *Dzieła*, VIII. 278; *Polen unter Stanislaus August*, 4.

[23] Burrow, Collini and Winch, *That Noble Science of Politics*, 188.

for Rousseau's claim that the culture of the ancient Poles most closely resembled that of the ancient Greeks, as shown by their preference for democratic assemblies.[24]

Although Lelewel praises individual achievements in Polish history, he nonetheless expresses a conviction that significant events were not the result of individual ambition or talents, however extraordinary; rather, they could be attributed to the influence of what he calls the 'public spirit' (*duch obywatelski*).[25] Despite his being a prominent representative of the republican tradition, Lelewel's beliefs were not predicated on the defence of outdated privileges and were therefore distinct from the republicanism of the eighteenth-century conservative magnates. In this context, his agenda was more radical than that of Enlightenment scholars because he did not consider citizenship to be contingent on property qualifications.[26] Social unity would be achieved by ennobling the entire population of Poland, thus restoring a condition inherent in the ancient democracy.

The majority of Lelewel's contemporaries, both fellow countrymen and foreigners, considered centralization a vital prerequisite for a strong and efficient state. Lelewel's position was at odds with this mainstream view, for he considered the cultural diversity of the former Common-wealth to be a model for a future Poland. Lelewel's preference was for a federal constitution with regional self-government, and three official languages: Polish, Lithuanian and Ruthenian.[27] He maintains that Poland's greatness rested on security from within and freedom from external threat, and not on violence and warfare. Poland's expansion into Lithuania and Ruthenia represented not a conquest, but a political necessity whose civilizing mission benefited the newly acquired nations, for example by allowing them to share in the advantages of political liberty associated with *szlachta* democracy.[28] He believes that people of various nationalities voluntarily identified with the customs, laws and values of the Polish state, but was oblivious to the contradictory implications of encouraging diversity, especially to the fact that accentuating differences

---

[24] Lelewel, *Polska, dzieje a rzeczy jej*, II. 252; *Betrachtungen*, 166.

[25] Lelewel, *Polska, dzieje a rzeczy jej*, III. 172–3; *Betrachtungen*, 105; quoted in Halina Beresnevičiūte, 'The Idea of the Nation in Joachim Lelewel's and František Palacký's Historical Works' (MA thesis, Central European University, Budapest, 1995), 36.

[26] Walicki, *Philosophy and Romantic Nationalism*, 32–33.

[27] Lelewel, 'Prawność narodu polskiego', in Andrzej Walicki and Jan Garewicz (eds.), *700 lat myśli polskiej: Filozofia i myśl społeczna w latach 1831–1864* (Warsaw, 1977), 779, quoted in Walicki, *Romantic Nationalism*, 70.

[28] Lelewel, *Polska, dzieje a rzeczy jej*, III. 164; *Betrachtungen*, 98.

could lead to the emergence of a more politically conscious elite among the non-Polish ethnic groups, and ultimately to the founding of new nations.[29]

Lelewel found that drawing a clear distinction between religion and politics, a manifestation of the 'national principle', contributed to the cohesion of the heterogeneous Commonwealth.[30] In his opinion, the Commonwealth distinguished itself by allowing all denominations to exercise their faith freely. He contrasts the tolerance shown towards the Jewish population in fourteenth-century Poland with the intolerance of the Spanish inquisition.[31] He also contrasts his homeland favourably to sixteenth-century Western Europe: while the latter was plagued by religious wars, in Poland King Bathory (a foreign ruler, whom he otherwise did not admire) declared that conscience belonged to God alone and hence nobody should be persecuted for their faith. Jews as well as Protestants and dissidents enjoyed security: 'apart from incidental atrocities, they were left in peace and considered Poland paradise on earth'.[32]

This leads us to consider what caused the decline and ensuing dismantling of a (supposedly) flourishing state, a question that was addressed by several prominent contemporary thinkers. Traditionally, anarchical and anachronistic forms of government have been held responsible.[33] The idiosyncratic *liberum veto* was specifically singled out. This allowed any deputy of the diet to force an immediate end to the current session and nullify all legislation passed so far. Some scholars, such as Bonnot de Mably, claimed that old Polish institutions were inherently inefficient, implying that they should be built on entirely new foundations. Lelewel took issue with Mably's position, insisting that Poland's demise was not due to republican institutions, which had functioned well, but their misuse and subsequent degeneration. He again appealed to Rousseau, 'the last defender of the Polish people', when asserting that the *liberum veto* was not inherently impractical, but in fact served to protect freedom and democratic principles; only in the seventeenth century was it abused to the extent that it disrupted the Diet.[34]

[29] Lelewel, *Polska, dzieje a rzeczy jej*, III. 167; *Betrachtungen*, 101.

[30] Lelewel, *Polska, dzieje a rzeczy jej*, III. 308; *Betrachtungen*, 214.

[31] Lelewel, *Dzieła*, VI. 210–11.

[32] Lelewel, *Polska, dzieje a rzeczy jej*, III. 180; *Betrachtungen*, 128.

[33] Jules Michelet, *A Summary of Modern History* (London, 1875), 4.

[34] Marian Henryk Serejski, *Naród a państwo w polskiej myśli historycznej*, 2nd edn. (Warsaw, 1977), 112; Walicki, *Philosophy and Romantic Nationalism*, 34.

In Lelewel's view, the principal reason for Poland's tragic fate lay in the expansionism of neighbouring powers. A further reason was the influx of foreign ideas, especially those of the Jesuits; their intolerance and manipulation were inimical to the ethos of the Commonwealth. To a lesser extent, Poland's unfavourable location contributed to its downfall, situated on a plain, and exposed on all sides, which made it an easy target for invaders. Lelewel's account, which primarily attributes responsibility to foreign powers, provides a useful contrast to Horváth's assessment of 'the death of a country, whose history displayed similarities with our country, both acting as a bulwark of Christianity'. Horváth argues that the selfish and dissolute nobility brought about their own downfall, by fighting amongst themselves, abusing their right of veto and oppressing the unprivileged classes. Nevertheless, the partitioning powers were also guilty: although the country was heading towards self-destruction, no one had the right to land the fatal blow.[35]

Lelewel's disillusionment with European politics in his émigré years is apparent in his revised views about the necessary conditions for Poland's re-establishment. After the partitions, the short-lived Duchy of Warsaw, a constitutional monarchy, was formed under the aegis of Napoleon, whilst the Congress Kingdom, an area approximately one-sixth of pre-partition Poland, was created by the Congress of Vienna. From 1830 to 1831, his awareness of the inflexibility of the European status quo led him to consider more limited boundaries, provided that some of the Lithuanian and Ruthenian territories would be annexed to the Congress Kingdom. Whilst in exile, however, Lelewel concluded that only the restoration of the Polish state to its historical boundaries of 1772 would be satisfactory.[36]

Disenchanted with Western diplomacy, after 1838 he vested his hopes in a greater cooperation between Slavic people.[37] On the whole, however, he insisted that Poles could only depend on their own efforts: 'Woe to that people which raises itself by the help of others! Such a nation will never be free. History has shown that reliance on diplomacy destroys every move. Such material is poor stuff to build with. From it can only arise, at best, a Duchy of Warsaw or a Congress Kingdom . . . structures of clay, which rain and sleet will wash away.'[38]

---

[35] Horváth, *Magyarország története*, VII. 449–51.
[36] Lelewel, *Dzieła*, VIII. 482.   [37] Skurnowicz, *Romantic Nationalism*, 97.
[38] W. J. Rose, *Poland's Place in Europe* (London, 1945), 17.

Lelewel's belief in the possibility of Poland being restored to its pre-1772 boundaries was unrealistic, but his stance should be set in the context of similar delusions harboured by the majority of Western radicals and socialists. Their ideal of a complete reinstatement of Poland was built upon the conviction that a strong, progressive and democratic state would counterbalance the intransigent ambitions of reactionary absolute monarchies in Europe.[39]

THE CZECHS: A SMALL NATION'S CONTRIBUTION TO LIBERTY

Palacký developed a new and compelling interpretation of Czech history, which is still influential to the present day. Several key elements of his scheme had already been formulated, or at least hinted at, by his predecessors, however. These include the idea that the Czechs, a peaceful agricultural people, were the first permanent settlers in the Bohemian lands, where they later founded their own state. The essence of Czech history as an eternal struggle with the Germans had also been conceptualized by earlier scholars, together with the cornerstone of Palacký's interpretation: the elevation of Hussitism into a unique and unrepeated internationally significant movement.[40] In contrast to the innovative quality of Palacký's writing, his periodization is somewhat bland and conventional. He initially distinguished between ancient, middle and modern eras which corresponded to the rules of the Přemysl (until 1306), Luxemburg (until 1526), and subsequently the Habsburg-Lorraine houses. He later modified this framework by extending the ancient period to 1403, and middle period to 1627, portraying the latter as the zenith of Czech history.[41]

In common with my other protagonists, Palacký's vision of early society is characterized by virtues, such as peace and democracy; in contrast, the medieval period is infected by harmful and foreign influences. The non-violence of the Slavs is also accommodated in the historian's vision; he draws a distinction between 'peaceful' and 'predatory' peoples. The Slavs are joined by the ancient Greeks and Jews

---

[39] Walicki, *Romantic Nationalism*, 73.

[40] For example, Palacký's predecessor, the historian František Martin Pelcl (1734–1801) thought highly of the Hussite movement.

[41] For a detailed breakdown of his periodization see *Myšlenka a dílo Františka Palackého* (Prague, 1926), I. 164–206.

in the first category, while the conquerors (*Raubvölker*) occupy the second and include the Germans, Romans, Huns, Mongols, Tartars and Hungarians.[42] Palacký's underlying belief that there was continuous contact and conflict between the Slavs is most evident in his assessment of the reign of King Charles IV (1347–78) in the fourteenth century. Typically, earlier historians, especially traditionalists, eulogized the king for instigating economic and cultural prosperity; for example, during his reign Prague became one of the most important cities of Europe and also a capital of the Holy Roman Empire, and he was also the founder of Prague University.[43] Whilst acknowledging these achievements and accepting that Charles (Bohemian in origin, but also German king and Holy Roman Emperor) 'was devoted to the Czech nation in his heart', Palacký regrets that his promotion of greater industry through the migration of foreign settlers, tradesmen and artisans resulted in colonization.[44]

Palacký shifts this conventional viewpoint by moving the zenith of Czech history to the early fifteenth century, when the Hussite movement was at its height, bringing about 'a watershed in the history of Christianity, but above all in the history of the Czech nation'.[45] The Hussites are acknowledged for attempting to rectify the disintegrated and corrupt state of the Church, by demanding the renunciation of its secular power and extensive wealth in an era when three people simultaneously claimed to be the legitimate pope. Yet, for Palacký, Hussitism had a wider significance beyond the mere demand for a renewed Church; it also espoused social and national ideas. As a 'democratic reaction to feudal and foreign influences', it served the cause of the Bohemian-Slav nationality.[46] Moreover, in Palacký's interpretation, Hussite doctrines are inextricably linked to ideals of modernity and progress, representing the first attempt in history to undermine the two main pillars of the medieval world: the Church (in the religious sphere) and the Holy Roman Empire (in the secular sphere).[47]

Palacký was responsible for winning sympathy for the movement's leader, John Hus, who became a potent national symbol. As well

---

[42] Palacký, *Geschichte des Hussitenthums*, 76.

[43] Miroslav Hroch and Jitka Malečková, 'The Construction of Czech History', *Historein* 1 (1999), 106.

[44] He tackles the reign of Charles IV in *Dějiny*, II. 471–530.

[45] Palacký, *Dějiny*, III. 3.

[46] Palacký, *Geschichte des Hussitenthums*, 59–66 and 158–60.

[47] Palacký, *Gedenkblätter*, 271.

as appreciating his role in initiating reforms from below, his dignity and great integrity, he also wrote highly of Hus's contribution to the promotion of Czech language and literature.[48] Palacký's account of the Hussite period, in which he wholly identifies with Hus's perspective, is infused with drama and pathos, particularly with regard to his poignant portrayal of Hus's martyrdom, which became one of the most defining moments of Czech historiography. Hus's courage positioned him as morally superior to the members of the synod who sentenced him to death on the pyre. He refused to renounce his doctrine to save his life, because:

As the founder and initiator of Protestantism, as the representative of spiritual liberty and freedom to choose one's religion, he would have betrayed his own spirit and ideals by renouncing his principles. Only two options were available to him: physical death and spiritual death. He chose the former. His decision ushered in a new era in the history of Christianity, one which was no longer limited to rigid, hierarchical authority, but open to new ideas of spiritual freedom.[49]

As this quote indicates, Palacký elevates Hus from a mere forefather of the Reformation to the founder of Protestantism and inventor of the doctrine of predestination, believing that his doctrines fully captured the essence of Protestantism, long before the arrival of Luther and Calvin. He emphasizes the continuity between Hus and Luther by pointing out that Luther saw himself as a Hussite.[50]

Hus's prominence in Palacký's view reveals his indebtedness to the 'great man' theory, which is also epitomized in his declaration that 'history is the final judge over those who distinguished themselves by their actions on the world-stage'.[51] Yet, in many ways, Hus did not fit the archetype of rulers, saints and warriors, but pre-empted the popularity that religious reformers and heretics enjoyed in the Romantic era. Jules Michelet, a Catholic historian, expresses admiration for both the forerunners and principal agents of the Reformation and, in addition to his *Mémoires de Luther*, entertained the idea of composing similar biographies of Wycliff and Hus. Nevertheless, Michelet's main preoccupation is with heresy, and, despite his admiration, he still views Hus as a heretic.[52] As the next chapter shows, Hus also has a place in the British Protestant tradition. On the other hand, it has been

---

[48] Palacký, *Dějiny*, III. 129–31.   [49] Ibid., III. 177–8.
[50] Ibid., VI. 269.   [51] Ibid., II. 3.
[52] Irène Tieder, *Michelet et Luther, Histoire d'une rencontre* (Paris, 1976), 15.

explained earlier that Palacký's censor and many of his colleagues, particularly those from Germany, remained thoroughly unimpressed by his interpretation, and saw Hus in a different light as not only a heretic but, in some cases, a common criminal.

The account of Hus's martyrdom is followed by an indulgent description of the Hussite wars, including the rivalry between various factions. Palacký believes that the antecedents of most modern political principles and philosophical systems, such as rationalism, socialism, communism, democracy, nationalism, pantheism and Panslavism, find some trace in Hussite doctrine.[53] In the moderate Hussite king Jiří of Poděbrady (1458–71) Palacký finds his secular hero. As an elected ruler, for Palacký he represents the ideal of constitutional monarch ruling with the consent of the nation, something which has obvious contemporary resonance, allowing Palacký to maintain a polemical distance from the policy of Habsburg neoabsolutism.[54]

Palacký ends his national history on the eve of the Habsburg accession in 1526, but his other works provided some further clues to his assessment of subsequent centuries, although these contain some inconsistencies. He includes the most traumatic event in Czech history, the defeat of the Protestants at the battle of White Mountain in 1620 and the Bohemian lands' subsequent assimilation into the Habsburg Monarchy, in his overview of conflict between Germans and Slavs. In seeking to account for the defeat, his rationale alternates between inner debasement exacerbated by the Pope's and Habsburgs' actions and reasons beyond Czech control, such as the absolutist and centralizing tendencies of the age.[55] The ensuing Counter-Reformation precipitated a new form of German feudalism, although this was ameliorated to some extent by the enlightened reforms of Maria Theresa and Joseph II, which Palacký, like Horváth, greatly appreciated. The national revival in Palacký's time represented the antithesis of these foreign tendencies. This is illustrated by Palacký's belief that, like the Hussite movement, the Revolution of 1848 represented an historical opportunity for the revival of the ancient liberties which the earlier Czechs enjoyed.

By concentrating on the history of the Czechs and writing in their language, Palacký distanced himself from the Bohemian identity of

---

[53] Palacký, *Dějiny*, III. 242; *Geschichte des Hussitenthums*, 186.
[54] Josef Válka, 'František Palacký—historik', in Mylan Myška (ed.), *Památník Palackého 1798–1968* (Ostrava, 1968), 53.
[55] Zacek, *Palacký*, 85.

the upper classes. His desire to overcome the limitations of territorial patriotism was evident, not just in the title of his national history, but also in the declaration that: 'my intention, from the beginning has been not to tear apart what God has joined together, and not to create barriers where none exist in nature; I am firmly of the conviction that being born a Moravian, I am of the Czech nation'.[56] Moravia retained a distinct regional identity, at least until the 1860s, together with a separate diet and a Moravian historiographer. In some respects, the region distinguished itself from the Bohemian lands: here the German inhabitants were a homogeneous group and the influence of Catholicism was more pronounced.[57] For Palacký, Moravia was an organic part of the Czech nation; his plea for unity was driven by appeals to the common language as well as to shared history. With few short exceptions, the two lands were governed by the same rulers, hence such a unity could not be accidental or arbitrary.[58] Palacký's ambition to integrate the history of Moravia is even more remarkable in the context of earlier accounts, which treated this region as an appendix to the history of Bohemia. In practice, however, he failed to fulfil his ambition, and Moravia retained only marginal significance to his argument, whilst the third constituent of the Bohemian lands, Silesia, received even less attention.[59]

Palacký takes a patronizing approach to the aspirations of the Slovak patriots, denying the existence of an independent Slovak nationality. For him, Slovakia's continued alliance with the Hungarian state, which lasted for a millennium, was overshadowed by cultural affinities. He considered the Slovak language to be a Czech dialect and argues that the distinction only evolved because of the separation of the two peoples through the migration of Hungarians into the Carpathian basin in the ninth century.[60] Most importantly, he sees the main role of the Slovaks as adding fortification to the Czech element in the region. Although he denies the Slovaks independent existence, Palacký champions the recognition of his nation's history as independent of the German realm,

---

[56] Palacký, *Dějiny*, III. 6.

[57] On developments in Moravia see Milan Řepa, *Moravané nebo Češi? Vývoj českého národního vědomi na Moravě v 19. století* (Brno, 2001).

[58] Palacký, *Geschichte von Böhmen*, I. 7; quoted in Jiří Kořalka, *Tschechen im Habsburgerreich und in Europa, 1815–1914* (Vienna, 1991), 59.

[59] Palacký was unsupportive of the Moravians' striving for autonomy; see *Gedenkblätter*, 156–63.

[60] Palacký, *Gedenkblätter*, 41.

and renounces identification with German aspirations. He addresses the German representatives in Frankfurt with the following words:

The object of your assembly is to establish a federation of the German nation in place of the existing federation of princes, to guide the German nation to real unity, to strengthen the sentiment of German national consciousness, and ultimately expand the power and strength of the German Empire. Although I respect such ideals and the sentiments upon which they are based, I cannot, precisely for this reason, participate in any capacity whatsoever. I am not a German, . . . I am a Bohemian of Slavonic origin (*Ich bin ein Böhme slavischen Stammes*).[61]

The appropriation of Bohemia for the purposes of German unification could be justified on the grounds that the Bohemian Crown had formed part of the Holy Roman Empire (of the German Nation) since the Middle Ages. Palacký refutes this rationale by appealing to natural rights: 'nature knows neither dominant nor subservient nations',[62] and by emphasizing that Bohemia had once been a sovereign and independent land: 'the whole union of the Bohemian lands, first with the Holy Roman (German) Empire, and then with the German confederation, was always a mere dynastic tie . . . the German emperors had never had, for the sake of their imperial dignity, anything to do with the Czech nation'.[63]

Palacký's Frankfurt letter was considered the first manifestation of the Czech idea of the federalization of the Austrian Empire, based on ethnicity. He believed that the nations of the Danubian region were too weak to counter Russian expansionist intentions alone. His later work, *Oesterreichs Staatsidee*, proposes another federal model, which placed more emphasis on traditional historical allegiances. He argued that the unique historical mission of the Austrian state—to defend Christianity against the Turks—had become irrelevant and the new raison d'être of the Austrian state was to ensure the protection and national equality of various ethnic groupings within a single political union.[64] Thus, until the mid-1860s, he believed that the Habsburg Empire was still necessary, but only if it could guarantee autonomy, a supranational government and equality to its constituent nationalities. The Austro-Hungarian Compromise of 1867 ignored the Czech demands by excluding them

---

[61] Ibid., 153. My translation is based on the excerpt in Trencsényi and Kopeček (eds.), *Discourses of Collective Identity*, II. 324–5.

[62] Ibid., 153.   [63] Ibid., 150; *Discourses of Collective Identity*, 325.

[64] Palacký, *Oesterreichs Staatsidee* (Prague, 1866), 4–5.

from political decision-making. This prompted Palacký to reconsider his position and fundamentally shift the focus of Czech history onto Prague instead of Vienna, as exemplified by his famous declaration: 'we were here before Austria and shall still be here after she has disappeared'.[65]

THE HUNGARIAN CONSTITUTION
AND THE SPIRIT OF LIBERALISM

Of the five historians, only Horváth succeeded in writing a comprehensive national history, extending from ancient times until the contemporary era and, uniquely among them, traced the most prosperous period of Hungarian history in the recent past, the Reform Period (1815–48) and the ensuing revolution and war of independence in 1848–9. In a similar chronological vein to Lelewel, he divides Hungarian history into alternating phases of 'foreign influence' and 'national counter-influence' and uses a metaphor to suggest the relationship between the two: like a piece of elastic, the harder it is pulled, the stronger it bounces back, the more intense the foreign influx, the greater the national counter-effect. According to this scheme, the era of state foundation represented a national period, which was succeeded by German influence, then another national period, followed by Byzantine, and so on. Throughout the course of Hungarian history, periods of German, Italian, Slavic and Turkish influences alternated with national eras.[66]

Nevertheless, in contrast to the account given by Lelewel, the national and foreign epochs did not necessarily coincide with prosperity and decay. The decades leading up to the damaging Battle of Mohács (1526) belonged to a 'national' era, yet were characterized, in Horváth's words, by the unruliness of the oligarchy. On the other hand, Horváth greatly admired the Anjou dynasty (the period of Italian influence) that reigned in Hungary during the fourteenth century, because they conferred on towns privileges which gave an impetus to industry and trade. They injected refined Italian manners into Hungarian customs, which still bore the imprint of oriental traditions.[67] Like the other historians, Horváth asserts that his country extended hospitality, and sometimes royal protection and privileges, to the Jews in the Middle Ages, as

---

[65] Palacký, *Oesterreichs Staatsidee* (Prague, 1866), 77.
[66] This scheme was applied in his eight-volume *Magyarország története*.
[67] Horváth, *Magyarország története* (Pest, 1871), II. 352.

opposed to the atrocities they suffered elsewhere in Europe, whilst not denying that this was motivated by vested interest, in return for their acting as creditors to Hungarian kings. He also charts the deterioration of their condition in the fourteenth century, when they were expelled from the country (to Poland).[68] Nonetheless, Horváth still maintains the belief that, whilst in other countries the Jewish population's wealth and property caused their harassment, an exaggerated religious devotion was the main reason for their persecution in Hungary.[69]

The language of commerce permeates Horváth's work. Adapting the Scottish Enlightenment's and the Göttingen school's trajectory of landmark developments in European history to the Hungarian context, Horváth found that to some extent even Hungary benefited from the invigoration of European trade and commerce which followed the Crusades.[70] At the same time, he argues that the morally beneficial effects of the Reformation were minimal in Hungary compared with other countries and, in fact, produced conflict and divisions. Nevertheless, he credits a distinct Calvinist culture for safeguarding national identity in the most precarious stages of Hungarian history.[71]

Horváth's argument was constructed in the framework of constitutionalism, and thus reforms, vicissitudes and abuses of the constitution were given prominence in his narrative. According to his interpretation, the constitution was his nation's unique heritage and instrumental in securing the unity and continuity of the Hungarian state. Correspondingly, he located its origins in the period of the conquest and perceived the Hungarian chieftains' legendary blood contract as a precursor to constitutional arrangements.[72] One of the main criteria for judging Hungarian rulers was whether they respected the constitution. Horváth greatly appreciated the Golden Bull of 1222, a document that endowed the Estates with the right to resist the ruler and also confirmed their already existing privileges. He noted that the Bull was protected as a cornerstone of the constitution in a way that paralleled the 'more fortunate English people's affection towards their Magna Carta of 1215'.[73] Horváth regretfully notes that the nobility sometimes violated the constitution, turning it into the stronghold of their outdated privileges. He believes that this strategy backfired by providing the government with an excuse for its autocratic rule in the eighteenth and nineteenth

---

[68] Ibid., II. 76.   [69] Ibid, II. 305.
[70] *Horváth Mihály kisebb történelmi munkái*, II. 21.   [71] Ibid., III. 393–4.
[72] Horváth, *Magyarország történelme*, I. 28.   [73] Ibid., I. 518.

centuries. Horváth concludes that the nobility's demand for proper conduct lacked a moral foundation, because their treatment of the lower classes was just as unconstitutional.[74]

One of the most celebrated figures in Hungarian history, the Renaissance king Matthias Corvinus (1458–90), is commended by Horváth for his legendary sense of justice, whilst simultaneously condemned for 'not being a friend of constitutional rule', as illustrated by his cunning tactic of exasperating the Estates by convening the Diet with such frequency that they ultimately begged for deferrals.[75] What makes Horváth's approach exceptional is the fact that the king's illegitimate son, János Corvinus, captured his attention to a greater extent than Matthias himself. Corvinus was only one of several heroes who merited an article from Horváth.[76] Others 'on the small scale' included the leader of the peasant uprising of 1514, György Dózsa, who was mentioned in the previous chapter. A book-length study recounted the life of a brave noblewoman of the seventeenth century, Ilona Zrínyi.[77] She defended the fortress of Munkács against the Habsburgs for two years, in the absence of her husband, who had been imprisoned by the dynasty. Last but not least, a sixteenth-century statesman and cleric, Cardinal Martinuzzi, was perhaps his most beloved character.[78] This was obviously no coincidence, as the similarity between the Cardinal's and Horváth's background is evident. Martinuzzi was born to a family of serfs; his exceptional career, culminating in elevated positions within the Church and State, was due to his own talent and efforts.

Horváth's historical-constitutional rhetoric is frequently combined with appeals to natural law (*természetjog*), whose principles, he believes, should govern relations between different social strata. For example, when assessing the law of 1514, which deprived Hungarian peasantry of the right of migration, his rhetorical question: 'how did this decree measure up in the tribunal of natural law?' shows his opposition to the regulation. He warns that 'the long-term violation of natural law cannot remain unpunished, because action results in reaction'.[79] Similarly, he also emphasizes the parity between rights and obligations, describing

[74] Horváth, *Magyarország történelme*, VII. 378.   [75] Ibid., III. 227.

[76] 'Corvin János élete', in *Horváth Mihály kisebb történelmi munkái*, I. 291–318.

[77] Horváth, *Zrínyi Ilona életrajza* (Pest, 1869).

[78] Horváth, *Utyeszenich Fráter György (Martinuzzi bíbornok) élete* (Budapest, 1882).

[79] Horváth, *Polgárosodás, liberalizmus, függetlenségi harc*, 43.

his (and the Hungarian liberals') desired society as one in which the contribution 'to public goods is in proportion to the advantages drawn from it, where the constitution serves, not just a few privileged individuals, but the entire nation'.[80]

In addition to the Reform era, two other epochs captured Horváth's imagination: the time of state foundation, and the early sixteenth century. The latter represented a critical juncture in Hungarian history, culminating in defeat by the Turks at the battle of Mohács in 1526, which led to the dismemberment of the Hungarian state, and Habsburg and Turkish occupation, whilst the Principality of Transylvania retained semi-independence. This development could be compared to the partitioning of Poland and to the consequences of the Battle of White Mountain for the Czechs; thus Horváth grappled with similar dilemmas to my Polish and Czech protagonists. Confronted with the question of responsibility for this fateful episode, which determined the course of Hungarian history for the next century and a half, Horváth was not slow to point the finger at the aristocracy and declare the Hungarians' cowardice, rather than the superior numbers of the Turks, as eliciting that tragic day.[81]

The Reform period, commencing with the convening of the Hungarian Diet after its long neglect in 1825, and extending to the revolutionary year of 1848, was, in Horváth's words, 'the most glorious epoch of the nation, characterized by a constitution founded on genuinely liberal (szabadelvű) principles'.[82] He notes with pride that such prosperity was particularly admirable because it was achieved entirely by the nation on its own, unsupported from above, despite many constraints. Horváth's account of these decades seeks to legitimize the liberal reform programme and reveals his affinity with the political credo of Louis Kossuth. His *Huszonöt év*, a monumental two-volume work, completed in exile, offers an extensive portrayal of how the crucial demands of liberals were gradually disseminated throughout the country. Central to his argument are: the issues of religious freedom (the emancipation of non-Catholic denominations); the imposition of tax on the nobility; the extension of civil rights to the people (the emancipation of the serfs); and the reform of the penal code. He sees this era through the

---

[80] *Horváth Mihály kisebb történelmi munkái*, I. 125.   [81] Ibid., III. 8–10.
[82] Horváth, *Magyarország történelme*, 2nd edn. (Budapest, 1873), VIII. 538.

eyes of a devoted liberal and explains the advancement of liberalism as an inexorable force, an imperative of the *Zeitgeist*. The more visible the contours of the 'progressive age' became, the more indefensible was the nobility's and clergy's unwillingness to surrender their privileges.[83] Horváth regrets that

(The Catholic clergy) were reluctant to accept that democratic freedom had become the guiding principle of the age, and consequently not only its advocates, but also its opponents, were progressing along its course. The latter were swept along against their wishes. The clergy were incapable of realizing that they too were just pawns in the hands of divine providence, that the ideals of equality and freedom were so all-encompassing that they extended beyond the reach of human will, and consequently they must have been commanded by divine providence itself.[84]

In Horváth's narrative the thread of continuity is especially evident in the resilience of ancient institutions, primarily the constitution and the diets. Social unity is advocated through Horváth's underlying theme of solidarity and the need for the harmonization of interests between various social strata. Horváth did not intend to use historical arguments to redefine Hungarian territory, and thus remained much less concerned with territorial questions than my other historians. However, ethnic variety could also act as an impediment to unity. Horváth touched upon this issue in his pre-1848 writings; nonetheless, as with most politicians of the Reform era, he tends to underestimate the potential problems resulting from the overlapping interests of Hungarians and other nationalities, and only occasionally hints at some awareness of these, albeit projected back to earlier centuries. For example, he surmises that the colourful mixture of various ethnic groups and the differences in their moral and civic condition, hindered the development of trade and industry in medieval Hungary.[85]

With hindsight, he showed greater understanding of the problem, noting that the Hungarians were so thoroughly engaged in their reform movement that, for a long time, they failed to recognize how quickly and successfully Panslavism had advanced in Europe, in particular among those nationalities who lived on the Hungarian border, under the protection of its constitution.[86] This viewpoint not only testifies to

---

[83] Horváth, *Magyarország történelme*, 2nd edn. (Budapest, 1873), VII. 378.
[84] Horváth, *Huszonöt év Magyarország történetéből*, II. 88.
[85] *Horváth Mihály kisebb történelmi munkái*, II. 54.
[86] Horváth, *Huszonöt év Magyarország történetéből*, I. 509 and II. 90.

Hungarian politicians' fear and loathing of Panslavism and, as Horváth puts it, 'Russian propaganda', but also to a paternalistic approach towards the nationalities, which informed Kossuth's principles in the Reform Era. Crucial to this was the assumption that the nationalities were not viable entities by themselves and that their only chance of obtaining political freedom and material development was under Hungarian protection. Thus, Horváth's attitude, in some respects analogous with Lelewel's patronizing views on the non-Polish population: both believed that the various nationalities could be reconciled by offering them the same civic liberties as the Hungarian and Polish dominant majority.

When Horváth embarked on his *Magyarország függetlenségi harcának története 1848 és 1849-ben* (History of the Revolution and War of Independence in 1848–9), his friends warned him that personal involvement and lack of hindsight would make his account too subjective. Against this scepticism, he succeeded in producing a creditable, albeit hagiographic, account of the War of Independence. He traces the role of leading personalities and their conflicting interests in the final outcome, citing selfishness and lack of solidarity as the main reasons for failure in this respect, causing him to overestimate the contribution of individuals at the expense of other circumstances. To neglect his own contribution would have been false modesty, and he refers to his own participation, with 'Minister Horváth'.

The decades following the suppression of the War of Independence witnessed the imposition of Habsburg neoabsolutism, but after its military defeat by Prussia at Königgrätz, the dynasty was compelled to search for a *modus vivendi* with the Hungarians, whose support it needed. The prominent, pragmatically minded politician of the era Ferenc Deák successfully negotiated the Compromise with Austria, which, in return for limited independence, guaranteed Austrian-Hungarian domination over the other nationalities. As we have seen, this had a traumatic effect on Palacký. The majority of the Hungarian public was satisfied with this arrangement, apart from the émigré Kossuth, who categorically renounced any alternative to full independence. At this stage Horváth's loyalty shifted from Kossuth's to Deák's camp. As Chapter 4 indicated, he praised the latter politician by borrowing Guizot's characterization of George Washington, as a considerate man who only took action if he was absolutely convinced that his intentions were right and just.[87] This

---

[87] Ibid., I. 345.

attitude led to criticism on Kossuth's part, to which Horváth responded vehemently:

When I wrote an account defending the Compromise, I was aware that it would not appeal to those who believe that our ancient liberties were buried with the Compromise in 1867, as this reduced our country to an Austrian province. Neither did I expect approval from those who try to steer our nation towards self-aggrandisement and behave as if it was one of the most powerful states in the world, on a par with England, Germany and France, as if there was no need to tailor our politics to our particular strengths and circumstances, leading to a sensible compromise.[88]

Horváth endorsed the Compromise by pointing out that, in the context of post-1848 Europe, the restoration of complete independence was even more illusory than at any time in the previous centuries. He believed that, if a state could gain greater prosperity in association with another one, then that option must be taken into account. In relation to this, he asked his readers to consider the Scottish example: although Scotland was a flourishing and influential part of Britain, it was not a state in itself.[89] His refutation of the unrealistic demands for independence was substantiated by a reference to Edgar Quinet's view that 'truth is a staple of nations that have reached a mature stage, whereas flattery, false promises and delusion suit the stages of childhood and youth', expressing his hope that his own nation belonged to the former group.[90] Additionally, Horváth couched his plea for pragmatism in terms of another beneficial aspect of the Compromise, a transparent regulation of rights and obligations. Appealing to the *historia magistra vitae* tradition, he highlighted cases in the course of Hungarian history when a reasonable compromise would have been more advantageous for the nation, rather than insistence on the unrealistic ideal of complete independence.[91]

ROMANIA: UNITED AND INDEPENDENT

Kogălniceanu's was a prime example of the politically motivated historian and, on both fronts, his principal concern was to provide historical

---

[88] Horváth, *Kossuth Lajos újabb leveleire*, 2nd edn. (Pest, 1868), 1.

[89] Ibid., 86.   [90] Ibid., 96.

[91] His main example was the Rákóczi War of Independence in the early eighteenth century.

justification for the necessity of the unification and, later, independence of the two Danubian principalities. He endowed the Romanians with illustrious ancestry through language, whilst drawing upon the Roman heritage, which evoked respectability and prestige, to culturally reorientate the Romanians from the Orthodox to the Latin world. This transformation, also underlined by Kogălniceanu's relinquishing of the Cyrillic alphabet in favour of Latin, was perceived as the restoration of an ancient, normative condition after a long epoch of cultural contestation.

Kogălniceanu divides Romanian history into three fundamental epochs: the ancient era from pre-historical times until the foundation of the principalities of Wallachia and Moldavia in 1290 and 1350 respectively; the medieval era, encompassing the history of principalities until the beginning of the rule of the Greek Phanariote princes in 1716; and the modern era from 1716 onwards.[92] Romanian historians wrestled with a major obstacle when reconstructing continuities with the national past, as they had to account for a dark millennium between the Roman withdrawal from Dacia in the third century and the foundation of the medieval principalities. In addition to the inadequacy of sources, they were confronted with an emerging hypothesis in the eighteenth century which disputed the continuity of the Romanians north of the Danube (in Transylvania) and suggested that they had migrated there from the south in the twelfth century. As we have seen, to counter the immigrationist theory and overcome the gap between the Romans' retreat and the foundation of the principalities, Kogălniceanu argues that, in spite of disturbances caused by the barbarian peoples (particularly the Hungarians, who established themselves in Pannonia in the ninth century), the Romanians withdrew to the mountains and organized themselves into two embryonic republics. He insists that these territories were independent and not, as Hungarian historians asserted, subjugated and paying tribute to Hungarians or Bulgarians.[93] Another solution involved exaggerating the Romanians' better-documented presences south of the Danube, a theory that Transylvanian scholars had already advanced, culminating in speculation that medieval Bulgarian tsardoms were actually Bulgarian-Romanian 'composite' states, in which the Romanian element occasionally dominated. Kogălniceanu subscribes to both tenets of this hypothesis. Firstly, he professed that after the Roman withdrawal, during the course of

---

[92] Kogălniceanu, *Opere*, II. 394.   [93] Ibid., II. 164.

struggles with Barbarian tribes, some Daco-Romans settled in the south. Secondly, in the medieval Bulgarian rulers Peter and Ivan Asen he detected these peoples' descendants.[94]

Kogălniceanu claims that Romanian history included many fascinating curiosities, surprising events, dreadful tragedies and hair-raising horrors. His account of 'the adventurous life and cruelties' of the prince Vlad Țepes, 'the greatest monster of nature and horror of humanity', combines revulsion with a degree of pride.[95] He asserts that the perverted barbarity of the prince, nicknamed Dracula, outdid even the deeds of Tiberius, Domitian, Nero and Ivan the Terrible. Habits of the prince included dining in a courtyard where Turkish hostages were tied to a stake, and inviting beggars for dinner and having them thrown onto a fire. Kogălniceanu also relates another tradition, according to which the prince would often order his servants to cut the feet of the Turkish hostages, sprinkle them with salt, and exacerbate the torture by sending sharp-tongued goats to lick the wounds. This latter episode substantiated Kogălniceanu's conclusion that the prince must have been mentally ill.[96]

A counterweight to such horrors is provided by a celebration of the deeds of Prince Michael the Brave, primarily for his achievements as a Christian warrior in the fighting against the Turks, an accomplishment that rendered him comparable to Themistocles and Achilles.[97] In the 1840s, Kogălniceanu's accounts of the prince began to place more emphasis on his short-lived unification of the three territories that were to form the core of modern Romania: 'Uniquely among the princes, he was the only ruler who succeeded in unifying the constituent parts of ancient Dacia, uniquely among them, he could address himself as Michael, the prince of Moldavia, Wallachia and Transylvania by God's grace.'[98] This change in emphasis corresponds to a shift in Romanian historiography between 1830 and 1860, whereby the perception of Michael underwent a metamorphosis from warrior and Christian hero to emblem of Romanian unity. Thus, Michael's unification could be interpreted in two ways: in retrospect it seemed like a short-lived resurrection of ancient Dacia; with foresight, it represents an antecedent of the future Romanian nation-state.[99] In that context, it provided a pillar of continuity between the ancient and contemporary eras, in the same way as the legacy of the Commonwealth for Lelewel and

[94] Kogălniceanu, *Opere*, II. 27–41. [95] Ibid., II. 112. [96] Ibid., II. 112–13.
[97] Ibid., II. 390. [98] Ibid. [99] Boia, *History and Myth*, 42.

the heritage of the Hussite movement for Palacký. The modern era, corresponding to the reign of the Phanariots in the eighteenth century, represented a downturn for the course of Romanian history. This was largely due to the ruling dynasties' corruption and immorality which had a detrimental effect on public spirit. Kogălniceanu believed that, during this era, most countries, including China, contributed to general development, whilst the despotism of the Phanariots made Romania an exception.

In addition to continuity, the other underlying theme of Romanian historiography was the need for national unity. Kogălniceanu saw the strength of regional loyalties as a serious obstacle and argued that these had to be subordinated to common national goals. He believed that the reluctance of the Spartans, Thebans and Athenians to unite under the banner of Hellas contributed to the fall of ancient Greek civilization.[100] In a similar vein, internal conflicts between medieval Lombards, Venetians and Neapolitans allowed the Germans to take advantage of political fragmentation. Kogălniceanu warned that even his ancestors suffered from lack of unity; they perceived themselves as Transylvanians, Moldavians and Wallachians, which was the source of their misfortunes.[101]

For Romanian scholars ancient Dacia became the expression of primordial unity, as well as being a vantage point for the definition of the national space. In 1834, unfolding the history of ancient Dacians, Kogălniceanu began his *Histoire* with the following sentence: 'In the first century AD a strong and powerful barbaric state shook civilized Rome. This state, which was independent, was to be located on the territory where Transylvania, the Banat, Moldavia and Wallachia are now situated: it extended from the Theiss (Tisza) and the Carpathians to the Danube, Dniester and the Black Sea.'[102] Using this demarcation of the lands of ancient Dacia, Kogălniceanu constructed a national desideratum about the borders of a future Romanian state. At the time when he was writing, the Romanian state did not exist, and the term *Dacia* was applied to the entire national territory, as illustrated by the title of Kogălniceanu's journal, *Dacia Literară*.[103] Kogălniceanu's designation of the national space testifies to contemporary fascination with 'natural borders', as manifested in the image of a perfect, almost

---

[100] Kogălniceanu, *Opere*, II. 394.   [101] Ibid.   [102] Ibid.
[103] The world *Romania* was first coined by a Transylvanian Saxon scholar in the eighteenth century; subsequently it was employed by a Greek historian in the early nineteenth century.

circular space, delineated by three great rivers: the Danube, the Dniester and the Theiss, and reinforced by the Carpathian mountains which pass right across it.[104] As well as geographical factors, the desired union of the two principalities was underlined by the condition that Wallachians and Moldavians were brothers in the cross, in blood, in language and in law; they shared the same hopes and anxieties.[105] Nevertheless, such a union was not inevitable: as with Bohemia and Moravia in Palacký's case, the history of the principalities of Moldavia and Wallachia was informed as much by rivalry and conflict as by political alliance. Furthermore, Kogălniceanu's historical and political endeavours were coloured by loyalty to his home region and Moldavia retained a degree of individuality in his work.

In 1859, the dream of Romanian politicians was fulfilled: the two principalities were united and Romania became a nation-state. Nevertheless, this was not yet the resurrection of 'ancient Dacia', as Transylvania remained a missing element in the desired geographical design. Transylvania had to be included because Kogălniceanu regarded all Romanian-speaking territories as his fatherland, and he actively promoted cultural ties between the principalities and Transylvania.[106] In his journal, the *Dacia Literară*, he often republished articles that had appeared in Transylvanian periodicals. His loyalty, however, did not manifest itself in concrete territorial claims. Since the dismemberment of the Habsburg Monarchy seemed illusory during this era, there could be no union between Transylvania and Romania. A federation seemed more feasible, and hence politicians sought the autonomy of Transylvania, or an autonomy that included all provinces of the Austro-Hungarian Empire with a Romanian population.

In 1878 the southern part of the former Ottoman province of Dobrogea was annexed to Romania, in return for Southern Bessarabia's seizure by the Russian Empire. The new arrangement disturbed traditional visions about national territory, as the region had never been considered to belong to it, and its attachment to Romania was initially an unwelcome development. As the British statesman William Gladstone noted, this province was as 'a gift ungraciously given and reluctantly received'.[107] Dobrogea's diverse ethnic composition was perceived as a danger to

---

[104] Boia, *History and Myth*, 132.

[105] Kogălniceanu, *Opere*, II. 394.   [106] Ibid.

[107] Constantin Iordachi, *Citizenship, Nation- and State-Building: The Integration of Northern Dobrogea into Romania 1878–1913* (Pittsburgh, 2002), 8.

the country's homogeneity and political stability. Nonetheless, after the initial shock, Romanian scholars began to focus their efforts on integrating the region into Romania, both geographically and historically, a motivation that informed Kogălniceanu's declaration that 'Dobrogea is not a Bulgarian land; in every corner . . . we find traces of our Romanian ancestors.'[108] Kogălniceanu supported this by augmenting the insubstantial evidence, noting Wallachia's temporary possession of the region at the beginning of the fifteenth century and the many ethnic Romanians in the province. He also called for archaeological excavations in order to find traces of the Romanian presence there. Later, the theory that Dobrogea had been an ancient Romanian land which returned to the 'mother country' took root in Romanian historiography, becoming an integral part of the national ideology.[109]

CONCLUSION

Whilst my protagonists attributed analogous qualities to the Golden Age, they simultaneously discerned aspects of that era in many diverse epochs and by appealing to different ideological traditions and political languages. Daukantas's account was indebted to the humanist heritage to a greater extent than that of his four colleagues. His veneration of paganism, and frequent parallels between ancient Greeks and Romans and ancient Lithuanians, resembled the stance adopted by some contemporary Irish historians, who asserted that the ancient kingdom of the Gaels had once been on an equal footing with the societies of ancient Greece and Rome and that paganism, an uncorrupted natural religion, was commensurate with the cults of the great ancient civilizations.[110]

Daukantas understated the continuity between the early modern Polish and Lithuanian states and forged a link between the era of the medieval Grand Duchy and contemporary Lithuanians, anticipating Lithuanian independence. Horváth believed that the Compromise provided Hungary with the arrangement best suited for the political circumstances of the age, whilst Palacký envisaged his nation's future

---

[108] Kogălniceanu, *Opere*, Vol. IV, pt. 4, p. 639, quoted in Iordachi, *Citizenship, Nation- and State-Building*, 14.

[109] Iordachi, *Citizenship, Nation- and State-Building*, 14.

[110] Colin Kidd, 'Gaelic Antiquity and National Identity in Enlightenment Scotland and Ireland', *English Historical Review* 109:434 (1994), 1202.

as part of a multi-national federation. Such dilemmas were characteristic of subordinate entities in composite states. Anti-unionists prized
national independence most highly; their counterparts believed that a
more advanced state offered benefits which outweighed the advantages
of (relative) autonomy. This preoccupation was by no means confined
to East-Central Europe; among other examples, it constituted the major
concern for Scottish historians after the Act of Union in 1707, as well
as for Norwegian scholars in the nineteenth century. In both cases,
advocates saw close coexistence with England and Denmark respectively
as an opportunity for modernization and the advancement of civilization; those who opposed it emphasized the colonizing nature of the
subordination.

In addition to sensitivity to national affairs, social concerns also
found an echo in my historians' representations of the Golden Age,
as illustrated by their admiration of rulers who acknowledged the
status of unprivileged people. To that end, Lelewel's veneration of
the Commonwealth's political institutions resonated with the native
republican tradition, and his attitude towards social reform evoked
radical Enlightenment ideals as well as those of contemporary democrats.
Horváth's emphasis on the originality of Hungarian political institutions
resembled the early modern feudal tradition of the 'ancient constitution',
but dovetailed with a modernizing, 'Whiggish' discourse. Rather than
defending the nobility's ancient privileges, it advocated the emancipation
of oppressed people. Moreover, uniquely among my historians, Horváth
argued in favour of industry and trade because they were perceived
to facilitate liberty, thereby endorsing the fundamental tenet of the
commercial tradition.

Only Palacký's narrative, infused with Protestant sympathies, was
markedly shaped by an explicit confessional orientation. His praise
of the Hussite movement and veneration of Jan Hus reflected the
Romantic era's fascination with heretics and religious reformers. Ranke's
rendering of Martin Luther as a symbol of German unity and Jules
Michelet's elevation of Joan of Arc into the most potent symbol of
French nationhood provided other examples of this trend. Heretics
distinguished themselves by their fearless opposition to the ruling
order (whether ecclesiastical or secular), evident in their willingness to
sacrifice their lives for their principles. Consequently, as the reaction
of the Austrian authorities to Palacký's portrayal of Hus indicates, they
could be appropriated to good effect by historians who opposed existing
regimes.

Kogălniceanu's appraisal of a 'traditional hero', Prince Michael the Brave, entailed redefining his original role from that of a Christian warrior into a proponent of Romanian unity. Perhaps the most obvious parallel to Romanian historians' preoccupation with unity and continuity is demonstrated by Greek historical writing. Whilst Romanian scholars sought to integrate their countrymen scattered throughout Moldavia and Wallachia and Transylvania, their Greek colleagues, believing that Greece should not be identified with the history of a small kingdom, strove to incorporate the Greeks of the Ottoman Empire. Furthermore, in both cases historians had to bridge a gap between ancient and modern times: in Romania this comprised asserting the existence of medieval embryonic republics, whereas in Greek historiography it encompassed the elevation of the Byzantine period, an epoch previously dismissed as a dark and barbarous age, into a crucial stage, the representation of the missing medieval link. Nonetheless, reflections on the national past were not exclusively inward-looking. On the contrary, as the next chapter will reveal, national self-images could only be defined through confrontation with 'others', by assessing the nation's relationship to foreigners, both inside and outside the confines of the national territory.

9

Perceptions of Others and Attitudes to European Civilization

IMAGES OF THE SELF AND OTHERS

National identity is by its nature contingent and relational and thus national communities are inclined to define other groups by the negation of their own self-image.[1] Following an assessment of self-perceptions in the previous chapter, as exemplified in the flourishing eras of national history, this chapter adopts a different approach to the subject, in relation to 'others': neighbours, dominant powers and (potential) enemies. This is accompanied by an exploration of my historians' orientation in the broader context of European culture and society and of their nation's perceived contribution to the cause of European civilization. Their perspectives embraced a wide spectrum and often shifted according to the changing political scene. Of these, I seek to focus on common trends and typical instances.

The construction of identities almost invariably involves asymmetric classifications. Reinhard Koselleck demonstrated that the first documented political concepts expressing this kind of relation were Hellene/Barbarian, and, later, the Christian/pagan pairings.[2] He termed these counterconcepts asymmetric because the qualities which communities ascribe to one another are not reciprocal. With some adjustment, Koselleck's scheme may be applicable to studies into national identities; as we have seen in the previous chapter, internal conflicts in national history were habitually imbued with appeals to antipodes, such as Protestants and Catholics, defenders and opponents of reforms,

---

[1] See for example Peter Sahlins, *Boundaries: The Making of France and Spain in the Pyrenees* (Berkeley and Los Angeles, 1989), 271.

[2] Reinhart Koselleck, 'The Historical-Political Semantics of Asymmetric Counterconcepts', in Koselleck, *Futures Past*, 158.

and foreign versus national ideas.[3] Perhaps even more significantly, the nation's relationship to external others was characterized by binary oppositions. The crystallization of the national territory, a corollary of administrative centralization since the Enlightenment era, resulted not just in the erosion (or at least fading) of regional frontiers, but also in a more precise demarcation of external borders vis-à-vis foreign nations.[4] The process of delineating previously amorphous and unsettled borders brought conflicting interests and overlapping territorial claims to the fore, and consequently neighbouring nations were inherently cast in the role of the significant 'external other'.

Even the history of Britain, an island geographically separated from the continent, overlapped with that of France and this encouraged British scholars to contrast a Protestant, robust Britain with an effete, Catholic France. They set honest manliness and simplicity against the perceived effeminacy and deceit of France and disparaged the artifice of French manners.[5] The late nineteenth-century historian Edward Freeman even declared that France was 'the undying curse of Europe'.[6] French historians, in turn, viewed Britain as their country's chief rival. For Jules Michelet Britain epitomized *l'anti-France*, a feudal nation where the appearance of liberty was obtained at the expense of injustice and inequality. He proclaimed that 'the war of all wars, the struggle of all struggles, is that between Britain and France, the rest(s) are minor skirmishes'.[7] Michelet reinforced his stance by 'pervasive metaphors': he portrayed the English as brutal transgressors and insatiable meat-eaters, whilst the French were vegetarian and lived in harmony with nature, subsisting peacefully on milk and cereals. Nevertheless, such stereotypes were not rigid and, with the onset of the Franco-Prussian war, Germany gradually replaced Britain as the most dangerous rival in Michelet's view. In a volte-face, he expressed hopes for a future reconciliation between the English and the French, underlined by an alimentary analogy: he noted that the English were introducing

---

[3] It has to be noted that Koselleck's scheme only includes pairs of concept which claim to cover the whole of humanity.

[4] R. J. W. Evans, 'Frontiers and National Identities in Central European History', in *Austria, Hungary and the Habsburgs. Essays on Central Europe c.1683–1867* (Oxford, 2006), 120.

[5] Burrow, *A Liberal Descent*, 209.

[6] *The Life and Letters of Edward A. Freeman*, ed. W. R. W. Stephens, 2 vols. (London, 1895), II. 10.

[7] Jules Michelet, *Le Peuple* (Paris, 1974), 224, quoted in Hans Kohn, 'France between Britain and Germany', *Journal of the History of Ideas* 17:3 (1956), 289.

increasing quantities of cereal into their diet, whilst the French were becoming more carnivorous.[8]

My protagonists' intellectual enquiries in this context encompassed corresponding dilemmas and anxieties, although they were conditioned by regional idiosyncrasies. Frontier regions have traditionally been cast as privileged sites for the articulation of national distinctions, and few countries other than Britain and Iceland could boast boundaries demarcated by the sea, and therefore beyond dispute. Most territories were riddled with enclaves and exclaves, and borders continued to fluctuate throughout the nineteenth century. Nevertheless, East-Central Europe distinguished itself even against this backdrop, as it displayed, in Louis Namier's words, 'more frontier and less coherence than any other state in Europe'.[9] Here, national histories did not merely overlap for a short period of foreign occupation, but territories as well as histories were literary 'shared'. Behind the unsettled borders resided a remarkably heterogeneous population, representing a wide array of languages, religions and customs. Typically, ethnic groups were not confined to clearly defined territories, but formed an inseparable patchwork of indivisible domains.

The demarcation of the national community vis-à-vis external others was entwined with an internal delineation against certain social, linguistic or religious groups who resided within the 'national' territory, but whose distinctive traditions and customs made them appear alien to the core. The Jewish population were a prime example of this: their unique traditions rendered them vulnerable to exclusion from eventual membership of the nation.

Perhaps surprisingly, members of the Jesuit order, a community notoriously hostile to the Jews, could also be cast in the role of the 'other' and thus regarded as an impediment to national unity. In this context, David Hume's statement entails an intriguing parallel: 'Where any set of men, scattered over distant nations, maintain a close society or communication together, they acquire a similitude of manners, and have but little in common with the nations amongst whom they live. Thus the Jews in Europe, and the Armenians in the East, have a peculiar character . . . The Jesuits, in all Roman Catholic countries, are also observed to have a character peculiar to

---

[8] Gossman, *Between History and Literature*, 199.
[9] Louis Namier, *Vanished Supremacies* (London, 1962), 139.

themselves.'[10] Additionally, ideas about women's roles in the national past and their status in contemporary society were also, to some extent, dictated by their 'otherness'.

When contextualizing their nations' status and attainments within the framework of European civilization, historians representing dominant nations tended to adopt a supremacist attitude and present these as exemplary for other ones. From this vantage point, other nations could be discerned not simply as inferior, but sometimes even as being 'in widely different stages of civilization', as illustrated by Macaulay, who asserted that, compared to the English, the native Irish were 'almost as rude as the savages of Labrador'.[11] Moreover, perceptions of civilization versus backwardness were also projected onto geographical divides, such as South and North and, from the eighteenth century onwards increasingly, West and East. As we shall see, my historians' attitudes to these perceptions diverged, but they were united in their efforts to refute the accusation of backwardness attached to their cultures by illuminating their nation's unique achievements in the history of European civilization.

EXTERNAL OTHERS: THE NEIGHBOURS

Whilst earlier chapters considered aspects of overlaps in national histories, the purpose of the following three instances is to review and further elucidate common patterns in the representation of those clashes. A central dilemma in this context arose from the conflicting nature of appeals to historical rights and natural rights. Horváth's account of Hungarian politicians' predicaments in the Reform Era aptly captures this complexity:

Fortunate are those countries, where the problems of language and nationality had been resolved before national jealousy emerged, for instance in France, where only a minority of people spoke the Paris dialect at the outbreak of the Revolution. Hungarians were not so blessed. Although their interest in the national language had already been aroused in the 1790s as a reaction to the centralizing and Germanizing attempts of the Viennese government, the

---

[10] David Hume, 'Of National Characters', in *Essays Moral, Political and Literary* (Oxford, 1983), 210.

[11] Burrow, *A Liberal Descent*, 41.

Hungarian language was prevented from becoming official until much later (i.e. before the Revolution of 1848). Thus, it was only natural that the Hungarians claimed their thousand-year-old historical rights and fought to strengthen the historical nation by emphasizing the legacy of their constitution . . . But whilst they drew upon *historical rights* in their endeavours, the nationalities' petition for greater recognition was founded on *natural rights*. Neither of the two parties was prepared to compromise in this matter.[12]

Horváth was sceptical about any cooperation between Hungarians and the nationalities. He characterized Kossuth's idea of a federation of Danubian peoples using a metaphor of 'six kitchens and twelve cooks', indicating that such a state formation would have been destined to provoke constant quarrels and thus was doomed to failure.[13]

Appeals to historical and natural rights were often incompatible when advanced by two different claimants; nevertheless, it was perfectly possible to amalgamate them *within* one particular national context. As we have seen, Romanian scholars fortified their postulate of antiquity and primacy of Romanian settlements with reference to the Romanians' majority status in the region and their exclusion from political representation. By contrast, Hungarian scholars refuted the theory of Daco-Roman continuity by advancing the immigrationist hypothesis, which held that Romanians appeared in Transylvania during the thirteenth to fourteenth centuries where their community of impoverished peasants and shepherds benefited from the superior status of the local population.[14]

Kogălniceanu's stance corresponded to this canonical Romanian view. Interestingly, Horváth's declaration that the Romanians constituted the most ancient and most populous community in Transylvania reveals that, at least in some of his works, he also seems to have subscribed to the theory of Daco-Romanian continuity.[15] His historical-constitutional approach, and confidence in the millennial Hungarian presence in the region, failed to take into account the implications of the Romanians' earlier occupancy for the status of Transylvania. It may be significant that in a posthumous edition of Horváth's work, the editor added a footnote to the relevant passage, expounding the tenets of the immigrationist hypothesis and declaring that 'new

[12] Horváth, *Huszonöt év Magyarország történetéből*, II. 116.

[13] Márki, *Horváth Mihály*, 213.

[14] Countless publications focus on this dispute, including László Péter (ed.), *Historians and the History of Transylavania* (Boulder, 1992).

[15] Horváth, *Magyarország történelme*, VII. 554 and VIII. 44.

evidence' invalidated my protagonist's argument on Daco-Romanian continuity.[16] Horváth sympathized with the complaint that despite representing the largest ethnic group, Romanians were not entitled to the political rights enjoyed by the Hungarians, Saxons and Seklers and also faced religious discrimination. At the same time, he noted that initially only a handful of intellectuals were concerned with those grievances and the overwhelming majority of the population remained oblivious to political issues.[17]

Lelewel's and Daukantas's conflicting approaches to the history of Lithuania typify another divergence between two strands of rhetoric, one highlighting the dominant nation's civilizing mission, the other construing the same tendency as an attempt to colonize the non-dominant group. As has been noted, Lelewel's interpretation, which saw Lithuania as a constituent of the Polish state, coincided exactly with the Polish territorial-patriotic stance. He put forward the claim that Polonization after the Union was entirely natural and beneficial and, in fact, the Lithuanians were fortunate to fall under the auspices of a more advanced civilization. Additionally, he interprets the Union of Lublin as a sign of brotherhood between the two peoples:

The change of nationality normally starts among the ranks of the higher classes. The influence of a superior foreign civilization makes it desirable. People usually retain their customs, language and religion for a long time but they do not actively resist if those are altered; they gradually become indifferent. This happened to the Lithuanians and Ruthenians when they were amalgamated with Poland. Despite the attempts of the Lithuanian aristocracy to overturn the union, in 1569 their tenacity was overcome and the association and fraternity of the two nations was finally sealed.[18]

Thus, for Lelewel, after 1569 Poland and Lithuania formed a single indivisible republic, governed by one ruler, who was elected by the common diets, and Lithuania constituted an inferior component of the Commonwealth.[19] Whilst the historical precedent of the Union was available to substantiate Lelewel's claim to Lithuania (and Ruthenia),

---

[16] This revision was based on the claim that the account of the medieval Hungarian chronicler, Anonymus, on the presence of the Romanians at the time of the Hungarians' conquest, was not reliable. See the comment of the editor, Gyula Sebestyén, in Horváth, *A magyarok története rövid előadásban*, 6th edn. (Budapest, 1887), I. 42–3.

[17] Horváth, *Magyarország történelme*, VII. 554–5. The nationalities' lack of political representation is also pointed out in *Huszonöt év*, I. 128.

[18] Lelewel, *Histoire de la Lithuanie et de la Ruthénie jusqu'à 1549* (Paris, 1861), 3.

[19] Lelewel, *Dzieła*, VII. 135–6; *Geschichte Polens* (Leipzig, 1846), 125–6.

linguistic and ethnic arguments were absent from his plea. Instead, he resorted to the ideological underpinning of the slogan 'for our freedom and yours', expressing the conviction that the non-Polish-speaking inhabitants of the former Commonwealth also benefited from the Poles' struggle for the restoration of the state.

Daukantas's assessment of the consequences of the Union for Lithuania represented a striking contrast:

> While the Union decreed that the two nations would protect each other, the Poles continually used the pretext of the Union as an excuse to reduce the size of Lithuania for their own benefit. Thus began the demise of the famous Lithuanian nation, which was not caused by the bravery and tenacity of her enemies, but by immorality and trickery ... from then on everything Lithuanian, language, character, and traditions, were ridiculed, while everything Polish was praised and honoured ... and though the Lithuanians agreed to obey the Polish king within the Union, they retained military and economic privileges and overall they maintained their old ways of rule.[20]

As we have seen, the same incompatibility characterizes the two scholars' views on feudalization in Lithuania. Daukantas professed that it was instituted under Polish auspices, whilst Lelewel specifically asserted that Polish influence led to its abolition. In seeking to trace instances that demonstrated the Lithuanians' advanced ways of life, Daukantas tried to counter Lelewel's patronizing attitude, claiming, for example, that the ancient Lithuanians had taught the Slavs how to cultivate the land,[21] and reprimanding the Poles for destroying and stealing archival sources. When contemplating setting up a new historical journal, the *Acta Lithuanorum* with his friend, Narbutt, he suggested that it should be published in Königsberg and not in Poznań because, 'if the Poles get hold of it, they will distort Lithuania's history'.[22] Scholars whose nation was subject to foreign occupation frequently voiced such grievances. For instance, in *A History of Scotland During the Reign of Queen Mary*, William Robertson likewise complains that in the late thirteenth century, Edward I of England challenged the independence of Scotland, and in order to strengthen his claim, he destroyed many historical monuments which supported the antiquity or freedom of the kingdom.[23]

---

[20] Daukantas, *Istorija Žemaitiška*, I. 408.   [21] Ibid., II. 68.

[22] Daukantas, *Raštai*, II. 734.

[23] William Robertson, *A History of Scotland during the Reign of Queen Mary* (Edinburgh, 1830), 8.

Central to Palacký's argument was the assumption that the ancient Czechs settled on an uninhabited land and that they were the first people to establish a state in that territory. As a corollary, the increasing German presence in the Bohemian lands was primarily the result of colonization.[24] Palacký's theory of the Czechs' and Germans' coexistence in Bohemia, encompassing a shared past fraught with conflict and trauma, is embedded in a philosophical framework:

The principal concern and the fundamental feature of all Bohemian-Moravian history is . . . continuous contact and conflict between the Slav, German and Romance characters. Because the Romance character does not exert a direct influence on the Czech, but does so indirectly through Germandom, it can be argued that Czech history is largely based on conflict with Germandom, in other words on the Czechs' acceptance or rejection of the German way of life . . . [It is] a struggle carried out not only on the borders of the Bohemian lands but also within them, not only against foreigners but also against compatriots, not only with the shield and the sword but also with word and spirit, institutions and customs, openly and covertly, with great zeal and blind passion, and not only for victory or subjugation but also for reconciliation.[25]

The use of polarity is clearly evident in this passage and has been attributed to Schelling's and Hegel's influence, but, as has been hinted, the eternal struggle with the German 'hereditary enemy' had already been outlined by one of Palacký's predecessors. Such appeals to the law of polarity (*lex contrariorum*) were commonly found in contemporary historical writing. Palacký's scheme resembles the Rankean dynamic rivalry, which presented a conflict not only between two peoples (the Germanic and Romance in Ranke's case), but also between religious denominations, those of Catholicism and Protestantism. Both Ranke and Palacký regarded this dynamic rivalry as a useful, even necessary, source of strength and vitality which maintained the balance of the universe. In the same vein, Palacký maintained that German influence was not entirely harmful; it had in fact forced the early Slavs to overcome their natural tendency towards anarchy, thus helping to ensure their survival.[26]

Descending from philosophical heights, my protagonist was confronted with the tangible conflict between the interests and future

---

[24] Štaif, 'The Image of the Other in the Nineteenth Century', 88.

[25] Palacký, *Dějiny*, I. 10–11; my translation draws on but is not identical with the excerpt in Trencsényi and Kopeček (eds.), *Discourses of Collective Identity*, II. 55.

[26] Palacký, *Radhost* (Prague, 1871), II. 491.

ambitions of the Czech and German inhabitants in his country. During the 1850s local borders in the Bohemian lands were redrawn and the Czechs demanded that the country be partitioned along the linguistic frontier.[27] Already in 1849 Palacký pointed out that the geographical peculiarities of the region rendered this unfeasible: 'I certainly do not oppose the separation of German-Bohemia and the Czech lands, and if this was realistic, I would definitely recommend it. However, Bohemia is a basin (*Kesselland*), and therefore, it is not possible to divide it without destroying it.'[28]

INTERNAL OTHERS: THE JEWS

The markedly distinctive religion, customs and way of life of the Jewish community almost unavoidably cast them in the role of the 'other' vis-à-vis the Christian majority. In the nineteenth century the legal status of Jewry in several countries was still regulated by anachronistic feudal laws, including restrictions on residence, exclusion from several professions and special taxation. In an era when the abolition of the remnants of feudalism constituted a crucial concern, approaches to the Jews in historical writing were inherently linked to debates about their legal situation. Because the Jewish population constituted a remarkably heterogeneous community, paradoxically, they could be singled out both for their reverence of ancient traditions and, later, for their pivotal role in economic progress and modernization. Although liberal historians tended to champion the emancipation of the Jews, their claims were predicated on the assumption that this would lead to cultural assimilation: the gradual abandonment of their language and ancient superstitions.[29] Nor were appeals for endowing the Jews with civil rights necessarily motivated by humanitarian concerns, but rather by the utilitarian expectation that their economic and cultural prowess would benefit the national community.

The magnitude and duration of this contribution should not be underestimated. In the absence of a desperately needed banking system in medieval Europe, where the Church prohibited Christians from lending at interest, money-lending became reserved for the Jews; and they also

---

[27] Evans, 'Frontiers and National Identities in Central European History', 130.
[28] Palacký, *Spisy drobné*, I. 79.
[29] Hoffmann, 'The Nation, Nationalism, and After: The Case of France', 225.

acted as creditors to royalty in return for protection and privileges.[30] Jewry's leading role in economic modernization increased the disparity between their actual economic influence and the outdated restrictions on their enterprises.[31] Moreover, their significant contribution towards modernization exposed them to the stereotype of 'capitalist corrupters'. Even in those countries where they were emancipated, new laws were not enforced and the legal separateness of Jewish society continued. The question of Jewish citizenship was a pressing issue even in societies where the Jews comprised a small minority of the population, for example in the German lands. Opponents believed that, by following their own religious laws, Jews were making themselves into a distinct and foreign nationality. For advocates of emancipation, religious conviction was not a precondition of citizenship and they also recognized Jewish military participation, particularly in the wars of liberation against France, an indication of their membership of the German nation.[32] In Britain, those who were hostile to their inclusion argued that Jews formed a community with their brethren scattered all over the world and not with their fellow countrymen. The following quote from Macaulay illustrates their perspective: 'an English Jew looks on a Portuguese Jew as his countryman, and on an English Christian as a stranger and this want of patriotic feeling, it is said, renders a Jew unfit to exercise political functions'.[33] Macaulay discredits this stance by underscoring the irrelevance of religion to civil status:

The points of difference between Christianity and Judaism have very much to do with a man's fitness to be a bishop or a rabbi. But they have no more to do with his fitness to be a magistrate, a legislator, or a minister of finance, than with his fitness to be a cobbler. Nobody has ever thought of compelling cobblers to make any declaration on the true faith of a Christian.[34]

A further objection to the Jewish population's incorporation into the nation revolved around disputing the voluntary aspect of membership. According to Michelet, France's core population was comprised of the

---

[30] Masha Greenbaum, *The Jews of Lithuania: A History of a Remarkable Community 1316–1945* (Jerusalem, 1995), 27.

[31] Magdalena Opalski and Israel Bartal, *Poles and Jews: A Failed Brotherhood* (Hanover and London), 15.

[32] For the German context see Peter Pulzer, *Jews and the German State: The Political History of a Minority, 1848–1933* (Oxford and Cambridge, MA, 1992).

[33] Thomas Babington Macaulay, 'Speech on Civil Disabilities of the Jews' (January 1831), in *Critical and Historical Essays*, 2 parts (London, 1933), II. 229.

[34] Ibid., 226.

native peasantry, whereas the roots and *patrie* of the Jews could be traced at the London stock exchange. His rumination: 'are the French all those who want to be French or those who are themselves products of French history, the descendants of the French?' indubitably implies the exclusion of the Jews from the nation.[35]

The Jewish population feature in my historians' writings in some prototypical ways. First, they all pride themselves on their nation's hospitality to the Jews in the past. Second, their assessment of the history of commerce and industry necessarily acknowledges the Jewish contribution, although usually in unfavourable terms. Third, they explore the relationship of the Jews to the rest of the population in both the past and present. In particular, they contemplate the question of emancipation, at which point their judgements diverge significantly. As we have seen in the previous chapter, my protagonists all professed that at some stage their national community extended hospitality to the Jews, in contrast to other countries where they suffered atrocities. Kogălniceanu recounts how the Dacian king, Decebal, invited Jews into his realm after their expulsion from Jerusalem in AD 70, thereby allowing them to avoid enslavement, and even offering them lands.[36] Daukantas praises the considerable degree of religious toleration and goodwill towards the Jews in pagan Lithuania, whilst Lelewel points to their autonomy and even professes that they considered the Polish Commonwealth a paradise on earth. Horváth reminds his readers that the privileges granted to the Jews by Hungarian kings were in return for services, especially delivering credit to the monarch.

Subtle and stronger hints in my historians' works reveal that they deemed the Jewish monopoly in commerce and industry, a corollary of the exclusion from many other professions, somewhat excessive. Daukantas notes that the Jews fled to Lithuania from Poland in ever increasing numbers during the medieval period; they were granted the right to farm customs duties and, at a later stage, become innkeepers.[37] Lelewel surmises that by the twelfth and thirteenth centuries only agriculture remained in the hands of the national population; commerce and trade were conducted by foreigners, especially Germans and Jews and, he added disapprovingly, 'neither of the two were lacking in

---

[35] Hoffmann, 'The Nation, Nationalism, and After: The Case of France', 232. Such a stance runs against the traditional view of French nationhood as voluntaristic.

[36] Kogălniceanu, *Opere*, II. 54.   [37] Daukantas, *Raštai*, I. 639.

numbers'.[38] He also alludes to the Polish landowners' practice of administering their estates through Jewish intermediaries, which often prompted anti-Semitic bias.[39] Horváth's more favourable assessment of the Jewish participation in trade and commerce was motivated by the high regard in which he held those activities. He lamented that, from the Middle Ages onwards, commerce enjoyed a poor reputation in Hungary, because the privileged classes remained oblivious to its potential to enhance the country's prosperity. According to Horváth, merchants and dealers were practically equated with cheats. He noted that in some individual cases Jews and Armenians might have deserved that verdict, but on the whole, he considered it unjust to hold an entire ethnic group responsible for individual instances of cheating and money-grubbing.[40]

My historians' attitudes ranged from pro-emancipatory rhetoric to opposition, or at least, reservations, towards granting civil rights to the Jewish population. Daukantas did not advance a specific argument in this context, but his remarks imply that he looked upon Jewry as a separate entity. Horváth and Lelewel wholeheartedly endorsed emancipation, Palacký expressed doubts about it and Kogălniceanu, yielding to domestic political pressure, concurred with the Romanian state's denial of civic rights to the Jews, despite this violating international agreements. Jews of the Congress Kingdom were emancipated, de jure, in 1807, but the new law was not enforced, causing Lelewel to lament that, despite their native status, after eight hundred years of residence, they were still treated as outsiders by the Polish population.[41] During the uprising of 1830 Lelewel published an essay 'To the People of Israel', in which he drew a parallel between the fate of the Jews and Poles: both had lost their homelands; whilst the Jews in ancient times had to endure oppression under the kings of Assyria, Egypt and Babylon, contemporary Poles suffered under the despotic rulers of Russia, Prussia and Austria.[42] He also juxtaposed the ruler Casimir the Great with King Solomon and compared the Poles' desire to liberate their land from

---

[38] Lelewel, *Dzieła*, VII. 93; *Geschichte Polens*, 68.

[39] Lelewel, *Betrachtungen*, 482; *Dzieła*, VIII. 115–16.

[40] *Horváth Mihály kisebb történelmi munkái*, II. 15 and 41.

[41] Lelewel, *Sprawa żydowska w 1859, w liście do Ludwika Merzbacha rozważana* (Poznań, 1860), 12; in German version, *Die Judenfrage im Jahre 1859, in einem Briefe an Ludwig Merzbach erörtert* (Lemberg, 1860), 12.

[42] Lelewel, 'Odezwa komitetu narodowego do ludu Izraelskiego', in *Polska. Dzieje i rzeczy jej*, Vol. XVIII/2 (Poznań, 1865), 147.

occupation to that of Judas Macabbeus.[43] The involvement of some members of the Jewish community in the uprising of 1830 confirmed Lelewel's hope that they would identify with the fate of the Poles, prompting them to join the struggle for independence, thereby securing civil rights for themselves.[44]

In 1859 the *Gazeta Warszawska* (The Warsaw Gazette) waged a vicious press campaign against the Jewish middle classes of Warsaw, which saw the Jews responding to the accusations and even suing the journal, although they subsequently lost the case in court.[45] Polish public opinion generally supported the assailants, but Lelewel was amongst a handful of intellectuals who sided with the Jews. Understanding that the origins of anti-Semitism were largely rooted in ignorance, he petitioned for the dissemination of the Jewish cultural heritage through the translation of poetry, prayers and even the Talmud into Polish.[46] Lelewel's support was greatly appreciated by the Jewish community; a rabbi attended his funeral and his attainments were praised, not just as an erudite man, but also as a friend of the Jewish people in several obituaries written by Jewish scholars.[47] One of these compared the Polish scholar to Moses, who delivered his nation from slavery but did not live to see the promised land.[48] In the 1860s, after yet another failed insurrection, the need to enlist Jewish support for Polish aspirations of independence once again became clear and a major shift in public opinion in favour of the Jews occurred. It was at this time that Lelewel's analogy between the fate of Jews and Poles became a widespread literary stereotype.[49]

In Hungary assimilation involved a linguistic dimension, entailing the renunciation of, not just Yiddish and Hebrew, but also the German of the Central European Jewish Enlightenment.[50] The Hungarian vested interest in emancipation was propelled by the need to redress the balance between the Hungarian-speaking population and the other nationalities, who slightly outnumbered them. Thus, the Hungarians' position was expected to be strengthened by the appropriation of the

---

[43] Lelewel, 144 and 154.

[44] Lelewel, *Dzieła*, VIII. 115–18; *Geschichte Polens*, 482–3.

[45] Opalski and Bartal, *Poles and Jews: A Failed Brotherhood*, 19.

[46] Lelewel, *Sprawa żydowska*, 6; *Die Judenfrage*, 6.

[47] Pinchas Kon, *Nekrolog hebrajski o J. Lelewelu* (1861) (Wilno, 1930). Lelewel's attitude to Jewish history and the Jewish question are discussed in R. Centnerszwerowa, *Stanowisko Lelewela wobec dziejów i spraw żydów polskich* (Warsaw, 1911).

[48] Brock, 'Joachim Lelewel', 83.   [49] Opalski and Bartal, *Poles and Jews*, 51–2.

[50] William O. McCagg, *A History of Habsburg Jews, 1670–1918* (Bloomington, 1989), 133.

Jewish contribution to economy and culture. For Horváth the essential nature of emancipation was self-explanatory, stemming from his conviction regarding religious toleration and equality between denominations. Nevertheless, he registers the voices of dissent in Hungarian public opinion. In the *Huszonöt év*, Horváth records the Jews' exposure to atrocities in March 1848, after the new laws declared the irrelevance of religion to civil status, rights and duties. He concludes that the middle classes, who were emancipated simultaneously, were unwilling to share their newly won rights with the Jews and, in their attacks, he discerns the hallmarks of hatred and prejudice, fuelled by shameful self-interest.[51]

Deliberations on Jewish emancipation in my protagonists' countries were often conducted in an anti-Semitic climate. Czech patriots expected that the Jews would relinquish their Jewishness in return for becoming Czechs and, unlike their Hungarian counterparts, Bohemian Jews tended to get absorbed into the German cultural sphere. In the 1840s violent outbursts gradually destroyed the hopes for assimilation of Bohemia's Jews into the Czech nation.[52] Towards the end of his life, the embittered Palacký railed against the perceived ability of the Jews to manipulate public opinion. He discerned in the newly emancipated Jews the prototypes of Shylock, bemoaning the fact that they satisfied themselves with the aspect of legality, whilst the concepts of generosity and honour remained alien to them.[53] On the whole, however, this uncharacteristic outburst is not representative of the Czech scholar's stance. Instead, his statement needs to be interpreted in relation to domestic politics, in particular his opposition to the Young Czech Party and his criticism of German liberalism.[54]

After the unification of the two Danubian principalities, one of the conditions imposed on Romania by the Treaty of Berlin was that the Jews must be granted civil rights. By contrast, in 1866, in violation of international guarantees, the government defined all Jews as members of a vagabond race, rendering them legally subject to expulsion.[55] Kogălniceanu tended to approve this illegal policy

---

[51] Horváth, *Huszonöt év Magyarország történetéből*, II. 669–70.

[52] Agnew, 'Czechs, Germans, Bohemians?', 69.

[53] Palacký, *Poslední mé slovo* (Prague, 1912), 58; in German version, *Politisches Vermächtnis*, 25.

[54] I am indebted to Michal Frankl for pointing this out to me.

[55] David Vital, *A People Apart: A Political History of the Jews in Europe, 1789–1939* (Oxford, 2001), 490.

because, as a politician, he was compelled to operate within the dual constraints of great power and domestic interests. He insisted that the Jewish question in Romania involved not a matter of principle but a question of numbers; that they were denied the same opportunities and guarantees as their fellow-foreigners, such as the Bulgarians or Armenians, because of their greater numbers.[56] At the same time, he condemned the Jewish community for appealing to foreign powers for protection instead of sharing Romanian hardships; this, in his eyes, constituted proof that they formed a separate nation. Consequently, according to Kogălniceanu, they could only be considered as inhabitants and not as citizens. Overall, he prioritized the pragmatic concerns of a young and unstable nation-state over the opportunity to extend full citizenship to the Jewish population. Especially revealing in this context is his appeal to the deputies in Parliament, with regard to the nationalization of the inhabitants of Dobrogea, urging them 'to make national laws before making liberal ones', a declaration that marked the eclipse of an era in which liberalism and nationalism could happily coexist.[57]

INTERNAL OTHERS: THE JESUITS

The Society of Jesus, founded by Ignatus of Loyola, received official recognition from the Pope in 1540, with a twofold mission: to educate and to evangelize. The Jesuits left an indelible mark on the history of education and scholarship, establishing and maintaining thousands of schools, colleges and universities throughout the world and significantly advancing the cause of the Counter-Reformation.[58] Among their ranks were numerous outstanding scholars and influential government advisors. At the same time, the Jesuits became infamous for their cunning and aggressive conduct and prompted association with the spirit of police, censorship, intrigues and the counter-revolution. Enlightenment scholars, such as William Robertson, viewed their uncompromising

[56] William O. Oldson, *A Providential Anti-Semitism: Nationalism and Polity in Nineteenth-Century Romania* (Philadelphia, 1991), 106.

[57] Kogălniceanu, *Opere*, V/I. 269, quoted in Constantin Iordachi, *Citizenship, Nation- and State-Building*, 26.

[58] See Christopher Chapple (ed.), *The Jesuit Tradition in Education and Missions: A 450-year Perspective* (Scranton, 1993).

fanaticism as antithetical to toleration, progress and, ultimately, to the maxims of reason.[59]

An aversion to the Jesuits constituted an almost indispensable ingredient in liberal historiography. They were often portrayed as the incarnation of reactionary evil; for example, Swiss radicals in the 1840s regarded them as the 'snakes in the heart of Switzerland'.[60] Michelet asserted that the Jesuits formed 'a secret army of parasites, infiltrating and undermining the healthy body of the nation'.[61] Furthermore, in a polemic on the Jesuits, a bestseller Michelet completed with Quinet in 1843, the authors stated that 'to whatever political form it (Jesuitism) is annexed . . . (it) secretly declares itself the enemy of this constitution and labours to undermine it'.[62] A principal concern of this book was the monopoly of secondary education and, in broader terms, moral and spiritual leadership, whose ultimate expression was control of the nation.[63] By the eighteenth century, so many educational institutions were operated by the Jesuits that their suppression in several countries, as a result of theological and political disputes, left a gaping hole. To try to redress this situation, governments often confiscated the order's vast holdings to finance a new state-run educational system.

The five historians' attitudes to the Jesuits largely reflect these archetypical antipathies, which posited them as constituting a foreign body within the state, entrenching themselves in every sphere of life. Horváth and Lelewel disapprove of their ambitions to extend their influence beyond their mandate; for example, Horváth discovered that in the late sixteenth century, the Prince of Transylvania secretly continued to follow the Jesuits' teaching even after their expulsion from the region.[64] Additionally, they were concerned not just with religious intolerance but even with violence. Both Lelewel and Horváth recount episodes in which Jesuits attacked Protestants and dissidents

---

[59] John Renwick, 'The Reception of William Robertson's Historical Writings in Eighteenth-century France', in Stewart J. Brown (ed.), *William Robertson and the Expansion of Empire* (Cambridge, 1997), 159.

[60] Zimmer, *A Contested Nation*, 128.

[61] Gossman, *Between History and Literature*, 179.

[62] Jules Michelet and Edgar Quinet, *Jesuits and Jesuitism* (London, 1846), 45. On Michelet's and Quinet's affair with the Jesuits see Geoffrey Cubitt, *The Jesuit Myth: Conspiracy Theory in the Nineteenth Century* (Oxford, 1993), 235–40 and 132–40.

[63] Gossman, *Between History and Literature*, 179.

[64] Horváth, *Magyarország történelme*, IV. 398.

in the sixteenth century.[65] For Palacký they were conterminous with censorship, and their conduct during the Thirty Years War, when the Jesuits confiscated and burnt Protestant books, particularly incurred his condemnation.[66] It may also be significant that on one occasion, when Palacký became especially irritated by the censor's intrusion into his work, he accused him of being a 'friend of the Jesuits'.[67] Meanwhile, Kogălniceanu registered the enmity of Orthodox people towards Catholicism: 'It is fair to say that the Jesuits were the cause of this antipathy, for there were no tricks which they would not employ ... they wanted to infiltrate in the country by any possible means ... but, with the notable exception of the Hungarian Szekler community in the Carpathians, they failed to gain auditors for their services'.[68]

Moreover, Lelewel went further still by assigning the Jesuits a crucial role in the decline and ultimately the fall of the Polish state. He asserts that Poland's misfortunes were directly linked to the Jesuits' appearance in the sixteenth century. Their ideology, as revealed through censorship and persecution, constituted an antipode of republicanism and was consequently inimical to the national spirit, ultimately leading to the violation of political freedom.[69] Interestingly, Lelewel discerns in the Piarists, the Jesuits' counterpart, a 'national order', who promoted knowledge and Enlightenment without extensive reliance on foreign ideas.[70] The Jesuits' contribution to scholarship was so great that not even disparaging accounts could afford to ignore it altogether. Lelewel admitted that their expulsion left behind a great hiatus in Catholic countries,[71] whilst Palacký set out his scholarly intentions in opposition to the Jesuits' accounts, even his harsh criticism implied a degree of grudging acknowledgement: 'That the monks, the Jesuits and their pupils, who, until now, have compiled our history, could neither comprehend nor appreciate the spirit of our ancestors, I do not wish to hold against them; but I must strive harder to banish the host of phantoms which their sectarianism has created, and to present the plain

[65] Lelewel, *Polska, dzieje a rzeczy jej*, III. 299–301; *Betrachtungen*, 206–7; Horváth, *Magyarország történelme*, IV. 398.

[66] Palacký, *Gedenkblätter*, 33.

[67] Jiří Kořalka, 'Bavorská a saská korespondence Františka Palackého 1836–1846', *Husitský Tábor* 5 (1982), 240.

[68] Kogălniceanu, *Opere*, II. 194.

[69] Lelewel, *Dzieła*, VIII. 143; *Geschichte Polens*, 135.

[70] Lelewel, *Dzieła*, VIII. 135; *Polen unter Stanislas August*, 56–7.

[71] Lelewel, *Dzieła*, Ibid.; *Polen unter Stanislas August*, Ibid.

truth to the friends of mankind to see'.[72] Nevertheless, on balance, my historians remained unimpressed with the Jesuits' attainments. Lelewel complained that they managed to attract talented people and even dissidents made the mistake (*sic*) of sending their children to Jesuit schools.[73] Although Horváth briefly acknowledged their contribution to culture, for example, by founding the first Hungarian university, he accentuated the manipulative nature of their activities.[74]

INTERNAL OTHERS: WOMEN

The length of this section testifies to the paucity of attention that women received in my historians' writings. This was not necessarily a manifestation of indifference or apathy; rather, it was conditioned by their subject matter: women only made occasional appearances in the then available historical sources and, apart from a few notable exceptions, primarily as wives of rulers and other prominent personalities. Liberal historians, whose assumptions my protagonists tended to share, assigned women a limited role in the national community. They also called for the improvement of their status, especially through education, though this did not imply the conferral of civil rights. Michelet's concept of the nation undivided, without disaffection or dissent, in which all Frenchmen would be united as brothers, implied an aspect of 'assimilation', whereby French women would realize their humanity by becoming more and more like French men.[75] Accordingly, when women received praise in my historians' writings, they were almost invariably hailed for their masculine behaviour, excelling either in warfare or in statesmanship. As we have seen in Chapter 6, they characteristically portrayed women in the context of early societies, endowing them with 'amazonian' attributes which were first employed in Tacitus's *Germania* to depict female figures, such as strength, courage and the willingness to follow men to battle.[76] Daukantas professed that early Lithuanian women were as strong and healthy as men. They returned to their duties three days after giving birth and took up arms to defend their

[72] Palacký, *Korrespondence a zápisky*, II. 81, quoted in Josef Zacek, *Palacký*, 33.
[73] Lelewel, *Polska, dzieje a rczeczy jei*, III. 206–7; *Betrachtungen*, 299–300.
[74] Horváth, *Magyarország történelme*, IV. 305.
[75] Gosmann, *Between History and Literature*, 179.
[76] Jane Rendall, 'Tacitus Engendered: "Gothic Feminism" and British Histories, c. 1750–1800', in Geoffrey Cubitt (ed.), *Imagining Nations* (Manchester, 1998), 58.

homeland whenever necessary. Palacký believed that Czech women in early history were free and treated with respect, in contrast to the situation of their German counterparts.[77] As we have seen, images of national self-gratification largely overlapped and sometimes conflicted, a tendency which also informed representations of women. Whilst Czech, and in more general terms, Slavic historians eulogized the freedom, peaceful spirit and industriousness of early inhabitants, as well as their respect towards women, Horváth portrayed the Slavs as diligent and hospitable, but simultaneously cowardly, servile souls lacking moral strength and notorious for their mistreatment of women.[78]

It is perhaps no coincidence that some of the rare appearances of women-amazons in my historians' writings belonged to the realm of mythology and fiction. Daukantas incorporates into his narrative a story of the medieval Lithuanian princess, Żywila, who distinguished herself by her heroism against the Russian enemy.[79] His source was in fact an early poem by the Polish Romantic poet Adam Mickiewicz which Daukantas mistakenly believed to be an authentic excerpt from an ancient chronicle.[80] Palacký's references to Libuša, the Slav ruler and founder of the ruling dynasty who also featured in the forged manuscripts, provide another instance of the integration and nationalization of legendary heroes.[81] Nonetheless, even Horváth's appraisal of a real heroine, Ilona Zrínyi, a noblewoman who featured briefly in the previous chapter, is based on her undaunted courage in battle, where she replaced her husband who had been taken prisoner by the Habsburgs.

The fair treatment of women, allegedly an attribute of early societies, was unanimously demanded by my historians but only very occasional hints in their writings address women's political participation. Chronicling the Diet of 1790, Horváth found it noteworthy that, for the first time, women were granted permission to follow proceedings from the balcony.[82] One version of Lelewel's national history includes

<hr/>

[77] Palacký, *Dějiny*, I. 63. See also Jitka Malečková, 'Where are Women in National Histories?', in Stefan Berger and Chris Lorenz (eds.), *The Contested Nation: Ethnicity, Class, Religion and Gender in National Histories* (Basingstoke, 2008), 171–99.

[78] *Horváth Mihály kisebb történelmi munkái*, I. 41.   [79] Daukantas, *Raštai*, I. 252–6.

[80] By the time Mickiewicz's authorship was established in 1884, the tale had secured a place in Lithuanian national culture.

[81] Jitka Malečková, 'Nationalizing Women and Engendering the Nation: The Czech National Movement', in Ida Blom, Karen Hagemann and Cathrine Hall (eds.), *Gendered Nations: Nationalisms and Gender Order in the Long Nineteenth Century* (Oxford and New York, 2000), 300.

[82] Horváth, *Magyarország történelme*, VIII. 28.

a half-page sketch on Polish women, illustrating their responsibility for patriotic education. He applauded women's sacrifices on the altar of the fatherland and their willingness to nurse wounded soldiers in the hospitals. Women merited praise because 'no weapon was too heavy for their delicate hands, no danger of war could frighten them off'.[83] Of the five historians, only Lelewel alluded to women's emancipation; unsurprisingly, he applied the same rationale in this context that he had used in relation to the Jews and the peasants: citizenship was made contingent upon their willingness to contribute to the Polish cause.[84]

SYMBOLIC GEOGRAPHY: EAST, WEST AND THEIR ALTERNATIVES

In his influential book *Inventing Eastern Europe*, Larry Wolff proposed that Eastern Europe was a concept invented by scholars of the Enlightenment era, epitomizing the first model of underdevelopment.[85] Barbarism and backwardness, qualities formerly associated with the North and juxtaposed with a civilized South, were now displaced onto Eastern Europe, thereby affirming the superiority of its Western counterpart. Wolff's thesis was based on perceptions of Westerners who travelled to Poland and Russia. Following the publication of his book, other prominent historians reversed this perspective with the aim of gauging how scholars in Central and Eastern Europe envisaged their societies' position in symbolic geographical terms and what strategies they devised to refute the assumption of backwardness.[86] Before applying a similar analysis to my historians' contexts, it may prove worthwhile to further qualify Wolff's theory in light of my findings.

As the title of Schlözer's celebrated volume, *Allgemeine Nordische Geschichte*, suggests, Russia, Poland and other territories inhabited by Slavic people were commonly aligned with the European North in the

---

[83] Lelewel, *Dzieła*, VIII. 119; *Geschichte Polens*, 487.

[84] Lelewel, *Dzieła*, VIII. 119; *Geschichte Polens*, 487.

[85] Wolff, *Inventing Eastern Europe*, 9.

[86] Among the most important ones are Lucian Boia, *History and Myth in Romanian Consciousness* and Jerzy Jedlicki, *A Suburb of Europe: Nineteenth Century Approaches to Western Civilization* (Budapest, 1999). For the Polish context see also an older book, Andrzej Wierzbicki, *Wschód-Zachód w koncepcjach dziejów Polski* (Warsaw, 1984).

late eighteenth century.[87] Such a classification originated in a tradition that distinguished between the former lands of the Roman empire north of the Mediterranean Sea (*Alteuropa*) and the regions which entered the European 'core' in the ninth and tenth centuries through the adoption of Christianity (*Neueuropa*).[88] I have observed that Lelewel's theory of dual development, in which the North epitomizes liberty and the South is characterized by rigid feudal structures, incorporated this concept, albeit with a twist. Nor does the North/South divide appear to have been (fully) eradicated in the nineteenth century. For example, Leopold von Ranke's rendering of the competing Teutonic and Latin elements as the core of European history, and relegating everything else as an unremarkable periphery, contained traces of this tradition.[89] Moreover, recent studies of Western travellers' experiences in the East, written from different vantage points to those of Wolff, have highlighted entirely different polarities, such as urban and rural culture, bourgeois and peasant milieu, as well as the differences between various religious denominations.[90]

Furthermore, even a commendation of Wolff's hypothesis about the metamorphosis of North/South domains into South/East leaves certain questions unresolved; for example, whether the qualities associated with the former geographical concept were fully transferred onto the latter or not. As we have seen, people of the North were traditionally cast in the role of uncivilized 'barbarians', whilst simultaneously being revered for their liberty, as manifested in the topos of the noble savage. Such admiration does not seem to have been extended to the inhabitants of Eastern Europe following the shift in symbolic geographical perceptions. Apart from a few apologists for the region, such as Herder, who implied that these underdeveloped, victimized and peaceful people's finest hours were yet to come, people of the East were typically regarded as *both* underdeveloped and oppressed. It was in this vein that Kogălniceanu complained that, in the 1830s, 'Moldavians and Wallachians are (still) regarded as savage people, brutalized, unworthy of liberty'.[91]

---

[87] See an interesting study, preceding Wolff's book, Hans Lemberg, 'Zur Entstehung des Osteuropabegriffs im 19. Jahrhundert. Vom "Nordern" zum "Osten" Europas', *Jahrbücher für Geschichte Osteuropas* 33 (1985), 48–91.

[88] Ibid., 60.

[89] Ranke, *Geschichten der romanischen und germanischen Völker von 1494 bis 1535*, I. iii–iv.

[90] Bernhard Struck, ' "Historical Regions between Construction and Perception": Viewing Poland and France in the Late-18th and Early-19th Centuries', *East Central Europe* 32:1–2 (2005), 79–88.

[91] Barbara Jelavich, 'Mihail Kogălniceanu Historian as Foreign Minister, 1876–79', in Dennis Deletant and Harry Hanak (eds.), *Historians as Nation-Builders* (London, 1988), 89.

Historians defined their position not just along concrete geographical lines, but also in terms of *isolation from* versus *exposure to* fundamental developments in Europe. Both of these directions could be conjoined with unique virtues. To that end, English historiography famously took pride in Britain's detachment from mainland Europe, a situation that enabled the country to avoid the wars, revolutions and conflicts which plagued the rest of the continent. In this spirit, Macaulay asserts that the English were 'islanders not merely in geographical position, but in their politics, their feelings and manners', a status affording them a unique constitution, 'which . . . deserves to be regarded as the best under which any great society has ever existed during many ages'.[92] A contrasting rhetoric derived moral capital from the suffering that a nation's exposure to battles and other conflicts generated. According to this rationale, the nation constituted a buffer zone and thus protected other societies from similar vicissitudes. This stance typically encompassed the perception of the national territory as a 'battlefield', 'crossroad of nations' or, as we shall see below, 'the bulwark of Christianity'. In this vein Kogălniceanu complains that:

It is perhaps the destiny imposed by God, it is perhaps a curse cast on this land, that from ancient times it should be trampled by the hooves and horses of invaders . . . it is enough . . . to gaze upon our chronicles, in order to see that each page is drenched in blood, since only battles between Hungarians, Poles, Turks, take place on our soil, or battles fought by our ancestors against the Poles, Hungarians, Cossacks, Tartars, Turks are spoken of on each page.[93]

A further strategy involved imagining one's own nation occupying a position at the *heart*—the centre—of Europe. This focal position also cast the nation in a mediating role, beneficially amalgamating distinct cultural values and forming a bridge between various cultures. Among my protagonists Palacký illustrates this approach most effectively: 'As the Bohemian lands are located in the centre, the heart of Europe, for many centuries the Czech nation has been the central point where elements and principles of national, State, and Church life in modern Europe, have come into contact, although not without struggle.'[94] As we have seen, Palacký's letter to Frankfurt specifically locates the focal

[92] Macaulay, *History of England from the Accession of James I*, 5 vols. (1849–61), I. 12–13.

[93] Démètre A. Sturdza (ed.), *Charles Ier: Roi du Roumanie: chronique—actes—documents* (Bucharest, 1899), Vol. II (1876–7), 649–50, quoted in Jelavich, 'Michail Kogălniceanu Historian as Foreign Minister, 1876–79', 97.

[94] Palacký, *Dějiny*, I. 10–11.

point of the region, and that of an eventual multinational federation along its major river: 'The vital artery of this necessary union of nations is the Danube. The focus of power of such union must never be diverted far from this river, if the union is to be effective and remain so.'[95] Interestingly, other plans for the federalization of the Empire, for example Louis Kossuth's dream of a federation of Danubian nations, also considered this river an axis of the region. The assumption of a central position and mediating role could also encourage scholars to assert that their nation acted as a 'sponge', absorbing a variety of influences, in the course of which negative qualities were neutralized and positive traits magnified. Lelewel professed that when the Poles adopted favourable elements from Western Europe (*sic*), they endowed those with even more dignity; when they borrowed certain superfluous rituals from the Orient, they refined and ennobled those conventions.[96]

THE CYRANO DE BERGERAC EFFECT

When comparing their nations' attainments against those of their more advanced 'Western' counterparts, my historians had a choice of two fundamental rhetorical strategies. One possible trajectory entailed affirmation of the normative nature of 'Western' civilization and applying it to the context of their own nation. Alternatively, categorical or outspoken aspersions could be cast on the legacy of exemplary standards, especially by underscoring the unparalleled values of one's own society. Nevertheless, as we shall see, even the apparent rejection of normative Western standards could indicate their implicit endorsement.

Disquieting as it may be to acknowledge the peripheral status of one's nation in the framework of European civilization, without such recognition no feasible programme of development could be devised.[97] My historians usually displayed acute awareness of their nation's status, but the way in which they communicated their concerns about domestic problems largely depended on their intended audience. In that context, Horváth's and Kogălniceanu's arguments in particular showed a propensity for what could be called the 'Cyrano de Bergerac' effect. In

---

[95] Palacký, *Gedenkblätter*, 152.
[96] Lelelwel, *Polska, dzieje a rzeczy jej*, III. 278; *Betrachtungen*, 188–9.
[97] Jerzy Jedlicki, *A Suburb of Europe*, xiii.

the renowned nose monologue from Rostand's play of the same title, the leading character, Cyrano, rejects critical remarks about his nose with the following words: 'While I sometimes choose to mock myself, I do not accept such pleasantries from others.'[98] In my protagonists' circumstances, this entailed a twofold attitude. When addressing their fellow patriots, they registered underdevelopment in their respective societies and endorsed it; for example in relation to the abolition of feudalism. On the other hand, in narratives aimed at a foreign audience (such as those that were published in German and French) they were inclined to prioritize what they perceived as the unique traits of their societies. Occasionally, they prided themselves on achievements which they believed even 'more developed' countries could not match. This was accompanied by sensitivity to criticism from abroad and regret about the ignorance of the Western public. Whilst Kogălniceanu lamented that the Danubian principalities were lesser-known than the smallest African and American states, Horváth specifically championed international recognition of the War of Independence of 1848–9: 'The foreign reader understands the cries of Ireland, the complaints of Venice and appreciates the heroic fights of the Poles, but is not sympathetic to the desires of our nation because he does not know its history in the past decades.'[99]

One of Kogălniceanu's parliamentary discourses, aimed at persuading his fellow countrymen of the urgent necessity of land reform, very clearly manifests the Westernizing paradigm. He expresses dissatisfaction with colleagues' 'reluctance to undertake those reforms which had been introduced in England, Belgium and Italy'; this he considered incompatible with his country's desire to occupy a place in the league of free and constitutional nations: 'May God help to promote these ideas among the Romanians and make them understood: Europe is willing to offer sympathy and extend support only to countries whose institutions are in accordance with the requirements of the civilized world.'[100] Horváth frequently buttressed his arguments with references to favourable foreign models: 'the emancipation of Irish Catholics in Great Britain was welcomed by every enlightened person; it also presented an opportunity for Catholic countries to urge their representatives to draft a proposal for extending the Protestants' religious

---

[98] Edmond Rostand, *Cyrano de Bergerac*, trans. Carol Clark (London, 2006), 33.
[99] Horváth, Introduction to *Huszonöt év*, Vol. I, without page number.
[100] Kogălniceanu, *Opere*, II. 602.

freedom.'[101] The 'free states of America' were, according to Horváth, commendable not only for the separation of church and state and respecting the freedom of religion and that of expression, but also because relations between various social strata were more harmonious than anywhere else, and social and material advancement had developed rapidly.[102] As we have seen in the previous chapter, Horváth expressed a preference for the Compromise over illusionary desires of Hungarian independence by pointing out the prosperity which Scotland enjoyed after its union with England.

For Lelewel and Kogălniceanu, Spain represented a particularly appropriate vantage point for conducting comparative enquiries. Lelewel juxtaposed the glory and decline of his homeland and that of Spain. Whilst his motivation was primarily theoretical and historical, Kogălniceanu was inspired by his sojourn in the country between September 1846 and March 1847. The two scholars' fascination was stimulated by the resemblance between Spain and their own countries. Kogălniceanu notes that 'I studied in Spain for a long time, a peculiar country that presents many similarities with ours, in language, character and even historical stage of development.'[103] In particular, the multiple layers of Spanish culture attracted his attention; its oriental heritage, neo-Latin language and undisputed position in the Western world. For him, Spain exemplifies a Janus-faced culture, exhibiting both genuine values and shallowness. In the former context, he remains unimpressed by the Spanish aristocracy. When, in 1864, the Romanian Parliament proposed the formation of a national guard, Kogălniceanu rejected this idea by recalling his encounters with the Spanish national guard, whom he characterized as 'an utterly useless group of people, doing little more than marching up and down on Madrid's streets'.[104]

The five historians made frequent, if not necessarily straightforward or consistent, references to 'Western' Europe and the 'Western' world. Mention of the 'East' usually alluded to the Russian Empire, albeit in multifarious guises. Daukantas's account, permeated with anti-Polish sympathies, displayed no hostility towards the Russian

---

[101] Horváth, *Huszonöt év*, I. 244.

[102] Horváth, *Az 1514-es pórlázadás, annak okai és következményei*, 9.

[103] Olga T. Impey, 'Mihail Kogălniceanu's Six Months in Spain: Their Consequences for His Life and Romania's Future', in K. W. Treptow (ed.), *Biography and Romanian Studies* (Iasi and Oxford, 1998), 61. Kogălniceanu's travel notes on Spain, 'Notes sur l'Espagne', can be found in *Opere*, I. 498–542.

[104] Kogălniceanu, *Opere*, III/1 (1856–64), 417.

Empire.[105] In his letter to Frankfurt, Palacký warned about the threat that the Russian Empire represented for the Danubian region if fragmented into small, non-viable states, but following his disenchantment with the Austrian idea he came to regard the Empire as a potential ally. Lelewel's attitude to the Russian Empire also underwent a shift, from participating in the anti-Russian uprising of 1830 to a greater emphasis on the brotherhood of Slavic countries in his mature years. Romanian culture was informed by the opposite tendency: initially the Russians were welcomed as 'liberating brothers' (ending the Phanariots' rule), but a growing emphasis on the Romanians' Latinity meant that they came to be associated with the spirit of Panslavism, with its attendant threat of assimilation.[106] Lastly, in Horváth's writings, Russia was primarily linked with Panslavism, which he saw as a potentially serious danger for the region.

Whilst in the *Histoire*, a book intended for foreign consumption, Kogălniceanu states that the Romanian principalities were among the first in oriental (*sic*) Europe to emancipate peasants, he tactfully conceals that this act created more problems than it resolved, because it was accompanied by the expulsion of peasants from lands that they had cultivated for centuries. In domestic politics, however, the Romanian scholar sought to highlight the gravity of the problem by reminding his contemporaries that even 'in the enormous empire of the Slavs, where no constitution, no parliament and no responsible government existed and where the Tsar was omnipotent, the problems of the peasantry were treated with more dedication and urgency than in his homeland'.[107] His article of 1862, dedicated to the improvement of the conditions of the peasantry, commences with the following words:

Gentlemen! If there exists a fundamental and difficult question in this country, then it is the one which I am submitting here: the improvement of the situation of the peasantry, that is to say improving the foundation of our national existence. No problem requires greater wisdom . . . it caused severe difficulties even in the most enlightened and developed countries of Europe. *(Even) in the Russian Empire* social conditions are to be reformed. In the principalities the question has been unresolved for a century . . . What happiness it would mean for our country and what a tribute to the educated and wealthy classes

---

[105] It is worth noting, however, that after the failed uprising of 1863 a policy of Russification was imposed on Lithuania which brought about a change in Lithuanians' loyalties.

[106] Boia, *History and Myth*, 37.   [107] Kogălniceanu, *Opere*, III/1, 171.

of Romania in the eyes of Europe if we could prove that we are able to initiate this fundamental social reform.[108]

NEGATION AND ANALOGY: THE NATION'S MISSION

As has been suggested, the standards of the 'Western' world were not necessarily deemed universal or irreproachable by my historians. Lelewel's attitude after the failed uprising of 1830 and the mature Palacký's writings in particular, were peppered with dismissive remarks, revealing a degree of scepticism about 'Western' values. To that end, we have seen that in the process of feudalization they discerned the harmful impact of occidental civilization.[109] Palacký cautioned that certain universally popular governmental models did not lend themselves to the special circumstances of multinational empires, and expressed dismay that others failed to recognize the unsuitability of the French and Belgian centralist constitution paradigm, hailed by liberals in 1848 as the pinnacle of political wisdom, for the Austrian multicultural context.[110] Lelewel's attitude runs counter to the standard Westernizing rhetoric culminating in the desire to be admitted to the concert of 'Western' nations. Not only does he dissociate Poland from the occident, but he also proclaims that Western countries could have learned from the legacy of the Polish past, in particular from the republican virtues, once deemed inherent in the Polish gentry democracy.[111] On this very point, however, it becomes obvious that Lelewel's and Palacký's explicit disapproval indicated an implicit acceptance of Western values: if Poland represented a model for Western countries, that implies a shared trajectory. Such paradoxes are typical of emancipatory rhetoric, especially the claim of 'being the first', i.e. that some fundamental tenets of contemporary European civilization had existed in my protagonists' countries long before their appearance elsewhere, or that they originated there. Consequently, there was no need to emulate foreign models, instead, it was sufficient to resolve the eventual contestation that affected the ancient traditions.[112]

[108] Kogălniceanu, *Opere*, III/1. 162.
[109] Lelewel, *Polska, dzieje a rzeczy jej*, III. 328; *Betrachtungen*, 232.
[110] Palacký, *Politisches Vermächtnis*, 15; *Poslední mé slovo*, 41.
[111] Walicki, *Philosophy and Romantic Nationalism*, 34.
[112] Jedlicki, *A Suburb of Europe*, 31.

In Palacký's view it was the 'irony of fate' that the qualities which he (but not his German contemporaries) regarded as characteristic of early Slavic societies were deemed to be quintessentially 'Western' and that, consequently, the Slavs were expected to emulate values which in fact were autochthonous in their own societies.[113] To that end, the historian asserts the unprecedented nature of the Bohemians' widespread resistance to the pillars of the medieval world, such as blind faith in authority, hierarchy and feudalism.[114] Furthermore, he believes that Hussite doctrines embraced a variety of fundamental religious views, political and social doctrines and even philosophical systems in embryonic form: rationalism, socialism, communism and democracy, as well as nationalism, pantheism and Panslavism.[115] He also detects a strong resemblance between the ideals of the Taborite wing of the Hussite movement and the ideology of French liberals after 1789. Kogălniceanu also puts forward a strong case for the primacy of Romanian achievements in certain fields, and their subsequent imitation by the 'West'. It is probably no coincidence that he advances this claim in an introduction to a volume aimed at the foreign public: the French edition of Romanian chronicles, published in 1845. Among such unique traits were military virtues, especially the Romanians' defence of religion and civilization against Islam and Asiatic 'barbarism', religious toleration and freedom of conscience, and the assertion that the Romanians were the first people in Europe to have a regular army.[116]

The second major direction pursued by my historians in their refutation of occidental superiority was the claim that their nations had been defenders of Western civilization. This sacrifice, which significantly aided the progress of Western powers, remained unacknowledged by these societies, thereby recasting my historians' nations in the role of moral creditors, and not 'debtors' to the West.[117] According to Horváth: 'Since the beginning of the fifteenth century Hungary was almost the sole guardian (on the mainland) of the peaceful progress of Christian civilization, which was in danger of being engulfed by the ominously expanding power of the Ottoman Empire.'[118] Kogălniceanu's grievance about the frequent foreign invasions suffered by his country in the past concluded with the allegation that: 'The victim in all these foreign

[113] Palacký, *Die Geschichte des Hussitenthums*, 89.   [114] Palacký, *Gedenkblätter*, 271.
[115] Palacký, *Die Geschichte des Hussitenthums*, 186.
[116] Kogălniceanu, *Opere*, II. 415–16.   [117] Boia, *History and Myth*, 156.
[118] Horváth, *Magyarország történelme*, VI. 242.

wars was always poor Romania, who paid for everyone, for the quarrels and the disagreements of others, who even paid with the loss of her territories, at one time Bukovina, at another Bessarabia.'[119] Another strand of this main theme is inherent in Lelewel's reinterpretation of the early modern concept of Poland as 'the bulwark of Christianity'.[120] According to this tradition, the Poles defended Europe against the Turks and Russians and, at the same time, they spread the light of Latin civilization in the Slavonic East. Nevertheless, there was no suggestion of Poland's role as the bastion of the *West*. On the contrary, this system of thought underlined the need to defend Poland's institutions and customs against dangerous Western influences.[121]

These examples of the nation's moral distinction formed part of a more encompassing strategy. The endowment of one's own nation with a unique, even providential, mission constituted a major tenet of Romantic historical writing, which can be most clearly observed in the Polish and Czech scholars' writings. Lelewel and his contemporaries reinterpreted the tradition of *antemurale Christianitatis* after the failed uprising of 1830 by linking the Polish struggle to the cause of humanity. To this end, the uprising assumed international significance because it prevented Tsar Nicholas I from his planned crusade against France, following the outbreak of the July Revolution.[122] Insurgents appealed to the international solidarity of free peoples, as exemplified in a Manifesto issued by the Polish Diet in 1831, a document authored largely by Lelewel:

Yet, if Providence has appointed this land for eternal subjection, if in this last fight Poland shall lay down her freedom amid the ashes of her towns and the corpses of her defenders, the enemy will extend his dominion over but yet another desert, and the true Pole will perish with joy in his heart that, if Heaven has not permitted him to save his own freedom and his Fatherland, he has at least in mortal combat protected the liberties of the peoples in Europe.[123]

The theme of mission took on another meaning towards the end of the 1830s, in the context of Lelewel's messianist worldview, influenced

[119] Jelavich, 'Michail Kogălniceanu: Historian as Foreign Minister, 1876–79', 97.

[120] This tradition of the *antemurale christianitatis* played a role in Polish, Hungarian, Croatian and Romanian national consciousness.

[121] Andrzej Walicki, *Poland Between East and West: The Controversies over Self-Definition and Modernization in Partitioned Poland* (Cambridge, MA, 1994), 9.

[122] Walicki, *Philosophy and Romantic Nationalism*, 78.

[123] R. F. Leslie, *Polish Politics and the Revolution of November 1830* (Westport, CT, 1969), 148, quoted in Walicki, *Philosophy and Romantic Nationalism*, 68.

by the famous Polish poet, Adam Mickiewicz, his old acquaintance from Vilna. Mickiewicz also resided in Paris after the uprising of 1830 and his lectures at the Collège de France made him well-known among French intellectuals, including Michelet and Quinet. In 1839 Lelewel delivered a speech commemorating the martyrdom of Szymon Konarski, a Polish activist, who had attempted to organize a new uprising in the Polish lands, but was caught and executed. Lelewel's discourse evoked a messianist topos, claiming that Poland had sacrificed herself for the cause of humanity but, like Christ, would one day be resurrected.[124] Nevertheless, as has been hinted in the previous chapter, in this epoch Catholicism did not yet form a quintessential tenet of Polish identity. Romantic historiography was characteristically imbued with a religious residue and an apocalyptic tone, which also entailed the cultivation of martyrdom. What distinguishes Polish appeals from the many outpourings of messianism prevalent after the revolutionary and Napoleonic upheavals, however, is that through Mickiewicz's lectures and Lelewel's writings a national philosophy was created. This worldview crystallized in the 1830s in an attempt to adapt classical German philosophy, especially Hegelianism, to the needs of Polish cultural self-determination. Its aim was to create a philosophy which would be distinctively national and universalist at the same time.[125]

Palacký's allusions to the mission of the Czechs spring from his reverence for the Hussite movement. They were also embedded in his overall vision of the Czechs as a small people greatly exceeding their potential in the grand scheme of the European Reformation. Not only does he attribute a 'diverse and special' destiny to the Czechs, but he also professes that their bravery in the Hussite wars presented an unparalleled instance of a small nation fighting doggedly, with devotion, skill and sacrifice. Palacký's view on the Czech contribution to the spread of Protestantism resembles a tradition in English historiography as expounded by John Foxe in the sixteenth century. According to this concept, England was *Prima provinciarum quae amplexa est fidem Christi* and the ancient Britons had been the first nation in the world

---

[124] Lelewel, *Polska, dzieje a rzeczy jej*, XX. 281–8; see also Marian H. Serejski, *Naród a państwo w polskiej myśli historycznej* (Warsaw, 1977), 128.

[125] Whilst for Mickiewicz Christianity provided the link through which Poland formed part of Western European civilization, Lelewel was not particularly interested in defining Poland's role in harmony with Western culture. See Andrzej Walicki, *Russia, Poland and Universal Regeneration: Studies in Russian and Polish Thought of the Romantic Epoch* (Notre Dame, IN, 1991), 11.

to embrace the Christian faith. Thus, England had a special place in the designs of Providence.[126] Foxe's concept of the elect nation, set out in his *Book of Martyrs*, promoted the cult of characters who were identified as forerunners of Protestantism. Interestingly, this tradition also accommodated Hus in the circle of English martyrs, probably due to his intellectual connections to Wycliff. In Foxe's famous interpretation: 'Wyclif begat Hus, Hus begat Luther and Luther begat the truth.'[127]

CONCLUSION

Some contemporary scholars have fallen into the trap of 'reading history backwards'; in that context the tragic episodes of the region's history in the twentieth century provoked a powerful presumption according to which xenophobic and paranoid overtones permeated East-Central Europe to a greater extent than the 'West'. Prejudice is undoubtedly a constituent of national historiography, this nonetheless appears be a ubiquitous phenomenon. For instance, Linda Colley has shown that Britain after the Union with Scotland (1707) was 'a markedly aggressive and predatory state', just like other composite nations, and that the political union forged between different peoples and cultures was accompanied by recurrent war against external enemies and persistent prejudice against the internal 'others'.[128] In my protagonists' contexts, partiality is especially evident in approaches towards cultures and states that evoked tragic episodes in their nations' past and presented—real or imagined—dangers; in particular, those that evoked the spectre of subjugation or even death of the nation. Attitudes towards these dominant nations often revealed a desire for status reversal, which was nevertheless informed by a resounding rhetorical appeal to self-sufficiency. Lelewel realized that the Poles could not expect help from 'Western' nations in order to regain their independence, and Palacký also emphasized the importance of self-reliance, although in his case this was underlined by pacific ideals and a focus on legality and morality, due to an awareness that five million Czechs surrounded by enemies were not in the position to achieve their intentions by force.[129]

---

[126] William Haller, *Foxe's Book of Martyrs and the Elect Nation* (London, 1963), 19.

[127] Ibid., 165.

[128] Linda Colley, *Britons: Forging the Nation 1707–1837* (New Haven, 1994), xiv.

[129] Palacký, *Spisy drobné*, I. 359, quoted in Josef Zacek, 'Palacký's Politics: The Second Phase', *Canadian Slavic Studies* 5:1 (1971), 68.

My historians drew the contours of the national community by adhering to a general mould, one which entailed elements of inclusion as well as exclusion. As we have seen in earlier chapters, one of the pivotal demands of liberal historians of the Romantic era was to include the history of the unprivileged classes in their analysis. At the same time, the redefinition of the criteria of nationhood from a phenomenon contingent on class into one dependent on ethnicity resulted in the rejection or questioning of the eligibility of certain groups for membership. To that end, it is not possible to classify the historians' concept of nationhood into the convenient 'civic' and 'ethnic' categories. Nor was the remarkable ethnic variety necessarily considered an impediment to progress, because, as we have seen, Lelewel believed it to be beneficial. Perhaps a more pronounced common denominator in these scholars' views is that membership of the nation was conditional on a significant contribution, whether cultural, material or, in the Polish case, participation in the restoration of the state.

Attitudes towards foreign cultures and values could be accommodating, but also conflicting and antagonistic, as exemplified by widespread appeals to binary oppositions. Although my historians' viewpoints undeniably expressed strong sentiments and biases, such contrasts are to be seen as much as rhetorical and stylistic devices as explicit pronouncements of enmity. To that end, because of its simple, effective and widely applicable nature, the law of polarity has been one of the most powerful rhetorical tools in historical narrative since antiquity. To greater or lesser degrees, the 'Manichean struggle' between two forces, such as liberty and faction, progress and stagnation, monarchism and republicanism, formed an organizing principle of the historical narrative.

The five historians were not just concerned with the demarcation of the national territory, but also imagined their nation's position in symbolic geographical terms. Divergent and even contradictory concepts characterized their orientations, including the desire to belong to the West, resistance to Westernizing discourses and the postulate of alternative concepts, such as the idea of Central Europe. The assessment of their nations' standing in European civilization was not devoid of exaggerations. To a certain extent, this was influenced by Romantic currents, and was employed as a device for converting feelings of inferiority into moral supremacy. Exaggeration also indicated a disjuncture between reality and ideal, providing yet another instance of the generally wishful nature of historical writing of the epoch.

Nevertheless, as we have seen, my historians aggrandized values were appropriated by the majority of European nations and thus represented universal ideals. Therefore, their historical vision was not autochthonous, but manifested a wish to occupy a respected position among European peoples.

Conclusion

My study has sought to unravel multifarious aspects of five historians' writings and to address these themes comparatively. It combines an assessment of the intellectual and institutional-professional background with an in-depth textual analysis and focuses particularly on the elucidation of the overall cultural context within which my protagonists' activities took place, as well as the intricate relationship between historical writing and nation-building. It remains for this final chapter to accommodate my findings in a wider setting. This entails contextualizing my historians' achievements within the broader realm of European historiography and exploring how my historians' work was received by subsequent generations. Lastly, the key questions of the book are revisited in light of my overall findings.

Like many of their contemporaries, my historians defined their innovative objectives—the democratization of the content, the medium, the scale and the audience of their historical writing—against the attainments of previous generations. They expressed a preference for national history over the earlier genres of dynastic, universal and general history. Such a shift should not be seen exclusively in terms of a narrow or even parochial worldview, but rather as evidence of scholars' awareness of the relative nature of historical knowledge and of the great variety of cultures, civilizations and languages, each possessing an individual character, or, in Herder's words, a 'centre of gravity'.

Despite adopting a critical approach towards their predecessors, the historians remained deeply indebted to them: they amalgamated several features of the Enlightenment's conceptual framework as well as the factual knowledge accumulated by the savants of the early modern period. In the late eighteenth century a celebrated figure with the Polish Enlightenment, the Piarist Stanisław Konarski (whose school, Collegium Nobilium, Lelewel attended), addressed the Poles with the following words: 'Let us govern ourselves like sensible people . . . For the God of nature did not search for different clay when he made the Poles from what he used for Englishmen.'[1] In this sense, the five historians, too, continued to accommodate their nation's trajectories within the common history of humanity. Although sometimes they perceived the 'otherness' of foreign cultures in unfavourable terms, nonetheless, the intellectual idioms so eagerly exploited by their successors, especially the concept of race and the tenets of national characterology, are entirely absent from their writings. A similar aspect of continuity informs their ambitions of professionalization, for example, their critical approach towards sources, and their intention to publish source collections. Furthermore, while the emerging new historiographical standards made style and presentation less significant, the genre of national history entailed paying renewed attention to these aspects. This seemingly paradoxical situation, simultaneously criticizing and relying upon predecessors, is by no means exceptional. As Donald Kelley has noted:

Historians are forever claiming to be unprecedentedly critical—but critical rejection is a rhetorical topos as well as a rational claim. They are forever pretending to overcome myth, but at the same time adept at devising alternative myths. And they are forever finding and asserting novelty; but novelty and innovation, too, represent an ancient trope as well as a modernist pose:—make it new.[2]

Given my historians' affinities with the intellectual world of the late eighteenth century, Reinhard Koselleck's famous concept of the *Sattelzeit*, which perceives the period between around 1750 and 1850 to be pivotal, and to constitute a distinct epoch, appears to be a more appropriate chronological scheme for our purposes than the traditional centennial divide. The vital importance of the year 1848, a watershed in the region, also reinforces its relevance.

It was within the framework of European civilization that my historians sought emancipation; their work was explicitly oriented towards change: domestic and international, societal and political. Consequently, their narrative was informed by prescriptive tendencies. In this context, the international situation in the first half of the nineteenth century offered more promise to historians who advocated radical change. After the failure of the Polish uprising of 1863, the establishment of the Austro-Hungarian dualistic arrangement in 1867 and German unification

---

[1] Hans Kohn, *The Idea of Nationalism* (New York, 1946), 522.

[2] Kelley, 'Ancient Verses on New Ideas: Legal Tradition and the French Historical School', 337–8, also mentioned in Frank Borchardt, *German Antiquity in Renaissance Myth* (Baltimore, 1971), 55.

following the French defeat in the Franco-Prussian war, the political scene became more rigid, leaving little hope for fundamental revision.[3] The nexus between my historians' activities in the cultural field and political fields has been emphasized throughout: their efforts to enrich national language and culture and to promote national scholarship can also be perceived in terms of their preoccupation with status raising. These pursuits were informed by wishful tendencies; for example, we have seen that they addressed journals to an anticipated audience, as did Daukantas in his educational works.

Overall, my historians' objectives were informed by a—latent or explicit—'Westernizing' trajectory. They adopted a twofold stance: on the one hand, they claimed that certain unique aspects differentiated their nation's past from that of 'Western' nations. On the other, those unique aspects were discerned in similar or even identical qualities to those that 'Western' historians reserved for their own nations. The same twofold perspective, negative *and* analogous, informed their cultural endeavours: they sought emancipation from a dominant culture (mainly but not exclusively German and Polish), but the arguments and strategies they employed for the enrichment of national culture were often taken from the precise culture whose impact they sought to undermine.

With the benefit of hindsight, the extensive scope of the five historians' accomplishments is beyond doubt. The juxtaposition of Czech political culture and academic life before Palacký's rise to prominence with its state after his departure helps to illustrate the extent to which an individual could make an impact upon national scholarship. In the 1820s, the time when Palacký commenced his national history project, he faced scepticism from his friends who believed that his attempt to revive the historical spirit in Bohemia came too late and thus was doomed to failure. As we have seen, he encountered similar incredulity when proposing that the Journal of the Bohemian Museum should appear not only in German, but also in a Czech edition. Some fifty years later, Palacký delivered a speech to inaugurate the National Theatre in Prague and recalled the time in his youth when Czech patriots were so few that if they had assembled in a single room, they could have been wiped out by a falling ceiling. In addition to the scepticism of his fellow countrymen, Palacký's aspirations were met by suspicion or

---

[3] Maciej Janowski, 'Three Historians', *CEU History Department Yearbook* (Budapest, 2001–2), 207.

even condemnation internationally. In 1852, Friedrich Engels (writing under Marx's name) declared in the *New York Tribune*: 'The chief champion of the Tschechian nationality, Professor Palacký, is himself nothing but a learned German run mad, who even now cannot speak the Tschechian language correctly and without foreign accent.'[4] Through his monumental lifework—the introduction of the 'Czech question' to the international agenda, the journals and institutions he helped establish and above all, the *Dějiny*—Palacký can take a great deal of credit for the fact that his successors' mindsets were no longer infused with the trepidation of decline or even extinction. Towards the end of his life, Palacký concluded optimistically that: 'Even if they (the Czechs) had to endure another testing time of blood and iron, they already have the necessary resilience and vigour to survive the ordeal and to spring back to new life whatever the conditions.'[5]

My other protagonists' achievements might have appeared less spectacular by comparison, but were equally significant. Lelewel died long before the restoration of the Polish state, but his oeuvre made a lasting contribution to Polish culture and scholarship, providing a privileged medium of continuity in the absence of the state. The numerous manifestos he authored ensured that the Polish cause did not fall into oblivion abroad, and his achievements in the field of geography and numismatics enriched international scholarship. If the Czechs had been exposed to the fear of extinction, this was even more true of the Lithuanians, whose prospects in the early nineteenth century seemed particularly bleak. Daukantas's multifarious efforts invigorated and transformed the intellectual landscape, albeit posthumously. Horváth represented a refreshing individual voice among Hungarian scholars as a promoter of a modern, secular society, continually emphasizing the beneficial societal effects of commerce and industry, whilst also rescuing the history of the peasantry.

Kogălniceanu is most renowned as an eminent organizer of culture, as well as the instigator of the unification and later the independence of the Romanian nation-state. Because he outlived his four colleagues, the final stage of his career can help to illuminate the transformation of the European political and intellectual climate in the last decades

---

[4] Friedrich Engels, *Revolution and Counterrevolution in Germany in 1848* (Chicago, 1919), 90.

[5] Palacký, *Politisches Vermächtnis*, 24, quoted in Richard Georg Plaschka, 'The Political Significance of Frantisek Palacký', *Journal of Contemporary History* 8:3 (1973), 54.

of the nineteenth century when national ambitions no longer rested upon appeals to the abstract ideas of freedom and justice. Instead, a more concrete definition of nationhood evolved, which designated a community united by language, inhabiting a specific territory and sharing particular customs and norms.[6] In addition, as Kogălniceanu's approval of the Jews' exclusion from citizenship (despite the guarantees given by the Romanian state to international bodies) confirms, historians who acted as politicians were often compelled to put political priorities ahead of their scholarly beliefs. As we have seen, the state-building project invariably entailed an element of exclusion and, once a nation reached a hegemonic position, this could easily be transformed into concrete political measures. In this context the sardonic observation of Baron Joseph Eötvös, an eminent Hungarian politician, that nations demand justice and equality while they are suppressed, and become intolerant and oppressive immediately upon being granted equal rights, proves highly relevant.[7]

Some of my historians' specific concerns are more analogous with scholarly preoccupations on the other 'margins' of Europe—Scandinavia, the Iberian peninsula, the Balkans, Ireland and Scotland—than with the shared agenda of nineteenth-century 'mainstream' historiography. In these territories, scholars were confronted with the potentially beneficial versus harmful effects of their homeland's status as an inferior member of a composite state; they also strove for equality with the dominant state. In earlier chapters I briefly considered Scottish historians' evaluation of the consequences of the Act of Union in 1707 as a possible basis of comparison. I also indicated in passing that Norwegian historiography represents another instance which invites useful comparison with my Lithuanian and Czech historians' trajectories. Among the parallels are Norwegian scholars' preoccupation with foreign—Danish and Swedish—political and cultural domination, and the perceptions of its impact: either in terms of colonization and cultural decline or, on the contrary, as a prerequisite for survival with benefits for the economy and education. Another correspondence can be perceived in the status of language: like their counterparts in Lithuania and Bohemia, Norwegian scholars regarded the peasantry as the true bearers of continuity

---

[6] Brian Porter, *When Nationalism Began to Hate: Imagining Politics in Nineteenth Century Poland* (Oxford and New York, 2000), 9.

[7] Maciej Janowski, 'Wavering Friendship: Liberal and National Ideas in Nineteenth Century East-Central Europe', *Ab Imperio* 3–4 (2000), 72–3.

and equality, hence they advocated the replacement of Danish (which remained the written language even after 1814, when the union with Denmark was dissolved) with a variant of Norwegian, which drew on rural dialects and preserved the traits of Old Norse.

As we have seen, the preoccupation with continuity and unity, as well as the way in which classical antiquity was evoked by Romanian scholars, offers a fruitful comparison with Greek historians' accounts. Both these countries struggled for international recognition under the influence of dominant Western powers, which helps to explain this emphasis on the classical tradition: it sought to underline their Westernizing orientation.[8] At first sight the historiography of Iberian countries may not appear conducive to comparison: Portugal and Spain had already achieved territorial unity in the Middle Ages, and the distinctive era of discoveries and overseas expansion followed. On the other hand, these countries' geographical position and their encounters with non-Christian peoples resulted in an emphasis on their achievements in the *Reconquista*, which they regarded as the triumph of European civilization over Arabic culture. Consequently, Spanish and Portuguese historians saw their nations as the bastion of Christianity in the same way as my protagonists highlighted their nation's contribution to fighting the Turks. The favoured strategies for elucidating the decline of these once prosperous two countries are also comparable to Lelewel's explanation of Poland's fall; arguments in both cases included the detrimental effects of absolutism and the dangerous influence of the Jesuits.

'Oppositional' and 'emancipatory' may be appropriate words to describe my historians' general attitude towards foreign powers, but should be qualified. First, it is necessary to note that this perspective also informed the work of scholars who took a stand against a *native* ruling regime. This was the case with representatives of the French liberal school until 1830, the year when the revolution yielded them important political positions and turned them into advocates of the existing order.[9] Second, we have seen that Horváth's discourse acquired a stance loyal to the Habsburg dynasty following the Compromise of 1867, and, after the creation of the Romanian nation-state, Kogălniceanu likewise identified himself with the actions of the governments in

---

[8] Effi Gazi, *'Scientific' National History: The Greek Case in Comparative Perspective 1850–1920*, 72.

[9] Pim den Boer, *History as a Profession: The Study of History in France, 1818–1914*, trans. Arnold J. Pomerans (Princeton, 1998), 64–5.

which he actively participated. I have also emphasized throughout that the agenda of 'oppositional' narratives did not necessarily contain a sovereign nation-state; it more often entailed a limited degree of independence. Nor should the differentiation between oppositional and loyalist historiography be taken too far: these two strands appear to have indicated specific rhetorical attitudes, rather than traits of genuinely distinct historiographical traditions.

More striking, however, are the manifold similarities in the representations of the national past *throughout* the entire European historiographical landscape. To a certain extent, these stemmed from historians' reflections on the common preoccupations of the age, particularly those of antiquity, unity, continuity and uniqueness. A comparable ideological orientation—in this context primarily Romantic-liberal—also contributed to the shared assumptions: antipathies as well as preferences were sometimes calculable, for example an aversion towards the Jesuits, even in Catholic countries such as Spain, Portugal and Poland. On closer inspection the historical narrative reveals the existence of a general template of national historiography in our era, which comprised a core story and numerous omnipresent tropes. Characteristically, the narrative was structured into three major phases: the ancient period, informed by liberty from time immemorial; the medieval epoch, often associated with the loss of liberty; and a subsequent period typified by the struggle for the restoration of liberty. This basic plot was then further embellished, depending on individual circumstances. Foundation myths, the claim of noble origins and the assertion of an early primitive democracy likewise belonged to the prevalent constituents. The portrayal of succeeding periods betrayed more variety: on the one hand, liberal scholars condemned the feudal system, on the other, they rehabilitated the Middle Ages, an era which in Enlightenment thought tended to be associated with barbarism and superstition. The zenith of the national past, the 'Golden Age', was considered to embody the unique qualities of the nation, and was typically traced back to epochs which were seen as most compatible with the respective historians' ideological orientations. It is also clear that historical accounts were often informed by tendencies towards hyperbole. In one respect, this was a common feature of the Romantic narrative. In another respect, it was due to the manifestly competitive nature of the genre: the desire to bolster self-images vis-à-vis other nations rendered the narrative especially prone to amplification, particularly in the case of scholars who sought to counter already pre-existing negative images.

Commonalities in the national variants of historical writing can be observed not only in the components of the historical narrative, but throughout the entire intellectual landscape: historians' educational backgrounds and intellectual frameworks, their intentions and attempts to fulfil them, their ideological orientations and their status in society. We have seen that nearly every historian of the era, including Macaulay and Michelet, called for the democratization of historical writing, and also that only very few succeeded in truly understanding the life of the common people. Historians' wholehearted identification with their subject matter has likewise been pointed out, as has their preoccupation with progress and their desire to reach a broad audience.

Regarding the structures of academic life, scholars of the Romantic era significantly contributed to the institutionalization and professionalization of the historical discipline. Although this process culminated in the subsequent epoch, and thus has traditionally been associated with the achievements of the positivist generation, historians in the first half of the nineteenth century prepared the ground for their successors by means of new methodological rules as well as through pragmatic incentives, above all, the editing of primary sources. This foundation allowed positivist scholars to devise a confident and more exclusive self-understanding of the profession which ultimately caused literary representation of history to be discarded. I have observed the earlier occurrence of this development in countries which had traditionally been considered (economically) 'backward'; in that context in East-Central Europe institutionalization was informed by emancipatory tendencies. On the other hand, the more established self-images found in Britain and France did not lend urgency to this process.

Countless tributes, including literary works, testify to the five historians' privileged positions in national memory.[10] The outstanding dramatist Stanisław Wyspiański (1869–1907), entitled his five-act play based on the events of 1831 *Lelewel*. The leading protagonist, who epitomizes national virtues, makes heroic efforts on behalf of the national cause but remains incapable of achieving his aim in the shadow of Russian canons. Justinas Marcinkevičius, one of Lithuania's foremost playwrights under Soviet occupation, produced a series of theatrical works about national heroes, thereby contributing to the maintenance of national identity in troubled times. One of these plays was named *Daukantas* and dedicated to its eponymous hero. Moreover, my

[10] Daukantas and Palacký also appear on the national banknotes.

protagonists' narratives influenced the storylines of historical novels: the books of the late-nineteenth-century writer Alois Jirásek primarily revolved around the Hussite period and reflected Palacký's interpretation, whilst some of the Nobel Prize winner Henryk Sienkiewicz's novels were indebted to Lelewel's vision of the past.[11] Representatives of other artistic genres seeking to construct a 'national style' also thematized my historians' leitmotifs: Daukantas's portrayal of pagan Lithuania inspired visual artists, and Palacký's advice was sought on the themes of the historical frescos decorating the National Theatre in Prague.

However, my historians did not entirely escape criticism, even during their own lifetimes, as illustrated by the example of Palacký's compromising involvement in the manuscript debate which rendered him into a frequent target of cartoonists. More importantly, in accordance with the 'dialectics' of academic scholarship, the positivist generation who succeeded my historians approached their legacy with an explicitly revisionist perspective. As has already been implied, positivist historians sought to apply a rigorous methodology and, in line with their ambition to write history 'without illusions', tried to deconstruct the myths produced by their predecessors. Yet, precisely because of their intense engagement with the Romantic legacy, they contributed greatly to its canonization. Furthermore, whilst the credibility of earlier myths was now being challenged, in their search for the 'naked truth' this generation created a new set of master narratives and myths, albeit wrapped in the language of the objective scientific method.

The tide turned after the restructuring of Europe following the First World War, which led to the restoration of Poland and the creation of Czechoslovakia and Lithuania. In addition, an independent, but radically truncated Hungary emerged on the ruins of the Habsburg Empire, triggering strong revisionist sentiment. During the interwar period the vulnerability of these states, together with the general political and intellectual climate in Europe, provided a fertile ground for the resurgence of political romanticism, albeit under a different guise: the progressivist framework of the nineteenth century was now replaced by cyclical-organicist models, and emphasis was placed on the historical role

---

[11] John Neubauer, 'Introduction' to the section on 'The Historical Novel', in Marcel Cornis-Pope and John Neubauer (eds.), *History of the Literary Cultures of East-Central Europe: Junctures and Disjunctures in the 19th and 20th Centuries* (Amsterdam, 2004), I. 463–7.

of the creative genius and irrational forces.[12] The communist takeover following the Second World War radically disrupted the continuity of academic life, pushing social questions and the satellite countries' relationship with Russia to the top of historians' agendas. Apart from these pivotal turning-points, anniversaries often served as occasions for revisiting the five scholars' work.

In their individual contexts the reception of my historians' undertakings could obviously occasionally deviate from this paradigmatic (chronological) scheme. In Poland, the anti-Romantic turn was triggered by the tragedy of the failed uprising in 1863. At the forefront of the positivist movement were a group of historians commonly referred to as the 'Cracow school'. Their most eminent representative, Michał Bobrzyński (1849–1935), produced a brilliant synthesis, *Dzieje Polski w zarysie* (Outline of Polish History, 1879) which aimed to discredit Lelewel's powerful legacy. Bobrzyński dismissed Lelewel's theory of unique early democracy as a myth and even claimed that, far from being malign, German feudalism in fact contributed to national survival. He defined his preferred political arrangement as an efficiently governed monarchic state, because he believed that republicanism was an anachronistic system based on the unhealthy dominance of the noble estates, which refused to accommodate essential political and social reforms. Contrary to Lelewel, he held the Poles themselves responsible for the partitions and considered Polish civilization to be underdeveloped, a circumstance he attributed to his nation's delayed integration into European civilization and to its distorted political evolution.[13] Lelewel came to be evaluated more favourably in the interwar period; subsequently, in the communist era, his work was assessed according to the dictates of Marxist ideology and terminology, focusing primarily on socio-economic conditions.[14] 1961 saw the hundreth anniversary of the Polish scholar's death, which sparked a renewed interest in his legacy.

Bobrzyński's Czech counterpart was Josef Pekař (1870–1937), who attacked Palacký's portrayal of Hussitism, and its further elaboration by Tomáš Garrigue Masaryk which placed the issue of humanity at the

---

[12] See Balázs Trencsényi's forthcoming book, *The Terror of History: Visions of National Character in Interwar Eastern Europe*.

[13] Piotr P. Wandycz, 'Historiography of the Countries of Eastern Europe: Poland', *American Historical Review* 97:4 (1992), 1015.

[14] Joan A. Skurnowicz, 'Lelewel in Polish Historiography in People's Poland', *Polish Review* 36:3 (1991), 269–82.

core of the Hussites' ideology. Pekař's highly original contribution to the interpretation of Czech history, *Smysl českých dějin* (The Meaning of Czech History)[15] argued that, far from being an early manifestation of the struggle for liberty and equality, the Hussite movement actually represented a medieval heresy. It followed that John Hus was not the forerunner nor the founder of the Reformation, but a Catholic with a fanatical devotion to church reform. Pekař also cast aspersions on the alleged universal significance of the Hussite movement, and disputed the connection which Masaryk established between Hussitism and national awakening. In addition, unlike Palacký, the Catholic Pekař held the Baroque culture of the Counter-Reformation period in high regard.[16]

As early as the 1890s, Palacký's polemical stance towards German culture provoked the burning of copies of his *Dějiny* in the squares of Sudeten German towns. During the period of the Nazi protectorate in Czechoslovakia (1939–45), his name was erased from public discourse. Following the rise of communism, scholars approached Palacký's legacy through the prism of Marxism, and encountered several obstacles when attempting to reconcile it with the new dominant ideology. They took issue with Palacký's restricted focus on the contemporary interests of his own social class, the Czech liberal bourgeoisie.[17] Nor did they endorse his disapproval of revolutionary means and disregard for social equality in favour of the equality of the rights of nationalities.[18] However, Palacký's anti-German biases could be productively transformed into tenets which resonated with the Czech communists' struggle against Nazism, while his Slavophile leaning could be interpreted as an early indication of brotherhood between the Czechs and Russians. Even the appropriation of the Hussite tradition presented no impediment to Marxist scholars, they simply focused on its social, revolutionary and anti-clerical aspects.

Daukantas was discovered by the first generation of Lithuanian 'national awakeners', who came to maturity after the failure of the (Polish) uprising of 1863. Lithuanians' participation in this event was punished by a regime of Russification, which entailed a ban on printing and importing Lithuanian books in the Latin alphabet (until 1904). Instead,

---

[15] The German version is entitled *Der Sinn der tschechischen Geschichte* (Brno, 1937).

[16] Janowski, 'Three Historians', 207.

[17] The Marxist reception of Palacký's ideas is discussed in Joseph F. Zacek, 'Palacký and the Marxists', *Slavic Review* 24:2 (1965), 297–306.

[18] Ibid., 300.

a specific version of the Cyrillic alphabet was prescribed. However, not only did this policy fail, but it also caused book smuggling to flourish, and helped to instigate the first short-lived but nonetheless important Lithuanian periodicals, *Aušra* (The Dawn, 1883–6), and *Varpas* (The Bell, 1889–1905). Both journals were published in Lithuania Minor, a Prussian territory, and then smuggled into Russian-dominated Lithuania.[19] *Aušra*'s inaugural volume contained an appreciative article which marked Daukantas's discovery by Lithuanian intellectuals. The journal's agenda revealed a clear line of continuity with his legacy: its efforts to standardize the Lithuanian language, its perception of the nation along ethnic lines, together with a veneration of the Grand Duchy of Lithuania stretching from the Baltic to the Adriatic Sea.

The second periodical, *Varpas* provides yet another instance of syncretism, the coexistence of different and often opposing intellectual currents in the cultural and intellectual life of East-Central Europe. Editors of the journal, which was launched only six years after *Aušra*, sought to relinquish the nostalgia for bygone times and strove to infuse historical writing with a more sober tone. Daukantas's vision of national independence proved particularly valuable to historians of the interwar period, faced with the task of providing a retrospective legitimization of Lithuanians' admittedly unexpected acquisition of independence. During the Soviet period, émigré scholars in the United States joined local historians in ensuring that my historian's legacy was preserved.

Horváth did not epitomize the quintessential Romantic historian, and this may be one of the reasons why his reception did not follow the typical Romantic-positivist-neoromantic path. Another reason may be connected with the peculiarities of Hungarian historical scholarship, the axis of which continued to revolve around the relationship with Austria, even after 1867 (when it became contractually regulated by the Compromise). Even in Horváth's own lifetime, a group of mainly Protestant historians had already begun to criticize this arrangement, asserting that it disadvantaged Hungary. The interwar period saw representatives of another orientation, who viewed the Habsburg Monarchy as a gateway to the West, and who displayed Catholic sympathies, gain influence. Horváth's endorsement of the Compromise must have proved unacceptable to the former faction, whilst the latter might have found his unfailing insistence on secularization and modernization indigestible. In

---

[19] Artūras Tereškinas, 'Between Romantic Nostalgia and Historio-Pedagogic Sentiments: A Few Ways to Discourse the Lithuanian Past', *Lituanus* 43:3 (1997), 11–48.

the second half of the twentieth century Marxist scholars came to admire Horváth's preoccupation with the peasantry, but his endorsement of the commercial tradition must have seemed too bourgeois and his veneration of the ancient constitution too reactionary for their purposes. Thus, it seems that Horváth's unique voice has caused Hungarian scholarship to overlook him.

Kogălniceanu's approach to historical writing was devoid of populist excesses, but nevertheless belonged to the Romantic brand of patriotic historiography. In Romania, representatives of the *Junimea* movement, who appeared on the intellectual scene in the 1860s, undertook a conservative-critical assessment of this tradition. They advocated a measure of detachment from history and questioned deep-rooted convictions in a tone that resembled that of Positivist scholars, although no major historians emerged from their circle. Junimists also sought to relate to contemporary problems without obsessively referring to historical precedents, whether to support the maintenance of ancient privileges or to advocate radical change.[20] After 1900, an autochthonist counter-current to Junimea became dominant, and accordingly, the Romanians' distinct legacy gained new emphasis. The twentieth century's foremost Romanian historian, Nicolae Iorga, added a new aspect to the historiographical tradition which predominantly revolved around the Roman heritage: he transformed Romanians into the inheritors of the historical and political tradition of Byzantium, in addition to emphasizing their European mission. Iorga genuinely appreciated Kogălniceanu's attainments, calling him the founder of Romanian culture and praising his initiatives to improve the situation of the peasant population.

As such generous engagement with my historians' legacy reveals, the 'national paradigm' by no means remained confined to the Romantic epoch. Not only did historical writing 'in a national key' survive, but it constituted the predominant tradition in Europe between approximately 1850 and 1950.[21] The next two decades saw the pluralization of historical discourses, through which national history either competed or formed alliances with rival master narratives, such as class and gender. Spatial alternatives, including local and regional history (Central Europe, the Mediterranean, etc.) also presented a challenge to the national

---

[20] Boia, *History and Myth*, 51–4.
[21] Stefan Berger, 'A Return of the National Paradigm?', *Journal of Modern History* 77:3 (2005), 631.

paradigm. During the 1980s, the decade culminating in the collapse of communism, national history experienced another revival, but in a diversified form: it now became impossible to return to the homogeneous models of earlier epochs.[22] The fact that the nation-state has remained the favoured legal, constitutional and bureaucratic framework in Europe justifies the survival of the genre in contemporary times. Nonetheless, more recently there has been a move away from essentialist arguments, and historical discourses have instead emphasized the constructed nature of the national heritage.

The enthusiastic reception and enduring status of my historians' legacy in the domestic academic context stands in sharp contrast with international scholarship's neglect of them. I have taken a decidedly revisionist stance towards their a priori dismissal as unoriginal, biased and irrational scholars. However, my motivation has not been to show at all costs that they were 'better' historians than they have previously been given credit for. Rather, I have sought to elucidate some fascinating aspects of their work and explore the complexity of their achievements, which can only be properly appreciated through comparison and contextualization.

In seeking to uncover what was groundbreaking about my historians' attainments, several problems have arisen. One of these concerns marginality, a concept which tends to invite the label of unoriginality: colonial hierarchies typically identify the 'core' with inventiveness, rationality and progress, whilst the periphery is usually assigned the qualities of imitativeness, irrationality and stagnation.[23] Against these assumptions, I sought to demonstrate that even dependency on other cultures, an engagement with something 'given' (for example, translations) can prove 'innovative', and 'original' if it results in a creation which fills a lacuna in the receiving culture. Furthermore, the contested nature of the concept of originality, which is paradigmatically associated with innovation, also becomes obvious when assessing the qualities of nineteenth-century scholars who occupy established and undisputed positions in the historiographical canon. The majority of these historians have become canonized not because of their innovative ambitions, which were rarely fulfilled, but due to their masterful and appealing style; an element through which they expressed continuity

    [22] Ibid., 661.
    [23] J. M. Blaut, *The Colonizer's Model of the World: Geographical Diffusionism and Eurocentric History* (New York, 1993), 17.

with an earlier historiographical tradition. Another problem concerns the presumption, tacit or otherwise, that reliance on a foreign culture is invariably 'imitational', and perhaps even 'unnatural'; a premise which implies that cultures are self-contained universes with very limited scope for interchange. In the same way, it is especially difficult to justify why borrowing from a foreign culture should be seen as imitational when borrowing from one's native predecessors or contemporaries is perceived as a 'natural' continuation of a given tradition. Lastly, it appears that an agreed standard of what constitutes scholarly excellence does not do justice to the diverse manifestations of prominence, which are often contingent on the structures of individual scholarly cultures. In that context, I have emphasized that my historians had no giants on whose shoulders they could stand. They excelled in laying the foundations of national scholarship, a venture which might appear less impressive than crowning the efforts undertaken by their predecessors.

No serious contemporary scholar would deny a strong element of invention in national historiography. But even speculations about the extent of fictionality may disclose value judgements. In this context, an overt or tacit implication in many accounts of nationalism is that historiography in East-Central Europe (and other 'margins') contained a greater degree of 'invention', hence it was of poorer quality. In particular, the absence of a continuous state tradition has been associated with such shortcomings, as the term 'nations with empty histories' implies. The analysis of my historians' narrative in a European context has confirmed the prevalence of specific tropes. This suggests that the typologies which are commonly employed to assess the varieties of nationalism, such as 'continuous' versus 'non-continuous' traditions, may have limited relevance in the realm of historical writing, even if, as we have seen, continuity represented one of the foremost political concerns of nineteenth-century historians. In light of my protagonists' accomplishments, another word of caution may be necessary. The relevance of the words which are omnipresent in the study of nationalism—constructing, imagining, inventing and dreaming—is undisputable. Nonetheless, at least on one point these words may not do justice to my (and other) historians' work: they fail to indicate the purposefulness, the very pragmatic and conscious nature of their endeavours, not to mention the painstaking work involved in their political, cultural, historiographical 'multi-tasking'. Their ambitious endeavours definitely needed vision, but daydreamers alone would have been unable to make the impact upon scholarship that my historians did.

The ultimate objective of my assessment of correspondences and divergences in historical writing has been to contemplate the question of whether it is meaningful to refer to East-Central European historiography as a distinct explanatory model. The more I have tried to find peculiarities, the more I realized that the alleged differences do not comprise an independent tradition; rather, they represent variations on a common theme. By and large, my case studies have confirmed Anne Marie Thiesse's declaration that 'nothing is more international than the construction of national identities'.[24] My historians might have played different instruments from those of their 'Western' contemporaries, but they certainly produced the same music.

[24] Anne-Marie Thiesse, *La création des identités nationales: Europe XVIIIe –XXe siècle* (Paris, 1999), 1.

Bibliography

PRINTED PRIMARY SOURCES

Because my historians' output was immense, I have listed below only those of their writings (in chronological sequence) which are directly relevant to my study. In addition to individual accounts and collected volumes, I include some excerpts (mainly in English). These are relatively easy to access and may offer a first insight into my historians' world, therefore, I also relied on them in the book.

Works by Joachim Lelewel

Throughout the book, whenever possible, I referred to the widely available modern edition of Lelewel's collected works, *Dzieła*. However, this is an incomplete collection, only nine volumes of the envisaged thirty were ever published. Therefore, I also found it necessary to avail myself of the far more comprehensive nineteenth-century edition, *Polska, dzieje a rzeczy jej*, which has a very restricted availability. Importantly, however, the Polish version of Lelewel's perhaps most significant book, *Uwagi nad dziejami Polski i ludu jej*, was published only in this edition. Works not included in these two collections as well as the books that I consulted in individual editions are listed separately, alongside the most important foreign versions of Lelewel's writings. A comprehensive bibliography of Lelewel's rich oeuvre, *Bibliografia utworów Joachima Lelewela*, edited by Helena Hleb-Koszańska (Wrocław, 1952) contains over a thousand entries.

Edda, cyzli księga religii dawnych Skandynawii mięszkańców (Vilna, 1807).
Bibliograficznych ksiąg dwoje, 2 vols. (Vilna, 1823 and 1826), reprint (Warsaw, 1980).
Atlas do Historyi i geografii starożytnej (Warsaw, 1828).
Atlas do Dziejów polskich z dwunastu krajobrazów złożony (Warsaw, 1829).
Geschichte Polens unter Stanislaus August (Braunschweig, 1831).
Numismatique du Moyen-Âge (Paris, 1835).
Études numismatiques et archéologiques (Brussels, 1841).
Histoire de Pologne (Paris, 1844).
Betrachtungen über den politischen Zustand des ehemaligen Polens und über die Geschichte seines Volkes (Leipzig, 1845).
Stracone obywatelstwo stanu kmiecego (Brussels, 1846).
Geschichte Polens (Leipzig, 1846 and 1847).
Polska wieków średnich (Poznań, 1846–51).
Examen géographique des voyages de Benjamin de Tudèle (Brussels, 1852).

Polska, dzieje a rzeczy jej, 20 vols., of which Vols. XIV and XV were never published (Poznań, 1855–68).

Cześć bałwochwalcza Sławian i Polski (Poznań, 1857).

Sprawa żydowska w 1859, w liście do Ludwika Merzbacha rozważana (Poznań, 1860).

Die Judenfrage im Jahre 1859, in einem Briefe an Ludwig Merzbach erörtert (Lemberg, 1860).

Histoire de la Lithuanie et de la Ruthénie jusqu' à 1549 (Paris, 1861).

Géographie du moyen âge, 5 vols. (Brussels, 1850–2), 2nd edn. (Amsterdam, 1967).

Dzieła, 9 vols. (I–VIII and X), ed. Marian Henryk Serejski (Warsaw, 1957–73).

Joachima Lelewela odpowiedź na anikietę historyczną François Guizota, trans. Marian Henryk Serejski (Wrocław, 1962).

Joachim Lelewel: Textes Choisis (Brussels, 1986), ed. Teresa Wysokińska.

Excerpts:

'Prawność narodu polskiego', in Andrzej Walicki and Jan Garewicz (eds.), *700 lat myśli polskiej: Filozofia i myśl społeczna w latach 1831–1864* (Warsaw, 1977), 779–98.

'Legitimacy of the Polish Nation', in Balázs Trencsényi and Michal Kopeček (eds.), *Discourses of Collective Identity in Central and Southeast Europe (1770–1945)*, Vol. II: *National Romanticism* (Budapest and New York, 2007), 33–41.

Works by Simonas Daukantas

The definitive edition of Daukantas's historical works can be found in *Raštai* and *Istorija Žemaitiška* (1993). I have relied on these volumes because they contain a critical apparatus, in addition to being more widely available. I also consulted and have thus listed the original editions of Daukantas's national histories; however, these are extremely rare and employ the old orthography, which makes it difficult to decipher them. Daukantas's dictionaries, folklore collections, translations and correspondence are listed separately.

Būdas senovės lietuvių, kalnėnų ir žemaičių (St Petersburg, 1845).

'Istorija Žemaitiška', under the title: *Lietuvos istorija*, 2 vols. (Plymouth, PA, 1893–7).

Darbai senujų lietuvių ir žemaičių (Kaunas, 1929).

Pasakojimas apie veikalus lietuvių tautos senovėje (Bitėnai, 1929).

Dainės Žemaičių (Petropilis, 1846).

Raštai, 2 vols. (Vilnius, 1976).

Žemaičių tautosaka, 2 vols. (Vilnius, 1983–4).

Vertimai ir sekimai (Vilnius, 1986).

Istorija Žemaitiška, 2 vols. (Vilnius, 1993).

Didysis lenkų-lietuvių kalbų žodynas, 3 vols. (Vilnius, 1993–6).
Laiškai Teodorui Narbutui: epistolinis dialogas (Vilnius, 1996).

Works by František Palacký
Palacký's magnum opus is undoubtedly his national history, which was published in numerous editions. Apart from the German version, below are listed the following Czech editions: the first one of 1848–57, as well as the edition of 1876–8, which is considered classical. Also included is the six-volume edition of 1939–40, which was published in Prague by Kvašnicka and Hampl. This version, which draws on the definitive publication of 1876–8, is more readily available than the earlier ones. I used it as my personal copy and my references in the book are also based on it. Palacký's individual monographs and pamphlets, the collections of his minor writings and correspondence are listed separately. A comprehensive biography of my historian's works can be found on the website of the journal *Dějiny a současnost* (History and the Present): http://www.dejiny.nlh.cz/Bibl/Palacky.html. A note on orthography: in non-Czech publications, in both primary and secondary sources, the accents are occasionally omitted from Palacký's name. Below I follow the spelling on the title-page of the publications.

Würdigung der alten böhmischer Geschichtschreiber (Prague, 1830).
Geschichte von Böhmen, grösstentheils nach Urkunden und Handschriften, 5 vols. in 10 (Prague, 1836–67).
Franz Palacky and Paul Joseph Šafařik, *Die ältesten Denkmäler der böhmischen Sprache* (Prague, 1840).
Archiv český, ed. Palacký, 6 vols. (Prague, 1840–72).
Dějiny národu českého v Čechách a v Moravě, 5 vols. in 10 (1848–67).
Idea státu rakouského (Prague, 1865).
Oesterreichs Staatsidee (Prague, 1866).
Die Geschichte des Hussitenthums und Prof. Constantin Höfler: Kritische Studien (Prague, 1868).
Zur Böhmischen Geschichtschreibung: Aktenmässige Aufschlüsse und Worte der Abwehr (Prague, 1871)
Radhost, 3 vols. (Prague, 1871–3).
Politisches Vermächtnis (Prague, 1872).
Urkundliche Beiträge zur Geschichte des Hussitenkriegs, 2 vols. (Prague, 1872–4).
Gedenkblätter (Prague, 1874).
Dějiny národu českého v Čechách a v Moravě, 5 vols. in 11, ed. Josef Kalousek (Prague, 1876–8).
Františka Palackého spisy drobné, ed. Bohuslav Rieger, Vojtěch Jaromír Nováček and Leander Čech, 2 vols. (Prague, 1898–1902).
Františka Palackého korrespondence a zápisky, 3 vols., ed. Vojtěch Jaromír Nováček (Prague, 1898–1911).

Poslední mé slovo (Prague, 1912).

Dějiny národu českého v Čechách a v Moravě, 6 vols., ed. Miroslav Novotný (published by Kvašnicka a Hampl, Prague, 1939–40).

Dílo Františka Palackého, 4 vols., ed. Jaroslav Charvát (Prague, 1941).

Palacký and Pavel Jozef Šafárik, *Počátkové českého básnictví, obzvláště prozódie* (Bratislava, 1961).

Geschichte der schönen Redekünste bei den Böhmen (Ostrava, 1968).

A Historical Survey on the Science of Beauty and the Literature on the Subject, ed. Tomáš Hlobil, translated from the Czech by Derek and Marzia Paton (Olomouc, 2001).

Short excerpts:
'A History of the Czech Nation in Bohemia and Moravia', in Balázs Trencsényi and Michal Kopeček (eds.), *Discourses of Collective Identity in Central and Southeast Europe (1770–1945)*, vol. II: *National Romanticism* (Budapest and New York, 2007), 50–6.

'Letter to Frankfurt, 11 April, 1848', ibid., 322–9.

Works by Mihály Horváth

In addition to the various versions of Horváth's national history, of which I primarily relied on the eight-volume version of 1871–3, I have listed his individual monographs, the four-volume collection of his minor writings and his articles which were not republished in collected volumes. Also included are two modern editions and the most important foreign-language versions of his writings.

Az ipar és kereskedelem története Magyarországban az utolsó három század alatt (Buda, 1840).

Az ipar és kereskedelem története Magyarországban a XVI század elejéig (Pest, 1842).

A magyarok története, 4 vols. (Pápa, 1842–6).

Geschichte der Ungarn, 2 vols. (Pest, 1851).

Magyar történelmi okmánytár a brüsseli országos levéltárból és a burgundi levéltárból (Monumenta Hungariae Historica), 4 vols., ed. Horváth (Pest, 1857–9).

Magyarország történelme, 6 vols. (Pest, 1860–3).

Huszonöt év Magyarország történetéből 1823-tól 1848-ig, 2 vols. (Geneva, 1864).

Magyarország függetlenségi harcának története, 3 vols. (Geneva, 1865).

Fünfundzwanzig Jahre aus der Geschichte Ungarns: von 1823–1848, 2 vols. (Leipzig, 1867).

'Horváth Mihály beszéde a Történelmi Társulat első közgyűlésén 1867-ki május 15-kén', *Századok* 1:1 (1867), 3–12.

Horváth Mihály kisebb történelmi munkái, 4 vols. (Pest, 1868).

Horváth, 'Miért meddő korunkban a művészet? S a történetírás miért termékenyebb remek művekben?', *Kisfaludy-Társaság Évlapjai* 4 (1868), 471–89.

Williams Roger, a,,szabad egyház a szabad államban" elv megteremtője s megtestesítője. Életrajzi vázlat (Pest, 1868).
Kossuth Lajos újabb leveleire, 2nd edn. (Pest, 1868).
Auf Ludwig Kossuth's neuere Briefe (Pest, 1868).
Zrínyi Ilona életrajza (Pest, 1869).
Magyarország történelme, 8 vols. (Pest, 1871–3).
Horváth Michele and Ribány Ferenc, *Storia degli ungheresi con introduzione ed aggiunte relative alla storia universale. Sulle orme di Horváth compilata dal Massimiliano Gresits* (Fiume, 1873).
A kereszténység első évszázada Magyarországon (Budapest, 1878).
Utyeszenich Fráter György (Martinuzzi bíbornok) élete (Budapest, 1882).
A magyarok története rövid előadásban, 6th edn. (Budapest, 1887).
Az 1514.-i pórlázadás, annak okai es következményei, ed. Gábor Szigethy (Budapest, 1986).
Polgárosodás, liberalizmus, függetlenségi harc, ed. Lajos Pál (Budapest, 1986).

Excerpt:
'History of the Hungarian War of Independence of 1848–49', in Balázs Trencsényi and Michal Kopeček (eds.), *Discourses of Collective Identity in Central and Southeast Europe (1770–1945)*, Vol. II: *National Romanticism* (Budapest and New York, 2007), 57–64.

Works by Mihail Kogălniceanu

Almost every item discussed in the book, with the exception of Kogălniceanu's source editions, can be found in *Opere*, the comprehensive and definitive modern edition of his literary writings, historical works and speeches. Additionally, I have included the original editions of his historical accounts. A book-length annotated bibliography, *Mihail Kogălniceanu 1817–91. Bio-bibliografie* by Alexandru Zub (Bucharest, 1971) offers a comprehensive overview of the Romanian scholar's writings.

Esquisse sur l'histoire, les moeurs et la langue des Cigains (Berlin, 1837).
Histoire de la Valachie, de la Moldavie et des Valaques transdanubiens (Berlin, 1837).
Fragments tirés des chroniques Moldaves et Valaques, ed. Kogălniceanu (Iaşi, 1845).
Letopiseţele Ţării Moldaviei (şi Valahiei), 3 vols. (Iaşi, 1845–52).
Chronicele României, 3 vols., ed. Kogălniceanu (Bucharest, 1872–4).
Romänische oder wallachische Sprache und Literatur: mit rumänischer Übersetzung (Bucharest, 1895).
Tainele inimei (Bucharest, 1973).
Opere, 5 parts, ed. Dan Simonescu (Bucharest, 1974–).

Short excerpt:
'Speech for opening the course on national history', in Balázs Trencsényi and Michal Kopeček (eds.), *Discourses of Collective Identity in Central and*

Southeast Europe (1770–1945), Vol. II: *National Romanticism* (Budapest and New York, 2007), 42–9.

SECONDARY SOURCES

ABRAMS, Bradley F., *The Struggle for the Soul of a Nation: Czech Culture and the Rise of Communism* (Oxford, 2004).

ADAMUS, Jan, *Monarchizm i republikanizm w syntezie dziejów Polski* (Łódź, 1961).

AGNEW, Hugh LeCaine, *Origins of the Czech National Renascence* (Pittsburgh, 1993).

—— 'Dilemmas of Liberal Nationalism: Czechs and Germans in Bohemia and the Revolution of 1848', in Sabrina P. Ramet, James R. Felak and Herbert J. Ellison (eds.), *Nations and Nationalisms in East Central Europe, 1806–1948: A Festschrift for Peter F. Sugar* (Bloomington, 2002), 51–70.

—— 'Czechs, Germans, Bohemians? Images of Self and Other in Bohemia to 1848', in Nancy Wingfield (ed.), *Creating the Other in the Nineteenth Century: Ethnic Conflict and Nationalism in the Habsburg Empire* (Oxford and New York, 2004), 56–81.

ALEKSANDRAVIČIUS, Egidijus, *Prieš aušrą: jaunieji Daukanto bičiuliai* (Vilnius, 1990).

ALEKSANDRAVIČIUS, Egidijus (ed.), *Lietuvių atgminimo istorijos studijos*, 11 vols. (Vilnius, 1990–6).

ALEKSANDRAVIČIUS, Egidijus and KULAKAUSKAS, Antanas, *Carų valdžioje: XIX amžiaus Lietuva* (Vilnius, 1996).

ANDERSON, Benedict, *Imagined Communities: Reflections on the Origin and Spread of Nationalism* (London, 1991).

ARNOLD, Thomas, *Lectures on Modern History*, 4th edn. (London, 1849).

ARSLEFF, Hans, 'The Rise and Decline of Adam and His Ursprache in Seventeenth Century Thought', in Allison P. Coudert (ed.), *The Language of Adam* (Wiesbaden, 1999), 227–95.

ASSORODOBRAJ, Nina, 'Wstęp', in Lelewel, *Dzieła*, Vol. II/1: *Pisma Metodologiczne* (Warsaw, 1964), 7–93.

AUER, Stefan, *Liberal Nationalism in Central Europe* (New York and London, 2004).

BARNARD, Frederick M., *Herder on Nationality, Humanity and History* (Montreal, London and Ithaca, 2003).

BARNES, Harry Elmer, *A History of Historical Writing*, 2nd edn. (New York, 1963).

BARZUN, Jacques, 'Romantic Historiography as a Political Force in France', *Journal of the History of Ideas* 2:3 (1941), 318–29.

BEAUVOIS, Daniel, *Lumières et société en Europe de l'Est: l'Université de Vilna et les écoles polonaises de L'Empire Russe (1803-1832)*, 2 vols. (Lille, 1977).

BECHER, Ursula A. J., 'August Ludwig v. Schlözer', in Hans Ulrich Wehler (ed.), *Deutsche Historiker* (Göttingen, 1989), Vol. VII, 7–22.

BECK, Thor J., *Northern Antiquities in French Learning and Literature: A Study in Preromantic Ideas*, 2 vols. (New York, 1934–5).

BECKER, Henrik, *Zwei Sprachanschlüsse* (Leipzig and Berlin, 1948).

BECKER-SCHAUM, Christopher, *Arnold Hermann Ludwig Heeren: Ein Beitrag zur Geschichte der Geschichtswissenschaft zwischen Aufklärung und Historismus* (Frankfurt am Main, 1993).

BĚLIČ, Jaromír, 'Zásady Palackého v otázkách jazykové kultury', in František Kutnar (ed.), *Tři studie o Františku Palackém* (Olomouc, 1949) Acta Universitatis Palackianae Olomucensis 1, 166–237.

BENTLEY, Michael, *Modern Historiography: An Introduction* (London, 1999).

—— *Modernzing England's Past: English Historiography in the Age of Modernism 1870–1970* (Cambridge, 2005).

BERESNEVIČIŪTE, Halina, 'The Idea of the Nation in Joachim Lelewel's and František Palacký's Historical Works', MA thesis (Central European University, Budapest, 1995).

BERGER, Stefan, *The Search for Normality: National Identity and Historical Consciousness in Germany since 1800* (Providence and Oxford, 1997).

—— 'Representations of the Past: The Writing of National Histories in Europe', *Debatte* 12:1 (2004), 73–96.

—— 'A Return of the National Paradigm?', *Journal of Modern History* 77:3 (2005), 629–78.

BERGER, Stefan, DONOVAN, Mark and PASSMORE, Kevin, 'Apologias for the Nation State in Western Europe since 1800', in Stefan Berger (ed.), *Writing National Histories: Western Europe since 1800* (London and New York, 1999), 3–14.

BERGER, Stefan and LAMBERT, Peter, 'Intellectual Transfers and Mental Blockades: Anglo-American Dialogues in Historiography', in Stefan Berger, Peter Lambert and Peter Schumann, *Geschichte, Mythos und Gedächtnis in deutsch-britischen kulturellen Austausch 1750–2000* (Göttingen, 2003), 9–61.

BERINDEI, Dan, 'L'activité de la section d'histoire de la Société Académique et l'Académie Roumaine jusqu'au parachévement d l'unité nationale (1867–1918)', *Revue Roumaine d'Histoire* 5:6 (1966), 963–79.

—— 'Societatea Academică Română (1867–1878)', *Revista de Istorie* 19:6 (1966), 1069–89.

BERKES, Tamás, *A cseh eszmetörténet antinómiái* (Budapest, 2003).

BETHLEN, Imre, *II. Rákóczi György ideje* (Nagyenyed, 1829).

BIELIŃSKI, Józef, *Królewski Universytet Warszawski 1816–31*, 2 vols. (Warsaw, 1907–11).

—— *Universytet Wileński 1579-1831*, 3 vols. (Cracow, 1899–1900).

312   *Bibliography*

BIERNACKA, Maria, *Joachim Lelewel: ksiegoznawca, bibliotekarz, bibliograf* (Warsaw, 1993).
BITTNER, Konrad, *Herder's Geschichtsphilosophie und die Slaven* (Reichenberg, 1929).
BJÖRK, Ragnar (ed.), *Contemplating Evolution and Doing Politics. Historical Scholars and Students in Sweden and in Hungary Facing Historical Change 1840–1920* (Stockholm, 1993).
BLACK, J. L., *Nicholas Karamzin and Russian Society in the Nineteenth Century* (Toronto, 1975).
BLACK, Jeremy, *Maps and History: Constructing Images of the Past* (New Haven, 1997).
BLANKE, Horst Walter, 'Verfassungen, die nicht rechtlich, aber wirklich sind. A. H. L. Heeren und das Ende der Aufklärungshistorie', *Berichte zur Wissenschaftsgeschichte* 6 (1983), 143–64.
——*Historiographiegeschichte als Historik* (Stuttgart, 1991).
BLAUT, J. M., *The Colonizer's Model of the World: Geographical Diffusionism and Eurocentric History* (New York, 1993).
BLOCH, Marc, *Feudal Society: The Growth of Ties and Dependences* (Chicago, 1964).
BLOCKMANS, Wim and GENET, Jean-Philippe (eds.), *Visions sur le développement des états européens: théories et historiographies de l'état moderne* (Rome, 1993).
BOBRZYŃSKI, Michał, *Dzieje Polski w zarysie*, 2nd edn. (Warsaw and Cracow, 1887).
BOCHMANN, Klaus, *Der politisch-soziale Wortschatz des Rumänischen (1821–1850)*, (Berlin, 1979).
BOER, Pim den, *History as a Profession: The Study of History in France, 1818–1914*, trans. Arnold J. Pomerans (Princeton, 1998).
BOHLEN, Peter von, 'Ueber die Werwandtschaft zwischen der Lithauischen und Sanskritsprache, vorgetragen am 6. November 1828', *Historische und Literarische Abhandlungen der Königlichen Deutschen Gesellschaft zu Königsberg* (1830), 111–40.
BOIA, Lucian, *History and Myth in Romanian Consciousness* (Budapest and New York, 2001).
BOJTÁR, Endre, *Foreword to the Past: A Cultural History of the Baltic People* (Budapest, 1999).
——, *Hazát és népet álmodánk"* (Budapest, 2008).
BOLINGBROKE, Henry, *Historical Writings*, ed. Isaac Kramnick (Chicago, 1972).
BONNOT DE MABLY, Gabriel, *Du gouvernement et des Loix de la Pologne* (London, 1781).
BOPP, Franz, *Vergleichende Grammatik des Sanskrit, Zend, Griechischen, Lateinischen, Litauischen, Alt-Slawischen, Gotischen und Deutschen* (1833–52).

—— A Comparative Grammar of the Sanscrit, Zend, Greek, Latin, Lithuanian, Gothic, German and Sclavonic Languages, trans. Edward B. Eastwick, 2nd edn. (London, 1854).

BORSODY, Steven Bela, 'The Foundation of the Hungarian Historical Association and its Impact on Hungarian Historical Studies', in Borsody, Clio's Art in Hungary and in Hungarian-America (New York, 1985), 17–34.

BORST, Arno, Der Turmbau von Babel: Geschichte der Meinungen über Ursprung und Vielfalt der Sprachen und Völker, 4 vols. (Stuttgart, 1957–63).

BOYLE, Nicholas, Goethe (Oxford, 1991).

BRANCH, Michael (ed.), National History and Identity: Approaches to the Writing of National History in the North-East Baltic Region, Nineteenth and Twentieth Century (Helsinki, 1999).

BREISACH, Ernst, Historiography. Ancient, Medieval and Modern, 2nd edn. (Chicago, 1983).

BREUILLY, John, 'Nationalism and the Making of Nationalist Pasts', in François Gemenne and Susana Carvalho, Nations and their Histories. Constructions and Representations (London, 2009), 7–28.

BRONOWSKI, Franciszek, Idea gminowładztwa w polskiej historiografii (Łódź 1969).

BROWN, E. A. R., 'The Tyranny of a Construct: Feudalism and Historians of Medieval Europe', American Historical Review 79 (1974), 1063–88.

BURKE, Peter, Languages and Communities in Early Modern Europe (Cambridge, 2004).

BURROW, John, 'The Uses of Philology in Victorian England', in Robert Robson (ed.), Ideas and Institutions of Victorian Britain: Essays in Honour of George Kitson Clark (London, 1967), 180–204.

—— A Liberal Descent: Victorian Historians and the English Past (Cambridge, 1981).

—— Whigs and Liberals: Continuity and Political Change in English Political Thought (Oxford, 1988).

—— The Crisis of Reason, European Thought, 1848–1914 (New Haven and London, 2000).

—— A History of Histories: Epics, Chronicles, Romances and Inquiries from Herodotus to Thucydides to the Twentieth Century (New York, 2008).

BURROW, John, COLLINI, Stefan, and WINCH, Donald, That Noble Science of Politics, a Study in Nineteenth Century Intellectual History (Cambridge, 1983).

BURY, J. B., The Idea of Progress: An Inquiry into its Origin and Growth (London, 1920).

BUTTERWICK, Richard, DAVIES, Simon, and SÁNCHEZ ESPINOSA, Gabriel, Peripheries of the Enlightenment, Studies on Voltaire and the Eighteenth Century 2008:1 (Oxford, 2008).

CAMPBELL, John C., *French Influence and the Rise of Roumanian Nationalism* (New York, 1971).

CAMPE, Joachim Heinrich, *Robinson der Jüngere* (Stuttgart, 2000).

CARLYLE, Thomas, 'On History', in Fritz Stern (ed.), *The Varieties of History, from Voltaire to the Present* (New York, 1973), 90–107.

CENTNERSZWEROWA, R., *Stanowisko Lelewela wobec dziejów i spraw żydów polskich* (Warsaw, 1911).

CESARZ, Elżbieta, *Chłopi w polskiej myśli historycznej doby porozbiorowej 1795–1864* (Rzeszóv, 1999).

CHALOUPECKÝ, Václav, *Fr. Palacký* (Prague, 1912).

CHALUPA, Ales, 'Frantisek Palacky and the National Museum', *East European Quarterly* 15:1 (1981), 85–101.

CHAPPLE, Christopher (ed.), *The Jesuit Tradition in Education and Missions: A 450-Year Perspective* (Scranton, 1993).

CHEYLETTE, Fredric L., 'Feudalism', in Maryanne Cline Horowitz (ed.), *New Dictionary of the History of Ideas*, Vol. II (Detroit, 2005), 828–31.

CHIROT, Daniel (ed.), *The Origins of Backwardness in Eastern Europe: Economics and Politics from the Middle Ages until the Early Twentieth Century* (Berkeley, CA, 1989).

COLLEY, Linda, *Britons: Forging the Nation 1707–1837* (New Haven, 1994).

CONRAD, Christoph and CONRAD, Sebastian (eds.), *Die Nation Schreiben: Geschichtswissenschaft im internationalen Vergleich* (Göttingen, 2002).

CRAIUTU, Aurelian, 'Introduction', in François Guizot, *The History of the Origins of Representative Government in Europe*, trans. Andrew R. Scoble (Indianapolis, 2002), vii–xvi.

CROCE, Benedetto, *History as the Story of Liberty* (New York, 1995).

CROSSLEY, Ceri, *French Historians and Romanticism: Thierry, Guizot, the Saint-Simonians, Quinet, Michelet* (London and New York, 1993).

—— 'History as a Principle of Legitimation in France (1820–48)', in Stefan Berger (ed.), *Writing National Histories: Western Europe since 1800* (London and New York, 1999), 49–56.

CROWLEY, Tony, *Language in History: Theories and Texts* (London and New York, 1996).

CRYSTAL, David, *Language Death* (Cambridge, 2002).

CUBITT, Geoffrey, *The Jesuit Myth: Conspiracy Theory and Politics in Nineteenth-Century France* (Oxford, 1993).

CYGLER, Bogusław, *Działalność polityczno-społeczna Joachima Lelewela na emigracji w latach 1831–61* (Gdańsk, 1969).

—— *Z wolnością mego sumienia: poglądy Joachima Lelewela na religię i na rolę Kościoła łacinskiego w dziejach* (Gdańsk, 1992).

DAHLMANN, Friedrich Christoph (ed.), *Die Protestation und Entlassung der sieben Göttinger Professoren* (Leipzig, 1843).

DAVIES, Norman, *God's Playground*, 2 vols. (Oxford, 1981).

DE SANCTIS, M., *Freeman and European History* (Farnborough, 1990).

DEME, Laszlo, 'Writers and Essayists and the Rise of Magyar Nationalism in the 1820s and 1830s', *Slavic Review* 43:4 (1984), 624–40.

DÉNES, Iván Zoltán, 'The Value System of Liberals and Conservatives in Hungary, 1830–48', *The Historical Journal* 36:4 (1993), 825–50.

DÉNES, Iván Zoltán (ed.), *Liberty and the Search for National Identity: Liberal Nationalisms and the Legacy of Empires* (Budapest and New York, 2006).

DRABEK, Anna M., 'Frantisek Palacky and the Beginning of the Austrian Academy of Arts and Sciences (Österreichische Akademie der Wissenschaften)', *East European Quarterly* 15:1 (1981), 103–16.

DRACE FRANCIS, Alex, *The Making of Romanian Culture: Literacy and the Development of National Identity* (London, 2006).

EBEL, Julia G., 'Translation and Cultural Nationalism in the Reign of Elisabeth', *Journal of the History of Ideas* 30:4 (1969), 593–602.

ENGEL-JANOSI, Friedrich, *Four Studies in French Romantic Historical Writing* (Baltimore, 1955).

ENGELS, Friedrich, *Revolution and Counterrevolution in Germany in 1848*, ed. Eleanor Max Aveling (Chicago, 1919).

—— 'Democratic Panslavism', in Marx and Engels, *Collected Works*, Vol. VIII (New York, 1977), 362–78.

ERIKSONAS, Linas, *National Heroes and National Identites: Scotland, Norway and Lithuania* (Brussels and New York, 2004).

ERNESTI, Johann August, 'Vorrede', in *Allgemeine Weltgeschichte ausgefertigt von Guthrie Gray und anderen in diesen Theilen der Wissenschaften berühmten Gelehrten*, Vol I (Leipzig, 1765), viii–ix.

ESPAGNE, Michael, *Les transferts culturels franco-allemands* (Paris, 1999).

EVANS, R. J. W., 'Die Universität im geistigen Milieu der habsburgischen Länder (17.–18. Jh.)', in Alexander Patschovsky and Peter Baumgart (eds.), *Die Universität in Alteuropa* (Constance, 2000), 183–204.

—— 'Language and State Building: The Case of the Habsburg Monarchy', *Austrian History Yearbook* 35 (2004), 1–24.

—— 'The Origins of Enlightenment in the Habsburg Lands', in R. J. W. Evans, *Austria, Hungary and the Habsburgs: Essays on Central Europe c.1683–1867* (Oxford, 2006), 36–55.

—— 'Frontiers and National Identities in Central European History', in R. J. W. Evans, *Austria, Hungary and the Habsburgs: Essays on Central Europe c.1683–1867* (Oxford, 2006), 114–33.

—— ' "The Manuscripts": The Culture and Politics of Forgery in Central Europe', in Geraint H. Jenkins (ed.), *A Rattleskull Genius: The Many Faces of Iolo Morganwg* (Cardiff, 2005), 51–68.

FENYŐ, István, *Haza és tudomány: A hazai reformkori liberalizmus történetéhez* (Budapest, 1969).

FISCHER, Josef, *Myšlenka a dílo Františka Palackého*, 2 vols. (Prague, 1926–7).

FLAIG, Herbert, 'The Historian as Pedagogue of the Nation', *History* 59 (1974), 18–32.

FLYNN, James T., *The University Reform of Tsar Alexander I 1802–1835* (Washington DC, 1988).

FODOR, István, 'Hungarian: Evolution–Stagnation–Reform–Further Development', in István Fodor and Claude Hagège (eds.), *Language Reform: History and Future*, 5 vols. (1983–4), Vol. II, 49–84.

FÖGEN, Thorsten, *Patrii sermonis egestas: Einstellungen lateinischer Autoren zu ihrer Muttersprache, Ein Beitrag zum Sprachbewußtsein in der römischen Antike* (Munich and Leipzig, 2000).

FRAKNÓI, Vilmos, *Emlékbeszéd Horváth Mihály felett* (Budapest, 1879).

——— *Horváth Mihály emlékezete* (Budapest, 1879).

FRANKEL, Jonathan, and ZIPPERSTEIN, Steven J. (eds.), *Assimilation and Community: The Jews in Nineteenth-Century Europe* (Cambridge, 1992).

FREEMAN, Edward, *The Historical Geography of Europe* (London, 1881).

FUETER, Eduard, *Geschichte der Neueren Historiographie* (Munich and Berlin, 1936).

FÜLÖP, Géza, *A magyar olvasóközönség a felvilágosodás idején és a reformkorban* (Budapest, 1978).

FUMAROLI, Marc, 'The Genius of the French Language', in Lawrence D. Kritzman (ed.), Pierre Nora (director), *Realms of Memory: The Construction of the French Past* (New York, 1998), Vol. III, 555–608.

GALL, Lothar, *Confronting Clio: Myth Makers and Other Historians* (London, 1992).

GANSHOF, F. L., *Feudalism*, trans. Philip Grierson (New York, 1964).

GARNIER-PAGÈS, Étienne (ed.), *Dictionnaire Politique; encyclopédie du langage et de la science politiques* (Paris, 1855).

GARRETT, Leah, 'The Jewish Robinson Crusoe', *Comparative Literature* 54:3 (2002), 215–28.

GASIOROWSKI, Zymunt J., 'The "Conquest" Theory of the Genesis of the Polish State', *Speculum* 30:4 (1955), 550–60.

GATTERER, Johann Christoph, *Versuch einer allgemeinen Weltgeschichte bis zur Entdeckung Amerikens* (Göttingen, 1792).

GAWLAS, Sławomir, 'Die Probleme des Lehnswesens und des Feudalismus aus polnischer Sicht', in Michael Borgolte (ed.), *Das europäische Mittelalter im Spannungsbogen des Vergleiches* (Berlin, 2001).

GAY, Peter, *Style in History* (New York, 1956).

GAZI, Effi, *'Scientific' National History: The Greek Case in Comparative Perspective 1850–1920* (Frankfurt am Main, 2000).

GELLNER, Ernest, *Nations and Nationalism*, 2nd edn. (Oxford, 2006).

GENZELIS, Bronius, *Švietėjai ir jų idėjos Lietuvoje (XIX a.)* (Vilnius, 1972).

GEORGESCU, Vlad, *Political Ideas and the Enlightenment in the Romanian Principalities 1750–1831* (New York, 1971).

GERŐ, András, *Modern Society in the Making: The Unfinished Experience* (Budapest, 1995).

GHOSH, Peter, 'Macaulay and the Heritage of the Enlightenment', *English Historical Review* 112:446 (1997), 358–95.

GLATZ, Ferenc, 'A Magyar Történelmi Társulat Megalakulásának Története', *Századok* 101:1–2 (1967), 233–67.

GOLDSTEIN, Robert Justin, *Political Censorship of the Arts and the Press in Nineteenth Century Europe* (New York, 1989).

GOLL, Jaroslav, 'Palackého program práce historické', *Český časopis historický* 4 (1898), 1–11.

GOOCH, G. P., *History and Historians in the Nineteenth Century* (London and New York, 1952).

GOSSMAN, Lionel, *Between History and Literature* (Cambridge, MA, and London, 1990).

GRABSKI, Andrzej Feliks, *Myśl historyczna polskiego oświecenia* (Warsaw, 1976).

——*Joachim Lelewel i demokracja niemiecka: z dziejów międzynarodowych kontaktów polskiej lewicy w dobie Wielkiej Emigracji* (Łódź, 1987).

GREENBAUM, Masha, *The Jews of Lithuania: A History of a Remarkable Community 1316–1945* (Jerusalem, 1995).

GREENFELD, Liah, *Nationalism: Five Roads to Modernity* (Cambridge, MA, 1992).

GRIGAS, K., 'Simonas Daukantas–Lietuvių Tautosakos Rinkėjas, Leidėjas ir Vertintojas', in J. Žiugžda (ed.), *Iš Lietuvių Kultūros Istorijos* (Vilnius, 1958), 270–86.

GUIZOT, François, *Historical Essays and Lectures*, ed. Stanley Mellon (Chicago and London, 1972).

——*The History of Civilization in Europe*, ed. Larry Siedentop (London, 1997).

GUTHRIE, William, and GRAY, John, *Universal History from the Earliest Account of Time to the Present* (London, 1764–7).

HALE, J. R. (ed.), *The Evolution of British Historiography: From Bacon to Namier* (London, 1967).

HALLER, William, *Foxe's Book of Martyrs and the Elect Nation* (London, 1963).

HAMBURGER, Joseph, *Macaulay and the Whig Tradition* (Chicago and London, 1976).

HAUPT, Heinz-Gerhardt, and KOCKA, Jürgen (eds.), *Geschichte und Vergleich, Ansätze und Ergebnisse international vergleichender Geschichtsschreibung* (Frankfurt and New York, 1996).

HAVRÁNEK, Jan, 'František Palacký a Univerzita Karlova', *Acta Universitatis Carolinae—Historica Universitatis Carolinae Pragensis* 21 (1981), 67–81.

——'Institutionen der tschechischen Geschichtswissenschaft bis zum Zweiten Weltkrieg', in Matthias Middell (ed.), *Historische Institute im internationalen Vergleich* (Leipzig, 2001), 173–84.

HEEREN, Arnold Hermann Ludwig, 'William Robertson, *Historical Disquisition on India*' (untitled review), *Bibliothek der Alten Litteratur und Kunst* 9 (1792), 105–21.

—— *Ideen über die Politik, den Verkehr und den Handel der vornehmsten Völker der alten Welt* (Göttingen, 1793).

—— *Handbuch der Geschichte des Europäischen Staatensystems und seiner Colonien* (Göttingen, 1809).

—— *Historische Werke*, 15 vols. (Göttingen, 1821–6).

HEGEL, Georg Wilhelm Friedrich, *Elements of the Philosophy of Right*, ed. Allen Wood, trans. H. B. Nisbet (Cambridge, 1991).

HERDER, Johann Gottfried, *Geschichte der Europäischen Völker* (Berlin, 1952).

—— *Auch eine Philosophie der Geschichte zur Bildung der Menschheit*, in *Werke in Zwei Bänden*, ed. Karl Gustav Gerold (Munich, 1953), Vol. II, 9–97.

HERMANS, Theo, 'Literary Translation: The Birth of a Concept', *New Comparison* 1 (1986), 34–8.

HILDERMEIER, Manfred, 'Von der Nordischen Geschichte zur Ostgeschichte. Osteuropa im Göttinger Horizont', in Hartmut Boockmann and Hermann Wellenreuter (eds.), *Geschichtswissenschaft in Göttingen* (Göttingen, 1987), 102–21.

HILL, Christopher, 'The Norman Yoke', in Christopher Hill, *Puritanism and Revolution: Studies in Interpretation of the English Revolution of the 17th Century* (London, 1965), 50–122.

HITCHINS, Keith, *The Romanians 1774–1855* (Oxford, 1996).

—— *A Nation Rediscovered: Romanian Intellectuals in Transylvania and the Idea of the Nation 1700–1848* (Bucharest, 1999).

HOBSBAWM, Eric, *Nations and Nationalism since 1780: Programme, Myth, Reality* (Cambridge, 1991).

HOFFMANN, Stanley, 'The Nation, Nationalism, and After: The Case of France', *The Tanner Lectures on Human Values*, Vol. XV (Salt Lake City, Utah, 1994), 215–82.

HÓMAN, Bálint, 'A történelem útja', in Bálint Hóman (ed.), *A Magyar történetírás új útjai* (Budapest, 1931), 7–52.

HORSMAN, Reginald, 'Origins of Racial Anglo-Saxonism in Great Britain before 1850', *Journal of the History of Ideas* 37:3 (1976), 387–410.

HROCH, Miroslav, *Social Preconditions of National Revival in Europe: A Comparative Analysis of the Social Consumption of Patriotic Groups among the Smaller European Nations* (Cambridge, 1985).

—— 'Historical Belles-Lettres as a Vehicle of the Image of National History', *National History and Identity, Studia Fennica Ethnologica* 6 (1999), 97–108.

HROCH, Miroslav, and MALEČKOVÁ, Jitka, 'The Construction of Czech History', *Historein* 1 (1999), 102–13.

HUMBOLDT, Wilhelm von, *On Language: The Diversity of Human Language-Structure and its Influence on the Mental Development of Mankind*, trans. Peter Heath (Cambridge, 1988).

HUME, David, 'Of National Characters', in *Essays Moral, Political and Literary* (Oxford, 1983), 202–20.

IGGERS, Georg G., 'The University of Göttingen 1760–1800 and the Transformation of Historical Scholarship', *Storia della Storiografia* 2 (1982), 11–37.

—— *The German Conception of History* (Middletown, CT, 1983).

—— 'The Crisis of the Rankean Paradigm in the Nineteenth Century', in Georg G. Iggers and James M. Powell (eds.), *Leopold von Ranke and the Shaping of the Historical Discipline* (New York, 1990), 170–180.

—— *Historiography in the Twentieth Century* (Hannover, NH, and London, 1997).

—— 'Nationalism and Historiography, 1789–1996: The German Example in Historical Perspective', in Stefan Berger (ed.), *Writing National Histories: Western Europe since 1800* (London and New York, 1999), 15–29.

IMPEY, Olga T., 'Mihail Kogălniceanu's Six Months in Spain: Their Consequences for His Life and Romania's Future', in K. W. Treptow (ed.), *Biography and Romanian Studies* (Iasi and Oxford, 1998), 54–71.

IONESCU, Virgil I., *Mihail Kogălniceanu: Contribuţii la cunoaşterea vieţii, activităţii şi concepţiilor sale* (Bucharest, 1963).

IORDACHI, Constantin, *Citizenship, Nation- and State-Building: The Integration of Northern Dobrogea into Romania 1878–1913* (Pittsburgh, 2002).

JANOWSKI, Maciej, 'Kozy i jiesoty', *Roczniki Dziejów. Społeczych i Gospodarczych* 56–67 (1996–7), 69–92.

—— 'Wavering Friendship: Liberal and National Ideas in Nineteenth Century East-Central Europe', *Ab Imperio* 3–4 (2000), 69–90.

—— 'Three Historians', *CEU History Department Yearbook* (Budapest, 2001–2), 199–232.

—— *Polish Liberal Thought before 1918* (Budapest and New York, 2004).

JARAUSCH, Konrad H., 'The Institutionalization of History in 18th Century Germany', in Hans Erich Bödeker, Georg G. Iggers and Jonathan B. Knudsen (eds.), *Aufklärung und Geschichte: Studien zur deutschen Geschichtswissenschaft im 18. Jahrhundert* (Göttingen, 1986), 25–48.

JARAUSCH, Konrad, and SABROW, Martin (eds.), *Die historische Meistererzählung: Deutungslinien der deutschen Nationalgeschichte* (Göttingen, 2002).

JASAITIS, Juozas (ed.), *Žalia bruknelė Daukantui* (Vilnius, 1993).

JEDLICKI, Jerzy, *A Suburb of Europe: Nineteenth Century Approaches to Western Civilization* (Budapest, 1999).

JELAVICH, Barbara, 'Mihail Kogălniceanu Historian as Foreign Minister, 1876–79', in Dennis Deletant and Harry Hanak (eds.), *Historians as Nation-Builders* (London, 1988), 87–105.

JENNINGS, J. R., 'Conceptions of England and Its Constitution in Nineteenth-Century French Political Thought', *The Historical Journal* 29:1 (1986), 65–85.

JOHNSON, James William, 'The Scythian: His Rise and Fall', *Journal of the History of Ideas* 20:2 (1959) 250–7.

JONES, Richard Foster, *The Triumph of the English Language: A Survey of Opinions Concerning the Vernacular from the Introduction of Printing* (Stanford, 1953).

JULKOWSKA, Violeta, *Retoryka w narracji historycznej Joachima Lelewela* (Poznań, 1998).

KAGAN, Alan S., *Aristocratic Liberalism: The Social and Political Thought of Jacob Burchhardt, John Stuart Mill, and Alexis de Tocqueville* (New Brunswick and London 2001).

KAMUSELLA, Tomasz, *The Politics of Language and Nationalisms in Central Europe during the Nineteenth and Twentieth Centuries* (Basingstoke, 2008).

KARAMZIN, Nikolai, *Histoire de L'Empire Russie*, trans. Jauffret [*sic*] (Paris, 1819).

—— *Istorija Gosudarstva Rossijskago* (Moscow, 1989).

KARLIK, J. (ed.), *Rukopisy Královédvorský a Zelenohorský* (Prague, 1936).

KAVKA, František, *The Caroline University of Prague: A Short History* (Prague, 1962).

KELLEY, Donald, 'Ancient Verses on New Ideas: Legal Tradition and the French Historical School', *History and Theory* 26:3 (1987), 319–38.

—— 'Tacitus Noster: The Germania in the Renaissance and the Reformation', in T. J. Luce and A. J. Woodman (eds.), *Tacitus and the Tacitean Tradition* (Princeton, 1993), 152–67.

—— *Fortunes of History: Historical Inquiry from Herder to Huizinga* (New Haven and London, 2002).

KELLOGG, Frederick, *A History of Romanian Historical Writing* (Bakersfield, 1990).

KENYON, John, *The History Men: The Historical Profession in England since the Renaissance* (London, 1983).

KEYLOR, William R., *Academy and Community: Foundation of the French Historical Profession* (Cambridge, MA, 1975).

KIDD, Colin, *Subverting Scotland's Past: Scottish Whig Historians and the Creation of an Anglo-British identity, 1689–c.1830* (Cambridge, 1993).

—— 'Gaelic Antiquity and National Identity in Enlightenment Scotland and Ireland', *English Historical Review* 109:434 (1994), 1197–214.

—— 'The Ideological Significance of Robertson's *History of Scotland*' in Stewart J. Brown (ed.), *William Robertson and the Expansion of Empire* (Cambridge, 1997), 122–44.

—— *British Identities before Nationalism* (Cambridge, 1999).

KIENIEWICZ, Stefan, *Joachim Lelewel* (Warsaw, 1990).

KIMBALL, Stanley B., 'Matice Česká, 1831–1861: The First Thirty Years of a Literary Foundation', in Peter Brock and H. Gordon Skilling (eds.), *The Czech Renascence of the Nineteenth Century* (Toronto, 1970), 53–73.

KLIMEŠ, Lumír, 'K Palackého překladu Dialogu Jana z Rabštejna', *Slovo a slovesnost*, 22:3 (1961), 181–6.

KŁOCZOWSKI, Jerzy (ed.), *Uniwersalism i swoitość kultury polskiej*, 2 vols. (Lublin, 1989–90).

KOCKA, Jürgen, 'Comparison and Beyond', *History and Theory* 42 (2003), 39–44.

KOHN, Hans, *The Idea of Nationalism* (New York, 1946).

—— *Nationalism: Its Meaning and History* (Princeton, 1955).

—— 'France between Britain and Germany', *Journal of the History of Ideas* 17:3 (1956), 283–99.

KOLÁŘ, Pavel, *Geschichtswissenschaft in Zentraleuropa: Die Universitäten Prag, Wien und Berlin um 1900*, 2 vols. (Leipzig, 2008).

KOMOROWSKI, Paweł, *Bolingbroke, Robertson, Gibbon: Znajmość i recepcja ich dzieł w Rzeczypospolitej doby Oświecenia (1761–1820)*, (Warsaw, 2003).

KON, Pinchas, *Nekrolog hebrajski o J. Lelewelu* (Wilno, 1930).

KOŘALKA, Jirí, 'Bavorská a Saská korespondence Františka Palackého 1836–1846', *Husitský Tábor* 5 (1982), 209–52.

—— 'Palacký a Frankfurt 1840–1860: husitské bádání a politická praxe', *Husitský Tábor* 6–7 (1983–4), 239–360.

—— 'Palacký, Sybel a počátky Historische Zeitschrift', *Husitský Tábor* 9 (1987), 199–248.

—— *Tschechen im Habsburgerreich und in Europa, 1815–1914* (Vienna, 1991).

—— *František Palacký (1798–1876) Životopis* (Prague, 1999).

—— *Frantisek Palacky (1798–1876): Der Historiker der Tschechen im österreichischen Vielvölkerstaat* (Vienna, 2007).

KOSELLECK, Reinhart, 'Historia Magistra Vitae: The Dissolution of the Topos into the Perspective of a Modernized Historical Process', in Koselleck, *Futures Past: On the Semantics of Historical Time* (New York, 2004), 26–42.

—— 'The Historical-Political Semantics of Asymmetric Counterconcepts', in Koselleck, *Futures Past: On the Semantics of Historical Time* (New York, 2004), 155–191.

KOSELLECK, Reinhart, MOMMSEN, Wolfgang J., and RÜSEN, Jörn, *Objektivität und Parteilichkeit in der Geschichtswissenschaft* (Munich, 1977).

KOT, S., *Five Centuries of Polish Learning: Three Lectures Delivered in the University of Oxford* (Oxford, 1914).

KRAPAUSKAS, Virgil, *Nationalism and Historiography: The Case of Nineteenth-Century Lithuanian Historicism* (New York, 2000).

KRATOCHVÍL, Václav, 'Palackého titul stavovského historiografa a statní rada', *Český Časopis Historický* 18 (1912), 321–31.

KULA, Witold, *An Economic Theory of the Feudal System: Towards a Model of the Polish Economy, 1500–1800* (London, 1976).

KUTNAR, František, and MAREK, Jaroslav, *Přehledné dějiny českého a slovenského dějepisectví* (Prague, 1997).

LASS, Andrew, 'Romantic Documents and Political Monuments: The Meaning-Fulfillment of History in 19ᵗʰ-Century Czech Nationalism', *American Ethnologist* 15:3 (1988), 456–71.

LEBEDYS, J., 'Simano [sic] Daukanto Biblioteka', *Lietuvių Literatūros Instituto Darbai* 1 (Vilnius, 1947), 51–72.

LEERSSEN, Joep, *National Thought in Europe: A Cultural History* (Amsterdam, 2006).

LEMBERG, Hans, 'Zur Entstehung des Osteuropabegriffs im 19. Jahrhundert. Vom "Norden" zum "Osten" Europas', *Jahrbücher für Geschichte Osteuropas* 33 (1985), 48–91.

LEONHARD, Jörn, *Liberalismus: zur historischen Semantik eines europäischen Deutungsmusters* (Munich, 2001).

LESLIE, R. F., *Polish Politics and the Revolution of November 1830* (Westport, CT, 1969).

LEVÝ, Jiří, *České teorie překladu* (Prague, 1957).

LIEDTKE, Rainer, and WENDEHORST, Stephan, *The emancipation of Catholics, Jews and Protestants: Minorities and the Nation-State in Nineteenth Century Europe* (Manchester and New York, 1999).

LINGELBACH, Gabriele, *Klio macht Karriere: Die Institutionalisierung der Geschichtswissenschaft in Frankreich und in den USA in der zweiten Hälfte des 19. Jahrhunderts* (Göttingen, 2003).

LIVESCU, Jean, 'Die Entstehung der Rumänischen Universitäten im Zusammenhang der europäischen Kulturbeziehungen (1850–1870)', in Richard Georg Plaschka and Karlheinz Mack (eds.), *Wegenetz Europäischen Geistes, Wissenschaftszentren und geistige Wechselbeziehungen vom Ende des 18. Jahrhunderts bis zum ersten Weltkrieg* (Munich, 1983), 19–35.

LÖNNROTH, Erik, MOLIN, Karl, and BJÖRK, Ragnar (eds.), *Conceptions of National History: Proceedings of the Nobel Symposium 78* (Berlin and New York, 1994).

LORENZ, Chris, *Konstruktion der Vergangenheit* (Vienna and Cologne, 1997).

LUDEN, Heinrich, *Geschichte des teutschen Volkes*, 12 vols. (Gotha, 1825).

LUKINICH, Imre, *A Magyar Tudományos Akadémia és a magyar történettudomány* (Budapest, 1926).

LUNN, Eugene, 'Cultural Populism and Egalitarian Democracy: Herder and Michelet in the Nineteenth Century', *Theory and Society* 15:4 (1986), 479–517.

MACAULAY, Thomas Babington, *History of England from the Accession of James I*, 5 vols. (1849–61).

—— 'Speech on Civil Disabilities of the Jews' (January 1831), in *Critical and Historical Essays*, 2 parts (London, 1933), pt. II, 225–36.

—— 'History', in Fritz Stern (ed.), *The Varieties of History, from Voltaire to the Present* (New York, 1973), 71–89.

MacDOUGALL, Hugh A., *Racial Myth in English History* (Montreal, 1982).

MACIEJOWSKI, Wacław, *Historya prawodawstw słowiańskich*, 2 vols. (Warsaw and Leipzig, 1832).

—— *Slavische Rechtsgeschichte*, 4 parts (Stuttgart and Leipzig, 1835–9).

MACKRELL, J. Q. C., *The Attack on Feudalism in Eighteenth Century France* (London, 1973).

MACURA, Vladimír, *Znamení zrodu. České obrození jako kulturní typ*, 2nd edn. (Prague, 1995).

—— 'Problems and Paradoxes of the National Revival', in Mikuláš Teich (ed.), *Bohemia in History* (Cambridge, 1998), 182–97.

MACŮREK, Josef, *Dějepisectví evropského východu* (Prague, 1946).

MAH, Harold, 'The Epistemology of the Sentence: Language, Civility, and Identity in France and Germany, Diderot to Nietzsche', *Representations* 47 (1994), 64–84.

MAIOR, Petru, *Lexicon Valachico-Hungarico-Germanicum* (Buda, 1825).

—— *Scrieri*, 2 vols. (Bucharest, 1976).

MALEČKOVÁ, Jitka, 'Nationalizing Women and Engendering the Nation: The Czech National Movement', in Ida Blom, Karen Hagemann and Cathrine Hall (eds.), *Gendered Nations: Nationalisms and Gender Order in the Long Nineteenth Century* (Oxford and New York, 2000), 293–310.

—— 'Where are Women in National Histories?', in Stefan Berger and Chris Lorenz (eds.), *The Contested Nation: Ethnicity, Class, Religion and Gender in National Histories* (Basingstoke, 2008), 171–99.

MALEČKOVÁ Jitka, and HROCH, Miroslav, 'The Construction of Czech National History', *Historein* 1 (1999), 101–12.

MARCINKEVIČIUS, Justinas, *Trilogija ir epilogas. Mindaugas, Mažvydas. Katedra. Daukantas* (Vilnius, 2005).

MARCOVICI, Simeon, 'Civilizaţia', in Paul Cornea and Mihai Zamfir (eds.), *Gîndirea românească în epoca paşoptistă*, 2 vols. (Bucharest, 1968), Vol. I, 230–9.

MARCZALI, Henrik, 'Horváth Mihály emlékezete', *Budapesti Szemle* 141 (1910), 161–84.

MARINO, Luigi, *Praeceptores Germaniae: Göttingen 1770–1820* (Göttingen, 1995).

MÁRKI, Sándor, *Horváth Mihály 1809–1878* (Budapest, 1987).

MASARYK, Tomáš Garrigue, *Palacky's Idee des böhmischen Volkes* (Prague, 1898).

MAURER, Michael, *Aufklärung und Anglophilie in Deutschland* (Göttingen and Zurich, 1987).

McCAGG, William O., *A History of Habsburg Jews, 1670–1918* (Bloomington, 1989).

McCLELLAND, Charles E., *State, Society and University in Germany, 1700–1914* (Cambridge, 1980).

McGREW, R. E., 'Notes on the Princely Role in Karamzin's *Istorija Gosudarstva Rossijskago*', *The American Slavic and East European Review* 18:1 (1959), 12–24.

MELLON, Stanley, *The Political Uses of History: A Study of Historians in the French Restoration* (Stanford, 1958).

MELMAN, Billie, 'Claiming the Nation's Past: The Invention of an Anglo-Saxon Tradition', *Journal of Contemporary History* 26:3–4 (1991), 575–95.

MERKYS, Vytautas, *Simonas Daukantas* (Vilnius, 1991).

MEYER, Frank, and MYHRE, Jan Eivind (eds.), *Nordic Historiography in the Twentieth Century* (Oslo, 2000).

MICHALSKI, Jerzy, *Z dziejów Towarzystwo Pryjaciól Nauk* (Warsaw, 1953).

MICHELET, Jules, *A Summary of Modern History* (London, 1875).

—— *Légendes démocratiques du Nord*, ed. Michel Cadot (Paris, 1968).

—— *Le Peuple* (Paris, 1974).

MICHELET, Jules, and QUINET, Edgar, *Jesuits and Jesuitism* (London, 1846).

MIELCKE, Christian Gottlieb, *Littauisch-deutsches und deutsch-littauisches Wörterbuch* (Königsberg, 1800).

MININGER, J. D., '*Nachschrift eines Freundes*: Kant, Lithuania, and the Praxis of Enlightenment', *Studies in East European Thought* 57 (2005), 1–32.

MISHKOVA, Diana, 'The Interesting Anomaly of Balkan Nationalism', in Zoltán Iván Dénes (ed.), *Liberty and the Search for National Identity. Liberal Nationalisms and the Legacy of Empires* (Budapest and New York, 2006), 399–456.

MOCHA, Frank, 'The Karamzin–Lelewel Controversy', *Slavic Review* 31:3 (1972), 592–610.

MOLNÁR, Miklós, *A Concise History of Hungary* (Cambridge, 2001).

MOMIGLIANO, Arnaldo, 'J. A. Droysen between Greeks and Jews', *History and Theory* 9 (1970), 139–53.

MONTESQUIEU, Charles de, *The Spirit of Laws*, ed. Anne Cohler, Basia Miller and Harold Stone (Cambridge, 1981).

MOSHEIM, Johann Lorenz von, *Versuch einer unpartheiischen und gründlichen Ketzergeschichte* (Helmstett, 1746).

MUHLACK, Ulrich, 'Klassische Philologie zwischen Humanismus und Neuhumanismus', in Rudolf Vierhaus (ed.), *Wissenschaftler im Zeitalter der Aufklärung* (Göttingen, 1985), 93–119.

—— 'Universal History and National History: Eighteenth and Nineteenth Century German Historians and the Scholarly Community', in Benedikt Stuchtey and Peter Wende (eds.), *British and German History 1750–1950: Traditions, Perceptions, Transfers* (London, 2000), 25–48.

MUSSOLINI, Benito, *Giovanni Hus il veridico* (Rome, 1913).

MUSZKA, Erzsébet, *A történelem és a történeti segédtudományok oktatása egyetemünkön, 1770–1848* (Budapest, 1974).

NAMIER, Louis, *Vanished Supremacies* (London, 1962).

NEUBAUER, Helmut, 'August Ludwig Schlözer (1735–1809) und die Geschichte Osteuropas', *Jahrbücher für Geschichte Osteuropas* 18 (1970), 205–30.

NEUBAUER, John, 'Introduction' to the section on 'The Historical Novel', in Marcel Cornis-Pope and John Neubauer (eds.), *History of the Literary Cultures of East-Central Europe: Junctures and Disjunctures in the Nineteenth and Twentieth Centuries* (Amsterdam, 2004), Vol. I, 463–7.

NIEDERHAUSER, Emil, *A történetírás története Kelet-Európában* (Budapest, 1996).

—— *The Emancipation of the Serfs in Eastern Europe*, trans. Paul Body (Boulder, 2004).

O'BRIEN, Karen, *Narratives of Enlightenment: Cosmopolitan History from Voltaire to Gibbon* (Cambridge, 1997).

OCHMAŃSKI, Jerzy, *Litewski ruch narodowo-kulturalny w XIX wieku (do 1890 r.)* (Białystok, 1965).

—— 'The National Idea in Lithuania from the 16th to the First Half of the 19th Century: The Problem of Cultural-Linguistic Identification', *Harvard Ukrainian Studies* (1986), 301–15.

ODLOŽILÍK, Otakar, 'A Czech Plan for a Danubian Federation', *Journal of Central European Affairs* 1:3 (1941), 253–74.

OEXLE, Otto Gerhard, and RÜSEN, Jörn (eds.), *Historismus in den Kulturwissenschaften: Geschichtskonzepte, historische Einschätzungen, Grundlagenprobleme* (Cologne, Weimar and Vienna, 1996).

OLDSON, William O., *A Providential Anti-Semitism: Nationalism and Polity in Nineteenth-Century Romania* (Philadelphia, 1991).

OLENDER, Maurice, 'Europe, or How to Escape Babel', *History and Theory* 33 (1994), 5–25.

OPALSKI, Magdalena, and BARTAL, Israel, *Poles and Jews: A Failed Brotherhood* (Hanover and London, 1992).

ORGELDINGER, Sibylle, *Standardisierung und Purismus bei Joachim Heinrich Campe* (Berlin and New York, 1999).

OSTERHAMMEL, Jürgen, 'Peoples without History in British and German Historical Thought', in Benedict Stuchtey and Peter Wende (eds.), *British and German Historiography, 1750–1950: Traditions, Perceptions and Transfers* (Oxford and London, 2000), 265–87.

OTÁHAL, Milan, 'The Manuscript Controversy in the Czech National Revival', *Cross Currents: A Yearbook of Central European Culture* 5 (1986), 247–77.

OZ-SALZBERGER, Fania, *Translating the Enlightenment: Scottish Civic Discourse in Eighteenth Century Germany* (Oxford, 1995).

OZ-SALZBERGER, Fania, 'Translation', in Alan Charles Kors et al. (eds.), *Encyclopedia of Enlightenment* (Oxford, 2003), Vol. IV, 181–8.

PAGDEN, Antony, 'Introduction', in Antony Pagden (ed.), *The Languages of Political Theory in Early Modern Europe* (Cambridge, 1987), 1–17.

PAJEWSKI, Janusz (ed.), *Z badań nad pracami historycznymi Joachima Lelewela* (Poznań, 1962).

PAMLÉNYI, Ervin, *Horváth Mihály* (Budapest, 1954).

PASCAL, Roy, 'Herder and the Scottish Historical School', *Publications of the English Goethe Society* 14 (1938–9), 23–42.

PEKAŘ, Josef, 'K sporu o zádruhu staroslavanskou', *Český časopis historický* 6 (1900), 243–67.

—— *Smysl českých dějin* (Prague, 1929).

—— *Der Sinn der tschechischen Geschichte* (Brno, 1937).

PÉTER, László (ed.), *Historians and the History of Transylavania* (Boulder, 1992).

PFITZNER, Josef, 'Heinrich Luden und František Palacký: Ein Kapitel Deutsch-Slawischer Kulturbeziehungen', *Historische Zeitschrift* 141 (1930), 54–96.

PHILLIPSON, Nicholas, 'Providence and Progress: An Introduction to the Historical Thought of William Robertson', in Stewart Brown (ed.), *Robertson and the Expansion of Empire* (Cambridge, 1997), 55–73.

PISKORSKI, Jan M., 'Medieval "Colonization of the East" in Polish Historiography', in Jan M. Piskorski (ed.), *Historiographical Approaches to Medieval Colonization of East-Central Europe* (New York, 2002), 96–106.

PLASCHKA, Richard Georg, *Von Palacký bis Pekař: Geschichtswissenschaft und Nationalbewusstsein bei den Tschechen* (Graz and Cologne, 1955).

—— 'The Political Significance of Frantisek Palacky', *Journal of Contemporary History* 8:3 (1973), 35–55.

PLATON, Maria (ed.), *Dacia Literară* (Bucharest, 1972).

POCOCK, John, *The Ancient Constitution and the Feudal Law: A Study of English Historical Thought in the Seventeenth Century*, 2nd edn. (Cambridge, 1987).

POMIAN, Krzysztof, 'Franks and Gauls', in Lawrence D. Kritzman (ed.), Pierre Nora (director), *Realms of Memory: Rethinking the French Past* (New York, 1982), 27–76.

PORTER, Brian, *When Nationalism Began to Hate: Imagining Politics in Nineteenth Century Poland* (Oxford and New York, 2000).

PORTER, Roy, and TEICH, Mikuláš (eds.), *Enlightenment in National Contexts* (Cambridge, 1981).

POTTER, Simeon, 'Palacký a anglické písemnictví', *Časopis Matice moravské* 53 (1929), 87–141.

PRINS, Yopie, 'Metrical Translation: Nineteenth Century Homers and the Hexameter Mania', in Sandra Bermann and Michael Wood (eds.), *Nation,*

Language and the Ethics of Translation (Princeton and Oxford, 2005), 229–56.

PRINZ, Friedrich, 'František Palacký als Historiograph der böhmischen Stände', in Ferdinand Seibt (ed.), *Probleme der Böhmischen Geschichte* (Munich, 1964), 84–94.

PROCHÁCZKA, Martin, 'Cultural Invention and Cultural Awareness: Translational Activities and Author's Subjectivity in the Culture of the Czech National Revival', *New Comparison* 8 (1989), 57–65.

PUKÁNSZKY, Béla, *Hegel és Magyar közönsége* (Budapest, 1932).

PULZER, Peter, *Jews and the German State: The Political History of a Minority, 1848–1933* (Oxford and Cambridge, MA, 1992).

PYNSENT, Robert, *Questions of Identity: Czech and Slovak Ideas of Nationality and Personality* (London and Budapest, 1995).

RANKE, Leopold von, *Geschichten der romanischen und germanischen Völker von 1494 bis 1535* (Leipzig and Berlin, 1824).

RATHMANN, János, *Herder eszméi–a historizmus útján* (Budapest, 1983).

REARICK, Charles, *Beyond the Enlightenment: Historians and Folklore in Nineteenth-Century France* (Bloomington and London, 1974).

REILL, Hans Peter, *The German Enlightenment and the Rise of Historicism* (Los Angeles and London, 1975).

REINHARDT, Angelika, *Die Karriere des Robinson Crusoe vom literarischen zum pädagogischen Helden* (Frankfurt am Main, 1994).

RENDALL, Jane, 'Tacitus Engendered: "Gothic Feminism" and British Histories, c. 1750–1800', in Geoffrey Cubitt (ed.), *Imagining Nations* (Manchester, 1998), 57–74.

RENWICK, John, 'The Reception of William Robertson's Historical Writings in Eighteenth-century France', in Stewart J. Brown (ed.), *William Robertson and the Expansion of Empire* (Cambridge, 1997), 145–63.

ŘEPA, Milan, *Moravané nebo Češi? Vývoj českého národního vědomi na Moravě v 19. století* (Brno, 2001).

REYNOLDS, Susan, *Fiefs and Vassals: The Medieval Evidence Reinterpreted* (New York and Oxford, 1994).

RHYZKOV, Vladimir, 'Enlightenment, Freedom, and Civic Society in Nikolai Karamzin's Political Thought', MA thesis (Central European University, Budapest, 2004).

RIGNEY, Anne, *The Rhetoric of Historical Representation: Three Narratives of the French Revolution* (Cambridge, 1990).

ROBERTSON, William, *A History of Scotland during the Reign of Queen Mary* (Edinburgh, 1830).

—— *The History of the Reign of Emperor Charles V* (New York, 1836).

ROBINS, R. H., *A Short History of Linguistics* (London, 1976).

ROMANI, Roberto, *National Character and Public Spirit in Britain and France, 1750–1914* (Cambridge, 2002).

ROSE, W. J., *Poland's Place in Europe* (London, 1945).

ROSTAND, Edmond, *Cyrano de Bergerac*, trans. Carol Clark (London, 2006).

ROUSSEAU, Jean Jacques, *The Government of Poland*, trans. Willimoore Kendall (Indianapolis and New York, 1972).

RÜEGG, Walter (ed.), *A History of the University in Europe*, Vol. III: *Universities in the Nineteenth and Early Twentieth Centuries (1800–1945)* (Cambridge, 2004).

RÜSEN, Jörn, BLANKE, Horst Walter, and FLEISCHER, Dirk, 'Theory of History in Historical Lectures: The German Tradition of *Historik*, 1750–1900', *History and Theory* 23 (1984), 331–56.

SADLAK, Jan, *Higher Education in Romania, 1860–1990: Between Academic Mission, Economic Demands and Political Control* (Buffalo, NY, 1990).

SAHLINS, Peter, *Boundaries: The Making of France and Spain in the Pyrenees* (Berkeley and Los Angeles, 1989).

SAJNOVICS, János, *Demonstratio Idioma Ungarorum et Lapponum Idem Esse* (Copenhagen, 1770).

ŠAMBERGER, Zdeněk, 'Mladý Palacký a jeho zakladatelský význam pro českou vědu', *Strahovská knihovna* 11 (1976), 17–48.

SAYER, Derek, *The Coasts of Bohemia: A Czech History* (Princeton, 1998).

SCHAMA, Simon, *Landscape and Memory* (London, 1996).

SCHAMSCHULA, Walter, *Die Anfänge der tschechischen Erneuerung und das deutsche Geistesleben (1740–1800)* (Munich, 1973).

SCHENKER, Alexander M., and STANKIEWICZ, Edward (eds.), *The Slavic Literary Languages: Formation and Development* (New Haven, 1980).

SCHIFIRNET, Constantin, *Civilizaţie modernă şi naţiune: Mihail Kogălniceanu, Titu Maiorescu, Mihail Eminescu* (Bucharest, 1996).

SCHINDEL, Ulrich, 'Christian Gottlieb Heyne und Göttingen as Mittler europäischer Aufklärung in Ungarn', *Ural-Altaistische Jahrbücher* 10 (1991), 53–70.

SCHLÖZER, August Ludwig von, *Tableau de l'histoire de Russie* (Gotha, 1769).

—— *Allgemeine Nordische Geschichte*, 2 vols. (Halle, 1771).

SCHÖTTLER, Peter (ed.), *Geschichtsschreibung als Legitimationswissenschaft: 1918/1945* (Frankfurt am Main, 1997).

SEBESTYÉN, Gábor, 'A magyar nyelvnek a mértékes versekre minden más nyelvek felett való alkalmatos volta', *Tudományos Gyűjtemény* 5 (1822), 50–8.

SEIER, Hellmut, 'Heeren und England', in Lothar Kettenacker, Manfred Schlenke and Hellmut Seier (eds.), *Studien zur Geschichte Englands und der deutsch-britischen Beziehungen: Festschrift für Paul Kluke* (Munich, 1981), 48–78.

SELIGER, M., 'Race-Thinking During the Restoration', *Journal of the History of Ideas* 19:2 (1958), 273–82.

SELLE, Götz von, *Geschichte der Albertus-Universität zu Königsberg in Preussen*, 2nd edn. (Würzburg, 1956).

SEREJSKI, Marian Henryk, *Koncepcja historii powszechnej Joachima Lelewela* (Warsaw, 1958).

—— *Swojkość a cudzoziemszczyzna w dziejach kultury polskiej* (Warsaw, 1973).

—— *Naród a państwo w polskiej myśli historycznej*, 2nd edn. (Warsaw, 1977).

SEREJSKI, Marian Henryk (ed.), *Historycy o historii, od Adama Naruszewicza do Stanisława Kętrzyńskiego 1775–1918* (Warsaw, 1963).

SETON-WATSON, R. W., *The Historian as a Political Force in Central Europe* (London, 1922).

SHEK BRNARDIC, Teodora, 'Intellectual Movements and Geopolitical Regionalization: The Case of the East European Enlightenment', *East Central Europe* 32: 1–2 (2005), 147–78.

—— 'The Enlightenment in Eastern Europe: Between Regional Typology and Particular Micro-History', *European Review of History* 13:3 (2006), 411–35.

SIEDENTOP, Larry, 'Two Liberal Traditions', in Alan Ryan (ed.), *The Idea of Freedom: Essays in Honour of Isaiah Berlin* (Oxford, 1979), 153–74.

SKURNEWICZ, Joan, *Romantic Nationalism and Liberalism: Joachim Lelewel and the Polish National Idea* (New York, 1981).

—— 'Lelewel in Polish Historiography in People's Poland', *Polish Review* 36:3 (1991) 269–82.

SŁOWIKOWSKI, Tadeusz, *Joachim Lelewel, krytyk i autor podręczników historii* (Warsaw, 1984).

SMITH, Antony D., *National Identity* (London, 1991).

—— *Chosen Peoples: Sacred Sources of National Identity* (Oxford, 2003).

SMITH, R. J., *The Gothic Bequest: Medieval Institutions in British Thought 1688–1863* (Cambridge, 2002).

SMITTEN, Jeffrey, 'Impartiality in Robertson's History of America', *Eighteenth-Century Studies* 19:1 (1985), 55–67.

SNYDER, Timothy, *The Reconstruction of Nations: Poland, Ukraine, Belarus, 1569–1999* (New Haven, CT, and London, 2003).

SPITZ, Lewis W., 'Natural Law and the Theory of History in Herder', *Journal of the History of Ideas* 16 (1955), 453–75.

STAFFORD, Fiona, *The Sublime Savage: A Study of James Macpherson and the Poems of Ossian* (Edinburgh, 1988).

ŠTAIF, Jiří, 'Konceptualizace českých dějin v díle Františka Palackého', *Český časopis historický* 89 (1991), 161–84.

—— 'František Palacký a česka historická pamet' (jublieum r. 1898), in Miloš Řezník and Ivana Slezáková (eds.), *Nations, Identities, Historical Consciousness: Volume Dedicated to Prof. Miroslav Hroch* (Prague, 1997), 229–50.

—— 'The Image of the Other in the Nineteenth Century: Historical Scholarship in the Bohemian Lands', in Nancy M. Wingfield (ed.), *Creating the*

Other: Ethnic Conflict and Nationalism in The Habsburg Empire (New York and Oxford, 2003), 81–102.

STANLEY, John D., 'Towards a New Nation: The Enlightenment and National Revival in Poland', *Revue Canadienne des Etudes sur le Nationalisme–Canadian Review of Studies in Nationalism* 10:1 (1983), 83–107.

—— 'Joachim Lelewel', in Peter Brock, John D. Stanley and Piotr J. Wrobel (eds.), *Nation and History: Polish Historians from the Enlightenment to the Second World War* (Toronto, Buffalo and London, 2006), 52–84.

STANZEL, Franz K. (ed). *Europäischer Völkerspiegel: Imagologisch-etnographische Studien zu den Völkertafeln des frühen 18. Jahrhunderts* (Heidelberg, 1999).

STEPHENS, W. R. W. (ed.), *The Life and Letters of Edward A. Freeman*, 2 vols. (London, 1895).

STEPHENSON, Carl, 'The Origin and Significance of Feudalism', *American Historical Review* 46:4 (1941), 788–812.

STRÅTH, Bo and SØRENSEN, Ø, (eds.), *The Cultural Construction of Norden* (Oslo, 1997).

STRUCK, Bernhard, 'Historical Regions Between Construction and Perception: Viewing Poland and France in the late-18th and early-19th centuries', *East Central Europe* 32:1–2 (2005), 79–88.

STUCHTEY, Benedikt, 'Literature, Liberty and the Life of the Nation: British Historiography from Macaulay to Trevelyan', in Stefan Berger (ed.), *Writing National Histories: Western Europe since 1800* (London and New York, 1999), 30–46.

STURDZA, Démètre A. (ed.), *Charles Ier: Roi du Roumanie: chronique–actes–documents*, 2 vols. (Bucharest, 1899).

SUBAČIUS, Giedrus, 'Three Models of Standard Written Lithuanian Language in the 19th Century: J. A. Pabrėža, J. Ciulda, S. Daukantas', *Lituanus* 43:1 (Spring 1997), 13–26.

SUGAR, Peter, F., 'The Influence of the Enlightenment and the French Revolution in Eighteenth Century Hungary, *Journal of Central European Affairs* 17 (1958), 433–55.

SUGAR, Peter (ed.), *Eastern European Nationalism in the Twentieth Century* (Washington DC, 1995).

SUNDHAUSSEN, Holm, *Der Einfluß der Herderschen Ideen auf die Nationsbildung bei den Völkern der Habsburger Monarchie* (Munich, 1973).

SVEJKOVSKA, Olga, 'The Relationship Between the German and Czech Versions of Palacký's *History of the Czech Nation*', *East European Quarterly* 15:1 (1981), 65–84.

SYBEL, Heinrich von, 'Vorwort', *Historische Zeitschrift* 1 (1859), iii–v.

TAZBIR, Janusz, 'Polish National Consciousness in the Sixteenth to Eighteenth Century', *Harvard Ukrainian Studies* (1986), 316–35.

TEICH, Mikuláš, 'Bohemia from Darkness into Light', in Roy Porter and Mikuláš Teich (eds.), *The Enlightenment in National Context* (Cambridge, 1981), 141–63.

TEREŠKINAS, Artūras, 'Between Romantic Nostalgia and Historio-Pedagogic Sentiments: A Few Ways to Discourse the Lithuanian Past', *Lituanus* 43:3 (1997), 11–48.

THIERRY, Augustin, *Dix ans d'études historiques* (Paris, 1834).

—— 'Letters from the History of France', in Fritz Stern (ed.), *The Varieties of History, from Voltaire to the Present* (New York, 1973), 63–70.

THIESSE, Anne-Marie, *La création des identités nationales: Europe XVIIIᵉ–XXᵉ siècle* (Paris, 1999).

TIEDER, Irène, *Michelet et Luther: Histoire d'une rencontre* (Paris, 1976).

TODOROVA, Maria, 'The Trap of Backwardness: Modernity, Temporality and the Study of Eastern European Nationalism', *Slavic Review* 61:1 (2005), 140–64.

TOLLEBEEK, Jo, 'Historical Representation and the Nation-State in Romantic Belgium (1830–1850)', *Journal of the History of Ideas* 59:2 (1998), 329–53.

TRAPP, J. P., 'Ovid's Tomb: The Growth of a Legend from Eusebius to Laurence Sterne, Chateaubriand and George Richmond', *Journal of the Warburg and Courtauld Institutes* 36 (1973), 35–76.

TREICHEL, Irena, *Pierwszy polski podręcznik bibliotekarski* (Wrocław, 1957).

TRENCSÉNYI, Balázs, 'The Terror of History: Visions of National Character in Interwar Eastern Europe', unpublished book manuscript.

TRENCSÉNYI, Balázs, and KOPEČEK, Michal (eds.), *Discourses of Collective Identity in Central and Southeast Europe (1770–1945)*, Vol. II: *National Romanticism–The Formation of National Movements* (Budapest and New York, 2007).

TREVELYAN, George, *Life and Letters of Lord Macaulay* (London, 1847).

TREVOR-ROPER, Hugh, 'The Invention of Tradition: The Highland Tradition of Scotland', in Eric Hobsbawm and Terence Ranger (eds.), *The Invention of Tradition* (Cambridge, 1983), 15–41.

—— *The Invention of Scotland: Myth and Identity* (New Haven, CT, and London, 2008).

TRUMPA, Vincas, 'Simonas Daukantas, Historian and Pioneer of Lithuanian National Rebirth', *Lituanus* 11:1 (1965), 5–17.

TUCZYŃSKI, Jan, *Herder i herderyzm w Polsce* (Gdańsk, 1999).

VÁLKA, Josef, 'La théorie de l'histoire chez Palacký', *Sborník prací filosofické fakulty brněnské univerzity* 14 (1967), 79–100.

—— 'František Palacký –historik', in Mylan Myška (ed.), *Památník Palackého 1798–1968* (Ostrava, 1968), 31–59.

—— 'Německá a česká verse Palackého Dějin', *Sborník prací filosofické fakulty brněnské univerzity* C 15 (1968), 79–91.

VÁLKA, Josef, 'Palacký a francouzská liberální historiografie', *Sborník prací filosofické fakulty brněnské univerzity* C 33 (1986), 101–9.

VARGA, János, *A Hungarian Quo Vadis: Political Trends and Theories of the Early 1840s* (Budapest, 1993).

VÁRKONYI, Ágnes R., *Pozitivista szemlélet a magyar történetírásban*, 2 vols. (Budapest, 1973).

VENTURI, Franco, *Italy and the Enlightenment: Studies in a Cosmopolitan Century* (New York, 1972).

—— 'Scottish Echoes in Eighteenth Century Italy', in Istvan Hont and Michael Ignatieff (eds.), *Wealth and Virtue: The Shaping of Political Economy in the Scottish Enlightenment* (Cambridge, 1986), 345–62.

VERBUNG, P. A., 'The Background to the Linguistic Concepts of Bopp', *Lingua* 2:4 (1949–50), 438–68.

VIERHAUS, Rudolf, 'Die Universität Göttingen und die Anfänge der modernen Geschichtswissenschaft im 18. Jahrhundert', in Hartmut Boockmann and Hermann Wellenreuther (eds.), *Geschichtwissenschaft in Göttingen, eine Vorlesungsreihe* (Göttingen, 1987), 9–29.

VINOGRADOFF, Paul, *Villainage in England* (Oxford, 1892).

VIROLI, Maurizio, *For Love of Country: An Essay on Patriotism and Nationalism* (Oxford, 1995).

VITAL, David, *A People Apart: A Political History of the Jews in Europe, 1789–1939* (Oxford, 2001).

VOČADLO, Otakar, 'English Influences upon Palacký', *Slavonic Review* 3:9 (1925), 547–53.

WACHSMUTH, Wilhelm, *Entwurf einer Theorie der Geschichte* (Halle, 1820).

—— *Europäische Sittengeschichte vom Ursprünge volkstümlicher Gestaltungen bis auf unsere Zeit*, 5 vols. (Leipzig, 1831–9).

WALICKI, Andrzej, *Philosophy and Romantic Nationalism: The Case of Poland* (Oxford, 1982).

—— *Russia, Poland and Universal Regeneration: Studies in Russian and Polish Thought of the Romantic Epoch* (Notre Dame, IN, 1991).

—— *Poland Between East and West: The Controversies over Self-Definition and Modernization in Partitioned Poland* (Cambridge, MA, 1994).

WANDYCZ, Piotr, P., 'Historiography of the Countries of Eastern Europe: Poland', *American Historical Review* 97:4 (1992), 1011–25.

—— *The Price of Freedom: A History of East Central Europe from the Middle Ages to the Present* (London and New York, 1992).

WEGELE, Franz X., *Geschichte der deutschen Historiografie seit dem Auftreten des Humanismus* (Munich, 1885).

WEINTRAUB, Karol, *Visions of Culture* (Chicago, 1966).

WELLENREUTHER, Hermann, 'Göttingen und England im achzehnten Jahrhundert', in *250 Jahre Vorlesungen an der Georgia Augusta 1734–1984* (Göttingen, 1985), 30–63.

WERNER, Michael, and ZIMMERMANN, Bénédicte, 'Beyond Comparison: Histoire Croisée and the Challenge of Reflexivity', *History and Theory* 45 (2006), 30–50.

WHITE, Hayden, *Metahistory: The Historical Imagination in Nineteenth-Century Europe* (Baltimore and London, 1973).

WIERZBICKI, Andrzej, *Wschód-Zachód w koncepcjach dziejów Polski* (Warsaw, 1984).

—— *Historiografia polska doby romantyzmu* (Wrocław, 1999).

WOLFF, Larry, *Inventing Eastern Europe* (Stanford, 1994).

WOOLF, Daniel, 'Of Nations, Nationalism and National Identity: Reflections on the Historiographic Organization of the Past', in Q. Edward Wang and Franz Leander Fillafer (eds.), *The Many Faces of Clio: Cross-cultural Approaches to Historiography. Essays in Honour of Georg G. Iggers* (New York, 2007), 71–104.

WRIGHT, Johnson Kent, *A Classical Republican in Eighteenth-Century France: The Political Thought of Mably* (Stanford, 1997).

WYSPIAŃSKI, Stanisław, *Dzieła zebrane*, Vol. III: *Lelewel, Legion* (Cracow, 1958).

WYSS, Johann David, *Der schweizerische Robinson* (Zurich, 1812).

ZACEK, Joseph F., 'Palacky and the Marxists', *Slavic Review* 24:2 (1965), 297–306.

—— *Palacký: The Historian as Scholar and Nationalist* (The Hague, 1970).

—— 'Metternich's Censors: The Case of Palacky', in Peter Brock and H. Gordon Skilling, *The Czech Renascence in the Nineteenth Century* (Toronto, 1970), 95–112.

—— 'Palacky's Politics: The Second Phase', *Canadian Slavic Studies* 5:1 (1971), 51–64.

ZEMLICKA, Josef, 'Die Deutschen und die deutschrechtliche Kolonisation Böhmens und Mährens im Mittelalter', in Jan M. Piskorski (ed.), *Historiographical Approaches to Medieval Colonization of East-Central Europe* (New York, 2002), 107–44.

ZIMMER, Oliver, 'In Search of Natural Identity: Alpine Landscape and the Reconstruction of the Swiss Nation', *Comparative Studies in Society and History* 40:4 (1998), 637–65.

—— *A Contested Nation: History, Memory and Nationalism in Switzerland, 1761–1891* (Cambridge, 2003).

ZINKEVIČIUS, Zigmas, *Lietuvių kalba XVIII–XIX a* (Vilnius, 1990).

ZUB, Alexandru, *Mihail Kogălniceanu, 1817–1891: Biobibliografie* (Bucharest, 1971).

—— *Kogălniceanu, istoric* (Iasi, 1974).

—— *A scrie și a face istorie* (Iași, 1984).

ŽUKAS, Saulius, *Simonas Daukantas* (Kaunas, 1988).

Index